World

ASTROLOGY

The astrologer's quest to
understand the human character

Also by Peter Marshall

Journey through Tanzania

Journey through Maldives

Into Cuba: Breaking the Chains?

Around Africa:
From the Pillars of Hercules to the Strait of Gibraltar

Celtic Gold:
A Voyage Around Ireland

William Godwin

William Blake

Demanding the Impossible:
A History of Anarchism

Nature's Web:
Rethinking our Place on Earth

Riding the Wind:
A New Philosophy for a New Era

The Philosopher's Stone:
A Quest for the Secrets of Alchemy

Peter Marshall

World

ASTROLOGY

The astrologer's quest to
understand the human character

MACMILLAN

First published 2004 by Macmillan
an imprint of Pan Macmillan Ltd
Pan Macmillan, 20 New Wharf Road, London N1 9RR
Basingstoke and Oxford
Associated companies throughout the world
www.panmacmillan.com

ISBN 0 333 90631 4

1 3 5 7 9 8 6 4 2

A CIP catalogue record for this book is available from
the British Library.

Typeset by SX Composing DTP, Rayleigh, Essex
Printed and bound in Great Britain by
Mackays of Chatham plc, Chatham, Kent

For Skipper Atman –
a shooting star

. . . Or let my lamp at midnight hour
Be seen in some high lonely tow'r
Where I may oft outwatch the Bear,
With thrice great Hermes, or unsphere
The spirit of Plato to unfold
What worlds, or what vast regions hold
The immortal mind that hath forsook
Her mansion in this fleshy nook;
And of those daemons that are found
In fire, air, flood, or under ground,
Whose power hath a true consent
With planet or with element.

JOHN MILTON, *Il Penseroso* (c. 1631)

Contents

Contents

Part Five
The Milky Way: Europe

List of Illustrations

Acknowledgements

I am indebted to countless individuals who have helped me in this long journey into the heart of astrology. They are too many to mention, but they will know who they are; please accept my warmest thanks.

On mainland China, I would like to thank Ming Zhiting, deputy director of the Taoist Association of China at the White Cloud Temple in Beijing, and Professors Zhao Kuang-hua and Zhou Jia-hua of the Institute for the History of Natural Science of the Chinese Academy of Sciences. In Hong Kong, I was helped greatly by Dr Chan Ki King, curator of the Hong Kong Space Museum, Choi Park-lai, author of the Chinese Almanac, Raymond Lo, astrology and feng shui expert, and Jacqueline Taylor-Smith, director of the Hong Kong chapter of the Royal Geographical Society. I am also grateful to the Needham Institute, Cambridge, for allowing me to reproduce illustrations from Joseph Needham's magisterial *Science and Civilisation in China*.

In India, I would like to thank Dr J. S. Shukla at the Samparnanand Sanskrit University in Varanasi and Professor Kamalesh Datta Tripathi at the Benares Hindu University for their enlightening conversations. Swami Yogi Prakash proved invaluable in explaining the intricacies of tantra and Indian astrology. Komilla Sutton, co-founder and chair of the British Association of Vedic Astrology, kindly clarified many issues for me.

In Egypt, I am indebted to Dr Zahi Hawass, Director of Antiquities at Giza, for allowing me to climb and explore the chambers of the Great Pyramid, and to Mohamed El Baili, Director of Antiquities at Luxor, for giving me permission to visit the tombs on the West Bank closed to the public. No student of Egyptian civilization and astrology could fail to be stimulated by the ideas and writings of John Anthony West.

Back at home, I would like to thank my former neighbours Brenda and David Thomas for many enjoyable discussions on astrology. I am particularly grateful to David for drawing up and interpreting horoscopes. My friends Graham Hancock, Joanna Sancha, Jonathan Lumby and Robin Waterfield have kindly lent me materials and pointed out leads. Dicker Feesey, Jeremy Gane, Dei Hughes, David Lea, John Schlapobersky, Peter Tutt and Jenny Zobel have all remained close and inspiring friends.

My wonderful children Dylan and Emily have kept my wits honed while my challenging brother Michael has kept my eye on the ball. The interest of the rest of my family, especially of Colette, Julie and Sylvie, has been much appreciated. Special thanks to my mother Vera for her loving support.

At Macmillan, I am indebted to William Armstrong, associate publisher, who encouraged me in the early stages, the copy-editor Christine Lee who did a fine job, and the editor Stuart Evers and the publisher Jeremy Trevathan who oversaw the whole project. Their incisive counsel and friendly co-operation have been invaluable.

Bill Hamiton, my literary agent at A. M. Heath, has as always been a fount of excellent advice, warm encouragement and sharp discernment.

Above all, I would like to thank Elizabeth Ashton Hill who accompanied me on my travels, helped me in my research and who has been my most affectionate and understanding critic.

May the stars shine on you all.

Peter Marshall

Little Oaks, 21 May 2003

Glossary

CHINESE ASTROLOGY

Ch'i: cosmic energy.

Ch'ien: the creative trigram associated with summer, South, fire and heaven.

Elements: there are five elements, each ruled by a visible planet: water (Mercury), metal (Venus), fire (Mars), wood (Jupiter), and earth (Saturn).

Feng shui: literally, 'Wind and Water'. The art and science of creating a dwelling in the landscape for the living and the dead. It arranges the environment to maximize the flow of ch'i.

H'sun: the gentle wind trigram associated with later summer, South-West and wood.

I Ching: *The Book of Changes*, ancient and revered text of divination.

K'an: the dangerous trigram associated with the autumn, West, metal and the moon.

Ken: the mountain trigram associated with early winter, the North-West and calm.

K'un: the receptive trigram associated with winter, the North, water and creation.

Li: the clinging trigram associated with spring, the East, wood and the sun.

Lo Pan: compass used by practitioners of astrology and feng shui.

Lo Shu: the magic square, said to have been discovered on a turtle's back.

T'ai Ch'i: the Ultimate.

Trigrams: the fundamental three-lined figure used to make the eight-sided hexagrams said to be the building blocks of all things. Used in the *I Ching* book of divination. The top line of the trigram represents heaven; the middle line, humanity; and the bottom line, earth.

Tao: indefinable, loosely 'The Way'. The Tao divides into the complementary forces of yin and yang which are found in all things and beings.

Tui: the lake trigram associated with early summer, the South-East, metal, joy.

Sha: unhealthy chi, literally 'noxious vapour'.

Yang: one of the two opposite but complementary forces which shape the universe. Associated with light, it is positive, creative, masculine energy.

Yin: associated with darkness, it is negative, receptive, female energy.

INDIAN ASTROLOGY

Artha: purpose or goal in life.

Atman: the Self in Hindu philosophy.

Ayanamsha: the 'portion of movement'; the difference in degrees caused by the precession of the equinoxes between the position of 0° Aries in sidereal (Indian) and tropical (Western) zodiac systems. Also known as Precessional Distance.

Ayurveda: the ancient Vedic science of medicine still practised in India today.

Bhava: literally a 'way of being'; the house of an astrological chart.

Brahma: the first god of the Hindu trinity, embodying the power of the creation. The others are Vishnu, the Preserver, and Shiva, the Destroyer.

Buddhi: the intellect.

Chakra: 'wheel'; name for the birth chart.

Chakras: energy centres in the body.

Chandra: 'Bright One'; the moon.

Chandra lagna: chart showing the moon as Ascendant.

Dashas: directions, planetary periods.

Dharma: untranslatable; variously describing the cosmic law, right conduct, religion, the way things are, way of life.

Gochara: transits of the planets.

Graha: literally 'seizer'; the usual Sanskrit word for a planet.

Gunas: 'threads' or 'qualities', the three fundamental aspects of the mind and existence consisting of *sattva*, goodness, purity, truth; *rajas*, passion, action; and *tama*s, attachments, darkness.

Jyotish: Sanskrit name for Vedic astrology. Originally, the study of the heavenly bodies, covering astrology, astronomy and mathematics.

Kalapurusa: 'Time-Man', cosmic being whose body is represented by the signs of the zodiac and whose emotions are symbolized by the planets.

Kali Yuga: the fourth, current age, equivalent to the Iron Age of the Greeks.

Kama: passion or desire.

Karaka: indicator.

Karma: 'actions'. In Hindu religion and philosophy: past actions, seen as influencing one's fortunes in the present or future.

Kendra: cardinal houses.

Ketu: the South node of the moon.

Kundalini: powerful energy within us, symbolized by a coiled serpent.

Lagna: 'that which meets'; variously, the moment of birth, the Ascendant, the horoscope.

Manas: the mind.

Mantra: sacred sound recited in meditation.

Manuyuga: sequence of four yugas, reckoned at 311,040,000 years. Fourteen Manuyugas make up the complete cycle, equivalent to a day in the life of Brahma.

Moksha: liberation, enlightenment.

Mooltrikona: 'root triangle', a position where planets become strong.

Nakshatra: lunar mansion, that is one of the twenty-seven or twenty-eight constellations through which the moon appears to pass through each lunar month.

Navamsha: the ninth division of a sign of the zodiac; ninth divisional chart.

Prana: solar energy.

Rahu: the North node of the moon.

Rajas: passion, action.

Rishis: seers or sages to whom the Vedas were allegedly revealed. Seven Rishis are identified with the stars of the Plough.

Sastra: branch of learning, science.

Sattva: goodness, purity, truth.

Shiva: one of the main Hindu trinity of gods; embodying the power of destruction and transformation.

Surya: the sun.

Tamas: attachments, darkness.

Tantra: 'weaving', 'thread'; a spiritual path which works with all parts of one's being – mind, body and spirit – by transforming rather than rejecting them.

Vargas: divisions, especially of the zodiac.

Yogas: planetary combinations.

Yuga: one of the four ages of the universe that make up the Manuyuga.

WESTERN ASTROLOGY

Affinity: see rulership.

Angle: the two axes of the circular birthchart form four angles within it. The top of the vertical axis is called the Midheaven (MC, *Medium Coeli*) and the bottom is the Lowerheaven (IC, *Imum Coeli*). They form the meeting point of the ecliptic and the local meridian. The left-hand point of the horizontal axis is the Ascendant and the right-hand point is the Descendant. They form the meeting point of the ecliptic and local horizon. They are the cusps of the angular houses one, four, seven and ten. Planets placed with in a few degrees of these points are considered particularly significant in a horoscope.

Ascendant: the degree or sign of the zodiac rising over the Eastern horizon at the moment of birth. Also the point at which the Eastern horizon intersects the ecliptic. Each degree takes about four minutes to rise, making 360° in a twenty-four hour day. The Ascendant is the cusp of the First House. The sign of the zodiac rising on the Eastern horizon is called the rising sign. The Ascendant is said to represent an individual's hidden qualities. In Greek, *horoscopos,* the First Place.

Aspect: the angle formed between two imaginary lines connecting two heavenly bodies or points with the earth. The arc between the two is measured in degrees around the circumference of the birthchart. The influence of aspects can be positive or negative in character, and powerful, strong, moderate or weak in strength.

Asteroids: a belt of a vast number of fragments, believed to be a disintegrated planet, between the orbits of Mars and Jupiter, some of which a few astrologers have integrated in their systems.

Cardines (Cardinal Points): the Ascendant, Midheaven (MC), the Descendant and the Lowerheaven (IC).

Cardinal signs: see quadruplicity.

Chaldean Order: the order of the planets as seen from the earth in their apparent distances and speeds. It refers only to the seven traditional visible planets: moon, Mercury, Venus, sun, Mars, Jupiter and Saturn.

Chiron: a planetoid, possibly a trapped comet, between the orbits of Saturn and Uranus. Taken by some astrologers to symbolize the wounded healer.

Chronactors: the 'Markers of Time' Jupiter and Saturn. The twenty-year Jupiter-Saturn conjunctions stay for around 200 years in the same element, forming an 800-year zodiac cycle. The cycles are said to mark the spirit of the age.

Conjunction: when two or more planets occupy the same point in the sky.

Cusp: the point in the zodiac which separates one house from the other in a horoscope. There are twelve cusps, one per House, four of them forming the Angles. The Ascendant is the cusp of the First House. It is misleading to say that 'I'm on the cusp between Leo and Virgo'. One is born either in the sign of Leo or that of Virgo.

Decans: the division of the 30° of a zodiac sign into three sections of 10°. Adapted from the Egyptian system of measuring time, the decans are usually ascribed to different planets.

Decumbiture: a chart cast for the time an ill person takes to his or her bed used for prognosis.

Descendant: the point at which the Western horizon intersects the ecliptic. On the birthchart, it appears opposite the Ascendant. Also called the Nadir and the Fourth House Cusp.

Detriment: the influence of a planet is weakened (in detriment) when it is in its polar sign, that is, opposite the zodiac sign it rules.

Dignity: planets are said to be in dignity when placed in signs they rule, or in which they are exalted, where their influence is strengthened. They are in debility and weakened in signs opposite their rulership (detriment) or opposite their exaltation (fall).

Directions: methods for timing events by moving (directing) planets and other factors into new positions and aspects in the horoscope. The movement may be derived from the diurnal rotation of the earth and sky in the hours after birth (Primary Directions), or from planetary motions along the ecliptic in the days after or before birth (Secondary Directions or Progressions). The latter has become the main method in contemporary practice.

Dodecatemories: twelfth-parts, originally referring to the twelve-fold division of the zodiac, but then to twelve parts within the signs, or smaller parts assigned to planets.

Ecliptic: the apparent path of the sun round the earth. The plane of the earth's orbit around the sun extended into space to meet the celestial sphere.

Elements: in India, the Middle East and the West, four elements are considered to be the fundamental principles of nature: fire, earth, air and water. Some Greeks added aether, sometimes translated as space. In Western astrology, they represent the fundamental nature of the twelve signs of the zodiac. Fire signs are Aries, Leo and Sagittarius; earth signs, Capricorn, Taurus and Virgo; air signs, Libra, Aquarius and Gemini; and water signs, Cancer, Scorpio and Pisces. A count of the distribution of the seven traditional planets among the elements indicates the balance of the elements in the horoscope. Traditionally the four elements were associated with four humours: fire with the choleric (driven and impulsive); earth with the melancholic (withdrawn and practical); air with the sanguine (optimistic and restless); and water with the phlegmatic (sensitive and reflective).

Elevation: the distance of a planet above the horizon. The planet nearest the Midheaven is said to be elevated.

Ephemeris: (plural empherides) table listing the precise positions of the sun, moon and planets on a daily basis in a particular year. It also contains information necessary to cast a horoscope, such as latitude, declination and sidereal time.

Epicycle: a circle with a centre moving around the circumference of a larger circle.

Equinoxes: the two days of the year in the spring and autumn when the sun crosses the equator and day and night are of equal length. At these times, the plane of the ecliptic intersects with the celestial equator.

Exaltation: the influence of a planet is stronger when it is in exaltation or exalted in a particular sign. Traditionally, the sun is exalted in Aries; the moon, in Taurus; Mercury, in Virgo; Venus, in Pisces; Mars, in Capricorn; Jupiter, in Cancer; Saturn, in Libra. Of the recently discovered planets, Uranus is said to be exalted in Scorpio; Neptune, in Leo; and Pluto, in Virgo.

Fall: the influence of a planet is weakened when it is in fall, that is to say, when it is opposite the sign in which it is exalted.

Genethialogy: natal astrology.

Great Year: the length of time taken by the planets to return to the same position in relation to each other, variously calculated from 1,000 to 30,000 years.

Heliacal rising: first rising of a star after its period of invisibility due to conjunction with the sun.

Horary astrology: a horoscope for a particular time and place about which an astrologer is asked a question.

Horoscope: (from the Greek, *horoscopos*, the First Place) a diagram, map or chart of the positions of the planets in the heavens at the exact time and place of a person's birth. It covers the whole sky, and within the 360° circle it shows the signs of the zodiac, the planets, the rising and culminating signs and the twelve Houses. Another name for a birthchart.

Houses (Mundane Houses): one of the twelve divisions made in the cycle of the earth's daily rotation. Each House represents a period of about two hours, during which one sign of the zodiac appears to pass over the horizon. Each quadrant of the horoscope is trisected to produce twelve Houses which represent different areas of concern in life, such as the home, work, relationships. The First House begins with the

Ascendant line and the rest follow in a counter-clockwise direction on the circle of the chart. There are different methods of determining their length, but the equal House system of 30° each is popular and easy. Tables of House, published for various geographical latitudes, list the degrees rising on the Ascendant and culminating in Midheaven, together with intermediate House cusps, at four-minute intervals over the twenty-four hour diurnal cycle. In ancient astrology, the Houses referred to the zodiacal Houses of the planets, that is the signs which they rule, while modern Mundane Houses were called Places.

Imum Coeli (IC): see Lowerheaven.

Katarche: astrology of initiatives, including hororary, decumbiture, elections and inceptions. They are charts cast for a moment other than the moment of birth intended to see what is the best decision to be taken in the situation.

Longitude: on the earth, the distance of any place East or West of Greenwich; in the heavens, the distance of any body from the first point of the zodiac (0° Aries), measured on the ecliptic.

Lots: theoretical positions in the zodiac, produced by an equation involving three significant factors in a horoscope, one of which is usually a cusp. Also known as Parts. See Part of Fortune.

Lowerheaven: (IC, from the Latin *Imum Coeli*), the meeting point of the ecliptic and the local meridian, directly below the observer. It is opposite the Midheaven on the horoscope. Also known as the Nadir and called the Fourth House cusp.

Luminaries: the sun and the moon.

Meridian: a great circle on the celestial sphere passing through the North and South points of the horizon and the zenith which is directly above the observer. In a birthchart the meridian is the line which connects the Midheaven (MC) with the Lowerheaven (IC), thereby bisecting the circle into two halves.

Midheaven: (MC, from the Latin *Medium Coeli*) the point where the meridian intersects the ecliptic. It is opposite the Lowerheaven (IC) on the horoscope.

Mid-point: the half-way point measured in degrees between any significant factors in the horoscope, such as two planets, two angles, or a planet and an angle. The mid-points are thought to express their energies. The technique, variously called cosmobiology or the Ebertin method, usually does away with intermediate Houses and the signs of the zodiac. Used in synastry charts.

Mundane astrology: the original kind of astrology applied to world events, politics and nations rather than to individuals.

Mundane Houses: see Houses.

Nadir: see Lowerheaven.

Nodes: the two points of the intersection of a planet's orbit through the ecliptic, one when it moves North and the other when it moves South. Nowadays only the moon's nodes tend to be used; the North Node is called the Dragon's Head; the South Node, the Dragon's Tail. Solar and lunar eclipses take place as a result of a node alignment of the earth, sun and moon on the plane of the ecliptic. The North Node is said to enhance success; the South Node, to accentuate problems.

Opposition: an aspect representing an angle of 180° between two planets. As a result, they face each other across the wheel of the zodiac and the birthchart.

Orbs: the number of degrees allowed on either side of an exact aspect for the aspect still to be operative. Usually taken to be 15°. The trine, for example, has an orb of 8° on either side of exactitude.

Paranatellonta: stars which rise and set at the same time as the sections of the ecliptic, but North or South of them.

Part of Fortune: theoretical position in the zodiac, calculated by the positions of the Ascendant, plus moon, minus sun. Other equations give other Parts or Lots used by Roman and Muslim astrologers, such as the Part of Marriage and the Part of Death. Its astrological symbol is the same as the astronomical one for the earth, a cross in a circle.

Planets: traditionally, five visible planets, Mercury, Venus, Mars, Jupiter and Saturn; and three recently discovered ones, Uranus, Neptune and Pluto.

Polarity: each sign of the zodiac has an opposite sign on the chart with which it is in polarity and has a special relationship. Also each sign is considered positive or negative and as such, male or female, extrovert or introvert, objective or subjective.

Precession of the Equinoxes: the gradual shift backwards of the signs of the zodiac against the backdrop of stars over long periods of time due to the earth's wobble on its axis. The retrogression of the equinoctial points when seen against the constellations has meant that the first point of Aries is actually now seen in Pisces. The phenomenon has given rise to the idea of the 'Ages'. Indian astrology takes into account the Precession of the Equinoxes; Western astrology does not.

Progressions: to understand past events and to make observations about the future, astrologers 'progress' a birthchart to represent a future period in time rather than the moment of birth. The most popular means is to count a day on the chart for a year in life; if someone is forty-six years old, the planets would be placed on a chart where they fell forty-six days after birth.

Quadrants: the four quarters of a birthchart. From any position of an observer on the earth, the heavens can be divided into four quadrants (Eastern horizon to upper meridian to Western horizon, with two comparable quadrants beneath the horizon).

Quadruplicity: see qualities.

Qualities: the signs of the zodiac are each assigned one of three qualities which reflect their mode of activity: cardinal (said to encourage action), fixed (resistance to change) or mutable (adaptability). Aries, Cancer, Libra and Capricorn are cardinal signs; Taurus, Leo, Scorpio and Aquarius are fixed signs; and Gemini, Virgo, Sagittarius and Pisces are mutable signs. A predominance of planets in one quality in a birthchart is called a cross.

Rectification: correcting the supposed time of birth in order to find the true time, usually deduced from the life events of the individual concerned.

Relocation: when the horoscope is redrawn for any place of significance in order to show a person's potential there.

Retrogression: the apparent backward movement of planets through the zodiac as seen from an observer on earth. It is an illusion produced by the relative speed of the planets in their orbits. A planet in retrogression is called retrograde.

Returns: the return of any planet to the position in the zodiac which it occupied at the moment of birth in a horoscope.

Rising sign: see Ascendant.

Rulership: every sign of the zodiac is said to have an affinity with or to be 'ruled' by a planet. The ruling planet of the rising sign is called the ruler of the horoscope.

Sidereal: referring to the stars. A sidereal month is the period of time taken by the moon to make one complete revolution around the earth, measured between two successive conjunctions with a particular star (approximately twenty-seven days, seven hours, forty-three minutes and eleven seconds). A sidereal year is the period of time during which the earth makes one revolution around the sun, measured between two successive conjunctions of a particular star (equal to 354.3671 days).

Solstices: the two days of the year in summer and winter when the sun is at its maximum angle of declination to the equator, resulting in the longest and shortest days.

Solar year: the period of time during which the earth makes one revolution around the sun, measured between two successive vernal equinoxes (approximately 365.256 days). Also called a tropical year.

Stellium: a group of three or more planets in conjunction which is thought to have a very powerful influence.

Sun signs: the twelve traditional signs of the zodiac through which the sun appears to pass in a solar year. The sun sign at a person's birth is now thought to represent his or her public image.

Synastry: the comparison of two or more charts in order to see their compatibility. A composite chart of a relationship between two people can be made from the mid-points of the common factors in their horoscopes.

Synodic: referring to a conjunction or two successive conjunctions of the same star or planet. A synodic month is a lunar month, the period of time taken by the moon to make once complete revolution around the earth, measured between two successive new moons (approximately twenty-nine days, twelve hours, forty-four minutes and three seconds).

Transit: a movement of a planet through a sign or house. Astrologers often use transits, comparing the positions of planets in the present with those in the birthchart, in order to interpret future trends and possibilities.

Triplicity: one of four fixed groups of signs, each containing three planets. They relate to the four elements – earth, air, fire and water. See also elements.

Trigon: a set of thee signs of the zodiac, 120° distant from each other, forming a triangle.

Tropical year: see solar year.

Vernal equinox: the intersection of the plane of the ecliptic with the celestial sphere. This intersection occurs once a year in spring in the Northern Hemisphere, at the moment the sun crosses the celestial equator, moving from South to North. The vernal equinox occurred at the first point of Aries (0°) about 2,000 years ago; since then they have gradually parted company due to the precession of the equinoxes.

Zenith: the highest point on the meridian directly above the observer.

Zodiac: the band of sky 18° wide along the ecliptic. It is divided into twelve parts, each 30° wide, which represent the twelve signs of the zodiac. The sun appears to pass through them in a year. Indian astrology uses the sidereal zodiac which is related to fixed star constellations.

ASPECTS

The Major Aspects (Ptolemaic)

Aspects	Symbol	Degree	Orb	Meaning
Conjunction	☌	0°	8	intensifies, identity
Opposition	☍	180°	8	very unhelpful, challenge
Trine	△	120°	8	very helpful, co-operation
Square	□	90°	6/4	unhelpful, struggle
Sextile	✶	60°	8	mildly helpful, creativity

The Minor Aspects

Aspects	Symbol	Degree	Orb	Meaning
Semi-Square	∠	45°	2	uneasy
Sesquiquadrate	⬦	135°	2	uneasy
Semi-sextile	⊻	30°	2	helpful
Quincunx	⊼	150°	2	stressful

HOUSES

First	life, constitution, self-expression
Second	finances, possessions and feelings
Third	siblings and relatives, communication

Fourth	home, family, responsibility
Fifth	children, creativity, games
Sixth	health, work and service for others
Seventh	relationships
Eighth	depth of feeling, death
Ninth	travel, education, religion
Tenth	standing in the world, career
Eleventh	friends, unorthodoxy
Twelfth	enemies, limitations, values

PLANETS

Planets	*Symbol*	*Meaning*
Sun	☉	purpose, creativity
Moon	☽	adaptation, receptivity
Mercury	☿	communication, intellect
Venus	♀	evaluation, relationship
Mars	♂	exertion, energy
Jupiter	♃	expansion, improvement
Saturn	♄	structure, limitation
Uranus	♅	deviation, unorthodoxy
Neptune	♆	refinement, sensitivity
Pluto	♇♀	transcendence, change

SIGNS

Sign	Symbol	Meaning	Affinity	Quality	Polarity	Element
Aries	♈	to initiate	Mars	cardinal	+	fire
Taurus	♉	to sustain	Venus	fixed	–	earth
Gemini	♊	to transmit	Mercury	mutable	+	air
Cancer	♋	to contain	Moon	cardinal	–	water
Leo	♌	to display	Sun	fixed	+	fire
Virgo	♍	to analyse	Mercury	mutable	–	earth
Libra	♎	to relate	Venus	cardinal	+	air
Scorpio	♏	to scrutinize	Mars/ Pluto	fixed	–	water
Sagittarius	♐	to extend	Jupiter	mutable	+	fire
Capricorn	♑	to construct	Saturn	cardinal	–	earth
Aquarius	♒	to innovate	Saturn/ Uranus	fixed	+	air
Pisces	♓	to merge	Jupiter/ Neptune	mutable	–	water

Introduction

What do you think of astrology? In my opinion it is a very great, very beautiful lady who comes from a time so distant that she cannot fail to hold me under her spell. I can see no finery or elegance in the purely physical world to match hers. Moreover, she seems to me to have in her possession one of the highest mysteries of the world. A pity that today, at least for the uncouth, a whore has been enthroned in her place.

ANDRÉ BRETON

WHY DO LOVERS check each other's birthcharts to see if they are compatible? Why do apparently rational men and women postpone operations because of the position of the planets? Why do presidents and military leaders consult astrologers before making crucial decisions which will affect the course of history? Has the world become star-struck? Despite the official disapproval of established religion and science, astrology has undergone an extraordinary renaissance in recent times.

Astrology is the study of the stars and planets and their effect on human behaviour. It assumes that there is a correspondence between heaven and earth, expressed in the phrase 'as above, so below', and that the position of celestial bodies influences personalities, events and affairs on this planet. It also believes that the microcosm of human beings mirrors the macrocosm of the universe, that is, 'as within, so without'. Born of magic and augury, astrology reflects a primordial drive to predict the future and is part of the age-old search for self-knowledge. Since ancient times, it has offered a way of attaining a higher form of consciousness, a mystic vision of the real. The stars have long been seen as doors to another world, even as the gates of heaven.

Astrology is older than civilization and still hugely popular throughout the world. It spans science and art and connects astronomy, mathematics, medicine, philosophy, religion, psychology, mythology and symbolism. It pervades every level of society. It is so much part of everyday culture that we all talk about 'starry-eyed' youth, an 'ill-starred' project or 'star-crossed' lovers. Few have not heard of the 'Age of Aquarius' and the prophecies of Nostradamus.

Yet many theologians and scientists reject astrology with an irrational hostility which borders on fury. Like alchemy and magic, it is seen as part of the sinister underground of the occult. For St Augustine it involved 'congress with demons', while for Pope Paul II it was a sin. If acknowledged by modern scientists at all, it is considered to be the 'primitive' study of celestial bodies which formed the basis of modern astronomy. It is shunted off into the 'lunatic' fringe of thought, rejected at best as a naive superstition or at worst as a dangerous heresy. The Astronomer Royal Harold Spencer Jones dismissed it as 'absolute rubbish'.[1] It has been called 'the most persistent hallucination that ever haunted the human brain'.[2]

So concerned were they about its growing popularity, that 186 scientists, including nineteen Nobel Prize winners, signed a manifesto in 1976 called 'Objections to Astrology'. Recklessly venturing outside their disciplines, they declared that there is 'no scientific foundation for its tenets' and dismissed astrologers as mere charlatans.[3] More recently, the zoologist Richard Dawkins, who 'detests' astrologers, has described the subject as an 'aesthetic affront' whose 'pre-Copernican dabblings demean and cheapen astronomy'.[4]

This new Inquisition has been no more successful in crushing astrology than the desperate efforts of earlier popes and emperors. Like alchemy and magic, astrology refuses to die. Presidents as disparate as Charles de Gaulle and Ronald Reagan have consulted astrologers. Politicians, generals and diplomats in India and Egypt do not move without consulting their personal astrologers. Meanwhile in China astrology is re-emerging after the Cultural Revolution despite official disapproval. In the humblest homes and in the palaces of the great, in corridors of political power and in the board rooms of international companies, astrology is alive and well. Astrologers are consulted not only for affairs of the heart and home, but for financial markets and horse races; not only for career and financial prospects, but for the course of history and the fate of nations. Millions of people regularly read their sun sign horoscopes in the press.

The poets W. B. Yeats and Ted Hughes took a great interest in the subject. Astrology inspired Holst's symphony *The Planets* and Constant Lambert's ballet *The Horoscope*, as well as the albums of the jazz supremo John Coltrane. Whatever the Astronomer Royal might say, Plato, St Thomas Aquinas, Dante, Marsilio Ficino, Goethe, André Breton and Henry Miller have all taken astrology seriously. Since such great thinkers, poets, writers, artists and musicians have drunk deep at the fountain of astrology, perhaps there is 'something' in it after all.

*

The words astrology ('the study of the stars') and astronomy ('the law of the stars') were used interchangeably until the Scientific Revolution in the seventeenth century. The ancient Greek for astronomer was *astrologos*. While the roots of Western astrology lie in the magical divination of Mesopotamia and the star religion of Egypt, Plato provided the philosophical framework of all later Western astrology. Ptolemy, usually considered the father of astronomy, went on to lay down the fundamental astrological principles which have changed little in the last 2,000 years.

After the collapse of the Greek and Roman Empires, the centre of astrology moved to the Islamic Empire and only returned to Europe in the Middle Ages via the Moors in Spain and Italy. It still remained an integral part of astronomy. The principal movers of the Scientific Revolution were deeply engaged in the subject. Tycho Brahe was a master astrologer. Johannes Kepler confessed his 'unwilling disbelief' and insisted that one should not 'throw the baby along with the bath water'.[5] Galileo, the founder of modern astronomy, had a lifelong interest in it. When an astronomer criticized Isaac Newton for his interest in astrology, the closet alchemist and author of *Principia Mathematica* is said to have replied: 'Sir, I have studied it, you have not.'[6] The same cannot be said of the modern scientists who object so strongly to astrology.

Astrology has made an enormous contribution to the history of science, not only to astronomy and mathematics, but also to medicine and psychology. Hippocrates, the father of medicine, allegedly declared that: 'A physician without knowledge of astrology has no right to call himself a physician.'[7] The psychoanalyst Carl Jung correctly saw astrology as the psychology of antiquity. The signs of the zodiac, he suggested, are 'archetypal images' or manifestations of the collective unconscious.[8] This no doubt explains the extraordinary power of astrological symbolism to kindle the imagination.

In the major traditions of astrology – in China, India, Mesopotamia, Egypt, the Middle East and Europe – there was an early move from predicting the fate of nations to divining the course of individual lives. As Western astrology split off from astronomy after the Scientific Revolution, the exploration of the psyche came to the fore. The emphasis shifted from delineating the machinery of destiny to interpreting human character, from predicting natural catastrophes to indicating the potential of an individual life. Despite its decline during the eighteenth and nineteenth centuries, astrology has risen like a phoenix as a great illuminator of the psyche at the dawn of the third millennium. In the Age of Aquarius it will undoubtedly play a central part in the emerging holistic and organic world view.

*

There are many currents in the great river of astrology. Early on this river divided into *natural* astrology and *judicial* astrology. The former predicts the motions of planets, and is now largely absorbed into astronomy, while the latter interprets the meaning of their influence on earth. The most important currents of *judicial* astrology are *mundane* astrology, dealing with the fate of nations, and *genethialical* astrology, the art of casting horoscopes of individuals. The most popular today is the latter which further subdivides into *natal* astrology, the birthchart as it influences the future personality; *hororary* astrology, the horoscope cast to answer a specific question concerning a particular time and place; and *electional* astrology, the horoscope cast to choose the right moment for an activity or enterprise. Then there is *medical* astrology which relates organs of the body to planets in the heavens and associates certain planets with the curative power of plants.

Among the plethora of astrological schools, societies and practitioners, four main trends in astrology have emerged in the twenty-first century. The first is to interpret the simplest factors in astrology in terms of popular psychology, using the sun signs of Western astrology and the animal signs of Chinese astrology as the main points in the horoscope. This type fills the newspapers, magazines and astrological 'cook books'. It is the most superficial, yet it can still help people to interpret their feelings and become clearer about their goals in life.

The second trend is an attempt to examine astrology on a statistical basis in order to give it a 'scientific' character and make it more acceptable to the academic community. But since astrology involves invisible forces, it is virtually impossible within the existing state of scientific knowledge to explain why and how it works.

The third trend recognizes the symbolic nature of astrology and uses it as a powerful technique to understand the character and destiny of human beings and their place within the universe. Ancient astrologers spoke of the planets as gods and classical astrologers gave them mythical names. Most modern astrologers see them as symbols, not referring to particular objects, but pointing to some more elusive reality in the collective unconscious. Indeed, as a symbolic language, astrology provides a great *mythos* that can inspire individuals to realize their full potential as social, psychological and spiritual beings.

Astrologers working in this area are often psychologists and therapists. They tend to offer generalities to cover all situations or subtly focus their interpretations according to their knowledge of their clients. A good astrologer assesses the character of her client, recognizes her problems and then fits them in to the horoscope. The extrapolated predictions are often wise counsel of what can be done in the context of her life. Obviously, the validity of this approach will depend largely on the astrologer's intuition and experience.

The fourth trend in modern astrology is to draw out its esoteric insights and hidden meanings. This approach sees the discipline as offering a process of initiation, a guide along the path of gnosis which leads to the illumination of the mind through knowledge. As such, it appeals particularly to those who wonder what the Age of Aquarius will bring, who believe in angels and spirits, and who see planetary energies in their bodies as well as in the heavens. Such individuals may live under the orange glare of cities, but they are continually looking up at the stars.

As we shall see, there is not one astrology but several – Chinese, Indian and Middle Eastern as well as Western. And just as there are several major trends in astrology, so there are many traditions. Even astrologers from the same school will make different interpretations of the same data. But they need not be exclusive and many astrologers work on several levels at once.

*

Clearly astrology has had its charlatans just as medicine has had its quacks. But at its best astrology can undoubtedly help individuals to make informed choices about the central concerns of life – work, love and health. From ancient times, it has been a vehicle for self-knowledge and offers the possibility of understanding oneself and shaping one's life. It addresses such central questions as 'Why am I here?', 'What is the purpose of my life?', 'How should I act?' It holds up a mirror in which individuals can see themselves and become aware of their potential. It can awaken and transform the self. Its symbolic language not only embodies ancient myths and symbols, but also points to hidden levels of consciousness. It appeals strongly to the heart and soul, to intuition and the imagination. Hence its perennial attraction for musicians, artists, writers and poets.

Astrology also raises many controversial questions. How do the heavenly bodies influence the personality of an individual at the time of birth? Does the horoscope really provide a map of the psyche? Is the foretelling of future events possible? Is the implied determinism incompatible with a notion of free will? How does the recent discovery of three new planets – Uranus, Neptune and Pluto – change the theory and practice of astrology? Above all, what does the persistence of astrology say about our condition and experience?

I set off on a world-wide search to answer these questions. Although somewhat sceptical at first, my researches and travels have led me to suspect that astrology contains, in a disguised form, the sacred science of the ancient world which is still highly relevant today. It not only conveys important truths about the structure of the universe, the character of human beings, and the course of history, but throws light on our rightful place within the cosmos.

Part One

Pillars of Destiny: China

1

Into the Dragon's Mouth

O N THE EDGE of the Gobi Desert on the ancient Silk Route, there is near Dunhuang an oasis, hidden among light brown dunes, called Crescent Moon Lake. In 1900 a Taoist monk called Wang Yuanlu came across a cave entrance set in some sandstone cliffs. With the flickering flame of his candle, he lit up exquisite Buddhist paintings on the walls of a great complex of temples. Even more startling, he discovered a vast hidden library which had laid untouched for more than a millennium. Called the 'Caves of a Thousand Buddhas', the temples had been founded in the fourth century by Buddhist monks as a centre for meditation, scholarship and artistic creativity.

The 750 caves, known today as the Magao Grottoes, were carved out of the sandstone. The library contained some 50,000 artefacts and their discovery was as important as that of the Dead Sea Scrolls.[1] The works included a Bible written in Syriac, a copy of the great Buddhist text known as the *Diamond Sutra* (the first printed book) and an ancient chart of the heavens.

In 1907 the archaeologist Sir Aurel Stein paid the Taoist monk who had made the discovery four silver pieces and carted off thousands of manuscripts and silk scroll paintings, including the star chart. These now lie in the Oriental and India Collections in the British Library.

The Chinese star chart, known as the Dunhuang star map, was drawn up around AD 940. When I went to see it, I was told by Graham Hutt, the curator of the collection, that it was so fragile that it could not be handled. The map is a cylindrical projection, similar to the kind Mercator developed in the sixteenth century, which presents the celestial globe projected on to a flat surface. The curator confirmed that it was the oldest known star map in the world.[2] The Dunhuang star map represented the fruition of thousands of years of patient star-gazing in China. It was drawn up at a time when Chinese astrology was at its peak and would have been used by the astrologers at the Imperial Court. It was a fabulous find.

What light could it shine on the Chinese understanding of the heavens and their influence on human destiny and character? I decided to go to China to find out.

The Soothsayers of Hong Kong

My first port of call was Hong Kong, a futuristic city of skyscrapers, where hordes of men and women, dressed immaculately in the latest designer clothes, stride purposefully to their work. It is a frenetic city, an unnerving city, a surreal city. It is called the dragon's mouth, with fiery energy flowing from its backbone along the mountains of mainland China, only to be stopped by the waters of the South China Sea.

Yet for all the post-modern architecture, the high fashion and the cutting-edge communication systems, ancient beliefs, arcane super-stitions and mysterious customs still flourish beneath the surface glitter. The headquarters of world banks consult experts in the ancient art of feng shui, a form of astro-ecology, about how best to position their skyscrapers and arrange their interiors in order to maximize profits. Many firms consult feng shui experts about the design and decoration of their offices. Executives check the Chinese almanac to find the right times for important events. Their employees visit astrologers to decide on the compatibility of partners, the most auspicious dates for weddings, and even the best time to conceive a child. They consult the ancient *I Ching*, the Book of Changes, to help them decide on career moves or when to travel. However large their salaries or however automated their lives, they travel to temples to divine the future and to heal themselves. They use astrology, often combined with other methods of divination, to explore their own personalities and to solve the difficult problems in their lives. By doing so, they come in contact with an ancient source of wisdom which reveals the ultimate nature of the universe and suggests that we must attune ourselves to it in order to live in peace and harmony.

The popular Wong Tai Sin temple on the mainland in Kowloon was founded in 1915 by a father and son who brought a portrait of the saint after whom it is named from the interior of China. A riot of colour, with red pillars, blue lattice work and yellow roofs, it is a typical Hong Kong temple, mainly Taoist, but mixed with Buddhist and Confucian elements. The Unicorn Hall, for instance, is devoted to Confucius and attended by students who want to do well in their studies. Its pavilions and halls are laid out according to feng shui principles; the main ones represent the five elements: metal, wood, fire, water and earth. It also has a typical Chinese garden with rugged miniature mountains and shapely evergreen trees. It contains a replica of the famous Wall of Nine Dragons in the Forbidden Temple which I had seen in Beijing. In the silent carp ponds, several large terrapins raise their enquiring heads among the lilies.

Wong Tai Sin is reputed to be an immortal being who cures illness and brings good fortune. His festival is on the twenty-third day of the eighth lunar month (usually in September). According to his autobiography, Wong Tai Sin was a poor shepherd boy born during the Tsun Dynasty: 'At fifteen, I was fortunate enough to have been blessed by a fairy who led me into a stone cave where I learned the art of refining cinnabar nine times into an immortal drug.' He became an adept in Taoist alchemy and lived in the cave for forty years until his brother, with the help of a fortune-teller, tracked him down. When asked where his sheep were, he took his brother to 'heaps of white boulders' which were quickly transformed into sheep at his call.[3] Fascinated by this impressive show, the brother took the necessary steps to become an immortal as well. This involved developing the 'pill of immortality', the Chinese equivalent of the Philosopher's Stone.

Inside the temple I joined the devout in their smart suits and dresses, both young and old, who laid out their offerings on a piece of newspaper on the ground in front of the pavilion containing the image of the saint. They prayed by moving their hands up and down with bowed heads towards the shrine. Before leaving, they placed burning joss sticks in sand held in great bronze urns.

I noticed that many people were shaking oval wooden cylinders full of bamboo sticks until one fell on the ground. A friend or a family member wrote its number down. They then repeated the same process many times. I learned that there are sets of forty, seventy-five or one hundred sticks, some of which are painted with black middles signifying yin (the female principle in the universe) while the plain ones are yang (the male principle). Each 'fortune stick' corresponds to Chinese characters which make a prediction. A medium is often consulted for the final interpretation.

The financial whiz kids and computer wizards of Hong Kong clearly hold superstitious beliefs and follow very ancient practises of divination which originated in Buddhist temples. Their practice with the fortune sticks would seem to be a simplified version of the *I Ching*, the oldest book in the world and still the most widely read book in China. But does it make sense? Is it possible to make any prediction about the future from an apparently random selection of sticks? Or does the process itself help the fortune-seeker become clearer about herself and her future?

These are not the only activities going on at the Wong Tai Sin temple. Attached to the temple compound is a rabbit warren of kiosks – about 160 in all – with men and women, heavy with years if not wisdom, offering you enlightenment and succour. As the English translation on a plaque puts it: this is a concrete village of 'soothsayers'.

Some are palmists, practising an art more properly called chiromancy which has been around for at least 3,000 years in China and India. I had already seen palmists at work in the gardens outside the Forbidden Palace in Beijing. The palmists take into account the shape of a person's hand and the lines on the palm to describe the owner's character and future, especially their relationships, career and prosperity. The size of the fingers and their fleshy mounds are said to indicate their characteristics. Not surprisingly, the Taoists were the first to use fingerprints as a means of identification in ancient China. I was also intrigued to discover that fingerprints are named after celestial bodies. The planets have the same associations as in Western astrology: sun, emotional stability; moon, emotion; Venus, romance; Mars, aggression; Saturn, prudence; Jupiter, wealth.

Other 'soothsayers' outside the temple were face-readers, experts in physiognomy. Again, this art was developed in ancient China by the Taoists. It was considered as a useful device in the 'tao of supremacy', that is the mastery of oneself and one's situation. A Taoist face 'map' was drawn up as early as 2500 BC. Clearly our faces provide an accurate guide to our moods, especially the lips and eyes, and our faces reflect our experience. The Chinese, however, believe that certain inherited facial features reveal your character: a pronounced forehead, for instance, indicates thoughtfulness; a short forehead, impulsiveness; a pointed chin, discontent; a dimpled chin, sensuality. Nevertheless, the Chinese are also aware that looks can be deceptive and no two faces are the same. A wise person does not judge by appearances alone.

However fascinating were the palmists and face-readers, I was chiefly interested in the Chinese 'astrologers'. I decided to sit down at booth thirty-nine which had a sign saying 'English'. Seated behind a desk was a small benign-looking man in his sixties. He wore a formal suit and tie and had thick-rimmed glasses. He gave me a pink card which declared: 'Speak English Teller'. As we discussed the fee – his English was certainly rudimentary – a stylish young woman came up and spoke to him rapidly in Chinese. Giggling, she withdrew. It seemed that most of the astrologer's clients were young women.

The price agreed (250 Hong Kong dollars), my astrologer asked me the hour and the date of my birth and tapped the details into a mini-computer. He then noted on a pink piece of paper the time, date, month and year of my birth, each written in two beautiful Chinese characters. He explained that each was a 'heavenly branch' and an 'earthly stem'. He then did the same for each year from 1960 to 2034. The piece of paper also had spaces to write the most significant signs for my life in ten-year-spans from the age of six to seventy-six. He was in fact practising the traditional astrology known as the 'Four Pillars of Destiny', popularly called the 'eight signs', which attaches an element, or a combination of elements, to different moments of time.

After analysing the chart in silence for a time and writing down signs in beautiful calligraphy with firm strokes, he lifted up his head and said gravely: 'You, Dog.'

This I assumed was referring to the year of my birth which, according to the Chinese zodiac, assigns twelve different animals to every twelve years, rotating in a complete cycle of sixty years.

'You belong, earth,' my astrologer continued. 'Your wife's position combined, right side, left side, water.'

And the conclusion: 'Unstable in love life. Earth, weak; water stronger.'

Having been divorced some six years earlier and having started a new relationship with Elizabeth who was travelling with me, this was not good news. The soothsayer looked at me with a side-long glance, as if to say: 'Women, trouble.'

All was not lost, however. He smiled and said: 'Lucky for you is fire, earth, wood.' I would at least get on with people of these signs. But then the bad news: 'Unlucky is gold, water. Gold: regress, sickness. Water: loss of capital'.

My astrologer then outlined on his pink chart the bad years in yellow and then the good ones in red. I was pleased to see that as he carefully marked the ten-year transits there was at least more red than yellow.

'Not special before thirty-six, better after sixty-six', he declared. Then he gave further details. 'Very special,' from 1964 to 1968 (when I had left boarding school, lived in London for a year, sailed around the world as a cadet in the P&O-Orient Shipping Company, and taught English in West Africa). 'Regress,' he claimed, had occurred between 1970 and 1972 (when I was researching my Ph.D.). It was very special between 1974 and 1979 (when I was involved in setting up a rural community and my daughter was born) and between 1980 and 1983 (when I was writing my first books and my son was born). He was silent about the years 1992–94 which were the most difficult for me after a circumnavigation of Africa which led to my divorce. Unfortunately, I was in the middle of another inauspicious period which would last from 2000 to 2003. During this period I had been working intensely on alchemy and astrology, moving house and starting a new life with my partner. But then it would be plain sailing until 2010 when things would deteriorate again for a further three years.

And what of my old age? The astrologer stressed that the period from 2020 to 2021 would be worrisome for my health (I would be seventy-four and seventy-five then). All would be fine again until 2030, when I would reach eighty-four. He made no mention of dates after that; I assumed that it was to be the year of my death. Years before in Sri Lanka, the astrologer-palmist of a friend's family had predicted the same date. I didn't believe it at the time, but now I began to wonder. It was extraordinary that astrologers from very different traditions should come to the same conclusion.

As for my overall situation, he said that my general fortune was normal and that I would be neither rich nor poor, but stable. My health was good and I would live a long life.

And my love life? I had, he said, more than two 'girlfriends' in the past (true) and that I was unstable in my relations with women (possibly . . .).

The final words of my Chinese astrologer were: 'Your general fortune, best before thirty-four!' That was not particularly good to know two decades later. I would clearly have to make the best of what remained, but at least I had been given a long life to enjoy and to prepare for the next.

Because of his broken English and the popular nature of his

approach, my astrologer at the Wong Tai Sin temple in Hong Kong could only give a very superficial account of my character and destiny. Nevertheless, he was part of a very ancient tradition that was full of deep meaning, and which had a long history stretching back to the earliest days of Chinese civilization. He insisted that his method was not a superstition but a science.

The method which he was practising is the most popular today in Hong Kong and Taiwan. Known as *Tzu P'ing*, it is based on the 'Four Pillars of Destiny' (*Ssu Chu*), that is the year, fortnight, day and time of your birth. It is sometimes called the 'eight signs' (*ba tze*): each pillar is designated by two 'signs' or Chinese word characters. It offers a detailed profile of your personality and indicates, among other things, your emotional and intellectual disposition at birth, as well as the kind of life which is most likely to fulfil your potential.

2

The Dog and the Tiger

WHEN MY HONG KONG soothsayer had said 'You, Dog' he was referring to the type of Chinese astrology most familiar to Westerners, known as *Ming Shu*, literally, 'Circle of Animals'. It is the easiest to understand as the dozen animals, with their associated personality types, are similar to the twelve sun signs in Western astrology. The Dog is my sign in Chinese astrology, just as Leo is my sun sign in Western astrology. One considers the solar year, the other the lunar month as the defining characteristic of your personality. The nature of the dog is to be patient, faithful and watchful.

Almost everyone knows that in Chinese astrology every year is associated with an animal, each with its own characteristics. What is less widely known is that they come around in a twelve-year cycle. This is sometimes called the 'Chinese zodiac', but the animals are not directly related to specific constellations in the sky as are the signs of the Western zodiac.

Where did the idea of the twelve creatures of the Circle of Animals come from? A popular legend in China credits Buddha with the origin of the system, no doubt because of his celebrated compassion for all beings. It is said that one day he invited all the animals on earth to visit him, but in the event only twelve turned up. As a show of his appreciation, he gave each animal a year with which they would be associated for ever. The order of the cycle of years reflects the order in which they arrived: Rat, Ox, Tiger, Rabbit, Dragon, Snake, Horse, Goat, Monkey, Cock, Dog and Pig. The year 2000, appropriately enough for the dawn of a new millennium, was the Year of the Dragon, the most auspicious sign and the most respected for its creative energy.[1]

The problem with this story is that Buddha was born in India around 563 BC and died around 483 BC. Buddhism reached China in the fifth century AD where it combined with Taoism to produce Cha'n

Buddhism, later known as Zen in Japan. Chinese astrology, however, is thousands of years older.

Another version of the origins of the Chinese 'zodiac' of twelve animals gives it a divine origin. In this version, it is said that, once upon a time, the Jade Emperor in Heaven wondered what the animals on earth were like. He called his chief adviser and said: 'I have reigned in heaven for a long time but I have never seen the animals on earth. What do they look like? What are their ways? Are they intelligent? How do they help humanity?'

The chief adviser replied that there were countless animals on earth and it would be impossible to see them all. He suggested inviting twelve of the most interesting up for a visit to heaven. The Jade Emperor readily agreed.

'Now, which animals shall I invite?' thought the adviser to himself. 'I know, I'll first invite the rat and ask him to give an invitation to his friend the cat!'

After more thought, he also decided to invite the ox, tiger, rabbit, dragon, snake, horse, goat, monkey and cock, asking them to present themselves at the gates of heaven at six o'clock sharp the next morning.

When the rat heard the news, he was delighted and rushed round to see the cat to tell him about their good fortune. Now the cat loved to roll up in a ball and sleep. Since he was a late riser, he asked the rat to wake him up well before six. When the rat went to bed that night, he could not sleep. Tossing and turning, he thought how sleek and smart the cat looked compared to himself. 'The Jade Emperor is bound to choose him before me,' he groaned. It was all too much; he finally decided not to wake the cat as agreed.

The next morning at six o'clock sharp all the other animals assembled at the gates of heaven and were welcomed into the imperial palace by the chief adviser.

The Jade Emperor was at first delighted with all the animals but when he counted them he began to frown.

'They're all very interesting, I grant you that, but why are there only eleven animals? You said there would be twelve.'

The chief adviser trembled and blurted out. 'There must be some mistake, your majesty, please wait a while and I will sort it out.'

He rushed out and told his servant to go down to earth and get the first animal he came across. It so happened that the servant met an old farmer taking his pig to the market. When he heard that the Jade

Emperor of Heaven would like to see his pig, the old man was only too pleased to oblige.

In the meantime, the rat was so concerned about being overlooked that he had jumped up on the ox's back and began to play the flute. The Emperor was amused and then enchanted. When it came to putting the animals in order, he decided to give the rat pride of place. Second place was given to the ox for being so generous and letting the rat clamber on his back. Third place went to the tiger because he looked so courageous; fourth to the rabbit because of his lovely white fur; and fifth to the dragon because of his fiery energy. The snake with his beautiful sinuous body was given sixth place and the horse with his handsome posture seventh. The ram was eighth because of his strong horns; the monkey ninth because he was so agile; the cock tenth because of his splendid feathers and the dog eleventh because of his watchful ways. And there stood the pig at the end of line, bewildered but happy to be called so suddenly to heaven. He was given twelfth place, last but not least.

After the Emperor had inspected all the animals and the parade was over, the cat suddenly arrived in heaven and began to knock as loud as he could on the gates. Unfortunately, cats' paws aren't very good for knocking on doors and it was a long time before he could get any attention.

When the chief adviser eventually opened the gates, the cat exclaimed breathlessly: 'I'm terribly sorry I'm late. I overslept, your honour. Rat was meant to wake me up but he didn't.'

'I'm sorry too,' said the chief adviser. 'I'm afraid you're too late. We already have all the animals we need, thank you.' And he closed the gates of heaven on the cat with a resounding thud.

Cat was furious. He never forgave the rat and that is why, to this day, cats and rats do not get on well with each other.

Poor old cat! But he is not alone in his love of sleep and his foibles. Every animal has its own weaknesses and strengths. Some are outward-going and assertive; others are more inward-looking and reticent. Some quickly become angry; others are more patient. Some get on with other animals; some don't. Compatibility is one of the main themes in this popular form of Chinese astrology. And the relationships apply to friends and colleagues, as well as to lovers. The Rat and the Dragon, for example, get on well on many different levels: they make good lovers, adventurous colleagues and steadfast friends.

In my case, my animal sign is the Dog and my partner is the Tiger.

Fortunately, Tiger and Dog get on very well. The Tiger likes to take risks; the Dog is more cautious and can warn of danger. The Tiger appreciates the Dog's watchfulness, while the Dog likes the Tiger's impetuous nature. But both can leap into action if need be, and together they make powerful allies. Both are idealists and are champions of the oppressed. The Tiger should remember that the Dog needs tender reassurance if the relationship is to succeed.[2] While being most compatible with the Tiger, Horse and Pig, the Dog also gets on well with the Rat, Rabbit and Monkey. I have no conflict with the Snake and Goat, although we might need to make an effort. I lack sympathy with the Ox and Cock and am downright antagonistic towards the Dragon.[3]

Compatibility is not the only preoccupation. Each animal is associated with an element, a colour, yin or yang, and a direction of the compass. The Rat, for instance, is associated with the element water (which works in harmony with wood), the colour black (connected with honour), receptive yin, and the direction North. He or she is linked with mid-winter when yin is at its strongest. As a Dog, my element is metal, my colour is black or dark blue. I'm more yang than yin (known as 'little yang'); my direction is West, and my season is autumn.

In this popular form of Chinese astrology, your fortune is influenced not only by your animal sign, but also by your position according to the year in a sixty-year cycle. The overriding unit for measuring the passage of time in China is the 'Great Year', based on the cycle of Jupiter, which takes approximately twelve years to revolve around the sun ($12 \times 5 = 60$). The years are often grouped into three, making up a cycle of 180 years.

The sixty-year cycle plays a key part in Chinese culture. There are sixty gods associated with the cycle and each year one of them takes centre stage. In Taoist temples, people often make offerings of incense, flowers, fruit and even money to their birth god to bring good fortune for themselves. In the White Cloud Temple in Beijing, the centre of Taoism in northern China, I saw young and old women burning incense in front of their 'divine protector' – pictured as a seated general – for the year in which they were born.

How does this fit in with the twelve animals signs? Within the sixty-year cycle, one animal sign will appear five times, but each time it will appear in a slightly different form. This helps to explain why two people with the same animal sign but born in a different year will experience different fortunes. In the case of the dog, for instance, the cycle begins with the year of 'Dog on Guard' (Chia Hsü), then 'Sleepy Dog' (Ping

Hsü) twelve years later, then 'Dog Going into the Mountain' (Mou Hsü), 'Temple Dog' (Keng Hsü) and finally 'Family Dog' (Jen Hsü). The cycle then begins all over again.[4]

Heavenly stems and earthly branches

The two Chinese characters for my year of birth, written in the Western alphabet as Ping Hsü, represent what is called a 'heavenly stem' (in this case, Ping) and an 'earthly branch' (Hsü). They not only unite heaven and earth, which is at the heart of Chinese astrology, but together represent a particular variation of one of the twelve animals. There are twelve heavenly stems and ten earthly branches which combine rather like two cogs in the sixty-year cycle.

Elizabeth, for example, was born in the 'Year of the Tiger'. According to the pairing of the stems and branches in the sixty-year cycle, it was the 'Year of Tiger Descending Mountain'. While there are general personality traits always associated with being a tiger, this particular variation is significant in forecasting family relationships, future well-being and job prospects.

Heavenly Stems	Number	Direction
Chia	1	ENE by E
Yi	2	ESE by E
Ping	3	SSE by S
Ting	4	SSW by S
Wu	5	Centre
Chi	6	Centre
Keng	7	WSW by W
Hsin	8	WNW by W
Jen	9	NNW by N
Kuei	10	NNE by N

Earthly Branches	Animal	Period of the Year	Direction
Tzu	Rat	mid-winter	N
Ch'ou	Ox	end of winter	NNE
Yin	Tiger	early spring	ENE
Mao	Rabbit	mid-spring	E
Ch'en	Dragon	end of spring	ESE
Szu	Snake	early summer	SSE
Wu	Horse	mid-summer	S
Wei	Goat	end of summer	SSW
Shen	Monkey	early autumn	WSW
Yu	Cock	mid-autumn	W
Hsü	Dog	end of autumn	WNW
Hai	Pig	early winter	NNW

To find out the particular variation of your animal type, you have to find your position in the sixty-year cycle. To do this, you consult the lunar chart for the year of your birth. According to the Western solar calendar, my partner was born on 20 July, 1950. The lunar chart tells me that it was the sixth lunar month in the twenty-seventh year of the sixty-year cycle, that is Keng Yin. The heavenly stem Keng is associated with the element metal, the colour white, and an acrid taste, while the earthly branch Yin is linked with the Tiger, early spring, and the direction East-North-East. Anyone born in the twenty-seventh year of the cycle is said to be tough, hard-working and generous. You can – like many Tigers – have sudden mood swings, reacting especially strongly when you are misled or offended, but your anger quickly dissipates. Family and friends appreciate your care and energy. On the other hand, if you were born in the 'Year of the Tiger in the Forest' or the 'Year of the Tiger Standing Still' you would be more observant and less volatile.[5]

In my case, I was born on the 23 August 1946, which is the seventh lunar month in the twenty-third year of the sixty-year cycle known as Ping Hsü, 'The Year of the Sleepy Dog'. The heavenly stem Ping is associated with fire, red, and bitter taste, while Hsü corresponds to the Dog, late autumn and the direction West-North-West. I am said to have a relaxed manner which enables me to listen to other people and help them with their dilemmas. But as a sleepy fellow, I do not like to be forced to meet deadlines or take decisions when I am not ready.

The System of Hours

A further dimension to your horoscope, based on the Circle of Animals, is added by the animal associated with your hour of birth. The Chinese day is divided into twelve units, each with a 'beginning hour' and an 'exact hour'. Each one corresponds to two Western hours on the twenty-four-hour clock, although the first spans from 23.00 to 01.00 hours and the last from 21.00 to 23.00 hours. The division is very ancient, made long before the first hours recorded on a Chinese calendar dating back to the fifth century BC. The twelve hours are named after the so-called 'earthly branches' which correspond to the twelve animal signs. The first two-hour period is therefore Tzu the Rat, and the last Hai the Pig.

Strictly speaking, to work out the animal sign for one's hour of birth, one must first convert the hour to Universal Time (Greenwich Mean Time) and then add nine hours to turn it into Chinese Coastal Time.[6] Most popular Western books on Ming Shu astrology do not, however, make the second conversion. Since I was born around 16.00 hours British Summer Time, if it is converted into Universal Time, my hour animal is Shen the Monkey, but if the conversion is made into Chinese time, I am Tzu the Rat.

Born in Shen hours implies that I have a lucky streak and find it easy to make a living, but I can also be extravagant. I need to give time to difficulties which might come in my love life. Elizabeth, born at 22.00 hours, and therefore corresponding to the earthly branch of Hai (the Pig), is likely to have a natural talent for handicrafts. Having begun something, she likes to complete it.

Most of the popular books on Chinese astrology use the twelve animals as emblems for the year and hour of birth. While the year animal is said to reflect your dominant personality and has implications for your love life and career, the hour animal is said to represent your

Hsai Hours		Animal	Element	Hours
1	子	Rat	Water	2300–0100
2	丑	Ox	Earth	0100–0300
3	寅	Tiger	Wood	0300–0500
4	卯	Rabbit	Wood	0500–0700
5	辰	Dragon	Earth	0700–0900
6	巳	Snake	Fire	0900–1100
7	午	Horse	Fire	1100–1300
8	未	Goat	Earth	1300–1500
9	申	Monkey	Metal	1500–1700
10	酉	Cock	Metal	1700–1900
11	戌	Dog	Earth	1900–2100
12	亥	Pig	Water	2100–2300

The Twelve-Hour System in the Hsia Calendar

'inner companion' and enhances, counterbalances or checks your main animal.[7] It therefore gives the final touch to your personality. In many ways, the animals are rather like the totem animals of shamans who act as guides and protectors in their vision quests.

I am a Dog by year, and a Monkey by hour according to this system. Elizabeth is a Tiger by year and a Pig by hour. Tigers and Dogs get on well, according to the traditional interpretations, and I like the idea that as a Pig she likes to look after me. I would like to be faithful, loyal and protective like the Dog. But then my Monkey side gets up to his mischievous tricks, and I like to swing from branch to branch around the globe without a care in the world . . .

As with the symbolism of animals in the West, the animals of the zodiac reflect the characteristics given to them by Chinese folklore. The Pig, for instance, has a much more positive image in China than in the West; its pictogram has a roof over it suggesting its home-loving qualities. The twelve animals are also heroes of old Chinese legends and in their different ways are all considered auspicious. The link with the heavens is established by the match between the twelve-year cycle of the animals with the twelve-year cycle of Jupiter.

The Circle of Animals is very ancient in China. A beautiful stone decorated with them has been discovered near Sian in the tomb of a T'ang princess, Chang Huai, who died in the seventh century AD. Another princess, Hun-shin Jun-ju (Kong Jo), who married the Tibetan king Srang-Tsan Gampo, introduced it around 642 into Tibet where it became known as *jung-tsi*. There is firm evidence that as early as the sixth century BC the twelve-fold division of the years became associated with the Circle of Animals.[8] But they probably go back thousands of years earlier and legend in China ascribes the beginning of the first twelve-year cycle to the semi-mythical emperor Hung Ti – the Yellow Emperor – in 2637 BC.

3

The Way and its Virtue

Ten Thousand things carry yin and embrace yang.

Lao Tzu

To understand Chinese astrology, it is essential to understand the Chinese notions of the Tao, yin and yang, and the five elements. They all have their roots in Taoism, the oldest philosophy in China. I had long been a student of Taoism. Its greatest text, the *Tao Te Ching* (The Way and its Virtue), is attributed to Lao Tzu, who is said to have died in the sixth century BC. It is one of the most beautiful, poetic and profound works of world literature. From the same tradition comes the ancient book of divination known as the *I Ching* (Book of Changes) which has had a strong influence on astrology.

It is important to realize that Taoism developed at a time when China was a country of farmers. Unlike pastoralists, who can order their animals' lives as necessary, farmers are dependent on forces they do not control. If they are to survive, they must co-operate more sensitively with the laws of nature. Whatever upsets the natural order is bad because it inevitably brings disastrous consequences. To achieve this peaceful harmony, the Chinese developed a love of compromise. The ultimate aim is to attain peace within oneself and around oneself. It is therefore essential to avoid extremes: the middle path, as for Buddha and the ancient Greeks, is the essence of wisdom.

The Tao

The natural order is called the Tao. This is best translated as 'the Way'
but there is a problem. As the great sage Lao Tzu observes: 'The Tao
that can be told is not the eternal Tao.'[1] The Tao cannot be explained
or described; it can only be sensed. The human mind, only one part of
the whole, cannot conceive of the One any more than a toad in a well
can understand the vastness of the ocean. But while the Tao cannot be
known, its dynamic effects can be felt. They appear as a kind of energy
or life-force which the Chinese call *chi*. Chi pervades everything and is
responsible for growth and regeneration. It also gives structure and
qualities to physical objects.

The Tao produces chi from nothingness and then reveals itself
through the two opposing and complementary forces of yin and yang
which are at work throughout the universe. The Taoist work *Huai Nan
Tzu* (c. 120 BC) describes how the Great Beginning was the source of all
things:

> Before heaven and earth had taken form all was vague and
> amorphous. Therefore it was called the Great Beginning. The Great
> Beginning produced emptiness and emptiness produced the universe.
> The universe produced material forces which had limits. That which
> was clear and light drifted up to become heaven, while that which
> was heavy and turgid solidified to become earth. The combined
> essences of heaven and earth became yin and yang, the concen-
> trated essences of the yin and yang became the four seasons, and
> the scattered essences of the four seasons became the myriad
> creatures of the world. After a long time, the hot forces of the
> accumulated yang produced fire and the essence of the fire force
> became the sun; the cold force of accumulated yin became water
> and the essence of the water force became the moon. The essence
> of the excess force of the sun and moon became the stars and the
> planets. Heaven received the sun, moon and stars while earth
> received water and soil.[2]

Yin and yang ebb and flow like a wave on the ocean. The *Tao te Ching*
says that living creatures are surround by yin and envelop yang and the
harmony of their life depends on the harmony of the two principles:

The Tao begot one.
One begot two.
Two begot three.
Three begot the ten thousand things.

The ten thousand things carry yin and embrace yang.
They achieve harmony by combining these forces.[3]

The process can be likened to the growth of a tree. From the earth emerges a shoot which splits into two leaves (yin and yang). The stem grows between the two leaves, combining to form three bodies in one. From these all the other branches and leaves grow.

The famous Taoist symbol shows how the forces of yin and yang are entwined, the one now waxing and other waning and vice versa. They may be likened to dolphins playing or lovers embracing. The black spot in the white and the white spot in the black show that they are not separate forces but aspects of the same reality. As the ancient text *Nei Ching* says: 'In yin there is yang and in yang there is yin.'

The Chinese name for the yin-yang symbol is *T'ai Chi T'u*. It is sometimes translated as 'The Great Ultimate'. *T'ai* means 'supreme'; *chi* here means 'pole'; and *t'u*, 'design'. Combined together, the three Chinese characters designate the North Pole, the axis on which the universe rotates. The practitioner of the martial art of t'ai chi thus copies the universe as she turns on her own axis. She also moves from yin to yang and back again.

The T'ai Chi T'u symbol is often surrounded by the eight trigrams which are said to represent all the possible combinations of yin and yang. The straight lines at the top represent Heaven and the South and the broken lines at the bottom, Earth and the North. When linked into pairs, they form the sixty-four hexagrams of the *I Ching* which allegedly contains the secret of 'all that is to come'. To discover what conforms to the natural order of the Tao, to find out what is in harmony with the universe, is the central aim of Chinese astrology and divination.

The roots of the Chinese characters for 'yin' and 'yang' reveal their meaning. The character for yin signifies the dark or northern side of a hill; yang, the sunny or south side. Extended to cover virtually the whole gamut of human affairs, yin represents the feminine, yielding, receptive principle and even numbers, while yang symbolizes the masculine, dominating, expanding principle and odd numbers. Yin is inward and introvert, yang is outward and extrovert. Neither yin nor yang are good or bad in themselves; only an excess of one or the other is potentially dangerous and harmful. This is true in acupuncture as well as in astrology. A woman should have some yang, although not too much. Even in love-making, a man should not exhaust his yang while assimilating his partner's yin.

This dualism is evoked by the yin images of the White Tiger (the colour of death) associated with the West and evening, and the yang image of the Green Dragon (colour of growth) associated with the East and morning. These images are sometimes painted on walls of houses. Within the Taoist religion, the oldest system of belief in China, the Queen Mother of the West is balanced by the Jade Emperor who dwells on the mountain peak of the East. Aware of the dualism of yin and yang in themselves, Taoists seek to recover the original oneness and harmony of the Tao.

The Five Elements

The chi of the Tao is first manifested by the interplay of yin and yang, but these are further subdivided into five forces – wood, fire, earth, metal and water. They are known as *hsing* which is usually translated as 'elements'. In Chinese, however, the term hsing means 'to march' or 'progress'. It reflects the flowing Taoist conception of nature which is not entirely captured by the Greek concept of the four elements which combine to form the substance of all things. Some have preferred to call them 'phases', 'agents' or even 'activities'.[4] I prefer to use the term 'element' since it is more familiar, but it should be remembered that in the original Chinese it always implies a dynamic process.[5] The five elements are powerful, invisible, interacting energies in ever-flowing cyclical motion. It is believed that not only time, space and nature can be explained in terms of the five elements, but also a person's character and destiny.

Each element has a particular 'virtue'. Water dissolves and sinks down; fire heats and rises; wood is alive and can be sharpened by a tool, metal is inert and can be moulded into a shape. Earth gives rise to the other four; it is the main point of reference and is identified with the centre.

The elements have a power to create and a power to destroy each other, depending on their particular natural virtue. They interact according to fundamental rules. From an astrological point of view, their interaction indicates the good or bad fortune which can befall a person or a place. The predicted pattern is:

wood produces fire	wood destroys earth
fire produces earth	earth destroys water
earth produces metal	water destroys fire
metal produces water	fire destroys metal
water produces wood	metal destroys wood

Their relationships may be illustrated by a Cycle of Creation and a Cycle of Destruction:

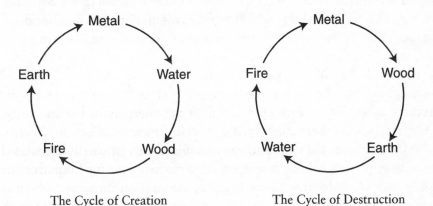

The Cycle of Creation   The Cycle of Destruction

According to the doctrine compiled by Chou Yen (305–270 BC), each element corresponds to one of the five seasons of the year (spring, summer, dog days, autumn and winter), the five compass directions, a colour, a prime number, a taste sensation, yin and/or yang energy, ages and one or more parts of the body.[6]

Since all is connected in the Tao, it is not surprising that there are certain relationships and affinities between the elements and other aspects of nature and the human body. Wood rules the liver, its colour is green, its taste acid and its number eight. Fire rules the heart, its colour is red, its taste bitter and its number seven. Earth rules the spleen and is associated with yellow, a sweet taste and the number five. Metal rules the lungs and is linked with white, pungent taste and the number nine. Water rules the kidneys and is connected to black, a salty taste and the number six. The five planets visible to the naked eye, called the Five Stars, are also associated with the elements. The Chronological Star is Mercury whose quintessence is water; Grand White is Venus (metal); Sparkling Deluder is Mars (fire); the Year Star is Jupiter (wood); and the Quelling Star is Saturn (earth). Since each planet is thought to have its own pitch, circling together they create the music of the spheres and show the inherent harmony of the universe. And the five intrinsic elements of a human being are essence, sense, vitality (ching), spirit (shen) and energy (chi). The first two give rise to the consciousness, while the other three are known as the three treasures.

The interaction of the elements is described in one of the oldest Chinese texts. The *Huang Ti Nei Ching Su Wen* (Handbook on Medicine of the Yellow Emperor), which reached its present form around the second century BC, describes their action. Fire, associated with summer and the South, symbolizes the 'great Yang'; water associated with winter and the North, symbolizes the 'great Yin'. Wood, connected with spring and the East, is the 'little Yin'. Metal is associated with the autumn and the West and is the 'little Yang'. Earth, situated in the centre, contains all the other elements and is related to them all.

The theory of the five elements forms the basis of Chinese medicine and acupuncture, as well as that of astrology. If the five elements assigned by Chinese medicine to each of the vital organs are balanced in a person and interact with each other according to the cycles of birth and destruction, he or she will enjoy good health. On the other hand, if one element grows too strong or too weak, it will upset the balance and illness will result. If the kidney is weak, for instance, water will not be able to keep the fire under control. The result will be a disease related to the heart, such as high blood pressure or an irregular heartbeat. The remedy would be to use medicine or acupuncture to regain the balance of the elements within the body.

The five elements pervade Chinese culture and way of life. They represent, for instance, five actions or gestures used in traditional *qigong* exercises. They were also associated with the feudal states of China, and have even been used by secret societies to show the relationship between their members: the head is metal, while the brotherhood is water.

The five elements have an effect throughout the year but, except for the element of the earth, they have a high and low ebb like the tide. Wood, for instance, has its maximum influence at the spring equinox and its minimum at the autumn equinox. Yin and yang also alternate during the day, beginning at 23.00 hours with the first element, water, which is yang, followed at 01.00 hours with earth, which is yin, and so on.

Through the creative interplay of yin and yang and the transformation of the elements into each other, the universe is in a constant state of flux. The change is not, however, random or arbitrary for it is part of the overall pattern. At the moment of creation, all things receive chi and are given a particular nature by a principle called *li*. This is usually translated as order but it is a spontaneous order and is not imposed by law. The philosopher Chu Hsi expressed well their interaction:

> Throughout heaven and earth there is *Li* and there is Chi. *Li* is the Tao (organizing) all forms from above, and the root from which all things are produced. Chi is the instrument (composing) all forms from below, and the tools and raw materials with which all things are made. Thus men and all other things must receive this *Li* at the moment of their coming into being, and thus get their specific nature; so also must they receive this Chi, and thus get their form.[7]

The Eight Trigrams

The constant process of change and the emerging order take place within a universal framework which is expressed from very ancient times by eight trigrams (*pa kuan*). The Great Commentary of the *I Ching* describes them:

> There is in the Changes the Great Primal Beginning. This generates the two primary forces (yin and yang). The two primary forces

generate the four images (major and minor yin and yang). The four
images generate the eight trigrams. The eight trigrams determine
good fortune and misfortune. Good fortune and misfortune create
the great field of action.[8]

Each trigram is made up of three lines, which can be either broken yin
lines (- -) or unbroken yang lines (–). The trigrams form the basis of
the *I Ching* which is at least 5,000 years old. Although the Great
Commentary is traditionally attributed to Confucius, the older layers of
the text assumed their present form a century before Confucius and his
pupils undoubtedly added their own interpretations later.[9] It dates back
to before first millennium and was written down with commentaries
and appendices by the time of the Han dynasty (206 BC–AD 220). As
a great classic of Chinese cosmology, it presents heaven, earth and
humanity as embodied in one organic system resonating with correspondences.

The main work is said to come from the legendary Fu Hsi who is
also remembered for inventing the Chinese calendar. He allegedly saw
the original eight trigrams marked on the back of a 'dragon horse'
emerging from the Yellow River. Their configuration is called the 'River
Chart' (*Ho T'u*). However, the real inspiration may have come from
the shapes on the back of tortoise shells which were used to predict the
future by heating them up and seeing how they cracked. In the Great
Commentary to the *I Ching* it is written:

> When in early antiquity Pao Hsi (Fu Hsi) ruled the world, he looked
> upward and contemplated the images in the heavens; he looked
> downward and contemplated the patterns on earth. He contem-
> plated the markings of the birds and beasts and the adaptations to
> the regions. He proceeded directly from himself and directly from
> objects. Thus he invented the eight trigrams in order to enter into
> connection with the virtues of the light of the gods and to regulate
> the conditions of all beings.[10]

This clearly demonstrates the intimate correspondence between heaven
and earth in Chinese thinking and astrology, expressed in the West by
the Hermetic dictum: 'As above, so below'.

Each trigram represents an essential aspect of nature: heaven, water,
mountain, thunder, wind, fire, earth and lake. Taken together, they are
considered to be a simplified model of the universe. They also came to

symbolize human relationships, the organs in the human body, various animals, shapes, colours and even trades.

The first ordering of eight trigrams was called 'The Former Heaven Sequence', with three yang lines at the top indicating South and three yin lines at the bottom indicating North. They represent the annual cycle of yin and yang as it waxes and wanes through the seasons, from the winter solstice when yin is at its greatest, to the summer solstice when yang is at its maximum, and to the equinoxes when they are balanced.

The trigrams were rearranged allegedly by Kin Wen (c. 1160 BC) into 'The Later Heaven Sequence'. It became clear that the eight trigrams were insufficient to represent the complexities and subtleties of life. So pairs of trigrams were placed together to form hexagrams (*kua*). By exhausting all the possible configurations of the trigrams, it was found that sixty-four hexagrams could be produced. They mirror the gradual movement in the universe from absolute yin to absolute yang and back again in a never-ending cycle.

The system clearly provided a much more refined model of both the universe and of human relationships. It formed the basis of the *I Ching* which became a divinatory tool since the hexagrams were thought to contain, in coded form, all the information about the universe. At first it was mainly used as an oracle to make decisions about politics and warfare, but today it is primarily used to ask a question about the future in order to decide on a course of action. It is a work consulted by feng shui experts and astrologers alike.

To consult the *I Ching*, it was the practice to cast fifty yarrow sticks to work out the relevant hexagram. But today many use an easier method of tossing three coins six times to establish the six lines of the hexagram. The meaning and interpretation of the hexagram can then be made by consulting the *I Ching*. To acquire a meaningful answer, however, it is first necessary to pose a clear question within a specific time frame. It is also a good idea to clear the head of all clutter by meditating in a quiet room beforehand, in order to be entirely focused on the question when tossing the coins. To interpret *I Ching* in the language of today, it helps to bear in mind that the original commentaries were written in the context of feudal China. Any interpretation requires imagination and intuition, as well as clear thinking and abiding calm.

The *I Ching* is not only one of the oldest works of Chinese metaphysics, but is also a crucible of profound wisdom. Jung considered it rightly 'a great and singular' work for lovers of self-knowledge.[11] It is still regarded in the East as a guide to social relations as well as an oracle. In the West, the dualism of yin and yang impressed the seventeenth-century philosopher and mathematician Leibniz, who developed the binary logic which gave rise to computer technology. It also finds an echo in modern science. The system of combining pairs of trigrams to form sixty-four hexagrams is similar to the configuration of DNA. Its dynamic and flowing understanding of nature anticipated quantum mechanics, and its vision of the One has inspired the search for a unified field theory of the universe.

4

Surveying the Infinite

The Red Road encircles the heart of heaven.

THE SUCHOW PLANISPHERE

AT DUSK IN BEIJING, the setting sun lights up on the skyline the rings of great armillary spheres mounted on the battlements of a watchtower, part of the original city walls. Known as the Ancient Observatory, it dates back to the days of Kublai Khan. The Great Khan and the later Ming and Qing emperors relied heavily on astrology before making any major decision. The present observatory was built from 1437 to 1446 to make astrological predictions as well as to draw up star charts to guide navigators across the seas.

It was not only in Beijing that the Chinese had observatories. The Jesuit Matteo Ricci observed in 1600 that on top of a high hall within the city walls in Nanking: 'There is an ample terrace, capitally adapted for astronomical observations, and surrounded by magnificent buildings erected of old. Here some of the astronomers take their stand every night to observe whatever may appear in the heavens, whether meteoric fires or comets, and to report them in detail to the emperor.'[1]

The use of astronomical instruments by Chinese astrologers goes back to ancient times. Jade rings dating from 1000 BC have been found, which were held out at arm's length and enabled the user to orientate himself among the constellations of stars in the heavens.[2] The jagged outer edges of the circular jade template would tally with the pattern of stars surrounding the Pole Star.

One of the most striking artefacts I discovered in the gardens of the Ancient Observatory in Beijing was a stone carving of a solar eclipse dating from the Han Dynasty (206 BC–AD 220). It depicts a bird covered by a toad – the inner symbol for the sun is a three-legged bird and for the moon a toad or sometimes a hare. The sun and the moon, like all the planets in the heavens, have a hidden meaning. As within yin and yang, each has enclosed within itself an indispensable germ of the other. The sun and moon represent the two different types of soul. The sun is the buoyant, volatile soul known as *hun* which is the 'cloud-soul', while the moon symbolizes the cool, receptive *p'o*-soul called the 'white soul'. The eighth-century astrologer Chang Kuo explains:

> Now the sun's cloud-soul (hun) and the moon's white-soul (p'o) are yang and yin – yang and yin are sun and moon. The sun is the yang and cloud-soul class, and the moon is of the yin and the white-soul class. There is a fowl in the sun: it is a representation of the Western Quarter, Metal, the lungs. It is of the yin class, and so the sun's cloud-soul stores the white-soul of the moon – and the white-soul is fulfilled by the cloud-soul. Therefore the sun is clarified by it. There is a hare in the moon: it is a representation of the Eastern Quarter, Wood and the liver. Liver is of the yang and cloud-soul class, and so the moon's white-soul stores the sun's cloud-soul – and the cloud-soul is fulfilled by the white-soul. Therefore the moon is illuminated by it.[3]

The passage seems opaque like the reflection of moonlight on water, but it demonstrates the hidden correspondences which run throughout Chinese astrological literature between the heaven and earth, the macrocosm and microcosm, yin and yang, the five elements and the five planets, and the organs of the body.

In the Ancient Observatory in Beijing I also came across a gnomon, dating from the Yuan dynasty (AD 1271–1368), brought from the Purple Mountain Observatory in Nanking. A large L-shaped instrument, some six metres long and three metres high, it measures the length of the solar shadow projected, at noon, on to a stone tablet at the base. The gnomon was used to determine the solstices, the equinoxes and the length of the solar (tropical) year, all essential for astrologers to establish a calendar, to make their calculations, and to determine the times for rituals. Many ancient Chinese observatories were giant gnomons in their own right. One such was the Gao Cheng Observatory near Kaifeng, built by the astronomer Gao Shoufing in thirteenth century. With the help of his giant gnomon, he calculated accurately that one complete revolution of the earth around the sun takes 365.2425 days.

Armillary spheres were made to establish the position of celestial bodies, the word armillary coming from the Latin *armilla*, meaning 'bracelet'. Such instruments were already in use in Han times, but were perfected in AD 125 by the astronomer Zhang Heng, who also invented the first seismograph to measure the severity of earthquakes. His ingenious instrument was rotated by water dripping from a clepsydra (water clock).

The spheres were assembled according to what is known as the 'equatorial' system of astronomy, a traditional Chinese system which goes back to at least 2400 BC. The celestial equator is represented by the broad horizontal circle around the outside of the instrument and the pole by the top point. In the early European tradition, the ecliptic, that is the circle described by the sun's motion in the sky against the back-drop of the constellations of the zodiac, was of primary importance. It was not until the seventeenth century that European astronomers realized that the Chinese system of the celestial equator was more convenient. Adopted by the Danish astronomer and astrologer Tycho Brahe, it became the foundation of modern astronomy.[4]

The main armillary sphere at the Ancient Observatory in Beijing was built about 500 hundred years ago during the Ming period. Although it looks complicated, it is comparatively easy to use. It is divided into three nests of rings. The outer nest comprises the fixed horizon circle, the outer equatorial circle and the meridian circle (the great sky-circle that passes directly over one's head and also through the pole). The middle nest consists of the equatorial circle, the ecliptic circle, and the two great circles (known as colure circles) which pass through the celestial poles and the equinoxes and the solstices, all pivoted on the polar axis. The sighting tube and the hour angle circle are in the inner nest.

By looking through the sighting tube at a celestial body and reading the graduations on the rings, one can obtain co-ordinates in order to fix its position. For the early Chinese, the most important rings of the armillary represent the 'Red Road' (the celestial equator), the 'White Road' (the lunar orbit), and the 'Yellow Road' (the ecliptic).

The modern telescope, invented by Galileo in the seventeenth century, made the old armillary spheres redundant. But did the Chinese have the telescope before it was discovered in the West? The first reference to the telescope in Chinese is taken to be in the 1615 translation of *Explicatio Sphaerae Coelestic* (*Thien Wên Lüeh*) by

Emanual Diaz (Yang Ma-No), where Galileo is said to have invented it because he 'lamented the weakness of the unaided eye'.[5] Robert Temple, author of *The Genius of China* and *The Crystal Sun*, is not so sure. When I met him in London he told me that in the Shanghai museum, he had been shown ancient bronzes from the Han Dynasty (the first two centuries BC and the first two centuries AD), which have decorations so minute that they could not have been done with the naked eye. It would seem that the Chinese made use of crystal lenses from early on. Certainly in the Taoist text *Huai-Nan Tzu*, dating from the second century BC, there is a reference in a discussion of the creation of the world to a concave burning-mirror (*fu-sui*) which shows that the ancient Chinese had advanced knowledge of optical instruments.[6]

Chinese Cosmology

With their advanced instruments and careful observation of the celestial bodies, what did the ancient Chinese infer about the origins, nature and structure of the cosmos? Clearly their view of the universe had important implications for astrology and for their understanding of the celestial influences on earth.

The best-known account of the origins of the cosmos emerges in the Taoist tradition, first in the *Tao Te Ching* and then in more detail in the *Huai-Nan Tzu*. At the very beginning there was the Tao. Although it cannot be described, it appeared as a void and was followed by chaos. From chaos emerged yin and yang, which finally gave rise to the five elements which produce the myriad forms of the universe. It was thought that 'The way of Heaven is to be round, while the way of Earth is to be square. Squareness dominates darkness, while roundness dominates light.'[7]

This view inspired the most popular of the three main schools of cosmology which evolved in China by the second century AD. Known as the School of the Hemispherical Dome (*Kai Thien*), it imagined the heavens to be round like an upturned basin and the earth square like a chessboard.[8] But there was a problem: how were the two connected? The heavens were said to be supported by eight pillars, rather like a pavilion, on the flat earth. In keeping with this view, most of the ancient palaces and temples of China were constructed as a round dome built on a square base to imitate the universe.

This model of the cosmos seems to have inspired a fascinating astrological game called 'image chess' (*hsiang hsi*), invented by Chou Wu Ti, the Northern Chou Emperor (561–578). The pieces represent the stars. As Wang Pao wrote:

> The first [great significance] of image-chess is astrological, for [among the pieces are represented] heaven, the sun, the moon and the stars. The second concerns the earth, for [among the pieces represented] are earth, water, fire, wood and metal. The third concerns Yin and Yang; if we start from an even number it signifies Yang and Heaven; if we start from an odd one it signifies Yin and Earth. The fourth concerns the seasons ... The fifth concerns the following of permutations and combinations, according to the changes of position of the heavenly bodies and the five elements. The sixth concerns the musical tones, following the dispersion of the *chi*.[9]

Since the dome model could not explain all astronomical phenomena, it was gradually replaced by the School of the Celestial Sphere (*Hun Thien*). The main exponent of the school, Zhang Heng of the Later Han Period (25–220 AD), argued that the heavens are like a hen's egg and that the earth within it is like the yolk at its centre. The heavens are said to be supported by chi (vapour) while the earth floats on the waters.

The third version of cosmology was known as the School of Infinite Empty Space (*Hsüan Yeh*). It visualized an infinite empty space in which the celestial bodies float freely. Yang Quan in the Three Kingdoms Period (221–265) further believed that stars appear spontaneously in the Milky Way. Although closer to the present understanding of Western cosmologists, it only remained a minor trend in China.[10]

Earliest astronomical observations

With their evolving views of the universe, their sophisticated instruments and their prolonged and careful star-gazing, the Chinese became the first great astronomers of the world, as well as the earliest astrologers. No other nation has built up such complete and comprehensive records of celestial phenomena. They also achieved a startling list of first discoveries. And since astronomy and astrology were not considered separate disciplines, they were all given an astrological meaning. What took place in heaven inevitably affected what took place on earth – and vice versa.

The oldest astronomical record in the world has been found in China: a solar eclipse recorded on oracle bones in 1300 BC during the Shang dynasty. It was thought that in a remote golden age when all was at peace, there were no eclipses. Their appearance was therefore a sign of the general decline of the world. Eclipses were said to be caused by a celestial dragon eating the sun; hence the earlier word for eclipse was *shih*, meaning 'to eat'. By the first century BC, it was understood that solar eclipses were brought about by the full moon covering the sun – as the stone carving of the toad covering the crow at the Ancient Observatory in Beijing so beautifully illustrates.

An oracle bone from the same period in the Shang dynasty records a new star appearing near Antares in the constellation of Scorpius – the oldest record of a nova in the world. The appearance of such 'guest stars' was regarded as a portent of great significance. There is a marvellous account of a nova interpreted by a court astrologer in 1054:

> In the fifth month of the first year of the Chi-Ho reign-period, Yang Wei-Tê (Chief Calendrical Computer) said, 'Prostrating myself, I have observed the appearance of a guest-star; on the star there was a slightly iridescent yellow colour. Respectfully, according to the disposition for emperors [the imperial colour being yellow], I have prognosticated, and the result said, "The guest-star does not infringe on Aldebaran [one of the brightest stars]; this shows that a Plentiful One is Lord, and that the country has a Great Worthy."
> I request that this prognostication be given to the Bureau of Historiography to be preserved.'[11]

And for our delight and instruction, it still is!

The Chinese were the most noted observers of comets in history. They made the earliest recording of Halley's comet in 613 BC. Comets at the time were considered messengers of doom: a tailed comet might sweep the sky clean, but the cleansing also meant death on earth. Early writers saw them as signs of disturbance and derangement in the heavens. In 1973 at Mawangui of Changsha in China, archaeologists unearthed the perfectly preserved body of Lady Tai and also discovered a book of silk pages which had a drawing portraying twenty-nine comets in different forms. As early as 2,200 years ago, Chinese astrologers were therefore making careful observations of the comets and interpreting their meaning. By the seventh century, they established the principle that the tails always point away from the sun, confirming their long-held belief that space is full of strong forces, if not an actual 'solar wind'.[12]

In Chinese literature, there is also a mass of information about meteors, which were known as *liu hsing*, 'shooting' stars, or *pên hsing*, 'energetic' stars.[13] They were often considered messengers of war. To give them the strength of the heavens, swords made from meteoric iron were most coveted by Chinese warriors in the Chou dynasty. Meteors were also thought to be souls descending to enter certain bodies – the great master of Taoism, Lao Tzu, was said to have been conceived by a meteor entering his mother.

Eclipses, comets, meteors, what next? The world's earliest precisely dated sunspot was made in China in 165 BC, although some sources suggest it was in 28 BC. Chinese records are certainly the oldest and longest continuous series of observations of sunspots in the world. The spots are sometimes referred to as *wu*, meaning 'crow' or 'black'. The name is probably inspired by the ancient myth that a three-legged crow dwells in the sun. I saw such a figure on the silk funeral banner placed in Lady Tai's tomb. The sunspots were probably observed through smoky rock crystal or semi-transparent jade. Since it was known that the eleven-year sunspot cycle affects the weather and therefore the harvests, the ancient Chinese astrologers had good reason to believe that changes in the heavens influence affairs on earth. The astrologer Kan Te of the Warring States period (480–221 BC) was the first to recognize that sunspots are features on the surface on the sun, a view rejected until the invention of the telescope in the West in the seventeenth century.

However, the most formidable discovery made by the Chinese astrologers was the detection, by the fourth century AD, of the precession of the equinoxes, one of the most complex phenomena of the heavens. It was a revelation which altered the traditional view of cosmic harmony by detaching the calendar from the fixed stars.

It was prompted by the observation that the 'Emperor Star' gradually lost its place and lustre as the polar star of ancient China. A year was defined as the time taken by the sun to complete one cycle along the ecliptic (the sun's apparent path against the sky), starting and ending from the point of the winter solstice. For a long time, the position was thought to be constant. By comparing the positions of the sun on the ecliptic at the winter solstice as recorded during the period of the Warring States to those recorded in the Later Han period (25–220 BC), the astrologer Yu Xi of the Chin Dynasty (265–317) discovered that its position was continuously drifting westward along the ecliptic at the winter solstice. The same was true at the spring equinox.

This precession of the equinoxes is due to a slight wobble in the earth's axis. Owing to the gravitational influence from the sun, moon and the planets, the earth's axis sweeps out the shape of a cone over a period of about 26,000 years. It is this precessional motion that causes the western drift of the points of the solstices and the equinoxes and alters the celestial north pole in the sky. Hence the dethronement of the Emperor Star from being a bright polar star 3,000 years ago to the lowest star in the rectangle of the Little Bear (Ursa Minor) today. The Pole Star (Polaris) is now the star α in Ursa Minor; in 13,500 years time, it will be replaced by Vega in the constellation of Lyra.

The first calendar in the world to take the precession of the equinoxes into consideration was *The Great Brilliance Calendar* drawn up by Zu Chongzhi of the Chin Dynasty. It is a lasting testament to the brilliance of the ancient Chinese astrologers.

The First Star Catalogues and Maps

With their advanced instruments and prolonged observation of the celestial bodies, it is not surprising that the Chinese made the first star maps in the world to be projected on paper – which they were also the first to invent.

The earliest humans must have been overawed by the vastness and splendour of the heavens and enthralled by the deep rhythms of the night skies. It cannot have been long before they discovered mysterious but subtle links between the seasons and the movements of the celestial bodies, and that the periodic changes in the weather were due to the journey of the sun and the moon during the year. The link between the rhythm of menstruation and that of the moon was made. And it was even observed that molluscs, sea-urchins and other marine animals grew fat and thin in response to the phases of the moon.

Very early on the Chinese astrologers noticed that the familiar group of stars known as the Plough or the Big Dipper (part of Ursa Major) changed orientation after sunset with the seasons. During the Warring States period (c.400 BC), it was written: 'When the handle of the Northern Dipper (as it was known in Chinese) pointed East, it was spring; when it pointed South, it was summer; when it pointed West: it was autumn; and when it pointed North, it was winter.'

The Chinese orientated themselves by the North Star and by the compass which they invented more than 2,500 years ago. At the Ancient Observatory in Beijing, I bought an exact replica of the first known compass in the world which consists of a spoon made of lodestar on a square of bronze. The handle of the spoon points south (Chinese maps are orientated towards the South) while the bulk of the spoon is drawn to magnetic North. The symbols of the cardinal points of the compass are the same as in the *I Ching* and were drawn up around 1400 BC: the North is represented by the Dark Warrior (a fabulous being, part tortoise, part snake) and the South is symbolized by the Red Bird. The Green Dragon stands for the East, and the White Tiger for the West. The same symbols were applied to the four directions of the regions in the heavens as well as on earth.

The first Chinese star maps, known as *gaitu,* appeared during the Warring States period when Kan Te (Gan De) and his contemporaries Shih Shen (Shi Shen-fu) and Wu Hsien (Wu Xian) created their own maps in order to draw up a calendar and to make astrological calculations. Projected on to a flat surface, they resemble modern planispheres. Kan Te and his group of astrologers were responsible for noting correlations between the elements and the planets, the so-called 'heavenly stems' and 'earthly branches', the lunar 'mansions', and the fortnightly periods which are central to the main astrological school known as the 'Four Pillars of Destiny'.[14]

The first star catalogue was drawn up by Shih Shen in 350 BC. Later, in the period of the Three Kingdoms, Chen Zhuo (c.230–320) combined three star maps to form a new star catalogue compromising 283 asterisms and 1,464 stars. One of the most famous of Chinese planispheres, prepared in 1193, was engraved on stone in 1247 in a Confucian temple at Suchow (Suzhou). It offers a wonderfully brief, if cryptic, exposition of the Chinese astronomical and astrological system.

Unlike the ancient Babylonians, Egyptians and Greeks who focused on the heliacal risings and settings of stars (i.e. as they rose and set with the sun), the Chinese concentrated their attention on the circumpolar constellations which travel around the Pole Star in full view during the hours of darkness. The innermost circle of the Suchow star map is therefore the circle of the circumpolar stars, within which the stars never set. The outer circle is what astronomers call the circle of 'perpetual occultation', that is, the boundary beyond which the stars are never seen to rise above the horizon. The middle circle is the celestial equator. Lines radiate from the central circle indicating the divisions of the twenty-eight lunar 'mansions' (*hsiu*). They are separated by hour-circles into hour-segments, rather like in an orange.

The text describes the celestial sphere, with its 'red' and 'yellow' roads (the celestial equator and the ecliptic): 'The Red Road encircles the heart of Heaven, and is used to record the degrees of the twenty-eight *hsiu*.'[15] The planetary portion is astrological and the text ends with correlations between regions in the sky and the Chinese cities and provinces thought to be affected by the celestial phenomena within them.

With such a phenomenal understanding of the heavens, how did the Chinese apply their astronomical knowledge in their astrological interpretations? How did they see the three great powers of the universe – heaven, earth and humanity – interact? To answer these questions, we need to delve deeper into the astrological history and literature of ancient China.

5

As Above, So Below

Grand White (Venus) will converse with me,
She will open the Barrier of Heaven for me.

LI PO

IN THE MUSEUM OF Chinese History, in Tianamen Square, Beijing, is a painted silk banner which once covered the coffin of Lady Tai. She died around 186 BC but her perfectly preserved body was only discovered in 1972.

The T-shaped banner presents a map of celestial phenomena. It is divided into three levels, the heaven of the immortals at the top, the earthly world in the middle and the underworld at the bottom. The sun with its three-legged crow is high up on the right, and on the left is the moon with its toad and hare, representing the cosmic forces of yin and yang. Just below them is a great dragon carrying Chang O with her elixir into the Palace of the Moon, and the Fu-Sang tree with its ten suns. In the centre is Fu Hsi, the organizer god with his serpent tail who allegedly discovered the trigrams of the *I Ching* and introduced the first calendar.

At the gates of heaven sit two guardian immortals. Lower down, Lady Tai, leaning on a stick and attended by three maids, discourses with two immortal envoys. In the underworld, strange creatures, all forms of Thu Po, the Earth Lord, do battle with the forces of evil.[1] Lady Tai is clearly destined to become an immortal being in the heavens, a destiny which all Chinese Taoists hope to achieve. Indeed, the Taoists regarded the stars as the souls of immortals beings. It was further believed that there is a ceremonial gateway called Ch'ang-ho, through which enlightened humans can pass.

But what is the exact nature of the relationship between heaven and earth in the Chinese scheme of things?

Throughout their history, the Chinese believed that the earth mirrors the heavens and there is a direct correspondence between the macrocosm of the universe and the microcosm of the individual. Indeed, humans were considered to be the universe in miniature, with different organs of the bodies associated with different celestial bodies. The Chinese word to describe the relationship between heaven and earth is *hsiang* which has a sense of a painted image.[2] Celestial events were therefore seen as 'counterparts' or 'simulacra' of terrestrial events. The two realms were closely attuned; indeed, since the universe was seen as a dynamic and organic whole, an event in one place would resonate with another elsewhere. And the process worked both ways: events in heaven not only influenced those on earth, but earthly happenings resonated in the heavens. It was the task of the astrologer to work out the exact resonance in the fate of nations and the destiny of individuals.

Astronomy in China was always practised in order to define the temporal order. Affairs on earth should mirror the harmony in heaven. The solstices and equinoxes were therefore key moments in each year and the time for important ceremonies and rituals. To ensure cosmic order, it was crucial that what took place on earth should be in harmony with what occurred in heaven. As Su Song observed in 1092: 'Those who make astronomical observations with instruments are not only organizing a correct calendar so that good government can be carried on, but also [in a sense] predicting the good and bad fortune [of the country] and studying the [reasons for] the resulting gains and losses.'[3]

In keeping with their view of the close correspondence between heaven and earth, the ancient Chinese projected the hierarchy of their feudal society into heaven. A Jade Emperor in the heavens mirrored the Emperor of China who was called the Son of Heaven.

The Naming of the Heavens

The sky was divided into four great precincts, sometimes called palaces, named according to the symbolic animals which preside over the cardinal directions: Green Dragon in the East, Dark Warrior in the North, White Tiger in the West, and Red Bird in the South. The sky was then further subdivided into three sets of smaller divisions, one of nine, one of twelve and one of twenty-eight. All these numbers are significant in the sacred numerology of Chinese astrology.

The astrologer Wang Xi-ming of the T'ang dynasty finally divided the sky into thirty-one regions called the Three Enclosures and the Twenty-eight Mansions. The Three Enclosures were called the Purple Forbidden Enclosure, the Supreme Palace Enclosure and the Heavenly Market Enclosure.

The Purple Forbidden Enclosure was a square which covered the region of the circumpolar constellations. The Pole Star was called the Emperor Star; three thousand years ago it was the star ß in Ursa Minor, although it is now inconspicuous due to the precession of the equinoxes. Stars in the Purple Forbidden Enclosure stood for the members of the imperial household, such as the empress, crown prince and concubines, while in the Supreme Palace Enclosure stars represented nobles and senior government officials.

Just as the Pole Star was known as the Emperor Star, so other stars were considered to be symbols of senior court officials. The Thian-Yang Shou star, for instance, was associated with the commander-in-chief and believed to govern the readiness of the country to withstand attack, as well as the preparation of armaments. According to the seventh-century astrological text *Chin Shu*: 'The two stars of Hsu (Emptiness, the eleventh lunar mansion) denote the officials in charge of ancestor worship. They govern northern cities, temples, and all matters pertaining to ritual and prayer. They also govern death and lamentation.'[4]

The Heavenly Market Enclosure was like a city of the people; it not only contained stars representing chopsticks, but also the lavatory and even faeces. The heavens reflected the whole gamut of life on earth, from the most humble to the most exalted.

The numerical divisions of the heavens was part of ancient Chinese sacred numerology. Twenty-eight is a key figure: the Chinese observed twenty-eight lunar mansions around the ecliptic (unlike twelve in the Middle East and the West) and the celestial equator was divided into twenty-eight mansions. They also divided the visible stars of the heavens into twenty-eight zones or constellations, with seven stars in each of the four directions (North, South, East and West). All the stellar zones are ruled by deities of an equal number: the twenty-eight constellations have twenty-eight deities.

In ancient Chinese astrology, every star in the sky was ruled by a deity who also had some influence on the life of the people beneath it.

The god of the Plough, for instance, was believed to hold sway over the death of humans, and those who prayed to him might be able to prolong their lives. The star of the South Pole – the South Polar Emperor of Longevity – was also supposed to determine how long a person might live. He was one of four Imperial Guards who carried out the orders of the Jade Emperor in heaven.

Some stars were considered to be luckier than others, especially the yellow ones. The most celebrated of all the lucky yellow stars was one of the fixed stars, Canopus, which is not familiar to most Northerners since it not visible above 37° latitude. The second brightest star in the sky, yielding first place only to Sirius which is almost due north of it, Canopus was called the 'Old Man Star' and sometimes the 'Longevity Star'.[5]

Star Lore and Taoist Adepts

There are many stories of star messengers in Chinese astrology and Taoist folklore. One sign of their arrival on earth was the sight of a flowing star entering the Southern Dipper. One story from the Sung period mentions four mysterious individuals who appeared in a wine shop in Szechwan. After consuming great quantities of the best local brew, they began to talk warmly of the seventh-century alchemist Sun Ssu-Mo. A local magistrate tried to find out who they were, but they suddenly disappeared, leaving behind a small pile of ashes. When the prince of the region asked the learned alchemist about the incident, he replied: 'These were the Transcendents of Great White (Venus) and the Wine Asterism.'[6]

The poet Li Po was also said to be a star spirit, the offspring of an ill-fated love affair between Venus and the moon. He described his journey to the stars in terms of a homecoming:

> Grand White will converse with me;
> She will open the Barrier of Heaven for me.
> Then I might ride off with the cooling wind,
> Straight out among the floating clouds,
> By raising my hand I could approach the moon.[7]

Female star visitors to earth were often called Jade Women and played an important role in Taoist star cults. They appear as divine guides and protectoresses. 'The Jade Women of the Luminous Star' await skilful adepts on Mount Hua, the sacred western prop of the sky, offering cups of the 'pale liquor' (the supreme elixir of the alchemists) which give everlasting life. They can also become directly involved with humans. One legend says the 'Jade Woman of the Occult Miracles' dreamed that she was visited by a 'streaming star' (a meteor?) which she swallowed. Eighty-one years later she allegedly gave birth to the greatest Taoist philosopher, Lao Tzu.[8] Some Jade Women are specialists in astral lore, such as 'The Jade Women of the Western Hua' who are placed in the 'Transcendental Metropolis' where they guard such wondrous titles as the 'Canons of Sky-hoards and Moon-crypts' and the 'White-silk Strips of the Flying Dragons'.[9]

These fairy figures are as insubstantial as snowflakes, congealed out of cosmic breath, yet as clear and luminous as shining jade. But how can one be sure of their identity? Easy. They are distinguished from ghost messengers by a piece of yellow jade the size of a millet grain placed above their noses!

From as early as Han times, Taoist adepts lived in monasteries on sacred mountains where they could draw on the energies of the stars. The original name of the 'monasteries' was *kuan*, which may best be translated as 'watch-place' or 'observatory'. They were often visited by lay seekers after wisdom as well as immortals flying down from heaven. The tenth-century poet Li Cung who lived in the state of Southern T'ang describes such a visit:

> I came at leisure to the Transcendent's Friary –
>   asked for Hsi-i;
> Clouds filled the altar of stars – water filled the pond.
> The 'feathered visitors' did not know whither he had gone.
> It was the season when, all at once, flowers fall in abundance
>   before the grotto.[10]

Within the sacred mountains, there are grotto heavens. In the far West of China there is a mountain which is a place of initiation, enlightenment and rebirth, where Huang Ti is said to have been given instruction about the nature of reality.

The nature of Taoist star and planet worship is vividly illustrated in an invocation to the Year Star (Jupiter) from around AD 900. Choosing the correct cyclic day in the spring, the celebrant first 'rectifies his heart' in meditation and then fixes his gaze on the planet and declares: 'I desire that the luminous star in the eastern quarter support my cloud-soul, unite with my white-soul, and make my longevity like that of pines and cypresses – a life extended through a thousand autumns, a myriad of years.'[11]

Many of the Taoist adepts flew beyond this world like the old shamans on their soul voyages, sometimes with their own burgeoning wings, sometimes with 'far-roving' star hats and 'flying-cloud shoes', sometimes on a star-raft to pass through a star gate to the realm of the immortals. The Taoist philosopher Chuang Tzu tells the story of a sage on Mount Ku Shê who nourished himself on wind and dew, rode astride a dragon and saved people from want and disease. There is a marvellous painting on silk from the Warring States period (475–221 BC) showing a human figure riding a dragon in interstellar space.

These adepts were also able to draw energy down from the stars by walking and dancing among symbolic stars drawn on the ground. A sudden surge of supernatural energy was the reward of the initiate who could dance the 'pace of Yü', sometimes called the 'shaman's step'. Great Yü's mother is said to have conceived him after seeing a shooting star in the constellation of Orion. The Grand Supreme Perfected Men (*t'ai shang chen jen*), the most exalted class of Taoist super beings, can allegedly summon the high polar deity Grand Monad (*T'ai i*) by 'pacing the road of the Nine Stars'. The advanced adept could also choose to make a circuit of the Five Planets, hopping along the ecliptic. Guidelines were even drawn up for navigating the heavens.

There is an extraordinary account of Taoists who could read messages in the colour of the stars without even looking at the night sky. Sitting in a dark place, pressing his eyeballs, the adept could see the powerful asterisms as points of coloured light. Prominent among them was the Stabilizer Star, supporter of the Northern Dipper. If it shone red, it meant virtue; if yellow, joy; if white, armed men; if blue, affliction; if black, malignancy. These internal stars were called 'spirit lights' (*shen kuang*).[12]

These magical stories of the supernatural feats of the ancient Chinese astrologers and Taoists are remarkably similar to Western descriptions of astral projection, in which people claim to leave their bodies and travel in space. The experience of stellar journeying may have occurred during long periods of meditation and fasting, or under the influence of powerful elixirs and magic mushrooms. Be that as it may, many Chinese still continue to believe in the possibility of drawing down the energies of the stars. Even temples, as I was to find out in Beijing, were designed to that end.

6

The Temple of Heaven

The astrologer foretells what the effects of heavenly phenomena will be on man; the sage foretells what the effects of man's actions will be on the heavens.

YAN HSIUNG

IT WAS THE PRIMARY duty of the Chinese emperor to perform the major rites of the year in keeping with the astrological calendar. This would ensure good harvests on which the whole of Chinese civilization was based. This was undertaken during the Ming dynasty in the Temple of Heaven in Tiantan Park, which is in the centre of modern Beijing. It is an extraordinary place, designed according to sacred geometry, numerology and acoustics, as well as being encoded with astrological signatures.

The Temple of Heaven (Tiantan) is set in 267 hectares of parkland with rows of straight trees, with the four gates placed in the four directions of the compass. It consists of three temples which represent the marriage of heaven and earth: from the air, the temples are round standing on square bases, embodying the ancient belief that the heaven is round and the earth is square.

In the South is the Round Altar, a magnificent white marble circular construction of three tiers which stands five metres high in a large square enclosure. The tiers represent the three great powers in the universe: heaven, earth and humanity. First constructed in 1530, it demonstrates the Chinese fascination with sacred numbers and the harmonious relationship between heaven and earth. Its three tiers revolve around the sacred number nine. Odd numbers are yang and therefore heavenly and the largest single-digit odd number is nine.

The top tier, which represents heaven, has nine rings of stones. Each ring is composed of multiples of nine stones, so that the ninth ring has eighty-one stones. The middle tier – earth – has the tenth to eighteenth rings, the bottom tier – humanity – has the nineteenth to twenty-seventh rings, ending with a total of 243 stones in the largest ring, or twenty-seven times nine. The number of stairs and balustrades are also multiples of nine. If you stand in the centre of the upper terrace and make a sound, the waves are bounced off the marble balustrades, making your voice appear louder.

Due North of the Round Altar, surrounded by a round wall, is an octagonal temple called the Imperial Vault of Heaven. The mastery of the acoustic engineers was so great that in the courtyard there are Triple Echo Stones: if you stand on the first one and clap, the sound is echoed once; on the second, twice; and on the third, three times. The temple used to contain the tablets of the God of Heaven which the emperor's ancestors employed in the winter solstice ceremony when prayers were offered on the altar of the 'Great Spirit who resides in Heaven'. The fact that it was held on the day of the winter solstice, the darkest day and the turning point of the year, shows how important the astrological calendar was in the life of the Chinese nation.

I walked due North from the temple along an impressive marble causeway – perfectly aligned, according to my compass, on a North–South axis – to a masterpiece of Ming architecture and one of the world's greatest astrological buildings. It is called the Hall of Prayer for Good Harvests. Originally raised in 1420 on a three-tiered marble terrace, it was rebuilt as an exact reproduction after a disastrous fire in 1889. Although thirty-eight metres high and twenty-four metres in diameter, no nails were used to hold the wooden structure together. Like the other two temples in Tiantan Park, it is a circular building on a square base, thereby uniting heaven and earth.

In the centre of the caisson ceiling of the hall is a wooden bas-relief of a dancing phoenix and wriggling dragon, the two great symbols of yin and yang. As such, the hall is astrologically a most auspicious building, a perfect place to pray for good harvests and to ensure the well-being of the Chinese people.

The hall is a magnificent architectural symbol of the Four Pillars of Destiny: the year, month, day and hour of one's birth. The four immense wooden pillars at the centre of the hall symbolize the seasons of each year, twelve in the next ring denote the months of the year, and the twelve outer ones represent the hour of the day which are paired into twelve 'watches'. The three rings of twelve also represent the thirty-six principle constellations.

As the Temple of Heaven beautifully demonstrates, the oldest astrology in China was concerned with the collective fate of the Empire rather than the destiny of individuals. It was used for making prognostications about the affairs of the Empire, the chances of war and the prospects of the harvest. The famous *Shi Chi* (Historical Record) of Ssuma Chien, written in the first century BC, but no doubt containing lore from much earlier, recorded such astrological predictions: 'If the Moon is eclipsed near Ta-Chio (Arcturus) this will bring hateful consequences to the Dispenser of Destinies (the Ruler).' On the other hand: 'When Mercury appears in company with Venus to the East, when they are both red and shoot forth rays, then foreign kingdoms will be vanquished and the soldiers of China will be victorious.'[1]

In an inverted form of astrology, Han Confucians developed the belief that any moral lapse on earth would also cause disturbances in heaven. If the emperor's speech was not rational, metals would not be malleable and terrible thunderstorms would occur. Even the irregularities of local officials could upset the movements of the planets. The mutual dependence between heaven and earth comes out well in a passage by Yang Hsiung in the fifth century:

> Someone asked whether a sage could make divination. [Yang Hsiung] replied that a sage could certainly make divination about Heaven and Earth. If that is so, continued the questioner, what is the difference between the sage and the astrologer?
>
> [Yan Hsiung] replied, 'The astrologer foretells what the effects of heavenly phenomena will be on man; the sage foretells what the effects of man's actions will be on the heavens.'[2]

Again, the causal link is not mechanical but a case of diffuse resonance. Any misconduct will disturb the harmony of the cosmos, which will have consequences in heaven as well as on earth.

The Son of Heaven

Chinese astrology was therefore integral to the State religion. As the 'Son of Heaven', the emperor was considered a cosmic figure, the equivalent of the Pole Star on earth and the main channel for the inflow of celestial energy from above. The dictates of this astrological religion even affected his sex life. For the health of the Empire and of the emperor, it was important that the yin and yang forces were balanced to maintain celestial and terrestrial harmony. The primary purpose of the lower ranks of the concubines would be to feed the emperor's powerful yang force with their yin. In the monthly cycle, the more common concubines would accompany the emperor at the time of the new moon. As the moon waxed, their numbers would grow less but their rank increase. Women of the highest rank were allowed to approach the emperor nearest to the full moon, when the yin influence would be at its height. Pai Hsieng-Chien observed in the ninth century: 'Nine ordinary concubines [slept with the emperor] every night, and the empress for two nights at the time of the full moon – that was the ancient rule . . . But, alas, nowadays all the three thousand [palace women] compete in confusion . . .'[3]

One of the astrologers' most important tasks was to record the position of the celestial bodies at the time of each consummation so that if the union produced any offspring the exact moment of conception would be known. Children conceived near the full moon were thought to have the highest virtue. Towards the end of the reign of an emperor, the nature of the asterisms which had been culminating at the time of a prince's conception would be taken into account in the final choice of a successor.

Since it was believed that the influence of celestial bodies on the lives of humans and the affairs of State was all-pervasive, knowledge of the stars in feudal China became a carefully guarded secret. To possess charts of the stars and to control the data revealed by the armillary spheres was therefore to wield great occult power. In the T'ang period (618–907) the Chinese equivalent of the Astronomer Royal was called 'The Board of the Gallery of Secret Writing' and the members of the imperial board were informally called 'star officers'. Their task was to observe the movements of the heavens in order to watch for happy omens and to foretell disasters. The latter consisted of a whole field of study known as *fen yeh*, translated as 'disastrous geography'.[4] The major responsibility of the court astrologer-astronomers was the compilation of an almanac which was promulgated by the emperor, the Son of Heaven, himself.

These practices were still being kept up in the seventeenth century. Nicolas Trigault observed disapprovingly during his travels in China:

They have some Knowledge also of Astrologies and Mathematikes . . . They reckon four hundred Starres more than our Astrologers have mentioned, numbring certaine smaller which do not always appeare. Of the heavenly Appearances they have no rule: they are much busied about foretelling Eclipses, and the courses of Planets, but therein very erroneous; and all their Skill of Starres is in a manner that which we call Judiciall Astrology, imagining these things below to depend on the Starres.'[5]

Individual horoscopes did not become really popular until the eleventh century, but as early as the first century the great sceptic Wang Chhung recognized the influences emanating from the stars on the fate of individual human beings. He argued that human destiny was not an inexorable decree of Heaven, but was dependent on three things: the spiritual essence (*ching shen*) of each individual, specific influences emanating from the stars, and the effects of chance. He believed that stars were among the most important of all influences upon humans during the formative period of their lives:

> As regards the transmission of wealth and honour, that depends on the *chi* which the nature obtains; it receives an essence (*ching*) emanating from the stars. Their hosts are in heaven, and heaven has their signs. If a man receives [at his birth?] a heavenly sign implying wealth and honour, he will obtain wealth and honour. If a man receives [at his birth?] a heavenly sign implying poverty and misery, he will become poor and miserable. Therefore it is said that [all dispositions depend on] Heaven. But how can this be? Heaven has its hundreds of officials and its multitudes of stars. Heaven sends forth its chi, and the stars send forth their essences, and the essences are in the midst of the chi. Men imbibe this chi and are born. As long as they cherish it they grow.[6]

The first known book to concern itself with horoscopes of individuals was the *Yü Chao Shen Ying Chen Ching* (True Manual of Determinations by the Jade Shining Ones), attributed to Kuo Pho of the third century. Interest in this area developed rapidly. In 732, during the T'ang dynasty, the voluminous encyclopaedia *Hsing Tsung* (The Company of the Stars) by Chang Kuo appeared. Important astrological works were still being produced at the end of the Ming dynasty and an astrological compendium was published in 1739.

These works refined the fundamental principles of the Four Pillars of Destiny (*Ssu Chu*) which had been established by Kan Te and his group of astrologers in the Warring States period. Still the most popular method of astrology in China, I had been introduced to it in a debased form by the temple soothsayer in Hong Kong. We are now in a better position to return to the subject with an increased understanding of its background and importance.

7

The Four Pillars of Destiny

WHILE THE 'CIRCLE OF ANIMALS' (*Ming Shu*) is the most widely known form of Chinese astrology in the West, the astrology of the Four Pillars of Destiny (*Ssu Chu*) is the most popular in Hong Kong, Taiwan and Mainland China. This form of fate calculation involves casting the 'eight signs' (*ba tze*) which are based on the four pillars of the year, month, day and hour of an individual's birth. They provide each person at the moment of birth with a kind of cosmic code, or elemental blueprint.

The lunar year of our birth is said to describe our underlying character; the month explains our main direction in life; the day indicates our self and emotional character, especially our attitudes to love, sex and friendship; and the 'hour' (twelve in a Chinese day) pinpoints our temperament. The method uses ten-year fate cycles in order to develop a personality profile and a life chronology.

Heavenly Stems and Earthly Branches

This method is not easy for Westerners to understand as it is based on a complicated luni-solar calendar. At its centre are two aspects – the ten 'heavenly stems' (*t'ien kan*) and twelve 'earthly branches' (*ti chih*), which are placed together in pairs. These are important to understand as they are associated with each of the Four Pillars of Destiny.

In general, the heavenly stems represent an element in its yin or yang mode and the earthly branches represent an element and an animal. Chinese astrologers claim that once they know the components of the five elements of your life, the rules governing the interaction of the elements and the pattern of change of the elements through time, they can understand your character and predict your future life.[1]

The heavenly stems are associated with the five elements (wood, fire,

Name	Ten Heavenly Stems	Twelve Earthly Branches	Name
chia	1 甲 Yang wood	1 子 Water (Rat)	tzu
yi	2 乙 Yin wood	2 丑 Earth (Ox)	ch'ou
ping	3 丙 Yang fire	3 寅 Wood (Tiger)	yin
ting	4 丁 Yin fire	4 卯 Wood (Rabbit)	mao
mou	5 戊 Yang earth	5 辰 Earth (Dragon)	ch'en
chi	6 己 Yin earth	6 巳 Fire (Snake)	ssu
keng	7 庚 Yang metal	7 午 Fire (Horse)	wu
hsin	8 辛 Yin metal	8 未 Earth (Goat)	wei
jen	9 壬 Yang water	9 申 Metal (Monkey)	shen
kuei	10 癸 Yin water	10 酉 Metal (Cock)	yu
		11 戌 Earth (Dog)	hsü
		12 亥 Water (Pig)	hai

The Ten Heavenly Stems and Twelve Earthly Branches

earth, metal and water) and the five directions of the compass (East, South, Centre, West and North), and are alternatively yang and yin. The earthly branches are associated with the twelve animal signs of *Ming Shu*, astrology, the elements, the directions of the compass and yang and yin.

The ten heavenly stems and twelve earthly branches combine alternatively to make sixty combinations to form a sixty-year cycle. They can be imagined as two enmeshed cogwheels, one having twelve teeth and the other ten. They are depicted by two different Chinese characters placed side by side.

In each sixty-year cycle, the signs of the ten-year series of heavenly stems repeat themselves six times (even and yin), while the twelve-year series of earthly branches repeats itself five times (odd and yang). In Chinese sacred numerology, six is the number of heaven and five the number of the earth; the cycles of stems and branches therefore point to the interdependence of heaven and earth.

The signs which make up the ten heavenly stems are to be found in inscriptions made on oracle bones 3,500 years ago and were used to count the days in the Shang period. The sixty-day count in six cycles was close enough to correspond approximately to the tropical year between the winter or the summer solstices. The sixty-day cycle also broke down into six periods of ten days, roughly approximate to two lunar months. This ten-day period is still used in some rural parts of China.

The Chinese characters of the heavenly stems are very graphic and poetic. The first yang one in the series, known as *chia*, is associated with wood and is depicted by a shape which represents a burgeoning bud; the second, *yi*, is yin and represents a sprout bursting from the bud. Both are clearly associated with the spring.

The twelve earthly branches did not emerge in written Chinese texts until the fifth century BC. They are related to the twelve hours of each day, the twelve months of the year and each of the twelve years of the Jupiter cycle – the sidereal period of Jupiter (the time it takes to travel around the fixed stars) is almost exactly twelve years. Since there are only five elements (wood, fire, earth, metal and water), each of which is applied to two of the twelve branches, the remaining two branches are assigned to the element earth.

Like the heavenly stems, the earthly branches alternate between yin and yang, and the Chinese characters for them are equally graphic and poetic. For instance the character *mao* is depicted as an open door to represent the beginning of spring, while *ch'en* which follows is a picture of a woman who hides her belly with her hands – she is both pregnant and timid. These twelve branches are the principal aspects for the study of the year, months and hours of the Pillars of Destiny.

The sixty-year cycle always begins with the heavenly stem *chia* (associated with the element wood, the colour green, the taste sour, East and yang) combined with the earthly branch *tzu* (associated with the rat, mid-winter, North-East and yang). The cycle ends with the heavenly stem *kuei* (water, black and salt) and the earthly branch *hai* (pig, early winter and North-North-West). The cycle then starts again.

Until the early twentieth century, the Chinese calendar was measured in this way and it is still employed in the astrology of the Four Pillars of Destiny. The year 1812, for instance, was the year *jen-yu* (in which *jen* was associated with water, black and salt, and *yu* with the cock, mid-autumn and West). Throughout the sixty-year cycle, the same combination of heavenly stems and earthly branches only occurs once. The year

2000, the first year of the new Christian millennium, was the year *keng-ch'en:* The Year of Dragon, The heavenly stem *keng* corresponds to metal and yang, and the earthly branch *ch'en* (the dragon) to earth and yang. Together, they are considered highly auspicious and are associated with wisdom, magic and generosity.

The Year Pillar

In a person's horoscope, the year pillar in the Four Pillars of Destiny indicates his or her general appearance, emotional disposition and pattern of behaviour. Born on 23 August 1946, my *Ming Shu* sign is the Dog, my element fire. My heavenly stem is *ping*, my compass direction is South and my chi is yang. My earthly branch is *hsü* and is associated with the element earth, West-North-West and yang. The relationship between the heavenly stem and earthly branch gives 'Earth of the Roof' and yang.

Earth, the element of my earthly branch, is the source of all the other elements. It corresponds to the afternoon, the 'dog days' of summer, the centre of the compass, both yin and yang, the colour yellow, the number five, the planet Saturn, sweet taste, the spleen, mouth and flesh. Taken together, my overall personality is said to be prudent, practical, reliable and conservative. I move with caution and like to delve deeply into things. My emotional state is one of desire. I am said to be of sallow complexion with thick features and round back.

Unfortunately, I don't recognize myself in this pen portrait. I am not saturnine in temperament. I have tended to be rash, idealistic and radical in my life and opinions, and I do not even like the colour yellow particularly! Perhaps my earth side will come out later in life . . . If the year of birth pillar is meant to define my pattern of behaviour and emotional state, then it should also do so for all the other millions born in 1946 who share the same element earth.

On the other hand, I feel my animal sign of the Dog indicated by the earthly branch for the year 1946 is more amenable but still, according to my own self-knowledge, inaccurate. I am said to be ambitious, faithful with a warm, loving nature, but liable to anxiety and pessimism. Combined with my element earth, I am meant to be secretive, bowing to consensus opinion while remaining true to my personal beliefs.[2] Again, I cannot recognize myself in this, except perhaps for having a loving nature.

The Month Pillar

While the year pillar indicates our emotional state and pattern of behaviour, the month pillar represents our destiny. It is used as a starting point to work out a personal chronology which is divided into ten-year cycles. Unlike Western astrology, it is based on information derived from the lunar and not the solar month of a person's birth. It is usually interpreted with other aspects of a person's horoscope. In my case, my month pillar is the seventh lunar month of the year of my birth.

I can of course simply look up the month on a chart which converts the Western solar calendar into the Chinese lunar calendar. To understand the principles behind the Chinese luni-solar calendar is not easy, but it is well worth the effort, for it throws fascinating light on the history of Chinese astrology, society and civilization.

Whereas Western calendars deal only with the arrangements of days and months, Chinese calendars also provide information on the movements of the sun, moon and the planets. Again, while the Western calendar is based on the cycle of the sun, the Chinese calendar takes into account the movement of the moon.

In fact the Chinese have developed two different calendar systems, one based on the moon and the other on the sun, and then combined elements of both to produce a luni-solar calendar. The one traditionally used by laymen is the lunar calendar which divides a year into twelve months. A solar calendar, used by farmers and fortune-tellers, is used to count the days. It is called the Hsia calendar as it has been employed since the Hsia Dynasty about 4,000 years ago.

The Hsia calendar is used for astrology and fortune-telling because it is closely related to the five elements. Each year, month and day is expressed in terms of two Chinese characters, each representing one of the elements. In this way any particular moment can be expressed in terms of the elements. By converting your date of birth – the four pillars of year, month, day and hour – into the format of the Hsia calendar, you get eight Chinese characters representing the eight elements prevailing at your birth.

Calendars, of course, are crucial not only for astrologers to determine the exact time of birth, but are also needed to organize our daily activities and to plan for the future. In ancient China, the emperor had to have a reliable calendar in order to perform the essential tasks for the well-being of the nation at the right time. Indeed, his most important task – his 'mandate from Heaven' – was to establish the calendar. The emperor would follow the progress of the sun by passing from the centre of his palace to the West, North, East and South quarters, before returning to the centre. He would dress in different colours and eat different foods; in summer, for instance, he would wear red and eat peas and chicken in the 'Palace of Clarity'. Some authorities say that the Emperor would also visit the four cardinal points of the Empire or made a pilgrimage to the sacred mountain peaks of the four points of the compass. This would ensure that order would reign on earth as it does in heaven.

The Chinese Calendar

To find out more about the development of the Chinese calendar, I went to the new Space Museum in Hong Kong near the Star Ferry terminus in the Kowloon district. There I met the curator, Dr Chan Ki Kung, an enthusiastic man who had devised an audio-visual programme on Chinese astronomy called 'The Dragon in the Sky'. Although the ancient Chinese system of astronomy was abandoned for the Western model, and the Western solar calendar officially adopted after the founding of the Chinese Republic of 1911, the traditional calendar is still widely used in the country and by astrologers.

The curator had no doubts about its importance: 'The highest attainments in ancient Chinese astronomy are to be found in Chinese calendar-making,' he declared proudly.

Ancient calendars were not only very complex but extraordinarily accurate: the Chinese Quarter Remainder Calendar, dating from the fifth century BC, put one tropical (solar) year at 365.25 days; we now know that one tropical year has 365.2422 days!

I asked the curator whether it was true that the Chinese used a lunar calendar, as opposed to the one based on the sun used in the West.

'Strictly speaking,' the curator insisted, 'the Chinese calendar should be called a luni-solar calendar.'

Although the Chinese calendar reflects the observed movements of the sun and the moon in the heavens, they cannot be equated.

The Chinese lunar year has twelve moons and each moon lasts for a little over twenty-nine and a half days (29.53 days). To make the days in each moon full days, Chinese astrologers decided that one year would be divided into six 'small' months, which would have twenty-nine days each, and six 'large' months which would have thirty days each. This adds up to a total of 354 days, eleven days short of the solar year (strictly speaking, twelve lunar months make 354.36 days, which is about 10.89 days less than a solar year). The length of the Chinese lunar year therefore varies and may comprise five 'large' months and seven 'small' months (a total of 353 days), or sometimes five 'small' and seven large months (355 days).

The lunar year falls short of the solar year by ten or twelve days every year. Two lunar years will therefore lag about twenty days behind a solar year while three years will be short by nearly a month. An extra lunar month is therefore added at roughly three-year intervals in order to harmonize the solar and lunar calendars. This is known as an 'intercalary' moon (also known as a 'embolism'). In a period of nineteen years, seven such moons are needed. The same system of calculation was developed by both the Jews and the ancient Greeks and is known in the West as the cycle of Meton.

The problem for the ancient Chinese astrologers was where to put the intercalary or leap month. The curator Chan Ki Kung pointed out that a very simple rule was devised: 'As two mid-periods are on average 30.44 days apart, which is longer than a synodic month of 29.53 days, every now and again there occur months which have no periods at all. Such months are made intercalary months. For instance, in 1995, the month after the eighth lunar month has no mid-period, so instead of the usual ninth lunar month, it's counted as the intercalary eighth lunar month.'

In Chinese astrology, each intercalary moon has no personality of its own and takes the number of the moon which precedes it. In 1987, for instance, the extra month was month six and followed the normal month six.

To link the lunar and solar aspects of the calendar together, it was decided that the spring equinox should fall in the second month and the summer solstice in the fifth, the autumn equinox in the eighth and the winter solstice in the eleventh moon. As a result, Chinese New Year's Day is not fixed and may be on any date between 21 January and 20 February. In 2001, the Lunar New Year's holiday began on 24 January, the day of the new moon.

The Cycles of Fate

The lunar months of the Chinese luni-solar calendar form the basis of the month pillar of the Four Pillars of Destiny. Like the year pillar, it too has a heavenly stem and earthly branch. Born on 23 August 1946, in the seventh lunar month of the year, my heavenly stem is the third, *ping*, the element of which is fire, and my earthly branch is the ninth, *shen*, the element of which is metal.

In most forms of Chinese astrology, and as my temple astrologer had illustrated, a person's life is divided into a series of ten-year fate cycles, beginning from the month pillar and placed within twelve houses of fate. However, the ten-year cycle does not always begin on a person's day of birth and so the second cycle could begin on his or her third birthday and finish on the thirteenth and so on.

To work out the time of the second fate cycle again is not easy. First, you look up the number of the heavenly stem of the year of your birth. If it's odd, it counts for one; if even, two. If the person is male, add one; if female, two. In my case the number is three; as it is odd, it counts for one, and as a male, I add one, making two!

Next you have to consult the solar aspect of the traditional Chinese luni-solar calendar. While a month in the Chinese calendar equals a lunar month of about twenty-nine days, it also contains 'fortnightly periods' closely related to the earth's revolution around the sun. Hence its 'luni-solar' nature. The solar calendar is divided into twenty-four periods (*chieh*), each of which is about fourteen days long. Their names, such as 'Movement of Insects' (beginning on March 5), 'Grain in the Ear' (beginning June 6), or 'Frost Descends' (beginning October 23) reflect the agrarian nature of Chinese society when these divisions were made. They are paired together into twelve monthly festivals which generally begin at the mid-point of one of the twelve Western zodiac signs.

In the Chinese calendar I bought in Hong Kong, approximately every fifteen days there are certain Chinese terms beside the dates which denote the fortnightly periods. The twenty-four fortnightly periods in a year are further subdivided into twelve sections and twelve mid-periods. Chan Ki Kung explained: 'Examples of sections are Beginning of Spring, Awakening of Insects, Clear and Bright, while The Rains, Spring Equinox, Grain Rain are mid-periods. Two consecutive mid-periods are about thirty days apart, so each mid-period is made corresponding to a lunar month. So, the First Lunar Month has the mid-period The Rains, the Second Lunar Month has Spring Equinox, the third has Grain Rain, and so on.'

To return to the ten-year fate cycle, if the calculation of the year pillar is odd, then you refer to the date of *chieh* (fortnightly period) immediately before the person's birthday. If the number is even (as in my case), you refer to the date of the *chieh* immediately after the person's birthday. The number of days between the person's day of birth and the chosen *chieh* date are counted and then divided by three.[3] The result is the age at which the person's second fate cycle begins. My temple astrologer began mine at the age of four.

Each cycle follows the numerical sequence of the heavenly stem and earthly branch of the month pillar: my second cycle is the third stem and ninth branch; the next ten-year cycle is the fourth stem and tenth branch and so on. This means different elements govern each cycle: fire and metal, next earth and earth, then earth and water, etc.

As with the twelve Houses of the Western horoscope, Chinese astrology employs twelve Houses of fate which influence the common areas of concern in a person's life. The descriptions of the twelve Houses of fate obviously reflect the interests of the privileged few in Chinese feudal society. They are: one, a person's ultimate destiny; two, wealth; three, brothers and relatives (also emotions and affections); four, land and dwelling (also possessions and legacies); five, sons and daughters (also charitable works); six, servants and slaves (also social status); seven, wives and concubines; eight, sickness and distress; nine, removal and change (also travel abroad); ten, official and reward (also profession); eleven, good fortune and virtue (also opportunities); twelve, manner and bearing.[4]

Clearly these Houses of fate were defined by court astrologers and were not intended for servants, slaves and concubines!

An astrologer uses the number of the progressed earthly branch of the monthly pillar to work out which House will be most influential during each ten-year cycle. In this way, he can build up a personal chronology. Assuming that my second cycle began at the age of four, from four to fourteen the most influential House was number nine, 'removal and change'; from fourteen to twenty-four, number ten, 'official and reward' as well as profession. I suppose it could be said that I laid down the foundation of my profession during this period, although I did not travel from my birthplace in Bognor Regis on the Sussex coast in the previous ten-year cycle. The monthly pillar is, however, interpreted together with the other three pillars of destiny to give an overall picture of one's life and expectations.

The Day Pillar

According to Tsu Ping, who lived around AD 800, the heavenly stem of the day (*hua*) pillar represents the self. The remaining seven of the eight signs (*ba tze*), each of which is associated with an element, symbolize relatives and friends. Used with the month pillar, it can help determine the pattern of the ten-year cycles.

To examine how strong or weak the self is among the other seven elements, the astrologer will look at the self element and its seasonal strength. For instance, fire is born in spring, prospers in summer, weakens in autumn and dies in winter. These seasonal changes in the cycle of the five elements have been embodied in the Hsia calendar.

With this information the strength of the self can be assessed. If the element symbolizing the self is fire, and the person is born in winter when fire dies, the self will be weak. On the other hand, if the fire person is born in the summer when fire prospers, the person will be strong. But the exact strength or weakness will depend on how supportive the elements are from the other seven signs.

The philosophy of the Four Pillars, like Chinese philosophy as a whole, is based on harmony and balance. Even the name of Tsu Ping, who established the method of the Four Pillars of Destiny in its present form, means 'balancing water'.[5] The element representing the self should be neither too strong nor too weak. If there is an imbalance, a person can be given medicine in the form of the other elements to improve the fortune of the self. The method can also indicate the ups and downs in a person's life. In 1993, the prevailing influence was metal and water and so it is likely that a weak fire person will have met with difficulties during that year.

The day pillar is easier to identify than the month pillar – a table provides the heavenly stem and earthly branch for each day of the year. Mine, on 23 August, are five and seven respectively, corresponding to the elements earth and fire. The outcome of events that might occur during each ten-year cycle indicated by the month pillar is interpreted in conjunction with the day of birth. This is done by exploring the relationship, during the course of each ten-year period, between the elements that influence the heavenly stem of the day pillar and the earthly branch of the month pillar and its fate house. Again, in my case, this means the relationship between the elements yang fire and yang fire in the first cycle. Fire enhances fire but the elements can stand in a positive, negative or neutral relationship with each other.

This is usually presented as a cycle of creation and cycle of destruction, depending on the relationship between the elements. For instance, the Chinese wood element produces fire, fire creates earth, earth begets metal, metal runs like water, water nurtures wood. They are in a positive relationship. On the other hand, wood burns earth, fire melts metal, earth absorbs water, metal cuts wood, and water douses fire. They are in a negative relationship. A neutral relationship can occur when three elements cancel each other out: in the case of wood, earth and metal, wood burns earth, but metal cuts wood.

An astrologer will look at the relationships between the elements in each ten-year cycle as it progresses through the twelve houses of fate. For instance, yin metal in the tenth House (official and reward) in the second ten-year cycle will tend to make a person determined and opinionated, if somewhat rigid. And if the element of his day pillar is yin water, the relationship between the two is positive, and one will enhance the other.

The strictly astrological element in the Chinese horoscope also involves the twenty-eight constellations associated with the element which rules the group of your day pillar of destiny. These determine the factor of chance in your life. The link is with the moon rather than the sun: the constellations are called lunar mansions or dwellings (*sieu*) through which the moon passes every day during each lunar month of twenty-eight days.[6] Each mansion is ruled by a fixed star and each fixed star is located in one of the four arcs of constellations in the four quarters known as the Green Dragon, the White Tiger, the Dark Warrior and the Red Bird. The twenty-eight constellations form a cycle of twenty-eight days which move in parallel with the overriding sixty-year cycle. Visible throughout the year, they were distributed along the celestial equator around 2400 BC, but because of the precession of the equinoxes they are no longer in their original positions.[7]

Each day's constellation, or lunar mansion, is associated with an animal and is considered auspicious or inauspicious. The first of the cycle is the auspicious Horn, associated with the crocodile; the fourteenth with the auspicious Wall (porcupine), and the twenty-eighth with the auspicious Chariot (earthworms). The first contains stars from Virgo; the fourteenth, from Pegasus and Andromeda; and the twenty-eighth, from Corvus. If a first reading of the constellations by an astrologer or feng shui expert is negative for the time of a key event or burial, he can look up the annual movement of the constellations in the Chinese almanac to find a more suitable time. The use of the lunar mansions was exported to Japan where it became very popular.

Another method uses the person's day pillar to plan daily activities by making a cross-reference between a person's day pillar (*hua*) and the fortnightly periods (*chieh*). A chart enables one to find the nearest fortnightly period that precedes the day under review. There are usually twelve indicators consulted for daily activities placed against the fortnightly periods, depending on one's earthly branch. One can then read off the auspicious and inauspicious times for different activities, such as settling bills, cleaning house, organizing social events (including marriage), undertaking long-distance travel, taking out loans, resting or even starting a diet.

As I write this on 15 May, by tracing the earthly branch of my day pillar and checking it against the fortnightly period which runs from 5 May to 21 May, I learn that it is an auspicious time 'for cleaning house or clearing the decks in preparation for things to come. Not a good time for doing business or socializing. Attend to personal health, fitness and appearance.'[8] It doesn't tell me that it's a good time for writing, but at least I am clearing away my research by writing it down.

The Hour Pillar

So far we have dealt with the year, month, and day pillars of the Four Pillars of Destiny. That leaves us the hour (*guo*) pillar. As we saw earlier, the Chinese day is divided into twelve periods of two hours of Western time each, beginning with the period from 23.00 to 01.00. Each period has two corresponding signs, one for the heavenly stem and one for earthly branch. For someone born outside China, it is first necessary to convert the hour of birth to Universal Time (UT) – the same as Greenwich Mean Time – and then add eight hours in order to convert it to Chinese Coastal Time (CCT). I was born at roughly 16:30 in August (British Summer Time) which is 15:30 (UT) and 23:30 (CCT). Taking into account the conversion, the number of my earthly branch is one, associated with the *Ming Shu* sign of the Rat and the element yang water. The heavenly stem of my hour pillar is nine, also associated with yang water. I am clearly very watery!

Once I know this information, I can work out what share of luck I was born with. Luck plays an important part in interpreting a Chinese horoscope. One of the oldest methods of calculating the portion of luck is by placing the earthly branch of the hour pillar on one of the four images of the Emperor Huang Ti, the semi-legendary 'Yellow Emperor' who reigned some 5,000 ago. Each image represents a particular season: spring, summer, autumn and winter. In Chinese almanacs, the four images are called the 'The Song of the Four Seasons'. The twelve earthly branches are distributed about the Emperor's body – head, shoulders, belly, hands, groin, knees and feet – which is yet another example of the microcosm reflecting the macrocosm of seasons defined by the movement of the earth around the sun.

To work out my portion of luck at birth, I find the season in which I was born (autumn in the Chinese year) and locate the earthly branch of my hour pillar which is on the shoulders of the Yellow Emperor. This indicates: 'Destiny improves with age . . . The person can improve on his or her fate by following two general rules: do not rely on other people for any reason, and avoid discouragement when encountering obstacles. This person's children will have a better fate.'[9] Very sage advice.

If your earthly branch is the Yellow Emperor's belly, you will be able to attain fame and fortune in the arts or music in later life; if the hands, business and trade are your main sources of fortune and you will do even better if you leave your place of birth; if the groin, you will be assured of wealth and high status in later life; if the knees, you will be unlucky, leading a restless and unfulfilled life. Finally, if your branch is the feet, you will only find happiness by renouncing all material and worldly aspirations, by developing your intellectual and spiritual aspects and by leaving your birthplace to live in the wilderness, although you might have two spouses! I would appear to be more of a foot man than anything else.

Once the Four Pillars of Destiny have been determined and the fate cycles worked out, the Chinese astrologer draws up a profile of the individual's personality. This is usually done on the three most important events in life: after being born, before getting married, and before being buried. With the information provided by the day pillar, the profile can also be used to make daily predictions.

It is not easy for a Westerner to appreciate the symbolic meaning of the eight signs (*ba tze*) made from the combination of the heavenly stems and earthly branches which symbolize the Four Pillars of Destiny.

Each sign has a magical value, like a gesture in a dance or an image in a painting. When the shamans dressed up as animals and danced and drummed, they knew it too. In many ways, the signs have the symbolic power of personal names.

8

Know All Things

No superstition is so common to the entire kingdom as that which pertains to the observance of certain days and hours as being good or bad, lucky or unlucky, in which to act or to refrain from acting, because the result of everything they do is supposed to depend upon a measurement of time.

MATTHEW RICCI

ANOTHER POPULAR TYPE of astrology is based on the Chinese calendar. It provides a method for planning daily activities, whether it be moving house, getting married or arranging a business meeting. It is based on the movement of the moon during the year as it passes through the twenty-eight constellations of fixed stars known as *sieu* (lunar mansions). This method of prediction uses a printed almanac for the current year.

The Chinese Almanac is very old. Indeed, it could be described as the oldest encyclopaedia in the world, for it has been published continuously since about 2250 BC. It was compiled by astrologers under the orders of Emperor Yaw who saw the advantage, especially to farmers, of the seasons being fixed. Although revised each year, the bulk of the text remains the same and its archaic language is difficult to understand. In Taiwan, it is known as the 'Farmers' Almanac'; in Hong Kong, as the *Tong Sing*, 'Know All Things Book'.[1] A compendium of information about astrology, divinatory procedures and traditional beliefs, it contains instructions for face and palm reading and embraces the wisdom of the Four Pillars of Destiny and of feng shui. It is basically a calendar which reflects the influence of the five elements at a certain point in time.

The sixteenth-century Jesuit Matthew Ricci disapproved of such works which were so popular in China. 'Every house has a supply of them [almanacs],' he wrote. 'They are produced in pamphlet form, and in them one finds directions as to what should be done and what should be left undone for each particular day, and at what precise time each and everything should be done. In this manner the entire year is carefully mapped out in exact detail.'[2]

I asked the curator of the Hong Kong Space Museum, Dr Chan Ki Kung, what he felt about the Chinese Almanac. A rational man with a background in physics and astronomy, he was not surprisingly sceptical. Nevertheless, he confessed: 'I looked at it the other day. There are lots of astrological terms in it. It's very popular with the old, but not many young people can read the terms. They know every word but when they come together they can't understand the meaning because they need a lot of background to interpret them. It's still widely read by parents for finding a good day for weddings. People move a lot in Hong Kong and it's also used to choose a good day to move house.'

The author in Hong Kong of the Chinese Almanac, the *Tong Sing*, is Mr Choi Park-lai. His office was on the eighth floor of the Hillier Commercial Building in the Central District. It was an open plan office stuffed with papers and covered with Chinese watercolours and drawings. Half a dozen men and women were working away. We were offered tea before retiring to his small office. Mr Choi, an octogenarian dressed in a brownish purple suit with a red tie, was an expert in feng shui as well as Chinese calendar-making. In keeping with his ancient art, he sat in a large chair covered with a white fleece in front of a large desk opposite the entrance to his office. He regularly appeared on television and was famous throughout Hong Kong. On his wall were photographs taken with various Western and Chinese celebrities.

I went to visit him with a young interpreter called Sherman. He told me through her that producing the almanac had been a family business for 120 years. His father had been his master. I read in a foreword to one of his diaries: 'The Choi family's knowledge of Fung Shui (geomancy), Yin and Yang (research into the positive and negative principles of nature), Ng Hang (the five primary elements) and "Date Choosing" has been handed down through three generations and I have been practising these theories professionally for several decades.'

In the same work, it was explained that: 'Fung Shui ("wind and water"), the name of the Chinese geomantic system, by means of which sites are determined for graves, houses and other buildings, and the Chinese Almanac are both ancient Chinese methods that utilize the highly sophisticated theories of "Yin and Yang" (the positive and negative principles of nature), and "Ng Hang" (the five primary elements, i.e. metal, wood, water, fire and earth) in order to help people to be harmonious with nature, and to pursue good fortune and avoid evil influences.'

I asked Mr Choi about the link between feng shui and the Chinese calendar.

'Feng shui is connected with the eight characters.'

This I knew was the popular term for the Four Pillars of Destiny in Chinese astrology. He pronounced feng shui in Cantonese as 'fung shoy'.

'The Chinese placement of things in the house,' Sherman translated, 'is connected with the four seasons. It involves the flow of chi, of energy. Sometimes it's good; sometimes not good. It's different for different persons; that's why it's connected with the eight characters.'

My translator soon began to perspire due to the difficulties of her task. Mr Choi remained totally calm and played with a small abacus on his cluttered desk as he talked.

'The eight characters are very personal. If you're born with eight good characters, you will be very successful and have a smooth life. If they are bad, you will have a very difficult life.'

'What about luck? Can that make a difference?'

'Your destiny is what you are born with. But luck is what you make of it. Luck can enhance prosperity. If you're born with good destiny and have good luck, your life will be even better.'

'And if you have a bad destiny?'

'Good luck can still help you.'

'What is the role of feng shui in all this?'

'Feng shui works like luck. It balances both sides. Good feng shui can help a bad destiny. If you have a good destiny, feng shui can make it even better. Feng shui offers a remedy for your life. It can multiply your earnings, maybe ten times as much. It's good for your health and for your relationships.'

'And if you don't apply feng shui?'

'If you don't apply it, you'll just go along with your destiny. But with feng shui you can enhance your life. You can not only avoid evil but also maximize your potential. You can get luck closer to your self.'

'What do you mean by evil?' I asked.

'A bad path. Feng shui tells a person to avoid a bad path. It's very general.'

'How do you do it?'

'By position and time. In this office one position is bad; another's good. If I don't use that corner, it helps to avoid evil. We can use decorations to counter the bad.'

I noticed that he had a feng shui compass, known as a Lo Pan compass, in his office and I asked how important it was.

'It's the most important. A feng shui master can't judge with his natural eye. There are twenty-four different directions according to the time of the year and different interpretations for the 360° – some good, some bad. There are also cycles of twenty years, nine years and one year. In 2004, for instance, we are at the end of a twenty-year cycle. There'll be a very big change.'

'What kind of change?'

'Feng shui doesn't make predictions of world trends; only for a country or a place.'

'How reliable are they?'

'The compass is only a tool to make calculations. Interpretations are made by humans,' he replied, smiling knowingly.

I then turned to what made Mr Choi a household name in Hong Kong – his almanac. I asked him whether it was based on the sun or the moon.

'Observatory people use solar calendar. In ancient times, Chinese farmers used the moon but it's not very accurate. We must use the solar.'

I asked him how his almanac worked.

'The Chinese almanac has 365 days. Some days are good, some are bad. On a bad day people can avoid doing certain things, daily things, like starting a business, moving house or travelling.'

'How do you decide what is a good or bad day?'

'According to my calculations. Every sixty years there's a cycle, and every 180 years a big cycle. This changes the days in different years.'

He was clearly referring to the so-called Great Year in the Chinese calendar.

'There's an entry for every day. It tells you the dos and don'ts, depending on your eight characters.'

'Can you interpret it yourself?'

'Yes. Just look into the book!'

The Good Luck Diary

Apart from his colourful and illustrated almanac in Chinese, Mr Choi gave me a 'Good Luck Diary' which summarized in Chinese and English many of the elements of the Chinese almanac. Many people take it seriously, even to such details as the best time for washing hair. The Chinese consider the beginning of any event as if it were its birthday.

As already explained, in the Chinese calendar there are a total of twenty-two characters, consisting of the ten heavenly stems and twelve earthly branches. The earthly branches are related to one another by clashing or harmonious relationships. The first rule in selecting a date for an important event is not to use days when the earthly branch clashes with the branch of the month; for example, you should not choose a day when the earthly branch is yin metal in a month which is yin wood, as metal, according to the cycle of destruction, cuts wood. In the same way, a clashing relationship between the birth years of the people involved should be avoided.

The 'Good Luck Diary' marks propitious days with red spot, a fairly good day with a red circle, and a bad day with a black spot. Good times are also given in red. Two symbols are also given for each day: one for an animal sign, the other for a taboo on a particular activity. If your animal sign appears on a particular day, you should not do anything important and you should avoid in particular the taboo of the day. The good hours during the day should also be consulted. Of course, if there is a very important thing to be done, such as a wedding, a burial or a contract, it is advisable to consult an expert to work out the most auspicious day and time.

Although written in Hong Kong for urban dwellers, the activities reflect the agricultural nature of ancient Chinese civilization. These include: marriage, going abroad, tilling soil, buying property, launching a ship, digging a sewer, fixing a door, building a stove, removing a bed, sinking a well, planting, brewing wine, making a net, cutting hair, litigation, an opening ceremony, laying a foundation stone, constructing a house, moving house, opening a store, trading, meeting a friend, enrolling in school, medical treatment, hunting, ancestor worship, making clothes, beginning work, house cleaning, and the burial of the dead.

In addition, the diary records the phases of the moon, the solstices and equinoxes of the sun, the fortnightly periods and the heavenly stems and earthly branches. Although primarily based on the modern solar calendar, it also contains lunar details and information from the Chinese calendar used in astrology from the earliest times.

I noted that in 2001, my birthday, 23 August, coincided with the fortnightly period 'Heat breaks up', which marks the end of summer. It was an auspicious red spot day, particularly between 01.00–03.00 and 05.00–21.00 hours. As for the taboos, it suggested that those with a Mouse (Rat) sign should not buy property on that day.

According to his diary and almanac, I met Mr Choi on a good day but at an inauspicious time. At the end of our interview, Sherman, the young translator, said she was going to Temple Street in Kowloon to have a 'face reading'. She certainly needed to relax after all her efforts in translating the cryptic words of such a famous figure as the author of the Chinese Almanac. Clearly in the heart of Hong Kong, astrology, feng shui and other divinatory practices are alive and well, despite the official atheistic Communism of the Chinese State and the materialistic capitalism of the island enclave.

9

Wind and Water

The energy of the dragon will be dissipated by wind and will stop at the boundary of water.

THE BOOK OF BURIAL

THE ASTROLOGICAL FOUR PILLARS mark out our destiny, but feng shui can influence our luck, which in turn can affect the workings out of our destiny. As the Cantonese say: 'Destiny comes first, luck, second and feng shui, third.' And, as the author of the Chinese Almanac told me, good feng shui can improve a bad destiny and make a good one even better.

In many ways feng shui complements traditional astrology. Both confirm the ancient Chinese belief that everything in the universe resonates with everything else and that there is an intimate link between heaven, earth and humanity. The Four Pillars show how the heavens influence our lives and feng shui shows how the earth affects the way we live. While we cannot change the former since it is based on the natural forces of the elements, we can the latter. Therein lies our area of freedom. Feng shui is a way of manipulating our luck.[1]

The Principles of Feng Shui

So what exactly is feng shui? Feng shui (pronounced as it is written in Mandarin and as 'fung shoy' in Cantonese) literally means 'wind and water'. The term seems to have been taken from the Chinese classic called *The Book of Burial* which offered guidelines for choosing a prosperous spot of land for ancestors. Such places were called 'dragons' lairs' where the energy of the mountain dragon accumulates. Clearly dragon energy will be blown away by the wind, hence the need for a well-sheltered spot. The boundary of water was interpreted to mean not only flowing water but also flat open space.

Feng shui is sometimes translated as geomancy but it embraces more than Western geomancy, as it is not only concerned with the earth, but also channels cosmic forces.[2] It is the ancient art and science of adapting the dwellings of the living and the dead to harmonize with the energy of their surroundings. It has become the study of the living environment. Its fundamental principles are based on the yin-yang philosophy, the five-element theory and the eight trigrams which are at the heart of Chinese astrology. It also takes into account the 'time-fate' of the main householder.

The bad siting of the tombs of the ancestors could lead to the disturbance of their souls and misfortune for their descendants. On the other hand, a good site will assist the well-being and prosperity of all. In a similar way, a dwelling with good feng shui will favour the health, prosperity and happiness of its inhabitants. The shape of Chinese houses, villages, palaces, cities and cemeteries have all been influenced by feng shui. Beijing in particular is protected from evil influences from the North by mountains and is situated on a gentle plain where it can enjoy the benign influences from the South.

Early Western commentators tended to dismiss feng shui as a superstition. In the sixteenth century, the Jesuit Matthew Ricci called it a 'superstitious rite'. In the nineteenth century, Ernest Eitel lamented how the 'system of superstition' was an obstacle to 'progress' as feng shui masters objected to the siting of telegraph lines, the construction of roads, the opening of mines, and the building of the railways. Even Joseph Needham, who appreciated its aesthetic influence on the Chinese landscape, called it a pseudo-science, a form of divination, and a 'grossly superstitious system'.[3] No doubt reflecting its increasing popularity, more recent Western interpreters have been more sympathetic, asserting that it is an 'astro-biological mode of thought' or a form of 'astro-ecology'.[4] It might be even better described as a kind of 'eco-astrology' for it recognizes the intimate link between the microcosm and the macrocosm (the person and the universe) and the close correspondence between the heavens and the earth (as above, so below). Furthermore, it offers a model of the cosmos on earth.

In many ways, feng shui is just plain common sense. We have all had the experience that some places are inspiring while other feel distinctly creepy. A house on damp, low-lying ground is likely to encourage ill-health and be flooded, while a sheltered South-facing house with a fine view gives a sense of security and well-being. Studying how the wind and water sculpt a landscape, feng shui has simply developed these intuitions into a system which is based on sound pragmatism and embodies the fundamental principles of ecology.[5]

Even before I came across feng shui, I would instinctively practise its principles. When camping with my children I would spend some time choosing a good site by taking in the wider topographical features and then walk around the immediate surroundings until I felt I had come across the 'right spot' to settle. Nomads and dogs do the same.

The principles are very ancient and the builders of megaliths throughout the world clearly understood them. There is evidence that in the Shang dynasty (1800–1200 BC) the establishment of settlements was a 'deliberate, planned event' and that they took the form of a walled enclosure aligned with the four cardinal directions.[6] The principles were being recorded in China as early as the fourth century BC and consolidated into a system in the Three Kingdoms period. The theoretical basis of feng shui is to be found in the *I Ching*, but the earliest reference to the discipline comes in a bibliography of Practical Arts in a work called the *Former Han Dynasty History* by Pan Ku (32–92). It mentions two lost works called *The Golden Box of Geomancy* and *Terrestrial Conformations for Dwellings* among others on astrology and calendars.

The *Imperial Encyclopaedia* refers to the fifth-century text known as *The Yellow Emperor's Dwelling Classic* by Wang Wei which discusses yin dwellings for the dead and yang ones for the living. It declares: 'A good earth will grow exuberant sprouts; a house with good fortune will bring prosperity.'[7] In the T'ang period, the delightfully named *Ching Nang Ao Chih* (Mysterious Principles of the Blue Bag) was attributed to the famous feng shui practitioner Yang Yün-Sung. In case you're wondering, the Blue Bag is the Universe!

After the Sung Dynasty (960–1292) two main schools of feng shui evolved. First was the Form School which took a more intuitive approach to the siting of a building. Later came the Compass School, said to have been developed by Wang Chi, which was more analytical and based on relationships between the five elements, the eight trigrams, the heavenly stems, the earthly branches and the constellations.

I was able to see a classic example of feng shui in practice in the Ming Tombs near Beijing. The location of the tomb of the first emperor is well protected on all sides by the mountains, and a lake is situated in front of the tomb, thereby creating a perfect dragon's lair. However, later emperors of the dynasty were buried further and further away from the original site and were no longer sheltered by the mountains or faced the lake. The thirteenth and last Ming emperor, who lost his country to the Manchurians from the North, is in the least favourable position, as if all thought of feng shui had been forgotten. Some masters consider this to be a metaphysical explanation of the fall of the dynasty: they no longer knew how to channel the energies of heaven and earth in favour of humanity.

Since both the energy of a place and the people who live there change over time, a feng shui expert must be schooled in Chinese natural philosophy (yin and yang and the five elements) and be a master of the calendar. The theoretical basis of feng shui is the concept of chi. Humans, both dead and alive, are under the control of the active energy of chi which is prevalent throughout heaven and earth. It flows underneath the surface of the earth in conduits known as dragon veins, rather like blood courses in the arteries and veins of humans. It is particularly concentrated in mountains, watercourses and vegetation. In general, it is responsible for growth and change in the natural world.

Chi varies not only in space but also in time in a cyclical manner, oscillating between yin and yang in different places throughout the year and in the great sixty-year cycle. This insight has given rise to what is known as 'flying star' feng shui in which the flying stars indicate how chi changes continuously over time and moves in space, affecting our well-being from different directions.[8]

There is earth chi in the landscape, heaven chi in the annual cycle of seasons, and the chi which flows in the watercourses. Its negative counterpart is *sha* (not to be confused with the same word for local eminences) which blows from the North, saps energy, travels along straight lines, pierces gaps and lies in stagnating pools.

In an ideal site, the chi of heaven and the chi of earth unite, accumulate and interact. As the *Chao T'ing-tung* put it, 'The earthly dwelling and the heavenly constellation should be in a productive relationship or in harmony.'[9] The most important features conducive to chi are the orientation of the site, the topography of the surroundings, the layout of the building, the time, and the occupants.

Every place on earth has special features which modify the local influence of the different types of energy or chi. The most important natural influences are made by the forms of the hills and the water-courses which are moulded by wind and water (hence the name feng shui). The heights, forms and orientation of buildings, and the direction of roads and bridges also play their part. Since the flow of chi in different localities is influenced by the positions of the celestial bodies, traditional astrology has also to be taken into account.

While a good site is the most important factor, remedies for bad feng shui can be taken, such as digging ditches and tunnels, creating ponds or re-orientating the direction of watercourses. Flowing water adjacent to a house is invariably good; isolated boulders are bad. Nothing should check the gentle flow of chi: it should not run away too fast, as on an escarpment; nor stagnate, as on marshy ground. Evil influences affecting a house that has already been built can also be counterbalanced by devices such as mirrors, wind chimes, tridents and talismans.

The ideal site takes the form of an 'armchair', protected on three sides by mountains or hills and open to the south with a watercourse in front. Here the earthly chi can ascend and the heavenly chi descend, meeting and uniting in the 'dragon's lair' of the dwelling. The tomb, house or village is then protected as in the crook of an elbow.

The two principal currents of life-giving chi in the earth are yin and yang, symbolized by the Green Dragon and the White Tiger who are associated with the Eastern and Western quarters of the sky. The strength of the yang Dragon and the yin Tiger should balance each other. In general, high escarpments are considered yang and round elevations and water yin (the sexual symbolism is obvious). Ideally, a site contains three-fifths yang and two-fifths yin. In urban sites, roads can take the place of watercourses, and other buildings can be consi-dered mountains.

The most important feature in the landscape is the dragon; it is linear and links all other shapes. Depending on its nature, it can enhance or destroy human fortune. Hills and mountain ridges are the veins and arteries of its body.

Rather than imposing an artificial grid on the landscape, the Chinese prefer winding roads, walls and buildings that follow the natural con-tours of the earth. I could see this in the siting of the older farms, houses and villages during my travels in China. Indeed, the move from geo-metrical gardens of the neo-classical period in Europe, like Versailles, to the picturesque, flowing gardens of the Romantic era may have been influenced by Chinese tastes first brought back by the Jesuits.[10]

Mountains protect chi from dispersal by calming the wind while watercourses block its movement and prevent it from running away. If there are too many channels the chi dissipates. The 'dragon's lair', on the other hand, is where chi has its positive and powerful influence. It is to be found on a good site and open to the South and shielded on three sides by mountains. The 'Mountain Dragon' brings harmony and 'Water Dragon' brings prosperity.

The five planets are used to describe different land forms and are associated with the five elements. Mercury is considered the Water Star, Venus the Metal Star, Mars the Fire Star, Jupiter the Wood Star and Saturn the Earth Star. If a mountain in the East is a Metal Star and one to the South is a Fire Star, it will be unfavourable because Fire destroys Metal. Ideally, Water (a rugged plateau) should be in the north; with Wood (blunt-ended) in the East; the land form associated with Fire (three peaks) in the South; and Metal (curved) in the West.

The ultimate goal of feng shui is to find a way of living harmoniously with the natural world, rather than dominating or conquering it. It provides a means of balancing the energies of the earth and the heavens and as such may been seen as the applied science of Chinese cosmology. Indeed, an auspicious dwelling for the Chinese is not just a symbol of the self but is nothing less than an *imago mundi* – an image of the universe.[12]

The Lo Pan Compass

The principal instrument for the feng shui expert to make his calculations is the Lo Pan compass. In order to align a dwelling correctly with the cosmic forces of the earth and the heavens, the feng shui expert makes use of information engraved on a series of concentric rings around the central magnetic compass. These include the directions, the trigrams and hexagrams of the *I Ching*, and the heavenly stems and earthly branches of the sixty-year cycle of the Chinese calendar.

A prototype of the Lo Pan compass, which reflected the close link between feng shui and astrology at the time, was the diviner's board known as the *shih*. Dating from at least the second century BC, it was made from two boards, the upper one shaped like a disc representing heaven and the lower one a square corresponding to the earth.

I acquired a Lo Pan compass in Hong Kong. Its square base contains many concentric rings around the central compass needle floating in oil – known as Heaven's Pool. I noticed that when I placed it near my computer, it vibrated gently, picking up the strong magnetic field and no doubt the radiation from my equipment.

Lo Pan compasses can have thirty-six rings, but the most simple have nine. Since they depict the hexagrams, the elements and the stars, they show how astrology and feng shui come together in finding an auspicious dwelling for the living or the dead. The compass encircles the three essential aspects of the universe – heaven, earth and humanity – which must work together to maintain the harmony which is essential for prosperity and well-being.

The first ring depicts eight trigrams of the early arrangement known as 'The Former Heaven Sequence' allegedly discovered by Fu Hsi. They depict the directions of the compass, with yang at its greatest height ($\equiv$) in the south and yin ($\equiv$ $\equiv$) in the north. The trigrams also symbolize natural phenomena: heaven, lake, fire, thunder, wind, water, mountain and earth. As symbols of natural forces, they are believed to protect the magnetic needle.

The second ring contains nine moving stars, believed to be the seven stars of the Big Dipper, plus two nearby stars which are mirrored by specific shapes in the landscape. Their names show their historical context: Covetous Wolf, Great Gate, Salary Preserved, Purity and Chastity, Destroying Army. The two extra stars are known as Left Reinforcement and Right Assistant. They represent favourable and unfavourable shapes in the landscape.[11]

The third ring enfolds the twenty-four 'mountains' composed of 15° sectors, which are directional points similar to the ones on a mariner's compass. The *San-ho* school of feng shui, which emphasizes the harmony between heaven, earth and humanity, has three rings of twenty-four mountains, but the *San-yüan* school, which stresses the influence of the cycle of time on the environment, has only one. The mountains correspond to four hexagrams from the Later Heaven Sequence, eight heavenly stems and twelve earthly branches. The heavenly stems Mou and Chi are missing because they correspond to the earth at the centre. The ring is used to establish the direction of dwellings and to measure the landscape and the mountain ranges.

The fourth ring contains the eight major stars from the astrology system of Tzu Wei (Master Wei). Tzu Wei is the name of the god who looks after what is variously called the Purple Star, the Purple Planet or the Pole Star. It is the centre of the astrological calendar. The life span of humans is symbolized by Ursa Major and Ursa Minor (Great and

Little Bear, or Dipper), the two closest constellations which are also called the North and South Measures. In the South Measure lives the god of birth and in the North Measure the god of death.

The next two rings – the fifth and sixth – list the sixty-four hexagrams (*kua*) of the *I Ching*. The hexagrams in the fifth ring offer a reading for the present, and the sixth, a reading for the future. Some feng shui masters associate different directions of the compass with *kua* numbers to represent eight twenty-year periods in the 160-year cycle. When selecting an auspicious place for burial, they will ensure that the positive energy – 'the incoming Dragon' – will come from a prosperous *kua* number and direction.

The seventh ring has the twenty-four terms or 'fortnightly periods' (*chieh*) of the Hsia solar calendar, each of which correspond to 15°, measured in longitude, of the movement of the sun on the ecliptic. In the calendar they take place every fifteen or sixteen days. Each term defines an activity in the agricultural year: the chi periods (such as 'Excited Insects' or 'Cold Dew') mark periods of growth and decay, while the fortnightly periods (such as the beginning of spring or the spring equinox) show the changes in the annual cycle.

The eighth ring encircles the twenty-eight constellations (*hsui*) which are used to determine the position and time of a burial. They are divided into sectors associated with the symbols of the four directions: the Green Dragon sector in the Eastern constellations; the Black Turtle (also known as the Dark Warrior) sector in the northern constellations; the White Tiger sector in the Western constellations; and the Red Bird sector in the Southern constellations. These are paralleled on earth, and in an auspicious house take up their rightful positions in the four cardinal directions.

The outer circle of the nine-ringed compass is divided into 360°. The original Chinese compass was divided into 365.25°, but it was changed after the arrival of the Jesuits in the sixteenth century with their telescopes and exact measurements.

There are other Lo Pan compasses with different arrangement of rings providing additional information. The thirty-eight ringed compass contains an astrology ring which is used to check the balance of the elements, yin and yang, heavenly stems and branches and the hexagrams to draw up a horoscope of the person in relation to a site.[12] There is also a Life Star Ring used to discover the Life Star or constellation of the deceased. The so-called Horse Palace Ring tracks the position of the travelling Horse Star in relation to the grave to make sure that the soul of the deceased will be content and not wander. This is important as the peace and happiness of the deceased will affect the fortune of the living members of the family.

The three main methods in the Compass School are the *San-ho, San-yüan* and *Chiu-hsing. San-ho* examines the feng shui site from four points of view: the dragon (the main mountain chain situated at the back of the site), the feng shui spot (*hsüeh*), local eminences (*sha*) and watercourses. The *San-yüan* method examines the situation within the sixty-year cycle which combines the ten heavenly stems and earthly branches based on the hexagrams of the *I Ching*. The *Chiu-hsing* method mainly considers the directional relationship of the house buildings and their elements.

The auspicious orientation of the house will depend on the 'life-fate' of the householder. His or her Four Pillars of Destiny must therefore be taken into account. The beneficial directions will depend on the age of the house (in which twenty-year period it was built within the cycle of 160 years), as well as the age of the householder and the particular stage he or she is at in the ten-year cycle. The Pa Che system, for instance, uses a personal compass to determine whether a person has an 'Eastern' or 'Western life', depending on the year of their birth. The compass indicates the elements which can bring about harmony or conflict in your life and what colours and numbers are most appropriate to you.[13] It also points out the favourable and malign directions of the compass for each individual. In my case, I am a 'Western life', my element is gold, my number six. Luck will come from the West (vitality), North-West (life), South-West (longevity) and North-East (good fortune). The other directions are unfavourable.

The Lo Shu Square

Another instrument used by the feng shui master to make his calculations is the Lo Shu square, which consists of nine squares within a square. The layout of cities, palaces and temples in China were traditionally based on this square. Even the provinces of the Empire had a similar pattern, with the emperor living in the middle square. In feudal times, the land-owner who could afford nine rooms adopted the layout, moving from one room to another according to the seasons. The Forbidden City in Beijing is based on the square.

While undertaking this research, I made the extraordinary discovery that the ground plan of my house in North Wales, designed by the Cambridge architect Keith Garbett in the 1960s, is based on the same model. The four outer walls are exactly aligned to the four directions of the compass. I sit writing this in the South-West square, facing West into a valley formed by an oak-covered hill and a rugged mountain.

The Lo Shu square is said to have been revealed to the legendary Emperor Yu by a turtle which emerged from the river Lo with it on its back. The Emperor is celebrated as the first man to control the flood-water of the great river by tunnelling through the Dragon Gate Mountain. The Jade Emperor himself rewarded him with a scroll with the sixty-four hexagrams, a jade tablet with twelve units which represent the twelve divisions of the day and of the year, and the turtle shell inscribed with the magic square. The supreme deity said: 'The hexagrams on the scroll will help you predict the auspicious years for your people, the jade tablet gives you the authority to govern wisely, the inscriptions on the turtle shell give you ability to plan well.'[14] These are still the principal tools of the modern Chinese astrologer and feng shui master.

The magical nature of the square is revealed in its special property of combining number and shape.

S

4	9	2
3	5	7
8	1	6

E (left) · W (right)

N

The odd, male and yang numbers are distributed at the four cardinal points and at the centre, while the even, female and yin numbers are placed at the corner of the square. The highest number, nine, is at the top; the lowest, number one, at the bottom, as they should be. One and nine are believed to be the most auspicious, because one is the beginning of all things, and nine represents completion. The number at the centre is five, the physical and mathematical mean and the most powerful. It is translated as *wu* in Chinese and it is no coincidence that characters for 'midday' and 'self' are also *wu*. If you add the numbers up along any line, including the diagonals, they make fifteen.

The four quarters symbolize the four seasons. Indeed, the numbers in a clockwise direction show the ratio of yang to yin in the annual cycle, yang being lowest in the winter when yin is highest and vice versa. The four quarters also represent the elements, with earth at the centre. And the square further arranges the trigrams of the Later Heaven Sequence with the directions and elements.

Where does the Lo Shu magic square come from? No one knows. The numbers might have developed from the divisions of the hand count, with the little finger down to the thumb representing the odd numbers, and the hollows between the fingers and the thumb being the even numbers. Certainly it was not confined to China. Arab alchemists also felt that it revealed the ultimate nature of the universe; Jabir ibn Hayyan even wrote a treatise on the square.[15] Many cities and temples in India, Egypt and even Ireland are designed to its principles.

10

Star House

I READ ABOUT RAYMOND LO on the day of my arrival in Hong Kong in an article in the *South China Daily Post* where he was pictured holding up a Lo Pan compass and grappling with the skyscrapers of the metropolis like King Kong. Having worked for the appropriately named China Light & Power company, he had decided to become a full-time practitioner of feng shui on 1 July 1997, the day Hong Kong was officially reunited with mainland China. He not only ran courses in Miami, Melbourne, Singapore, London and the University of Hong Kong, but had also become an English-speaking pundit in the world's media, appearing on CNN, ABC's *Good Morning America* and BBC's *Whicker's World.*

He lived on the mainland in the district of Kowloon (literally, 'nine dragons'). I took one of the famous 'star ferries' from the main island of Hong Kong and tracked down Raymond Lo's office in Star House opposite the terminal. It was on the eighth floor, just down a corridor from a company called Oracle Sourcing and Development. The name Fung Shui and Destiny Consultant was over the glass door. He liked to be known as Fung Shui Lo, pronouncing it in Cantonese style as 'fung shoy'.

His office was decorated in light grey and white. Although it had the minimum of furniture, there were many model lions and tortoises, as well as miniature sphinxes and pyramids brought back as souvenirs from Egypt. His desk was positioned sideways along a long window which faced East. The back of his chair was against the wall, which protected him and gave him support. His entrance was placed in the South-West. Good energy comes from both of these directions.

My Destiny Consultant was a short, chubby man dressed in a dark green shirt and black trousers. His small, smiling eyes and oval mouth were set in a round face. He had just returned from Egypt and was suffering from jet lag and a stomach upset. 'I shall have to get some good Chinese herbal medicine for it!' he joked, making light of it.

He explained that his office was decorated in grey and white because he needed more metal and water elements in his life.

It was 2001 and the Chinese New Year's Eve had been on 25 January when the first new moon of the year rose in the sky. It had marked the beginning of a two-week festival which lasted from the new to the full moon. The many festivities included dragon-dancing, house-cleaning (to sweep away ill fortune), flower-decorating, feasting, lantern parades, firecrackers, 'fortune cookies', and red 'good-fortune scrolls' hung from the walls.

Lo, however, insisted that 4 February was the beginning of spring and the real first day of the Year of the Snake: 'The people use the lunar calendar, but the real calendar is the solar one. The farmers use this Hsia calendar which should be used for the almanac and auspicious days.'

He was, of course, referring to the calendar developed during the Hsia dynasty which dates from 2205–1766 BC .

'We are in the dragon's mouth,' Lo announced. 'The tail of the dragon is in the North-West. The dragon energy of China passes down the central mountains to the South-East and stops at the sea. The mountains shelter and protect the energy in the harbour. That's why Hong Kong is so auspicious a site.'

'Are there other sources of energy which affect us?' I asked.

'There are three kinds of influence: earth, heaven and man. Most energy comes from heaven, but earth energy influences the whole landscape. Heaven's energy changes from time to time, but in the landscape there is no change for millions of years.'

'What determines a person's character and fate, then?'

'There are three aspects. The first is destiny, the inborn quality of your personality, which does not change. It is fixed by your date of birth. We call this the Four Pillars of Destiny.'

'Is that what you mean by the Chinese horoscope?'

'Yes, that's it. The second aspect is luck. After you're born, luck influences your experience and passage through life. It's not random but determined. It provides you with opportunities.'

I knew that *joss*, meaning luck, is the most important word in the Chinese religious vocabulary. Since it cannot be left to chance, gods must be appeased and bad spirits and hungry ghosts dispersed. To attract luck, people go to temples and burn incense, present gifts and say prayers to the immortals and the gods.

'The third aspect is feng shui,' Lo went on. 'It shows how a positive environment can affect your destiny and luck and how you can relocate your self.'

'Can you change your destiny?'

'We use the word improve, not change.'

'Does that mean your destiny is predetermined?'

'Not exactly. It's like the inborn quality of an artist. In the case of a banker, if he works hard and makes good decisions, he can minimize difficulties and improve on his luck.'

'So you can affect the direction of your life, then?'

'Your situation in this life is like a fish. A fish can enjoy its freedom to swim, but the undertow goes to the sea.'

'So even if you swim against the current, you'll still go in the same direction as the river in the end?'

'Yes. Another way of looking at it is like driving a car. Your destiny is the car; it can be luxurious or old and uncomfortable. Your luck is the road you travel on; it can be a smooth highway or a rocky road. Even if the car is excellent, if the road is bad your journey will not be comfortable!'

Lo explained you have 'luck pillars' derived from the month pillar of the Four Pillars of Destiny. Each one will show a ten-year period when you come under the influence of the two elements in each luck pillar. To be very fortunate, you need a good set of pillars of destiny as well as good luck pillars.

'And how does feng shui fit in?'

'Feng shui consists of your driving skills and the parts you need for the car!' He laughed in reply, clearly enjoying his analogy. His general approach echoed the ancient Taoist view that a wise person will not oppose the flow of nature but go with it.

I asked Lo how he deals with someone who comes to him with a problem.

'I have three methods: destiny analysis using the Four Pillars, based on my client's date of birth, feng shui to improve their situation, and the *I Ching* to help them if a particular choice has to be made.'

He dismissed the popular system of the 'Circle of Animals' which is usually taken in the West to be all there is to Chinese astrology: 'It's like the sun signs of the Western zodiac. They're very superficial and only deal with one aspect.'

He insisted that true astrology should be based on the solar-lunar calendar and not the lunar one associated with the Circle of Animals.

'It's a total misconception to say that the Chinese work on a lunar system. The lunar system is very artificial for it only adds up to 360 days in the year and for the excessive days you have to have a thirteenth month every few years. I prefer the Hsia calendar based on the sun and used by the farmers. Today, 4 February, is the real New Year. It is the beginning of spring, exactly one and a half months before the spring equinox!'

'What do you think of the feng shui being practised in the West?'

'A lot of it is false. An emperor in the T'ang Dynasty issued a false book of feng shui for the people. It's very simple and ninety per cent false. It was called *Killing the Barbarians* to fool foreigners. To become an expert you must learn from a master, not from books. Most of them are superficial and wrong.'

'When did feng shui begin in China?'

'It's very old. The feng shui symbols of a dragon on the right and a tiger on the left have been found on tombs of ancestors from around 6000 BC. The philosophy of yin and yang and the *I Ching* emerged about 4500 BC. Turtle shells were used for oracles; their shape perhaps gave the idea for the trigrams. The Yellow Emperor mentions a feng shui compass around 2000 BC. The first book was written by Ko Po in 250 AD. It was a book for burials, on how to choose the right environment. The concern was originally with the dead and only later with the living. It was not just concerned with the physical directions of a dwelling, but also with the influence of time.'

I had come to Hong Kong because I thought practices such as astrology and feng shui would be considered irrational beliefs from the past in Communist mainland China. I was right.

'It's not banned in mainland China,' Lo said, 'but the old practitioners have died away. Only those in Hong Kong and Taiwan have continued.'

'When you see a client, what do you do?' I asked.

'I advise him on the site of his building: where the energy of the heaven and earth mingle. You have to find a good spot. I suggest the arrangements in the office – where the boss should be, the marketing and conference rooms, the entrance. I also advise on the interior design: where to put the furniture, what colours to have, what kind of plants and objects to use and where to place them. The idea is to increase the flow of energy and to make the business prosperous.'

Prosperity was clearly the main goal of feng shui for business managers. Lo had specifically written a book for them. I wondered at this uncritical acceptance of capitalism. The original aim of feng shui was to attain harmony with the environment and well-being for the living and the dead.

He explained that there are two main schools of feng shui. The physical 'form' school works by eyesight alone, while the 'compass' school works with directions and time. In both, the symbols are the same. A mountain, for instance, represents human harmony, while water stands for prosperity.

'In Hong Kong, the mountain dragon is weak and the water dragon is strong. We have a lot of money but not much family harmony. But it will change.'

Lo was not wary of making broad generalizations about the sweep of history and the direction of the future. In the year 2000, for instance, the two elements metal and earth were in harmony and it was relatively peaceful. It all depends on whether the elements clash or support each other. Referring to the year 2001, Lo declared: 'Now that we have entered the year of the Snake whose element is fire, it will clash with the Pig whose element is water. Therefore there will be more disasters and more accidents in air and on sea. Fire, on the other hand, is good for economic activity, but the new economy is metal which is not doing so well as fire attacks metal. Energy will, however, shift in 2005 which is the beginning of a new twenty-year cycle.'

That was enough for the time being. Lo was visibly wilting; his chi was low. Egyptian food and crossing the world in a silver bird were taking their toll. We agreed to meet later in the week.

Lo gave me some of his books to read before we met again: *Feng Shui: The Pillars of Destiny*, *Feng Shui and Destiny for Managers* and *Feng Shui and Destiny for Families*. The last one taught how to 'choose a compatible life partner, protect and enhance family health, detect and encourage your child's talents, and create a harmonious and successful home' – what most humans are interested in!

He claimed that our true self is reflected 'in the elements that constitute our body and soul'.[1] He confirmed that the Four Pillars is a system based on five basic driving forces – the elements – in the universe and the principles of yin and yang. Although the elements change over time, they interact with one another in the form of the two cycles that my temple soothsayer had first shown me: the Cycle of Creation and the

Cycle of Destruction. The Chinese calendar carries information about the five elements and indicates which ones are prevailing during a particular time.

Once you have worked out your Pillars of Destiny, you can then work out your 'luck pillars' – the pairs of elements which affect your journey through life for every period of ten years. They therefore represent the cyclical changes in your life.

The different pillars represent different relations of yourself: the hour pillar, your children; the day pillar, your self (heavenly stem) and spouse (earthly branch); the month pillar, your father and mother; and your year pillar, your grandparents. The elements for each pillar will indicate how you get on with them according to the Cycles of Creation and Destruction. If the day pillar is wood (the self) and the month pillar is metal (father), then it indicates that my father will try to dominate me (metal destroys wood). If the earthly branch of the day pillar (spouse) is water, then he or she will support your wood.

The Four Pillars can help you find the right partner by seeing if the elements are compatible between you. The basic rule is to find some exhaustive elements if the self is too strong and some supportive elements if the self is weak. The time to meet a partner or get married can be indicated by the luck pillar of the ten-year cycles. Although the animal sign has a deep-rooted tradition in Chinese match-making, Lo argues that 'animal sign astrology' is 'as illogical as newspaper astrology in the West'. It refers to the earthly branch of the year pillar, thereby giving only one eighth of the required information to be found in the eight signs of the Four Pillars of Destiny. Lo does not mince his words here: 'It is preposterous to believe that the entire human population has only twelve types of fate!'[2]

The Three Periods and the Nine Ages

Reading Lo's books, I noted that he defined feng shui as 'the power of abstract energies coming into contact with physical surroundings'. While these energies are governed by yin and yang and the Cycles of Creation and Destruction of the five elements, they also change over time in a fixed and predictable pattern known as the 'Three Periods and Nine Ages'. This pattern takes its name from the division of the traditional Chinese 180-year cycle into three periods of sixty years, which are further divided into three twenty-year ages. Each of the nine ages is assigned a number from one to nine, and carries the meaning of one of the trigrams of the *I Ching*.

This book is published in the Age of Seven, which runs from 1984 to 2004. The trigram for the Age stands for female power, the mouth, technology and the West. For Lo this explained why numerous female leaders have come to the fore and world communication systems like the Internet have developed. According to Lo, the trigram for the Age of Eight – the young son, the hand and the North-East – means that young men will come to power, machinery and robots will develop, and China will grow in strength.

The concept of the Three Periods and the use of the Lo Shu square add the dimension of time in the 'Flying Star' school of feng shui to which Lo belonged. At the end of each twenty-year Age, the number of the new Age is placed in the centre of the square. All the numbers in the square then change accordingly as in a game of musical chairs. The meaning of the numbers, as they move around the square, will therefore change with time, as the number of the prevailing Age will always be the most prosperous number. As we are in the Age of Seven, any number below seven is unfavourable and a square representing a room in a building with that number should not be used for anything important.

Two 'flying stars' are distributed in each square according to a set method. They are represented by the first nine digits and symbolize the elements expressed in the trigrams. Those on the left of each square are quiet 'mountain stars' representing harmony, and on the right, active 'water stars' symbolizing prosperity. Like the numbers in the Lo Shu square, the flying stars change in a predictable pattern. Rooms should be arranged according to their required use: a living room is best with an active water star and the bedroom with a quiet mountain star. The flying stars carry with them elements which can be strengthened or weakened by appropriate objects and colours. Since the water star eight is an earth element it can, for instance, be supported by yellow colours. Since the flying star two is earth and symbolizes sickness, it can be checked by talismans such as a string of six metal coins. A wind chime counteracts the influence of the bad star five.

The kitchen, master bedroom and sitting room are considered the most important rooms in a house. The last touch of feng shui in a house is the placement of furniture, decorative objects and plants to enhance good energy and to minimize the harmful effects of bad energy. The top left-hand corner of the sitting room, for instance, is considered the place of prosperity and a healthy, growing plant there will actively encourage it. A desk is best placed in the diagonally opposite corner to the entrance, against the wall, at a right angle to one side, with the back of the person using it against a wall. The best position for a bed is similar to a desk, but sleeping below an overhead beam is to be avoided. Again, much of this would appear to be common sense. But it was fascinating to see it confirmed in Lo's works, which are intended for a modern, urbane audience.

Lo was fully recovered when Elizabeth and I met him a few days later. Chinese herbal medicine had restored the balance in his body after his Egyptian bout of food poisoning. He was now wearing a white collarless shirt, a black sleeveless pullover and black trousers. Green had given way to black.

I had read in one of his books that the five elements are expressed in colours: metal (white, gold, silver, shiny colours), wood (green, blue, dark brown), water (black, grey), fire (red, purple, pink), earth (yellow, beige, light brown). I assume that when I first met him, he needed more wood; now it was the time for water.

I told Lo that I had discovered that my house in North Wales was based on the Lo Shu magic square and asked him about the arrangement of my rooms. At the time, I had been writing in the South-West corner and sleeping in the South-East. The entrance was in the South.

As an exponent of the Flying Star School of feng shui, he argued that the feng shui of a house changes over time. It was therefore essential to consider the age of a house and its place in the 180-year cycle. In the case of my open-plan home, it was built in the early 1960s, during the Age of Five. After careful calculations, he concluded that I was working in the wrong place and would be better off sleeping there. I should work in the North-West square, which had previously been my dining area. The entrance, unfortunately fixed for ever in concrete in the middle South square, should be in the South-West. He warned that the energy of the Age of Seven was waning at the end of the twenty-year cycle and that when we turned into the Age of Eight in 2005, the energy would also turn and it would be advisable for me to change the use of my rooms again.

I next asked Lo to work out my horoscope according to his system of the Four Pillars of Destiny. I told him I was around 16.00 on 23 August, 1946. Lo took away an hour to adjust it according to Greenwich Mean Time or Universal Time, but he did not seem to add

eight hours as some purists do to convert it into Chinese Coastal Time.
Obviously, that time would throw up a very different horoscope.

He then drew up the elements for the hour, day, month and year
(the four pillars), matching them with the appropriate elements. The
result below represented my destiny, the qualities with which I was born
and which I would carry with me throughout my life. The heavenly
stems are on the second line and the earthly branches underneath.

Heavenly Stems			
Hour	*Day*	*Month*	*Year*
Water	Earth (Self)	Fire (Father)	Fire

Earthly Branches			
Hour	*Day*	*Month*	*Year*
Metal	Fire	Metal	Earth
Children	Myself/Spouse	Father/Mother	Grandparents

I was, Lo explained, primarily 'yin earth' which stands for intellect.
That seemed appropriate enough for a philosopher and author.

'You were born in August when it is autumn for the Chinese,' he
said. 'Since metal dominates earth, your energy is a little weak and
therefore you need fire to support and strengthen you.

'You have three fire signs, but in autumn fire is not strong. You need
more earth, more fire, and wood is good for you. They stand for friends,
resources and power. Bad for you is water and metal, which represent
money and intelligence. You have some of metal, but not much water . . .'

So much for my destiny. I was fated to be intelligent but poor. And
what about my luck during my journey through life?

Like my soothsayer at the Wong Tai Sin temple, Lo appointed an element for every ten years of my life, starting from the age of five and continuing to eighty-five. Looking back, he declared that from twenty-five to thirty-five, there was tension between earth and water, which gave rise to struggle in my life. From thirty-five to forty-five, metal and water were in opposition, which meant that I had a demanding life and limited resources. He declared that from forty-five to fifty-five was a period of metal and earth, during which earth was giving me some support and things were improving . . .

I was not so sure about this. The first five years of the ten-year cycle had proved to be the most difficult time in my life. I had gone through separation and divorce and the loss of a beloved home in the Welsh mountains. But there was no looking back, it seemed. Lo declared: 'Your luck should steadily improve for the rest of your life, with water supporting wood from fifty-five to seventy-five and wood feeding fire. From eighty-five, you also have wood and fire. Fire stands for resources, earth for friends, wood for power, metal for intelligence, and water money.'

'Do you have any advice?'

'As a weak earth person, you need a warmer climate and warm colours like red, pink or purple, no black or white, to enhance your energy level.

'Each of the elements,' Lo said, 'carry meaning. Fire gives support, strength and resources, and represents abstract knowledge and education. It stands for house, clothes and your mother. The earth stands for friends and people around you. Wood is the power element; it conquers earth. It is your status, your duty. You have no wood, which means you have no social power; you're not made out to be a politician. Metal is your creative and productive side, your intelligence and skill.'

'What do my signs imply about my work?'

'The double metal in you means that you are a scholar and conservative. You could be in a profession like an architect or doctor. You show knowledge.'

I was indeed a scholar, but in feudal times in China a Confucian scholar would be part of the civil service and a supporter of the status quo, and I was far from conservative in my life and opinions.

'And my health?'

'Your fire is weak. Your stomach is weak. You need to replenish your energy, not cool down.'

Again, this didn't seem to be the case as I was prone to raised blood pressure, a sign of too much yang fire.

'Your children are water and you are earth. They are too aggressive and are exhausting you. They do not listen to you as a teacher.'

This was certainly not the case.

He then turned to Elizabeth and drew up her Four Pillars of Destiny based on her date of birth at 21.00 on 20 July, 1950. He announced: 'You are a fire lady. You have three fire elements; you're yang fire. You're warm and straightforward with an open mind. But you have only one wood; you need more wood and water. You're more commercial than Peter; your fire can support Peter. It was a struggle for you from thirty-four, but luck is coming. If you take note, you'll be able to maximize your good fortune. From sixty-four it will be better with more water and from seventy-four you're totally water! At the end of your life, you'll have an earth problem. You need wood so you should wear green!'

Before we left, I asked him how popular the astrology of the Four Pillars was in Hong Kong.

'It's very important for couples as the Chinese do not usually divorce like in the West. Many people check the birthday of their baby. They try and choose the right time. It's most important as the destiny of a child affects the parents.'

'Who comes along to see you?'

'I have more women than men clients; even for feng shui.'

'Do you use the *I Ching*?'

'Yes. It's a very useful tool. It fills the gap. The Four Pillars of Destiny and feng shui can't answer questions. The *I Ching* can help you in your choices, to make a decision if two things seem equally good.'

Science or Superstition?

Before taking my leave, I asked Lo whether astrology was a science or a superstition. He was adamant in his reply: 'It's totally objective and scientific, not intuitive. I only read the signs.'

I was unsure. There can be no doubt that the astronomy and astrology of China have the same root in the careful observation of the processes of nature. Its astrology, moreover, is based on a persuasive metaphysics and a profound understanding of human nature. The dynamic and organic world view underpinning Chinese astrology,

Armillary sphere for measuring the movement of the celestial bodies.
Made by Kuo Shou-Ching (AD 1276) and copied by Huangfu Chung-Ho (1437).
Beijing Ancient Observatory, China.

Carving of a solar eclipse, dating from the Han Dynasty (206 BC–AD 220).
It shows the moon, symbolized by a toad, covering the sun,
represented by a bird. Beijing Ancient Observatory.

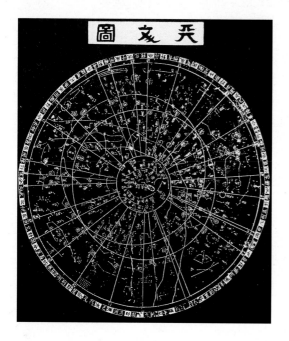

The Suchow planisphere of
AD 1193, portraying the stars,
the ecliptic and the curving
course of the Milky Way.

Feng shui practitioners,
c. fourth century, surveying an
auspicious site. The leaning figure
is consulting his Lo Pan magnetic
compass. Feng shui is often used
to improve the findings of a
Chinese horoscope based on
the Four Pillars of Destiny.

Coiled Serpent, representing kundalini
energy, a manifestation of the Hindu
goddess Shakti. In Indian astrology,
the nodes of the moon, Rahu and Ketu,
indicate a person's kundalini.
Seventeenth century, Gujarat.

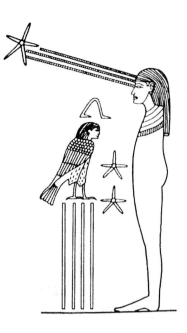

Detail from the second
golden shrine of Tutankhamen.
Eighteenth dynasty
(1333–1323 BC), Egypt.

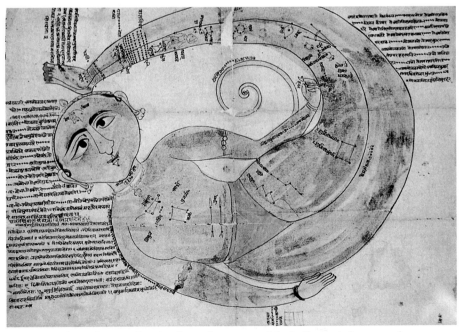

Astrological Man, showing how the twenty-eight Indian nakshatras or lunar
mansions are related to the human body. Eighteenth century, Rajastan.

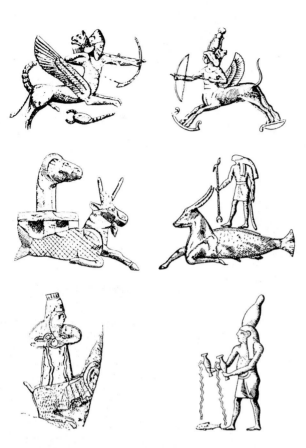

The zodiacal signs of Sagittarius, Capricorn and Aquarius from Babylon (left) compared with those from Egypt (right), before their final shapes were settled.

Egyptian sky goddess Nut, from a coffin dated from the eighth to the eleventh century BC.

North Polar constellations depicted on the tomb ceiling of Seti I.
The standing hippopotamus on the right probably represents the constellation of Draco, while the 'thigh' on which it rests its forefoot is usually considered to be the Great Bear (Ursa Major). The crouching lion outlined by stars is almost certainly Leo, while the standing man is probably Orion and the bull possibly Taurus.
Nineteenth dynasty (1306–1290 BC), Valley of the Kings, Luxor.

inspired by Taoism and embodied in the *I Ching*, not only coincides with the findings of modern physics but anticipates the best of Gaia theory. There is, as all astrologers claim, undoubtedly a close correspondence between heaven and earth. And if we are influenced by our terrestrial environment, it is not so far-fetched to believe that the celestial environment should have an effect on us as well.

Chinese astrology does not follow the mechanical causality of much Western science, but recognizes a variety of influences at work. While much scientific thinking in the West is content to isolate, weigh, measure and classify, the Chinese mind believes that the events in heaven and earth resonate together. They see countless interacting ingredients being involved in an event at any particular moment. In this they recognize something like Carl Jung's 'synchronicity', an acausal principle that takes the coincidence of events in space and time as meaning something more than mere chance. Such coincidences have 'a peculiar interdependence of objective events among themselves as well with the subjective (psychic) states of the observer or observers'.[3] My own experience suggests that what appears as a 'coincidence' is often very meaningful and has an underlying pattern.

Chinese astrology may not be a science in the conventional Western sense, but if you take science in its original meaning as *sciencia*, knowledge acquired by study, then astrology undoubtedly offers much wisdom about our condition and place within the universe. Indeed, its many insights may well be the disguised remnants of a lost 'sacred science'.

Chinese astrology, like Chinese metaphysics, assumes that everything in the universe (symbolized by the five elements and their configuration expressed in the sixty-four hexagrams) do indeed follow certain tendencies (the oscillation between yin and yang and the Cycles of Creation and Destruction). By understanding these rules, we can have a better understanding of our destiny.

However, for the Chinese, fate is never completely settled; if it were, they would not be so interested in divination and gambling. Chinese astrology is based on the Taoist insight that it is better to go with the flow of nature than against it. If we go with the flow, we will be more effective and attain our end. If we let ourselves drift, we will be taken out to sea, but we can also row against the tide if necessary and reach the haven of our choice. Either way, it helps to know the direction of the prevailing current.

As in Western astrology, any apparent 'negative' elements in a reading of the Four Pillars of Destiny are not really negative. No chart is good or bad; it is a simply a guide to your potential. Whether your life becomes good or bad is still up to you. If anything, such indications can be positively helpful. By becoming aware of potential difficulties, it is easier to deal with them and eventually overcome them. Indeed, an awareness of potential difficulties could help us by providing an impetus to sort things out and bring about change.

For astrologers like Raymond Lo, the ultimate goal is to improve our destiny by obtaining a clearer view of our future. Yet even he admits that the astrology of the Four Pillars of Destiny is not entirely accurate. It is merely one of several equations which can cast light on human destiny. There are other variables which affect our fate; such as 'feng shui, the fortune of the land, individual effort and, of course, free will'.[4] By allowing individual effort and free will into the picture, he is of course recognizing that humans are at least partially responsible for their actions. We may be products of our terrestrial and celestial environments, but we can also be active agents in shaping our future. Although the method of the Four Pillars of Destiny may indicate our inborn qualities and potential and predict the ups and downs in the different phases of our life, it cannot predict the details of the outcome. Therein lies our freedom.

For the Chinese everything is in a state of flux, everything is changing. The natal horoscope is not, therefore, a kind of photograph which gives a static image of your character and destiny. It does not even offer the elements of a complex compound but rather 'the forces of action and interaction which are indissolubly tied to all the energies of the universe'.[5] When we come to understand them, our will is able to make use of these forces and to turn them to our benefit. Indeed, although according to Chinese divination our family circumstances and personality traits have been determined at birth, our future destiny is not fixed. 'You continue to shape your fortune through the actions you take during your lifetime,' Man-Ho Kwok wrote, 'and thus the final version of our life ultimately remains in our hands.'[6]

We are born into a situation with certain qualities and potential – physical, intellectual and emotional. The wider environment, both earthly and heavenly, undoubtedly influences our make-up and the stages in our life's journey. But I believe that because we have consciousness and are capable of making conscious choices, we can ultimately shape our future. The configurations of stars and elements may incline us towards a particular course of action, but they do not compel. As the fourth-century astrologer and alchemist Ko Hung wrote: 'The span of life is up to me, not heaven!'[7]

Part Two

Lord of Light: India

11

Wisdom of the Heavens

Fools obey the planets while wise men control them.

B.V. RAMAN

ONE COLD AND misty morning in January, just before dawn, I joined the crowds hurrying down the narrow streets in Varanasi in North-East India towards the slowly moving waters of the Ganges. They poured down the steps of the ghats which stretch for miles along the banks of the river under the decaying palaces of the rajas. Just as night is about to end, the devout turn towards the East. As the sun rises, they take to the cold waters of the sacred river to purify themselves of their sins. Afterwards the holy men sit and meditate as the rays of the rising sun began to burn away the morning mist.

The Ganges is also the site of the greatest pilgrimage known to the world. Twenty-two million devotees flocked on 24 January 2001 to the confluence of the rivers Yamuna and Ganges near Allahabad. According to Hindu astrologers, it was the most auspicious planetary configuration to occur for 144 years. The festival began as soon as the sun moved into Aquarius to join Jupiter. Countless *sadhus*, naked holy men, wandered around the crowds and the leading gurus held forth in the city of tents. By the end of the festival, known as the Kumbh Mela – *kumbh* means a pot that is thought to contain *amhrit*, the nectar of immortality – most pilgrims had taken to the sacred waters of the Ganges to wash away their sins, have their prayers answered and prepare for the coming journey after death. The daily and annual pilgrimages to the Ganges demonstrate the ancient correspondence between heaven and earth and the deep spirituality at the heart of Indian astrology.

Unlike in the West, Indian astrology continues to be held in high esteem by the educated elite as well as the wider public. The former Indian Prime Minister Nehru wrote to his sister, referring to the birth of his first grandson in 1944: 'In my letter to Indu I suggested to her to ask you to get a proper horoscope made by a competent person. Such permanent records of the date and time of birth are desirable. As for the time, I suppose the proper solar time should be mentioned and not the artificial time which is being used outside now. War time is at least an hour ahead of the normal time.'[1] The tradition continues: the late Prime Minister Indira Gandhi was famous for her reliance on astrologers.

Astrology is not only officially approved by the Indian Government but there are calls for it to become part of the academic curriculum. The University Grants Commission invited India's universities to set up departments of Vedic Astrology leading to doctoral degrees. The circular declared: 'There is urgent need to rejuvenate the science of Vedic astrology in India, to allow this scientific knowledge to reach the society at large and provide opportunities to get this important science exported to the world.'[2]

Astrology in India is traditionally used to help attain the four main goals of life: *dharma* (work and religious merit), *artha* (acquiring wealth), *kama* (worldly enjoyment) and *moksha* (liberation). Parents will consult an astrologer at the birth of their children, not so much for material questions of wealth, marriage and worldly success, but to understand their destiny so that they can more easily help the children to realize their potential. Astrology can also be used to promote good health and is an integral part of the traditional Ayurveda medicine of India.

Wherever astrology has developed, it inevitably reflects the social and cultural values and preoccupations of the society in which it flourishes. In many ways, India is a conservative country and Indian astrology mirrors the social structure and concerns of traditional India. This is particularly evident in the horoscopes of women. It is assumed by most astrologers, as well as their female clients, that a fulfilled life consists of finding a compatible husband, having many male offspring, and living a life of modesty and service. Many women, despite the tendency to the contrary, still hope that they will die before their husband.

As for the public at large, ninety-five per cent of Indian marriages take into account astrological considerations. The final pages of most Indian dailies are devoted to astrology. Parents publish classified announcements of the horoscopes of their daughters and sons of marrying age. Couples planning to marry must ensure their horoscopes are compatible and must marry on an auspicious day. Every aspect of family life and work, from the time to build a house to the time to conceive children, has its astrological dimension. One astrological website offers 15,000 possible names for children.[3]

Hindus believe that there are sixteen important functions in their lives (*shodasa karmas*), such as being educated, getting married and having children, and astrologers use their birthcharts as well as the transiting planets to make sure that these functions are carried out at the most auspicious times. Vedic astrologers are prepared to predict the time of your death, thereby helping you to prepare for your journey into rebirth. They can even suggest what world you came from in your previous life and what world you are heading for in the next. With a population of more than 1,000,000,000, Indian astrologers clearly have their work cut out.

The celebrated Indian astrologer B.V. Raman, in the ninth reprint of the twenty-sixth edition of his *Astrology for Beginners* printed in 1998, admits that a number of quacks have earned astrology a bad name, but nevertheless argues that astrology should be ranked among the exact sciences. Indeed, as the science which records the influence of planets on terrestrial phenomena, he insists that:

> It throws light on the dark recesses of the gloomy future. It attempts to foretell the future history of man, the fate of nations, empires, kingdoms, wars, revolution and other terrestrial phenomena. It tells us these things not by vague guesses or gesticulations but on the adamantine basis of pure mathematical calculations. By observation, by education and most important of all by induction, the astrologer has actually found a correspondence between the movement of planets and events in the life of each individual.'[4]

Raman bases his case on universal determinism (every cause must produce an effect), the circulation of energy in the universe, the gravitational waves described in relativity theory, and the fact that man is the microcosm of the macrocosm of the universe.

While Raman is unusual in stressing the scientific nature of astrology, all Indian astrologers assume that the energies coming from the sun, moon, planets and stars (all of which have their own magnetic and gravitational fields) affect the physical, environmental, mental and spiritual state of beings on earth. Since every one is a microcosm of the macrocosm, each individual has a planetary constitution which endows a unique personality and potential. The exact nature of that constitution depends on the specific time and place of birth.

Jyotish

Despite Britain's long association with India, it is only in recent times that the technical complexities and deep spiritual concerns of Indian astrology have been conveyed to the West. In fact, it has been practised in its present form for at least 1,500 years and was probably evolving thousands of years earlier. While its roots are in ancient Vedic civilization, Indian astrology has borrowed many aspects from the Greeks (who in turn had been influenced by the Babylonians) after the conquest of India by Alexander the Great.

It uses the same signs of the zodiac as in the West, although some of the constellations are seen to form different patterns in the sky. Again, while it employs a similar system of houses (each house deals with a particular concern of life), the concerns of some of the houses are not the same. The main differences are that the horoscope reflects more accurately the reality in the heavens and that the moon plays a more important role. Above all, the ultimate aim is not so much worldly success on earth, but self-realization and spiritual enlightenment. It teaches how to live in harmony with the One. Indeed, it has been argued that Indian astrology offers one of the highest forms of human endeavour – a *sadhana*, 'a spiritual path that can transform your life'.[5]

It is no accident that Ganesh, the Hindu god with an elephant's head, is the deity of astrology. Ganesh is the god of wisdom and success who can guide us on the path towards enlightenment. I have often seen him worshipped in Hindu temples dedicated to Shiva, the god of destruction and rebirth.

The Indian word for astrology is *Jyotish*. It comes from Sanskrit, the ancient language of India. It has two roots: *jyoti,* meaning light, and *Isha*, meaning Lord or God. As such, it can be translated as 'Lord of Light' or 'Wisdom of the Heavens'.[6] It also means candle-flame, light which banishes darkness. A renowned astrologer used to say: 'When you see the *jyoti* [light], then you become a *jyotishi* [astrologer].'[7] In modern Hindi, an astrologer is called a *josis*.

Jyotish originally referred to astronomy as well as astrology. Indeed, the two subjects, only recently separated, were considered inseparable. *Jyotish* is also an intrinsic part of India's cultural and religious experience. It finds its written source in the ancient sacred texts known as the *Vedas*, generally considered to be the fountain head of Hinduism. Some call *Jyotish* simply Vedic or Hindu astrology, but since it is also practised by Jains, Sikhs, Buddhists and Christians, I prefer to call it Indian astrology.

Karma and the self

Indian astrology cannot be understood without an understanding of the notion of karma. Karma assumes that everything in the universe is interconnected in place and time. This applies not only to heaven and earth, but also to the past, the present and the future. Karma also assumes a belief in reincarnation or the transmigration of souls. In the *Bhagavad Gita* ('The Songs of God') the idea is expressed in a homely image: 'As a man leaves an old garment and puts on one that is new, the Spirit leaves his mortal body and then puts on one that is new.'[8]

Karma has been called the universal law of cause and effect and is very similar to Newton's famous Third Law of Motion: 'For every action there is an equal and opposite reaction.' In less abstract terms, karma implies that we invariably reap what we sow. All our actions have a knock-on effect, rather like the ripples spreading out from a pebble tossed into a pond. The actions of our past lives (karma) influence our present actions (dharma), which in turn affect our future lives. Life on earth is seen as just one of many lives, as one stage in the long journey of the soul towards enlightenment. Our planet is called *mrityisthana* or the 'place of death', since everything that lives on earth must die. In a very real sense, we are all born astride the grave. Only if we can become sufficiently enlightened will we be able to escape the cycle of birth and death and all the suffering it entails.

How does Indian astrology fit in with this scheme of things? Since life on earth is one of many lives, we all bring into this world a certain consciousness shaped by our previous lives. By delineating our character and potential, by revealing the nature of our past karma, astrology can help us develop remedies to counterbalance negative influences, and ultimately to liberate ourselves from the attachments and coils of the world. At its best, it offers a voyage of self-discovery which entails the progressive unfolding and realization of one's potential.

Hindu astrologers recognize three main forms of karma. The first is *sanchita* ('heaped together') *karma* – the sum total of past actions (both conscious and unconscious) which we inherit at birth from previous lives. We can no more change this karma than we can alter the colour of our eyes. The second is *prarabdha karma*, the kind of karma we are going to encounter on earth, whether we like it or not. It appears in the form of fate or personal destiny and assumes that it is impossible to change the type of experience we are going to have, such as being born blind or unable to have children. The experience can be both positive and negative. Natural disasters or accidents, as well as unexpected successes, fall into this category.

But does this mean that we are entirely in the grip of past karma and present circumstances? In the endless karmic chain of causes and effects, are we no different from a billiard ball hit by other billiard balls? Not entirely. There is fixed karma and changeable karma, and our life is a dynamic interaction between the two. Our freedom lies in the third form of karma, known as *kriyamana karma*, the effects created by current actions which will becomes causes in our future. This is the kind of karma that enables us to choose between the different courses of action which are presented to us and respond to the different events in our lives. It is equivalent to the Western notion of 'free will'. There is also *agama karma*, actions we can imagine performing, even though we do not put them into practice. This is involved in any form of planning. To be effective and successful, it makes sense to plan our work (*agama karma*) and work out a plan (*kriyamana karma*).

By developing our consciousness, planning for the future, and making the right choices, we can improve our *prarabdha karma* and build up positive *sanchita karma*. In this way, we can take up our past and launch ourselves into the future. The more we understand ourselves and the karma we have inherited, the easier it is to realize our potential and transform our lives.

Jyotish is not fundamentally fatalistic. Even for B.V. Raman, who claims everything in the universe, including humankind, is subject to mathematical laws, it does not follow that we are merely passive victims of such laws: 'Fools obey the planets,' he declares 'while wise men control them.' Another contemporary astrologer has observed that it is 'not man being controlled by stars, but man using the stars to enhance his life.'[9]

Apart from its notion of karma and general spiritual orientation, Indian astrology differs from Western astrology in two important details. Whereas Western astrology makes great play of our sun sign (the place of the sun in a particular sign of the zodiac at our birth), Indian astrologers, like the Chinese, pay special attention to the cycle of the moon as well. The Indian religious calendar has always been a solar-lunar one. Rituals are carried out on a particular day of the lunar month, particularly after the new or full moon. The ancient astrologers made a careful study of the rhythm of the moon, and found out early on that it takes almost nineteen solar years to complete its full cycle, moving from South to North and back again, with major and minor standstills on the way.

It is a common misconception that *Jyotish* is a purely lunar astro-logy. It was the sun's movement that inspired early Indian astrologers to use the twelve constellations (signs) of the zodiac and twelve houses, and the time units of the day. At the same time, it was the moon's monthly movement along its path through the constellations in the heavens which inspired the use of twenty-seven or twenty-eight 'lunar mansions' known as *nakshatras*.

Indian astrology treats the North and South nodes of the moon (in the West sometimes called the Dragon's Head and the Dragon's Tail) as if they were 'shadowy planets'.[10] Known respectively as Rahu and Ketu, they are considered as important as the visible planets. Neither are beneficial: Rahu is considered malefic and feminine and associated with corruption and renunciation, while Ketu is malefic and hermaphrodite, associated with selfishness and dark forces. In fact, they have no physical existence at all. Rahu is the Northern intersection and Ketu the Southern intersection of the moon's orbit through the earth-sun orbital plane of the ecliptic. Solar and lunar eclipses, however, occur due to an earth-sun-moon node alignment on the plane of the ecliptic.

Another distinctive feature is that Indian astrology traditionally only uses the sun (a star), the moon (the earth's satellite) and the five planets (called in Sanskrit *grahas*) that are visible to the naked eye: Mercury, Mars, Venus, Jupiter and Saturn. It ignores the planets that have been discovered since the eighteenth century with the use of the telescope: Uranus, Neptune and Pluto. They are considered by many to have no effect on human affairs.[11]

The *Jyotish* term for planet is *graha*, which is used in the sense of a celestial body (or point in the case of the nodes) that has the property of attraction. In Sanskrit, *graha* literally means 'seizer'; its effect is to hold us in its power. The planets are believed to correspond to every aspect of life on earth and their energies imperceptibly affect our perceptions. Indeed, each represents one of the 'seven levels of consciousness that encase the living soul'.[12] When benefic, they encourage higher consciousness; when malefic, they check the flow of energy. To study the influence of the planets is therefore to become acquainted with our potential, our strengths and our weaknesses as inherited at birth.

Astrologers recommend a variety of remedies (known in Sanskrit as *upayas*) to rectify the negative impact of planets as well as past karma. Some temples are dedicated to the planets and worship in them will help. Diets and fasts and specific acts of charity can be effective. The wearing of gemstones is common, such as a diamond to correct the excessive influence of Venus. The saying of mantras is often recommended; each planet has a *bija mantra* (seed sound) which when repeated can create the energy of a planet in the consciousness. Astrologers themselves often worship an *ishta devata*, a personal deity who represents the Absolute One to reduce the baneful effects of certain combinations in their work.

The disturbing effects of certain planets can cause an imbalance of energies in the body, which can, in turn, result in ill-health. According to Ayurveda, there are seven tissues of the body which can be influenced by the planets: the sun influences consciousness and eyes; the moon, the mind; Mercury, the intellect; and Jupiter supervises knowledge. Mars influences the blood and liver; Saturn, the neuromuscular systems. Venus governs the reproductive system. Ayurvedic doctors, like astrologers, recommend remedies such as fasting, meditation, rituals and mantras, as well as the use of certain stones, gems, crystals and metals to restore the natural harmony of good health. Recognizing the importance of astrology for medicine, one Ayurvedic expert has called *Jyotish* a 'wonderful healing science' which embraces the whole human being.[13]

The Branches of Indian Astrology

The basis of the most popular form of astrology in India today is the birthchart, known as *jataka*, which focuses on the time and place of birth when the soul is believed to enter a new body and the individual ego is formed. As such, it offers a map of the heavens at the time of birth which is said to reveal the fixed karma inherited from previous lives and our set of qualities and possibilities for this life. By understanding our make-up with the aid of an astrologer, the birthchart can help us find our direction in life and realize our potential.

Within mainstream Indian astrology there are four other fundamental branches. *Prashna* (hororary) explores the relationship between
the planets at the time a client asks a particular question. Little of this
type of astrology has been written down and astrologers will often
consider many variables before giving an answer, such as how the
question is asked, what parts of the body the questioner touches, and
what direction of the compass she might be in when asking the question.
Even the words she utters, the first letter of her name or the numerical
value of her full name are taken into account. These factors are sometimes used to reconstruct the horoscope of a person who does not know
their time or date of birth, a situation which is still common in many
parts of rural India.

Muhurta ('right' moment) is a form of electional astrology which
maximizes the effects of remedies (*upayas*) and calculates the right
astronomical moment for religious and social rituals to be performed.
This was probably the first kind of *Jyotish* to be developed by the
ancients and the reason why it was called the 'eye' of the Veda.[14] Even
the moment of independence of the modern State of India in 1947 was
decided after consulting *muhurta* astrologers. Muhurta still plays an
important role in calculating the best time for the main functions and
celebrations of life. *Vihaha* ('marriage') is one of the most popular
forms of Indian astrology, especially in arranged marriages, which are
still common. *Vihaha* contains aspects of *jataka* and *muhurta*: not only
are the natal charts of the would-be bride and groom compared to see
if they are compatible, but also the most auspicious time for the
wedding has to be decided upon.

Less in vogue today, *varshaphala* (predictive) astrology seeks to
anticipate future events. *Yatra* ('campaign') is concerned with the
military fate of nations and was much more widely practised when India
was ruled by rival dynasties and kingdoms.

Indian *Jyotish* often supplements all these approaches with palmistry,
numerology and other forms of divination such as omenology (*nimitta*).
I can remember well when I visited the 'family astrologer' of a friend in
Sri Lanka, the ancient sage consulted my palms as well as my natal chart
to draw his conclusions about my past and future. I was in my thirties
at the time and somewhat sceptical. With hindsight, he was extraordinarily accurate, predicting that in my forties I would find 'literary'
success, break up with my wife and meet the second great love of my
life. I wait to see if his prediction that I will live to eighty-four is realized!

Each branch of astrology has further subdivisions. *Jataka* (natal astrology), for instance, has sixteen *sodas vargas* or divisional charts (each representing an area of life, such as destiny, education and marriage), which are used to draw up a personality profile. There are also definite rules for ascertaining the relative strengths and weaknesses of different planetary positions and their relationships with each other (known as *yogas*).

The two most commonly used *sodas vargas* are the sign chart (*rasicakra*) and the house chart (*bhavacakra*), which are employed to delineate the overall personality of an individual at birth. While some charts are concerned with more mundane subjects such as the ability to acquire wealth, find a good partner or to have offspring, the *vimsamacakra* chart deals with spiritual potential. This is considered the most important of all and is essential if one seeks to escape the cycle of birth and rebirth and attain enlightenment and liberation (*moksha*).

Another important branch of Indian astrology is Tantric *Jyotish*. Its exact origins are unknown, but Tantric here implies a mystical and intuitive approach towards *Jyotish*. *Tantra*, meaning 'weaving', involves transforming the physical desires, rather than repressing them in the pursuit of spiritual enlightenment. Tantrikas recognize the close correspondence between the body and the universe: 'As in the body, so in the universe' (*Yatha pinde tatha Brahmande*, literally 'As in the lump, so in Brahma's egg').[15] Counterparts of astrological planets, signs and houses are to be found in the human body: the divine power of the universe is within all. Tantric astrologers use such techniques as reading omens, special breathing, clairvoyance and even astral travel to receive information and inspiration from ethereal beings. Tantrikas seem to have been mainly responsible for making the invisible South and North nodes of the moon as it crosses the ecliptic – Rahu and Ketu – carry the same weight as the visible planets in a horoscope.

The Tantric cult of the planets was given supreme expression in the Sun Temple at Konarak in Orissa. Built for King Narasimhadeva (1238–64), the colossal temple was built in the form of a chariot and dedicated to the sun god Surya. Now in ruins, the chariot had twelve enormous wheels carved round its base and was drawn by seven giant horses. All the luminaries of the sun and the moon, the five planets and the 'invisible planets' Rahu and Ketu are represented, making nine figures in all, which symbolize the eight directions (the cardinal and intermediate points of the compass) as well as its centre. Tantrikas engage in ritualized sex to mirror the union of the male and female aspects of the universe, Shiva and Shakti, and in true Tantric fashion, the Sun Temple at Orissa is decorated with playful and delicate scenes of love-making.

Although there are ancient and modern texts on astrology, Indian astrologers argue that it is impossible to learn the intricacies of the subject by reading alone. All the texts insist on the need for the guidance and blessing of a guru who can interpret their meaning. In this way, the accumulated wisdom of the tradition is passed down orally from master to apprentice. A *Jyotishi* has great responsibility and should be devout as well as skilled. He or she should not be concerned with narrow material gains, but be 'intent upon the worship of the Gods, religious vows and fasting'.[16] As with alchemy, the inner meaning of Indian astrology is a carefully guarded secret. No one can therefore expect to understand it without the guidance of a guru.

12

Far-seeing Eyes

A king without an astrologer is like a boy without a father.

ATHARVA VEDA

IN JAIPUR THERE IS a remarkable observatory made of masonry instruments. The Samrat Yantra, which acts like a giant sundial, has a gnomon ninety feet high. The beautiful Yantra Raj is an ancient instrument used to find the altitude and position of heavenly bodies. It represents every aspect of the ecliptic and is ideal for reading off the Ascendant (*Lagna*), the part of the ecliptic rising in the east. It can be corrected, by subtracting the requisite number of degrees, to find out the first point of Aries (*Aswini*).

The observatory was built by Maharaja Sawai Jai Singh II (1688–1743) in Jaipur. Other smaller ones were built in Delhi, Ujjain (the Greenwich of India), Banares and Mathura. Models of the astronomical buildings at Ujjain can be seen in the Science Museum in London.

Having discovered errors in the tables of the Portuguese astronomer De La Hire and being unsatisfied with the instruments of Ulugh Beg, the astronomer of Samarkand, and those used by the Turkish astronomers, Maharaja Sawai Jai Singh decided to develop his own. In 1723 he published his tables *Zeech Mohammed shahi* (Movements of Heavenly Bodies).

Sawai Jai Singh was an exceptional man. He not only built observatories but inns for travellers in various parts of his dominions. He led a luxurious life and had a great love of music and women, with thirty-one wives and numerous concubines. A steadfast Hindu, he particularly favoured the Jains who practise the most extreme form of *ahimsa* (non-injury) by refusing to kill even a fly.

I found it very revealing that the author of the official guide to the Jaipur observatory, B.L. Dhama, former Superintendent of the Archaeological Survey of India, should openly declare his faith in astrology: 'The life of all creatures, vegetables or living, given birth on the face of the earth by the heavenly bodies, is composed of five Tatvas or elements, namely (1) Fire, (2) Air, (3) Water, (4) Earth, and (5) Sky, and their actions, auspicious or inauspicious, are governed by them which are determined from correct measure of time of the movement of the heavenly bodies through the twelve signs of the zodiac.'[1]

He also gives the horoscope of Sawai Jai Singh II. His love of luxury and fondness for women, as well as his interest in astronomical works, is explained by Aquarius being in the fifth house. His love of women is further indicated by Scorpio being in the second House. The fact that he was born under the Tula or Libra Rashi, gives him the following general character: 'Generous nature, easily influenced by women, disposed to extravagance, clever in business matters, changeful and restless, kind and amiable nature, harsh natured (sic), fond of travels, virtuous, respected by his kinsmen, sensitive and of keen sympathies, joyous, spirit, self-indulgence, influenced by the flattery of women, sincere religious tendencies, and favoured by persons of high ranks.'[2] The personality sketch, with its occasional contradictions, gives a vivid flavour of Indian astrological readings.

The findings of Copernicus and Galileo clearly had not reached Sawai Jai Singh for he believed that the earth was set in the centre of an enormous hollow sphere, on the inner surface of which were situated the stars. The whole celestial sphere rotated on its axis which passed through the poles once in a day. This accounted for the daily motion of the stars, rising in the East and setting in the West.

The earth itself was seen as a sphere, immovably fixed in the centre of the universe. The planets (Mercury, Venus, Mars, Jupiter, sun and moon) moved in orbits around the earth. The fixed stars were contained in an eighth orbit or sphere and beyond that was the ninth and last orbit which was of infinite dimension. The whole heavens, including all the orbits, rotated daily around the earth from East to West, causing the rising and setting of the stars. This is still the world view held by practising astrologers in India.

The Roots of Indian Astrology

The Jaipur Observatory represented the zenith of Indian astrology, but where did it come from? Indian astrology is as old as Indian civilization itself. Its roots are obscure but they undoubtedly developed independently of China and the Middle East. The date of the most famous astronomical and astrological text, the *Surya Siddhanta*, is said to be more than 2,000,000 years old (2,163,102 BC precisely), although it is now thought to be mostly from the sixth century AD.[3] Again, it has been argued that the astrological text known as the *Paitamahasiddhanta* is as old as 3000 BC, but recent research has suggested that it is of a much later date.[4]

Certainly, Indian astrology deals with vast periods of time. The present epoch of history, the Kali Yuga (Iron Age), began on 18 February 3102 BC at Ujjain in Central India. It will last 432,000 years. The Age of Brass, which preceded it, lasted twice as long, the Silver Age before that was three times as long, and the Golden Age, when humans lived to 400 years, was four times as long. The present age of Kali Yuga is only one tenth of a *mahayuga*, and 1,000 *mahayugas* make a *kalpa*, at the end of which the world is destroyed by fire and recreated.[5] There is still some time to go.

The first written sources of Indian astrology come in a series of hymns known as the *Vedas*. These are the oldest Indian texts, widely believed to have been written about 3,000 years ago and undoubtedly handed down orally from much earlier times. Written in Sanskrit, they allegedly contain sacred knowledge revealed by ancient sages and seers, known as the *Rishis*. It is said that they were so adept and clairvoyant that they were able to draw up horoscopes of individuals not yet born! It is still widely believed that the *Rishis*, with their superior consciousness, knew the answers to all the problems of life which modern science with its limited knowledge is still vainly trying to solve.[6]

The gods, being alarmed at the power of the *Rishis*, sent a great fire to destroy their birthcharts but a few survived and were passed down by *Nadis* (meaning 'destined' in Tamil), a school of astrologers, who still guard their secrets and name themselves after gods, sages and planets. Written down on palm leaves, *Nadi* astrology is mainly practised in Southern India. The palm leaves are held by certain families who interpret them by taking a thumb impression or by reading the palm of the hand and the birthchart.

The *Vedas* not only describe the powers of heavenly bodies, but also place great emphasis on the right times to perform certain rituals – a key part of all subsequent astrology. They reveal a profound awe and reverence for the forces of nature. The most important deities are linked in some way with the heavens or earth. All the planets appear as gods or demigods and have their own myths, in which they are represented in human form with all-too-human strengths and weaknesses. The *Vedas* are personified as a human being and the art of *Jyotish* is considered to be his far-seeing eyes. Early Indian astrology was also known as *jyotshi vedanga*, one of the 'limbs of the Vedas'.

Not only are gods considered to be stars, but the Seven Sages (*Rishis*), the mythical founders of astrology, were the Seven Stars of Ursa Major (Big Dipper) which are so dominant in the night sky of the northern hemisphere.[7] The bright star Canopus was also identified with the sage Agastya, who is said to have taken Vedic teachings to southern India where it rises. On the other hand, some stars were felt to be humans. Any changes in the appearance of the stars were seen as omens, anticipating the weather or epidemics.

The sacred knowledge of astrology was a carefully guarded secret and passed down orally from master to pupil. Maharishi ('Great Rishi') Parashara, one of the founding fathers of *Jyotish*, declares at the end of one of his works: 'The knowledge I have imparted to you is that same science of Jyotish that Lord Brahma [the Creator] spoke to Narada [the Divine Messenger], and that Narada spoke to Shaunaka and other sages, from whom I received it. I have narrated it to you as I learnt it from them.'[8]

The fourth-century astrologer Minaraja also begins his classic poem in Sanskrit on natal astrology with the words:

> Praise to you, Shiva, Creator of the Worlds, unperishing through the times of Issuing forth, Continuance and Destruction: perpetually present in all things, spotless Sun containing the three Vedas.
>
> That teaching on astrology in 10,000 verses which the Sages of old spoke to Maya, Minaraja has studied assiduously and by his own intelligence has put into just 8,000 verses.
>
> That destiny, fulfilled of the power of actions done in past lives [karma], which is written on one's forehead by the Creator, astrology reveals, just as a lamp in darkness reveals a mass of things.[9]

In its present form, the treatise contains ninety-seven chapters with more than 2,000 verses on natal astrology. Scholars believe that it probably dates from the fourth century AD, but it is not certain whether it was written before or after the court astrologer Varahamihira worked for the celebrated Emperor Chandragupta II. Like all the main texts on *Jyotish*, it is written in Sanskrit.

Many legends explain the creation of the starry heavens. The *Bhagavata Purana,* for example, says how the virtuous Prince Dhruva was appointed by the gods to be the Pole Star. His particular virtue was to have stood immobile on one leg for more than a month. It was therefore said: 'The stars, and their figures, and also the planets shall turn around you.' He ascended to the highest pole 'to the exalted seat of Vishnu, round which the starry spheres forever wander, like the upright axle of the corn mill circled without end by the labouring oxen.'[10] Newlyweds are still encouraged to look at the Pole Star together in order to be inspired to remain as constant as Prince Dhruva.

The *Vedas* refer to 'fire' to describe the great circle reaching from the North Pole of the celestial sphere to its South Pole. In the *Rig Veda* (Veda of Hymns), which is primarily concerned with metaphysical knowledge, it is written enigmatically: 'Agni! How the felly, the spokes, thus surround the gods.'[11] Agni is the 'fire' god, the gods are the stars, while the felly is the rim of the wheel in which the spokes fit. Agni has three mothers, corresponding to three birthplaces: in the sky, on earth and in the waters. Agni's son Skanda is the planet Mars, borne by the Krittika, the Pleiades. Agni moreover offers what many seek to gain from astrology: 'May one obtain through Agni wealth and welfare day by day, which may bring glory and high bliss of valiant offspring.'[12]

The *Vedas* declare that the sun god, Surya, is 'the god among the gods, the highest light':

> Thou risest toward the host of gods
> And toward the race of men: toward all,
> That they may see the heavenly light.[13]

The ancient astrologers would have been able to observe the glory of the heavens without the light pollution of modern cities. They felt at one with the universe during the day and night. Indeed, the night was not a period to be feared but revered. The Night (*Ratri*) is not a figure of darkness, but a bright goddess covered with the glories of the stars and planets: 'The goddess Night has drawn near, looking about on many sides with her eyes. She has put on all her glories. The immortal goddess has filled the wide space, the depths and heights. She stems the darkness with her light.'[14]

The *Atharva Veda* (Veda of the Spells), which is particularly concerned with medicine and science, states that the fire sticks belong to *skambha*. The word in Sanskrit means 'support' or 'pillar' and it refers to the axis of the world, the frame of the universe. A hymn in the *Atharva Veda* is dedicated to skambha, 'In whom earth, atmosphere, in whom sky is set, where fire, moon, sun, wind stand fixed, that Skambha tell . . .'[15]

One of the principal tasks of *Jyotish* was to calculate the right times for rituals and sacrifices. A later supplement to the *Atharva Veda* declares: 'A king without an astrologer is like a boy without a father.'[16] It was essential to find as accurately as possible the dates of the equinoxes and solstices for the Vedic sacrifices. The Vedic months were synodic months, reckoned from one full moon to the next one.

The observation of the seasonal sacrifices led the astrologers to notice certain changes due to the precession of the equinoxes. The winter solstice occurred when the moon was full in the constellation of Maghâs, of which, around 2344 BC, the principal star was Regulus. The asterism gave its name to the month of Magha, which at first was meant to run from the full moon in conjunction with Regulus. However, owing to the precession of the equinoxes it became necessary to reckon it from the preceding new moon to keep the month close to its asterism.

It would also seem that in Vedic times the Indians could calculate the periodical return of eclipses in different parts of the zodiac. The modern Indian scholar R. Shama Sastry, for instance, has given an astronomical interpretation of the myth of Rohita and to the Sunhahsepa hymns. Aditi (Unity), the mother of the gods, represents the fifty-eight eclipse cycle, while Rohita becomes a reddish-coloured eclipse recurring in 1,000 days. Visvamitra's cursing fifty of his 101 sons encodes the fact that fifty of the 101 eclipses in a twenty-year cycle are invisible from any given place.[17]

From early on Indian astrologers divided the circle of the zodiac into twenty-seven or twenty-eight asterisms known as *nakshatras* (lunar mansions) through which they measured the monthly passage of the moon. The first known reference of the asterisms as a complete set comes in the *Atharva Veda*. At this stage, all the asterisms are auspicious, and it was only later that the influence of some became malefic.

The *Upanishads*

The other great text of ancient Indian astrology, the *Upanishads*, was written down around 600 BC, but dates from much earlier. *Upan* means 'to sit near' and *shad* means 'destruction'. The *Upanishads* are concerned with the destruction of ignorance, the development of consciousness and the liberation of the soul. Unlike the *Vedas*, with their songs to particular forces of nature, the *Upanishads* focus on the ground of being prior to all existence. They do not separate humans from the rest of creation and emphasize the close correspondence between the micro-cosm (humanity) and the macrocosm (universe). Indeed, in the claim that 'in the beginning this world was Self alone in the form of a Person', humanity is seen as part of a gigantic organism.[18]

How does the individual self relate to the universe? Central to the *Upanishads* are the notions of *atman,* the personal self, and *Brahman*, the all-pervading Absolute or Universal Self. The two are not separate for the Absolute manifests itself in every individual self. The exact nature of *Brahman* is obscure; it is described in the *Upanishads* as 'Hidden in all beings, all-pervading, the self within all beings, watching over all works, dwelling in all beings, the witness, the perceiver, the only one, free from all qualities. He is the one ruler of many who does not act; he makes the one seed manifold.'[19] What unites the vast diversity of things and beings in the world is *prana*, which is similar to the Chinese notion of all-pervading chi. This energy links the animate to the inanimate. In its external form it is the sun; in its internal form, it is consciousness. *Prana* supports life, sustains evolution and reveals itself in our desires and thoughts. The *Upanishads* build around the notion of *prana* a theory of seamless life:

> The Self asked himself, 'What is that makes
> Me go if it goes and stay if it stays?'
> So he created *prana*, and from it
> Desire; and from desire he made space, air,
> Fire, water, the earth, the senses, the mind . . .[20]

Astrology is one of several methods developed in ancient India to help one to know oneself and to realize the self-in-the-Self – that is, *atman* in *Brahman*. This realization frees us from the cycle of death and rebirth and the chains of illusion. Above all, it enables us to recognize ultimate reality as the dwelling of pure being (*sat*), pure consciousness (*cit*) and pure delight (*ananda*). It involves the joyful release from the suffering imposed by our ego through ignorance.

This can be achieved by channelling passions, not repressing them; by directing thoughts, not suppressing them. Once unity with *Brahman* has been attained, rituals become superfluous, death loses its sting, and the mind becomes calm, contented and free. Only those who find out who they are and what they want find freedom. As a result, one's whole being is transformed. Indeed, the *Upanishads* claim that the knower of *Brahman* has a shining face, feels healthy and even smells good!

Purusha and *Prakriti*

While the *Vedas* and the *Upanishads* provide the metaphysical background, Indian astrology also embodies a psychology largely based on Kapila's *Samkhya* system of philosophy which was developed in the seventh century BC. This teaches that there is an Absolute Reality beyond time, space and causality known as Brahman. The cosmos itself results from the union of *Purusha* and *Prakriti*, which loosely speaking might be called 'consciousness' and 'nature'. Although complete in itself, *Purusha* desires to experience itself. This desire gives rise to *Prakriti*. The cosmos we inhabit is therefore the result of the meeting of *Purusha* and *Prakriti*, the male and female principles. While the former is unknowable, the latter produces the known world.

The awareness of separateness (*buddhi*) in the realm of *Prakriti* produces *ahankara,* literally the 'I-creator'. This is our sense of being a separate individual. It gives rise to the personal ego which is responsible for the actions which make up our karma. In a striking image in the *Srimad Bhagavata, buddhi,* the faculty of discrimination, is likened to a charioteer, the *manas* (mind) to the reins, and the senses to the horses. Behind the charioteer, directing his actions, stands the individual soul (*atman*).

There are three attributes of *ahankara* and three principles of *Prakriti* known as *gunas*. These are *sattva* (essence of intelligence), *rajas* (essence of energy) and *tamas* (essence of matter). At the beginning of the cosmic cycle all three were in perfect equilibrium until disturbed by *Purusha*. They then combined in different proportions to produce all the diversity of the world and the variety of human character.

Every individual is made up of the three *gunas*. The exact combination in any one person is symbolized by the relationship between the planets at his or her birth. Each planet, house and sign is associated with a particular *guna*.[21]

When I was in Varanasi in India, Vaidya (Dr) J.S. Shukla at Samparnanand Sanskrit University explained to me his own understanding of the three *gunas* and how he applied them in Ayurvedic medicine:

> *Sattva* stands for goodwill and ideas, *rajas* is dynamic vitality, and *tamas* means stagnation. All aspects are omnipresent in an individual. The combination of *sattva* and *rajas* give rise to the five sensory organs, while the combination of *rajas* and *tamas* results in the five functional organs. The mind is the finest organ in humans. Although it relies on our functional and sensory organs, it is very fine and very fast. If it doesn't send an order through your body, you won't be able to move your finger!

Sattva produces the mind (*manas*) and the senses. *Sat* means 'pure being' and *va* 'where it dwells'. In general, it represents moral and spiritual qualities. It is associated with equilibrium, truth and purity. Sattvic people look for enlightenment, cause minimum harm and wish to help others. They are calm, fearless and generous. They are not interested in fame and fortune and little upsets their peace of mind. They can become ascetics. Sattvic food is pure and plain.[22]

Rajas stands for the quality of taking action and is associated with restless searching. It can be translated as 'pollen of the flowers'. The ego has rajastic tendencies, especially when it is constantly striving and grasping. Rajastic people tend to want material success and can easily be disappointed or distracted. They can lack peace of mind because they do not always know what they want.

Tamas gives rise to the five objects of the senses – sound, texture, form, flavour and smell. It can be translated as 'ignorance'. This is considered the physical realm of darkness. Tamasic people are usually driven by their physical desires and tend to be materialistic and sensuous. They like food which is hot and spicy.

In Indian astrology, the qualities of the three *gunas* are attributed to different planets, signs and *nakshatras* (lunar mansions). Although the personality of each person will be the result of a combination of the *gunas*, one quality usually tends to be dominant. But it need not remain the defining characteristic. If you are a sattvic person, for example, it does not mean that you will automatically attain higher consciousness, any more that a tamasic person will always be ignorant, materialistic and sensuous. A natal chart is a map of our psyche at birth; it is not an excuse to do nothing in life. Indian astrologers insist that we can always transcend the characteristics inherited from previous lives and realize our full potential.

The Greek Connection

It is clear that astrology developed very early on in India. Some Indians even claim that the science of astronomy and astrology was actually discovered in India and from there travelled to other countries via Arabia.[23] But India had wide trading links, especially with the Middle East, and it has been suggested that there was an early influence from Babylon, particularly during the period following the Persian conquest in 539 BC. Both civilizations seem to have had a similar level of scientific knowledge and a shared interest in calendar cycles. But the origins of Indian astrology are undoubtedly in India, especially with its preoccupation with the lunar mansions which is not found in early Babylonian astrology.[24]

The case for Greek influence is more clear cut. While the *Vedas* demonstrate a keen interest in the movement of the sun and moon and the stars, there is little mention of the planets. Early Indian astrology was primarily a system for regulating the calendar and for interpreting omens in order to establish favourable times for key rituals within the community. The importance given to planets and to individual horoscopes in later works of astrology would seem to have been a direct influence of Greek astrology, which reached the sub-continent after the arrival of Alexander the Great in the fourth century BC.

Indian astrologers not only came to use a similar zodiac and the same planetary rulerships as the Greeks, but also borrowed from them many technical terms. They called the early texts on natal astrology *Yavanajataka* – *Yavana* means literally 'Ionian', the Indian name for the Greeks. The oldest surviving work on natal astrology by Sphujidhvaja was dated year 191 of the Saka Era (AD 269–70), but the author claims to have versified a text translated 120 years earlier by one Yavanesvara, 'Lord of the Greeks'. Yavanesvara, who was no doubt a member of the Greek community settled in Western India at the time, claims to have received his knowledge from Surya the sun god, who received it from the Asvins, who learned it from the creator god Prajapati.[25] The work contains much Indian material as well as an overlay of Greek.

Many technical terms were taken over directly from the Greek: *lipta* for minutes, *trikona* for trigon, *jamitra* for diameter (or opposition), *panaphara* for rising. Even the art of drawing up a horoscope is called *hora*, Greek for hour. The *Romaka Siddhanta* cites the length of the tropical year in the same figures given by the second-century BC Greek astronomer Hipparchus, who is usually considered to have first discovered the precession of the equinoxes. The figures for precession given in the *Surya Siddhanta* (mostly dating from the sixth century) are more accurate than those of the second-century Alexandrian, Claudius Ptolemy, so-called 'father of astronomy' and the greatest authority for Western astrology. The Indian text gives it as $54'$ per annum against Ptolemy's $36'$. The correct figure today is $50.2°$.[26]

It seems likely that the Indians took the signs of the zodiac from the Greeks. This is confirmed by the existence of two sets of names, one transliterated from the Greek, probably before the exact meanings were known, and the other a translation into Sanskrit. The Greek name for Aries, for instance, was spelt in Sanskrit as *Kriya* and given the Sanskrit name *Mesha*, meaning Ram.[27] More than any other people, however, the Indians have used each of the twelve names of the zodiac to describe an arc of $30°$ on any circle and not only along the ecliptic.

All the fundamentals of Indian astrology as practised today can be found in the *Vrddhayavanajataka* (Great, or Old, Greek Astrology) written in the fourth century by Minaraja. The greatest authority is considered to be Varahamihira, probably the court astrologer to Emperor Candra Gupta II (c.376–415) who was a great patron of the arts and sciences. Amongst his many astrological writings (which include astronomical theories, correspondences, omens, military astrology and marriage) his work on natal astrology, *Brhajjataka*, became the inspiration for much later Sanskrit literature on the subject.

Despite the influence of Greek astrology of the Hellenistic and Roman period, summarized in the work of Ptolemy, the Indians continued to adapt it to their own tradition. Indian cosmology had formerly imagined a flat earth with the sun, moon and planets orbiting a vast mountain called Mount Meru, but the impetus of the new ideas from the Middle East led to the abandonment of the old world view in favour of a spherical earth. This explained more convincingly the differences in the stars visible in Alexandria in Egypt and in North and South India. The earth-ball was now imagined as hanging in the centre of a world-egg.

The great fifth-century astronomer Aryabhta boldly suggested that it was the earth that revolved while the skies remained stationary, just as for a sailor on a boat land appears to be moving backwards. The celestial North Pole, the axis around which the stars revolved, was thought to be Mount Meru, the sacred mountain at the centre of the world. The *Jyotishi* chose Ujjayini (modern Ujjain in Madhya Pradesh) as their 0° longitude, which they thought passed through Sri Lanka with its 'Adam's Peak' where the first man set foot on Earth.

Although the Indians adopted the Greek twelve-sign zodiac they still retained their older system of lunar mansions. They found ways of linking the two, counting both circles from 0° Aries, which in the Greek method coincided with the position of the sun at the vernal equinox. The circle of lunar mansions was started with Asvini (β and γ Arietis), which was at the time closest to the point. But despite a fashion for the Greek 'tropical' zodiac in which the year was measured by the passage of the sun, the Indian astrologers soon dropped it in favour of their more traditional 'sidereal' zodiac, which measured the ecliptic from a certain point among the stars. As a result, the two systems have been drifting apart at a rate of 1° every seventy-two years. 0° Aries (the vernal equinox) in the Western system, is now close to 7° Pisces in the Indian system. As a result, the Indian zodiac reflects more accurately the position of the stars in the sky.

Once civilizations meet, influences travel in both ways and during the Middle Ages, Indian learning reached Europe via the Muslims who occupied Spain and Southern Italy. The Arabic system of lunar mansions was probably adopted from India and passed into Europe. During the Renaissance, European astrologers used the Sanskrit word *ucca* (high point), Latinized as *aux*, to describe the 'exaltation' of a planet as it reaches its highest point in the heavens.

While conveying aspects of Indian astrology to Europe, the Arabs influenced Indian astrology in turn. *Tajika Jyotish* is a late development (from about the thirteenth to the eighteenth centuries) inspired by Arabic astrology (*Tazig* is an Iranian name for Arabs). It has a common root with Western astrology and is based on the solar year. One of its special concerns is the calculation of anniversary charts or 'solar returns', described in Sanskrit as *varsaphala*, 'fruits of the year'.

The continuity of the oral tradition of Indian astrology is illustrated by Lieutenant Colonel John Warren who came across an astrologer and calendar-maker in Pondicherry in 1825.[28] He calculated for him, without the use of books, the time of an expected eclipse by arranging shells on the earth. His method of working showed that it had been passed down directly to him from the works of Varahamihira in the sixth century. The oral tradition still continues today, forming an unbroken link to the time of the *Vedas* at least 3,000 years ago. And the teachings of the legendary *Nadis*, first inscribed on palm leaves, can be accessed on the Internet.[29]

13

The Wheel of Life

LIKE WESTERN ASTROLOGY, *Jyotish* recognizes the zodiac as a broad band in the heavens extending about 8° on either side of the ecliptic. In the *Vedas*, the ecliptic is called the *Sudarshan chakra*, the wheel in the hand of the Lord Vishnu, the Creator of the universe. It is divided into twelve sections or *rashis* of 30° each. They represent the twelve signs of the zodiac which consist of twelve constellations in the heavens. Each *rashi* rules one house of the natal chart.

Although the *rashis* bear the same name as the signs in Western astrology, it is important to remember that they represent constellations, that is, groups of stars. How a planet acts in the horoscope depends on the nature and meaning of the constellation in which it is placed.

As in the West, the Indian zodiac begins at *Mesha* (Aries) and ends in *Meena* (Pisces). Each sign has its own characteristics. My sign *Simha* (Leo), for instance, is 'fixed, odd, masculine, cruel, fiery, of long ascension, barren, rising by the head'.[1] On the other hand, my partner's sign *Kataka* (Cancer) is 'even, movable, feminine, mild, watery, of long ascension, rising by the hinder part and fruitful' – clearly the opposite of me, except for our 'long ascension'!

Indian astrologers further mark the ecliptic by twenty-seven constellations (sometimes twenty-eight) or stellar points, which are measured at intervals of 13.33° of longitude along the ecliptic. Each constellation is further subdivided into four quarters: each quarter is equal to 3.33° of longitude on the ecliptic. The signs and the constellations are both measured from the same point, the 0° of longitude of the sign *Mesha* (Aries) and of the constellation *Aswini*.

Although the twelve signs of the zodiac bear the same names as in Western astrology, different shapes for a few of them are discerned in the constellations in the heavens. *Mithun* (Gemini), for instance, is a male-female couple; *Makara* (Capricorn) is a mythical beast that resembles a crocodile with an elephant's trunk, and *Kumbha* (Aquarius) is a water pot. The Sanskrit names for the *rashis*, and not the symbols given in the West, are used in the charts. The same is true for the planets. On the other hand, the planetary rulers of the twelve signs of the zodiac follow the traditional Western pattern: Mars for Aries, Venus for Taurus, Mercury for Gemini, Moon for Cancer, Sun for Leo, and so on.

The cardinal signs are Aries, Cancer, Libra and Capricorn, which are positive and directed towards action. The fixed signs are Taurus, Leo, Scorpio and Aquarius which are thoughtful and stable. The mutable signs are Gemini, Virgo, Sagittarius and Pisces which are negative and changeable. The male signs are the odd-numbered signs: Aries, Gemini, Leo, Libra, Sagittarius and Aquarius. They are described in Vedic literature as 'cruel'; they are action-orientated and outgoing. The female signs are even-numbered: Taurus, Cancer, Virgo, Scorpio, Capricorn and Pisces.

Each sign also takes on the qualities of one of the elements: fire, earth, air and water. The fire signs are Aries, Leo and Sagittarius. People born under these signs tend to be dynamic and determined. The earth signs are Taurus, Virgo and Capricorn. They are practical and reliable. The air signs are Gemini, Libra and Aquarius. They are communicative and creative. The water signs are Cancer, Scorpio and Pisces. They are intuitive and caring.

Ayanamsha or Precessional Distance

Despite the similar meaning and use of the signs of the zodiac, planets and houses in Indian astrology, there is one fundamental difference with the Western system which produces very different results for a horoscope. If you thought you were a Leo in England, you may well turn out to be a Cancer in India!

This is because Western astrology uses the 'tropical' or solar year, that is to say, the time the earth takes to make one revolution around the sun. The time is measured between two successive vernal (spring) equinoxes and is equal to 365.24219 days. Indian astrology, on the other hand, uses the 'sidereal' year, during which the earth makes one revolution around the sun, measured between two successive conjunctions of a particular star. This is equal to 365.25636 days.

Western astrologers use the vernal equinox as the beginning of the zodiac – the first point of Aries. This point, however, is not strictly speaking fixed. Due to a tilt in the axis of the earth, which makes it wobble, when the sun returns on the vernal equinox its position is out by about 50° and 3′ of longitude. As a result, the equinoctial point in relation to the backdrop of constellations is gradually moving backwards from East to West.

This process is called the precession of the equinoxes. The 'first point of Aries' now appears in the constellation of Pisces (about 7°). It lasts 2,160 years in each constellation, marking an Astrological Age – we have been in the Age of Pisces since AD 150 and are approaching the Age of Aquarius (in 2010). It also takes 25,920 years to move backwards through all the twelve signs to return to the first point of Aries, marking the Great Astrological Year.

Western astrologers are not unduly upset by the break between the signs of the 'tropical' zodiac and the actual position of the stars in the sky (the astronomical zodiac). They say that our sun signs are in tune with the earth's seasonal and monthly changes. The Indian astrologer, however, believes that the precession of the equinoxes should be taken into account when calculating the horoscope of an individual. The tropical and sidereal zodiacs coincided in 285 AD, but now there is about 24.5° of longitude difference. The difference is called *Ayanamsha* or Precessional Distance. The calculation is not difficult, but to construct a Hindu chart all the planets on the Western chart are moved backwards.[2] Clearly this will give a very different interpretation but it is arguably closer to the real state of affairs in the heavens. When the sun passes through the constellations, it is said, it enhances the emanations from the stars which affect our energy on earth.

Rashis: the Signs of the Zodiac

The cycle of the zodiac – the Wheel of Life – describes the journey of the soul through the world.[3] Since every birthchart contains the twelve signs, we are affected by them all to different extents. With *Mesha* (Aries), the first sign of the zodiac, there is a new beginning, full of promise, but with it comes the danger of being too impulsive. It is male and rajastic. Its ruler is Mars which gives strength and courage. The Sun is exalted in Aries.

Vrishibha (Taurus) stands for creative potential on a practical level; its symbol, the Bull (Nandi, the animal of Shiva) suggests the power of procreation. It is androgynous and contains all three *gunas* (*sattva, rajas* and *tamas*). Ruled by sensuous Venus, it likes the finer things in life. The Moon is exalted in *Vrishibha*.

Mithun (Gemini) stands for the birth of the intellect. Its emblem of the twins symbolizes the coming together of the spiritual and physical to give birth to the personal ego (*ahamkara*). *Mithun* people tend to be intellectuals, but as their sign suggests, they are often dual-natured and ambivalent. Mercury, the planet of communication, rules *Mithun*. Like *Vrishibha*, *Mithun* is androgynous and contains all three *gunas*.

Kartaka (Cancer) represents the next stage in the development of the soul. Its symbol, the crab, lives in the water (universal consciousness) but also walks on land (everyday reality). Its ten feet stand for the ten sense organs of the human body, both external and internal. Ten is a perfect number; those born in *Kartaka* seek perfection. Being sattvic, they are idealistic but can also be very practical. With *Kartaka* ruled by the moon, which waxes and wanes, they can have changeable moods.

Simha (Leo) expresses a person's individuality. Having the lion as a symbol, it suggests power and strength. It is sattvic and therefore idealistic, but it can also put ideals into action. Ruled by the sun, with their element being fire, *Simha* people are independent and reject any constraints.

Kanya (Virgo) is the Virgin, the pure feminine. *Kanya* people are deeply involved in the practical world, often with considerable material success, but at a cost to their inner selves. Since world involvement can be an obstacle to spiritual development, they may be frustrated and discontented at times. *Kanya* is a tamasic sign, associated with earthly attachments and darkness. Mercury, the planet of intellect and communication, rules *Kanya*, which makes *Kanya* people good planners.

Halfway through the zodiac, *Tula* (Libra) marks the point when the soul can leave the darkness of world entanglements and move towards spiritual light. It offers a fine balance (a pair of scales is its symbol) of enjoying the material life without being too attached by it. On the other hand, those in *Tula* find it difficult to decide, seeing both sides of a question, and often swinging between the two. Although under the sign of relations, they can appear detached in their search for balance. *Tula* is rajastic, concerned with action and searching. It is ruled by Venus who, according to the *Vedas*, advised the demons who had lost their way in the spiritual quest. Gloomy Saturn, who can help towards liberation, is exalted in *Tula*.

Indian astrologers see *Vrishchika* (Scorpio) as a difficult and complex sign. As a water sign it wants to flow, but as a fixed sign there is a danger that it may stagnate. Ketu is exalted and Rahu debilitated in *Vrishchika*, the tail and head of the serpent Vasuki Narga. Just as the serpent churns the oceans with his tail, so *Vrishchika* churns our emotions. The symbol of *Vrishchika* is a scorpion, a creature which lives in a hole and which can sting with its tail. It has Kundalini energy which can both destroy or lead towards enlightenment. After mating, the female scorpion kills the male; this implies that having embarked on our spiritual path, we must become dead to the world. Our old self must die in order for us to be created anew. Mars rules *Vrishchika*, offering courage and strength to overcome worldly desires for wealth and power.

Next comes *Dhanus* (Sagittarius), the Centaur with a bow and arrow. Half-horse and half-man, it illustrates the stage in our journey where we can begin to leave our animal appetites behind and become a truly spiritual being. One must become a cosmic warrior and aim straight. Self-discipline and self-denial will help in the struggle. The great teacher Jupiter rules *Dhanus*, standing for expansion and good fortune. Being orientated towards the mystic, it is not surprisingly sattvic.

Makara (Capricorn) is a bridge between the human and the super-human. It is a female, cardinal and earth sign, the sign of duty, hard work and responsibility. *Makara* people are serious in working out their salvation, but they must face the consequences of their past actions if they are to transcend them. It is ruled by Saturn, the planet of karma, who makes sure that it is not an easy task. The symbol of *Makara* is the crocodile. Appropriately enough, it stands opposite *Kartaka* (Cancer) in the wheel of the zodiac. While the crab lives in water (universal consciousness) and ventures on the land (the earth), the crocodile lives on land but dives into the water. It stands for the transitional stage between heaven and earth. Between two worlds, it is tamasic.

Kumbha (Aquarius) is an air sign. Its Sanskrit name is associated with *kumbhaka,* a technique of breath control. By controlling our breath in yoga, we learn to draw on the energy of the universal breath known as prana. The emblem of *Kumbha* is a pitcher holding water. Water gives life and purifies and, as such, symbolizes universal consciousness. *Kumbha* water-bearers carry what they are seeking. But to merge themselves in the water of universal consciousness, they must first break the pitchers of their individual egos. Their goal is the ultimate one of enlightenment and liberation, so the sign is tamasic. The path is not without difficulty and danger. Those born in *Kumbha* tend to work with their heads more than their hearts. Saturn rules *Kumbha*, ensuring that they will have to shoulder great responsibility in their work for others.

The twelfth sign *Mina* (Pisces) completes the wheel of life. It marks the last stage in the journey of the soul when the individual becomes part of the universal whole, when *atman* merges with *Brahman*. *Mina* is symbolized by two fish facing in opposite directions. Those born in *Mina* swim with ease in the ocean of Being; they can dive down into the cool, calm depths below the wave-tossed surface. As their sign is female and mutable, they can move this way and that but risk being swallowed up by others. They are sattvic, concerned with purity and truth. The great teacher Jupiter rules *Mina*, bringing expansion and wisdom, while Venus is exalted in the sign, symbolizing desire for a new life as the old one comes to an end.

Vargas: the Divisions of the Signs

Apart from the *rashis* or signs of the zodiac, Indian astrologers make use of at least five other divisions or *vargas* of the circle of the ecliptic. The most popular are the *hora*, the half sign; the *drekkana*, the decan (the division of the sign into three segments of 10° each); the *navamsa*, the ninth-sign (the division of the sign into nine segments); the *dwadashamsha*, the twelfth sign (the division of the sign into twelve segments); and the *trimsamsa*, or degree. Like the *rashis*, each of them has its own planetary ruler. The *vargas* fill in the detail of the horoscope and show in a more subtle way how the planets act in the chart. The *varga* charts reveal the real strength of the planets according to whether they are enhanced or reduced by their positions.[4]

The *hora* is produced by the division of the signs into solar and lunar halves of 15° each. The simple divisions symbolize male and female energies. In masculine signs, the first *hora* belongs to the sun and the second to the moon, and vice versa in feminine signs. The *horas* thus go round the zodiac in the order of sun, moon, moon, sun and so on. There are twenty-four *horas* in a full circle of the zodiac, corresponding to each hour of the day, and they give an idea whether you are an active or passive person and how easily you will acquire riches.

While the *hora* is not generally used in Western astrology, the *drekkana* or decan has a long history in both traditions. It comes from the Greek *dekanos,* meaning a division of 10°, which in turn derives from Egyptian astrology which allotted a deity to each one. The *drekkana* chart helps give detail to the third House, referring to siblings and friends.

Each decan has a planetary ruler. The most popular formula for their distribution is as follows: the three decans of each sign correspond in order to the sign itself and to the two other signs of the same triplicity. The three decans of Aries, for example, will be given to 1. Aries, ruled by Mars; 2. Leo, ruled by the Sun; and 3. Sagittarius, ruled by Jupiter.

Each decan is associated with a symbol. A sixth-century text by Varahamihira describes the first of Aries as:

> A fierce black man, like one able to protect [many], red-eyed, wearing a white cloth round his waist, holds an axe upraised. The form of the middle decan of Aries as taught by the Yavana [the Greeks] is a pot-bodied, horse-faced woman, dressed in red, fond of ornaments and food, standing on one foot. The third decan in Aries is described as a man, cruel, skilled in arts, reddish, seeking to act but foiled in his attempts, angry, holding a stick upraised, dressed in red.[5]

Some of the images are striking. The second decan in Cancer is 'a roughly behaved woman, her head adorned with lotus-flowers, her body entwined with a snake', while the first in Scorpio is 'a beautiful woman, naked and without ornaments, coming ashore from the ocean, with a snake curled around her legs'. The third decan in Leo, relevant to my birthday on 23 August, is 'a man with a bear-like face and the movements of a monkey, with a beard and curly hair, armed with a club and holding meats and fruits'.[6]

Of the other six divisions, the most important after the sign itself is the *navamsha* or ninth sign, extending for 3° 20′, and known in the West as the 'subdecanate'. The 108 *navamshas* correspond to the signs of the zodiac, repeated nine times over. The first corresponds to Aries, the second to Taurus, and so on. They fulfil an important role in reconciling the twelve divisions of zodiac with the twenty-seven divisions of the lunar mansions (*nakshatras*). Traditionally, Indian astrologers mark the positions of the planets in signs and *navamshas*, both noted by numbers. Any planet in the same sign and *navamsha* is seen as strong.

The *dwadashamshas* or twelfth signs, extending for 2° 30′, are again allotted to the twelve signs of the zodiac. They are mainly used for indications of health and development, such as life expectancy or the growth of a baby in the womb. Each *trimsamsa* or degree is allotted to one of the star-planets. They are particularly used in the charts of women for discovering the prospects of marriage, and give details on the twelfth House, especially your past karma. It is usually considered to be the 'mother and father chart', since according to Hindu belief your choice of parents in this incarnation is a result of the karma of your previous lives.

There is even a chart for sixty parts of 0° 30′ each known as the *shastiamsha* chart which is often used in electional astrology and to differentiate between twins. Clearly the exact time of birth is required, defined in India by the moment of the first breath.

Bhavas: the Houses

As in Western astrology, the planets are placed not only in the signs of the zodiac or twelve constellations (*rashis*) but also in twelve Houses around the circle of the ecliptic. The Houses, known as *bhavas*, focus on the main areas of concern in human life. The Sanskrit word *bhava* means both 'a state of existence' as well as 'a state of mind'. They represent the external condition of life as well as our internal state of mind; indeed, they have been described as 'the cosmic looms on which the grahas weave the tapestry of your life from the yarn of your karmas.'[7]

Although both twelve in number, the Houses (*bhavas*) do not overlap with the signs (*rashis*). While each sign is always 30° of longitude, a House can vary in length, depending on the time of the birth and the latitude of the place of birth. Nevertheless, many astrologers divide them into twelve equal sectors of 30° each.

Each House is measured from the Ascendant of your horoscope, known as *lagna* in Sanskrit. Your Ascendant is the degree of the zodiac intersected by the Eastern horizon at the place and time of your birth. It therefore establishes which planets are placed in the different Houses in your natal chart. The word *lagna* has a sense of being 'tied down': the Ascendant thus ties the position of the planets to the place and time of birth.

Different astrologers vary slightly the meaning of the *bhavas*, but in general they stand for the following:[8]

First House	Birth, body, appearance
Second House	Family, death, wealth, eyesight
Third House	Intelligence, brothers, sisters
Fourth House	Happiness, education, mother, land, vehicles
Fifth House	Children, memory, discernment
Sixth House	Debts, diseases, misery, enemies
Seventh House	Spouse, desire, journeys, death
Eighth House	Accidents, inheritance, loss, death
Ninth House	Religion, virtue, father, guru, good fortune, foreign travel
Tenth House	Occupation, fame, philosophical knowledge
Eleventh House	Gains, wishes
Twelfth House	Losses, misfortune, *moksha*

Although the significance of the *bhavas* is similar to that of the Houses in Western astrology, the spiritual emphasis is particularly Indian. The *bhavas* reveal the four fundamental human objects in life known as *dharma, artha, kama* and *moksha*. *Dharma* Houses are one, five and nine. They point to your path through life. *Dharma* is usually translated as 'duty' but really means 'doing what you are born to do'.[9] The *dharma* of a river is to flow, of the sun to shine. *Artha* Houses are two, six and ten. They indicate your likely resources, including wealth. *Kama* Houses are three, seven and eleven. *Kama* means 'desire', not so much in sexual terms, but in attaining one's aspirations. Finally, *moksha* Houses are four, eight and twelve. *Moksha* is 'liberation', that is, being liberated from the chains of illusion and slavery to the material world. It involves going beyond the conditional and limited worlds of *dharma, artha* and *kama* and reaching Absolute Reality.

Although the meanings of the eighth House are similar to those of the sixth House, the former are usually longer and more intense than the latter. The ninth is the most advanced House, pointing to the spiritual path. While it stands for the peak experience of *dharma*, the tenth is the peak of *artha*, the zenith of human experience. The eleventh House is the apex of *kama*. The twelfth and last House represents *moksha*, the completion of life on earth and the beginning of the next life.

But this not all. There are certain kinds of Houses in Indian astrology. Planets will vary in strength depending on what Houses they are in. The fourth, seventh and tenth Houses are known as *kendras* or angles (also known as quadrants in the West). They indicate conscious, self-initiated actions. Planets that rule *kendra* Houses become benefic if they are naturally malefic. On the other hand, naturally benefic planets ruling *kendra* Houses become malefic.[10]

The first, fifth and ninth Houses are called *trikonas* or trines. They indicate unconscious actions. Planets that rule these Houses are always benefic. The second, the eighth and the eleventh are known as *panaparas* or succedent Houses. The rest are *apoklinas* or cadent Houses.

The third, sixth, eighth and twelfth Houses, known as *dusshanas*, indicate what is most likely to cause a person suffering in life, while the second and seventh Houses, known as *maraka* (killer), indicate the length of life.

Planets in *trikonas* are very strong; in *kendras*, fairly strong; in *panaparas*, slightly strong; and in *apoklinas*, they are extremely weak. Planets that rule the malefic Houses (the third, sixth, and eleventh) are always malefic, while rulers of the second, eighth and twelfth Houses are neutral.

Of course, Indian astrology shares much with Western astrology here. But I found particularly interesting the notion that planets have 'directional strength' (*dik bala*) – that is, their energies grow when placed in certain Houses of the birthchart. Each planet is strong in a particular direction of the four cardinal points – Mars in the South and Venus in the North, Mercury and Jupiter in the East and Saturn in the West. The Sun grows in the South, the moon in the north. The direction of a planet is defined by the House it finds itself in: the first House is East, the fourth, North; the seventh, West; and the tenth, South. If at the time of birth, a planet is in the House of its own direction (the moon in the fourth House, or Mercury in the first House), it gains considerably in strength.

As in feng shui, Indian astrologers believe that the direction of a House can affect its residents. Front doors in the North and East, the directions of Venus and Jupiter, are regarded as auspicious.

14

The Family of Planets

IN ASTROLOGY THROUGHOUT the world, the influence of the planets plays a key role in shaping our personality and destiny. Indian *Jyotish* is no exception. As we have seen, planets are considered as astral forces which can 'seize' our being. They are agents of the Universal Law of Karma and influence us through their emanations. A horoscope may thus be described as 'a map of your karmas, drawn to the specifications of the Nine Seizers'.[1]

Nine Seizers? These, of course, are the sun and the moon, the five planets Mercury, Mars, Venus, Jupiter and Saturn, and the 'invisible planets' Rahu and Ketu (the moon's North and South nodes).

Astrology in both the East and West considers the movement of the planets as seen from the earth. It follows the findings of ancient astronomy which assumed that the sun moves around the earth rather than the other way round. The rotation of the earth from West to East makes it appear that the sun, moon and the planets pass over the earth from East to West. This takes place each day and is called diurnal motion. At the same time, the same planets appear to move in the opposite direction, from West to East, through the constellations of the zodiac. This is known as proper motion. Diurnal motion is always faster than proper motion. On average, the sun, Mercury and Venus take thirty days to pass through a constellation or sign of the zodiac. The moon takes two and a quarter days, while Mars takes one and a half months, Jupiter a year, and Rahu and Ketu one and a half years. Slow Saturn takes about two and a half years per constellation.

The *grahas* are not only associated with gods, but take on human characteristics and a sexual dimension. The sun, Mars and Jupiter are masculine; the moon, Venus and Rahu are feminine; Mercury and Ketu are hermaphrodite. The sun, Mars, Saturn, Rahu and Ketu are called malefics. In general, they exert a harmful influence, causing problems and creating obstacles, although their mischief can be alleviated. Jupiter and Venus are benefic. They generally do good, but in certain relationships they are capable of harm. The moon is benefic when waxing, but malefic when waning. Mercury is often taken to be neutral, taking on the temperament of the planet with which it is placed.

In Indian mythology, the solar system is often seen as the personification of the Divine Person of Time known as *Kala Purusha*. The planets rule different parts of his being and are responsible for different parts of his personality. The fiery sun rules the soul and the receptive moon rules the senses and the emotions. Valiant Mars rules power and strength. Quick Mercury rules the rational mind and speech, while cheery Jupiter rules knowledge and fortune. Youthful Venus rules desires and yearnings, and gloomy Saturn rules sorrows and misfortunes.

Indian astrologers often use stories to teach the cosmological meaning of the planets. One delightful tale describes the character of planets and relates how they came to rule different constellations in the zodiac. The story has only just been written down.[2]

In the beginning the sun and moon, king and queen of heaven, ruled the constellations of Leo and Cancer respectively. Not wanting to be left out, Mercury asked the sun (Mercury rules communication) for a place in the zodiac for himself. Being naturally generous, the sun gave him Virgo, the constellation next to his. Being a cunning fellow, Mercury then waited for the night and graciously asked the moon for another place. The sun is the soul and the moon is the emotional mind (which shines by reflected light), but she does not like to be outdone. She therefore said: 'If you really want one, have Gemini, the plot next to mine.' In this way, Mercury, the thinking mind, acquired two signs: Virgo and Gemini.

Now Venus (desire) observed what had happened and felt moved to ask for the same. The sun replied that he had already given away the plot next to him, but Venus could have the next space – Libra. The moon likewise gave her Taurus on her side. Mars (action) did not want to miss out and the sun and the moon generously gave him Scorpio and Aries respectively. Nor could they refuse Jupiter (wisdom) who received Sagittarius and Pisces. Finally even Saturn, slow and given to renunciation, was given Capricorn and Aquarius, which were left on either side of the sun and moon. The circle was then complete. There were no more planets (Uranus, Neptune and Pluto had not been discovered) and there were no more places free.

The order of the *grahas* reflects the distances of the planets from the sun as seen from the earth: Mercury, Venus, Jupiter and Saturn. It also shows the planetary ruler for each of the constellations of the zodiac. Above all, the story beautifully illustrates the evolution of consciousness as it takes on bodily form, moving from the soul (sun), the emotional mind (moon), the thinking mind (Mercury), desire (Venus), action (Mars) and finally the result of experience and thought – wisdom (Jupiter). One aspect of the mind gives rise to the other. Time (Saturn) brings the whole process to a close until it begins again in a new life.

In India the nine planets or *navgrahas* play an important role in everyday rituals. Temples throughout India are dedicated to different planets where people come and say prayers and make offerings in the hope of attracting their positive influence in their lives. Many women wear rings or pendants studded with jewels which symbolize the *grahas*. There is also a mandala called the *Navgraha Yantra* which has a certain combination of numbers which symbolize the different energies of the planets.

As in European languages, the days of the week are based on the *grahas*. The word *Vaar* (day) is added to the Sanskrit name for each of them: *Ravivaar* (sun's day), *Somvaar* (moon's day), *Mangalvaar* (Mars' day; in French, *mardi*), *Budhvaar* (Mercury's day; *mercredi*), *Brihaspativaar* (Jupiter's day; *jeudi*), *Shukravaar* (Venus' day; *vendredi*), and *Shanivaar* (Saturn's day). On a planet's special day, its energies are believed to be stronger; its strength can be further enhanced by fasting or rituals. Important activities (such as a marriage ceremony, setting off on a journey or opening a business) are rarely performed on the days of the malefic planets Mars and Saturn. On the other hand, some astrologers claim it is fine to move house on Saturday and have an operation on Tuesday!

The Sun

India's many legends are associated with the *grahas* and reflect their astrological symbolism. The sun (*Surya*) is understandably important. Without the sun there would be no life. The sun is *Purusha*, the male principle of the universe, and symbolizes the eternal soul. The sun also represents the father, authority, vitality and courage. Psychologically, all planets have a positive and negative side: the sun can be generous and creative, but also proud and despotic.

The sun is pure (sattvic), but it can create problems because it is so fiery. Vedic myth has it that the wife of the sun left him and the Creator had to reduce some of his brightness before she came back, but even then he was too hot.

A strong sun in our chart suggests that our inner and outer selves will be harmonious and we will have a highly developed consciousness. On the other hand, too strong a sun means that we can be authoritarian and overbearing. A weak sun implies that we lack vitality and need to increase our solar energy, for example by wearing dark red colours and jewellery made with gold, rubies or garnets. Living in a warm climate or even sun-bathing can also help! The sun is strong in Leo (which it rules), neutral in Gemini and Virgo; strong in third, sixth and eleventh Houses, but strongest in the tenth. It is weak in Libra and in the fourth House.

In India the solar day lasts from sunrise to sunrise and the solar month, thirty solar days, the sun's transit from zero to 30° of one sign. The moon (Chandrama or Soma) does not shine with its own light, but only by the reflection from the sun.

The Moon

While the sun gives life to the universe, the moon is responsible for life on earth. It is *Prakriti*, the female principle, the cosmic mother. It controls life and death, birth and rebirth. In Vedic literature, the moon is Soma, a god (not a goddess). Although he has feminine energy, he likes to enjoy himself and has twenty-seven wives (the lunar mansions or *nakshatras*). At best, he can be receptive and imaginative; at worse, hyper-sensitive and over-reacting.

While the sun represents the soul, the moon symbolizes the embodied mind. When strongly placed, it can overcome many problems. But it also waxes and wanes and when its light is dim, our desires and appetites can overcome us. It represents the ebb and flow of our feelings from day to day in the cycle of the lunar month. Its *guna* is sattvic.

In the lunar cycle, a new moon travels 13° 20′ a day and takes two and a quarter days to transit one House or zodiac sign (30°). It circles the ecliptic, passing through all the signs of the zodiac, and returns to its original position in twenty-seven days. But since the sun also appears to have moved, the moon requires another two and a half days to catch up with it for a new moon. A lunar month is therefore twenty-nine and a half days. In the Indian almanac, a lunar month is thirty days, known as *tithis*. The waxing phase of the moon is considered to be a period of increasing outgoing energy, while during the waning moon it decreases and turns inward. The five days over the full moon is when the mind is at its best.

In astrology, the waxing moon is considered benefic; the waning moon, malefic. The moon represents the mother. A strong moon in our chart suggests that we were well cared for by our mother; a weak one implies a difficult relationship with our mother, and a tendency to depression and agitation. This can be counteracted by meditation and surrounding ourselves with white, the colour of the moon, or wearing jewellery made from silver, pearls or moonstones. The moon further stands for the emotions, liquids and the sea.

The moon is strong in Cancer (which it rules), and when 72° away from the sun. It is weak in Scorpio and when less than 72° from the sun. It is strong in the fifth, ninth and eleventh Houses but strongest in the fourth.

Mars

As in the West, Mars (*Kartika*) is a warrior. According to myth, the demon Taraka once terrorized the world. It was said that the only being who would destroy him would be a seven-day-old son of Lord Shiva. Kamadeva, the god of love, hit Shiva with an arrow which aroused him, whereupon the furious Shiva killed the god with his third eye. The seed which was produced was so hot that it had to be cooled in the river Ganges. At the time, the Krittikas (six stars, known as the Pleiades in the West) were bathing in its waters and were fertilized by Shiva's semen. They produced Kartika (Mars) who fulfilled the prophecy and killed the demon Taraka when he was seven days old.

As a male planet, Mars stands for action and his qualities are courage and strength. While purposeful and passionate, he can also be irritable and impatient. He signifies the position of brothers in the birthchart; traditionally, he does not, as in the West, indicate the male partner in a woman's chart. His presence is seen generally as malefic, creating problems in life. But Martian valour and perseverance can help to overcome the obstacles on the path towards enlightenment and self-realization.

A strong Mars indicates a good relationship with brothers and determination in achieving our goals. In the seventh House, however, it can mean a tendency to dominate; if this is the case, calm music and cool colours can counteract it. A weak Mars, on the other hand, suggests that our energy may be easily be blocked or dissipated. In this case, dressing in bright red colours and wearing coral can help.

Mars is strong in Aries and Scorpio (which it rules); strong in the third, sixth and eleventh Houses, but strongest in the tenth. It is weak in Cancer and in the fourth House.

Mercury

Whereas the sun represents the individual soul (*atman*), the moon, mind (*manas*), Mercury (*Buddha*) stands for awareness (*buddhi*). Together they produce *ahamkara*, the personal ego. Mercury is the son of the moon and the star Tara, Jupiter's wife. Soma, the moon god, seduced Tara, but Jupiter wanted her back and declared war on him. The gods sided with Jupiter while the demons opted for Tara and in the ensuing conflict threatened to destroy the world. Brahma, the Creator, fearful of the outcome, obliged Tara to return to her husband, Jupiter, but she had already conceived *Buddha*. Jupiter eventually accepted him. The story relates symbolically how the encounter between the pure soul of Tara and the emotional mind of Soma produces the rational intellect.

Because it orbits close to the sun and conjoins with it three times a year, Mercury is considered to be the messenger of the gods. Vedic literature describes him as a eunuch; he is androgynous. He represents childhood, and like many children, is quick, changeable and endearing. He is characteristically rajastic, that is, full of dynamic vitality. A strong Mercury suggests a keen intelligence and an ability to communicate, but if too strong it can indicate a lack of emotion. His wit and intelligence can degenerate into aloofness and expediency. A weak Mercury can mean that we are too easily persuaded and too reliant on our feelings. This can be counteracted by developing the intellect through meditation and yoga and wearing his colour, green.

Mercury is strong in Gemini and Virgo (which it rules) and in the second, fourth, fifth, ninth, tenth and eleventh Houses, but strongest in the first. It is weak in Pisces, in the sixth, eighth and twelfth Houses and weakest in the seventh.

Jupiter

Jupiter (*Brihaspati*) is the teacher (guru) of the gods. He is a *Brahmin*, that is, one who has knowledge of Brahma, the Creator. He stands for growth, expansion, joviality and wisdom. He is the most benefic planet; if we have a strong Jupiter in our chart, we should be able to surmount the difficulties we encounter in our lives. In addition, it suggests that we will have material prosperity which should enable us to focus on our spiritual development.

In a woman's chart, Jupiter stands for relationships and a son. His position is carefully studied, for it offers answers to the two questions most often asked by clients in India: Will I marry? Will I have a son? Representing expansion, he also rules obesity! A strong Jupiter implies higher knowledge and an ability to use it for the well-being of others. A weak Jupiter can suggest difficulties with relationships and a possible tension between one's ideals and everyday life. Greed and extravagance can creep in. This can be counteracted by wearing the colour yellow, gold, topaz or citrine gems and by deliberately working for others.

Jupiter is strong in Sagittarius and Pisces (which it rules) and in the fifth, ninth, tenth and eleventh Houses, but it is strongest in the first. It is weak in Capricorn and in the seventh House.

Venus

Venus is the guru of the demons as Jupiter is the guru of the gods. The demons are evolved souls who have lost their way; Venus tries to bring them back to the true path. Of all the planets, he is the only one who has the secret of immortality.

Although male, Venus has feminine energy; he is benefic and rajasic. At the same time, he represents refinement, love and gentleness. But while he can help us realize our material desires, he cannot always ensure contentment. He can bring us fame and popularity, but not peace of mind. At worse, he can encourage vanity and corruption. This is well illustrated by the story of the daughter of Venus, who fell in love with a king and insisted that her father arrange the marriage. The prospective bridegroom felt unable to refuse but he was already in love with another woman and was unable to show affection towards his new bride.

A strong Venus will attract the opposite sex towards us and bring grace and luxury into our life. A weak Venus can make relationships difficult for us. To strengthen our Venus, we need to develop our self-esteem and make the best of our potential. Wearing white or variegated colours and adorning yourself with silver and diamonds or white sapphire will help. In all charts, Venus stands for marriage; in a male chart, Venus represents the wife.

Venus is strong in Taurus and Libra (which it rules) and the first, fifth, ninth, eleventh and twelfth Houses, but strongest in the fourth. It is weak in Virgo and in the sixth, eighth and tenth Houses.

Saturn

Saturn (*Shani*) stands for restriction, limitation and heavy responsibility and therefore is considered malefic. It is the most feared planet in India. In Vedic literature, Saturn is the son of the sun and of his shadow wife Chayya. The story goes that one day Chayya secretly went to visit her parents and left her shadow behind; the sun took it for real, made love to it, and the result was Saturn. When the sun realized his error, he rejected both his wife and offspring.

Not surprisingly, the relationship between the sun and Saturn is problematic. If Saturn is placed with the sun in the ninth House, it implies that we will have a rift with our father. The most fraught relationship, however, is with the moon. If conjunct with the moon or placed in the twelfth or second House from the moon, Saturn can create loneliness, melancholy and rigidity. His colour is black and his gems are sapphire and lapis lazuli. Whether weak or strong, Saturn brings difficulty. If anything, a weak Saturn is the worst. It is then best dealt with by fasting and meditation.

Saturn causes separation whenever he is present. But while he gives rise to frustration and suffering, the obstacles he places in life's journey can help us to detach ourselves from the entanglements of the world and to transform ourselves. By moving more slowly than the other planets, he offers plenty of time to come to terms with our karma from previous lives. If we are careful, we can emerge from the experience stronger and more complete.

Saturn is strong in Capricorn and Aquarius (which it rules), strong in the third, sixth, tenth and eleventh Houses, but strongest in the seventh. It is weak in the first House.

Rahu and Ketu

The last two *grahas*, Rahu and Ketu, are the names given to the North and South nodes of the moon. The nodes are two points on the ecliptic, 180° apart, where the path of the moon around the earth traverses the apparent path of the sun around the earth. The axis, sometimes known as the karmic axis, passes through the zodiac signs in retrograde motion, taking about eighteen years to complete the cycle.

Rahu and Ketu are known as shadow planets (*chayya grahas*) although they have no physical reality. They are considered the most powerful *grahas* in the zodiac because they are believed to 'swallow' the sun and the moon during eclipses. Solar eclipses (on a new moon) take place within a band of zero to 18° from the nodal axis; lunar eclipses (at full moon) take place within a band of 0° to 11°. During this period, the three most significant influences in our lives – the sun, earth and moon – come together in powerful alignments.

Working in unison at two opposite points in the zodiac, Rahu and Ketu disturb our lives in order to help us realize our inner potential. Ketu allegedly contains knowledge of our past lives while Rahu brings out into the open our karmic weaknesses, thereby helping us to transcend them. As such, these two *grahas* have been called the ultimate controllers of destiny.[3]

They are powerful but also potentially dangerous. The Vedic symbol of Rahu is Naga (the snake) representing knowledge which, like venom, can both kill and cure. While reminding us of our mortality, the way a snake sheds its skin is also a symbol of death and rebirth, of leaving the envelope of our mortal body to find a new life in another body.

According to myth, Naga Vasuki was the demon snake who governed the Underworld. In the war between the gods and the demons for control of the universe, Vasuki at first assisted the gods. They tied him around the cosmic mountain Mandara and used his body to churn the ocean – a reference, it would appear, to his role in making the planets and stars go round in the firmament. In the meantime, the gods went in search of *amrita*, the nectar of immortality. They gave wine, women and song to the demons to keep them occupied, but the cunning Vasuki was not to be fooled. He secretly drank the nectar of the gods and became immortal himself.

The sun and the moon complained to Lord Vishnu, the Creator of the Universe. Furious at Vasuki's deception, he hurled a wheel, known as the *Sudarshan chakra* (the ecliptic), at him, which cut him in two. But since he was now immortal he did not die. Instead, Rahu (the head) and Ketu (the tail) remained forever cut in two in the heavens. And there they remain, constantly moving backwards, a reminder to the other gods, and ourselves, of the dark side of our nature which we must overcome in order to attain immortality. In the churning ocean of our feelings, we have the capacity for good or evil. While Rahu symbolizes our attachment to the material world, Ketu stands for liberation and self-realization (*moksha*).

As the two poles of the karmic axis, Rahu and Ketu always fall six Houses away from each other and highlight the areas in our life where we must struggle to overcome the consequences of our past karma. Together they represent the Kundalini energy within us – also symbolized by a snake – which when awakened can either destroy us or lead us to enlightenment. Its power is not to be taken lightly and needs careful channelling, but its effects can be transcendental.

Rahu is strong in Virgo and weak in Scorpio and Sagittarius. Ketu is strong in Pisces and weak in Taurus and Gemini. They are unable to act on their own, and tend to adopt the characteristics of the planet that rules the sign they are in. At best, Rahu can bring originality and independence; at worst, confusion and neurosis. Ketu can lead to spirituality and compassion, but it can also encourage fanaticism and violence. Planets in the same Houses as the nodes indicate the karma we bring into this life from previous lives which has to be worked through. Rahu usually enhances the essential quality of the planets, while Ketu overshadows them. Rahu rules agate, and Ketu turquoise. The sun and the moon particularly suffer from conjunctions to Rahu and Ketu since they were so hostile to the demon snake Naga Vasuki. Nevertheless, since Rahu enhances the qualities of the sun, if they are in conjunction in our chart, we are likely to make a mark on the world.

Planetary Aspects

To refine his interpretation of a horoscope, the Indian *Jyotishi* will explore the aspects or relationships between the planets, their combinations (*yogas*) and consider their influence at different periods (*dashas*) in a person's life. The whole has been developed into a profound and subtle art.

The fourth-century astrologer Minaraja wrote: 'A planet is said to have one [kind of] strength in a sign or *navamsa* which it rules, or in which it is exalted, or which is ruled by a friend; or when aspected by a benefic. The moon and Venus are strong in the feminine signs, and the others in the masculine signs.'[4]

In fact, the planets can be friends, enemies or simply neutral.[5] They can even be, like many of us, friends on some occasions and enemies on others. Mars, for instance, has Jupiter, the moon and the sun as friends, Mercury as an enemy and Saturn and Venus as neutrals. Venus has Mercury and Saturn as friends, the moon and the sun as enemies and is neutral towards Jupiter and Mars. Some Westerners may think that men are from Mars and women from Venus but, in the Indian scheme of astrology, they are both male and indifferent to each other! The moon, representing mind and water, has no enemies.

But friendships and enmities are not always firm and the planets, just like humans, form temporary relationships. Those found in the second, third, fourth, tenth, eleventh and twelfth signs of the zodiac from any other planet become the latter's temporary friends. The others become its enemies. To complicate matters further, Indian astrologers believe in mixed or compound relations. These are formed by combining the natural and temporary relationships: when a natural friendship is mixed with a temporary friendship, the result is, not surprisingly, a great friendship; enmity and friendship cancel each other out to have a neutral influence; and neutral and friendship means friendship.

These temporary and mixed relationships mirror the changes which occur in the character of the planets in the chart of a particular individual. The relationships a planet has with others will alter its habitual influence. A malefic planet like Mars may have a beneficial effect if its relationships are positive; the opposite can occur with a benefic planet like Jupiter, if it is badly related.

Relationships exist between planets and signs too. The four most important kinds of relationships are those of ownership, exaltation, debilitation (well known to Western astrologers) and *mooltrikona* (an Indian speciality).

First, ownership. Particular planets are said to 'own' or 'rule' particular signs. Another way of putting it is to say that a planet is the lord of a sign. It means that they have a special affinity with each other.

A planet in its own sign is strengthened to do good. The sun owns Leo, the moon, Cancer. Mars owns Aries and Scorpio; Mercury rules Gemini and Virgo; Jupiter owns Sagittarius and Pisces; Venus rules Taurus and Libra; Saturn is lord of Capricorn and Aquarius.

Next, exaltation. When in a particular sign, a planet is said to be exalted, that is held high. Such a planet is thought to be in its best position. Its power to do good is greater when it is exalted than when it is in its own sign. It is even more powerful when it is placed in a particular degree in the sign; it is then said to reach its maximum exaltation. The sun, moon, Mars, Mercury, Jupiter, Venus, Saturn, Rahu and Ketu are in high exaltation in the degrees of the following signs: Aries, 10°; Taurus, 3°; Capricorn, 28°; Virgo, 15°; Cancer, 5°; Pisces, 27°; Libra, 20°; Taurus, 20°; and Scorpio, 20° respectively.[6] An exalted sun in Aries, for example, makes a person learned, religious, strong, placid and charitable. The moon in Taurus renders someone rich, sedulous and creative.

By contrast, debilitation – a weakening of energies – occurs when the planets are situated in opposition to the optimum position of exaltation, that is 180° away. When in this situation, the planets give the opposite results to when in exaltation. Rahu and Ketu are exalted in Taurus and Scorpio and debilitated in Scorpio and Taurus respectively.

Finally, the intriguing-sounding *mooltrikona*. These are the positions of planets in a range of degrees in signs where they do well. They extend from 4° to 20° of longitude. The sun's *mooltrikona* is in Leo (0° to 20°); the moon in Taurus (4° to 20°); Mars in Aries (0° to 12°); Mercury in Virgo (16° to 20°); Jupiter in Sagittarius (0° to 10°); Venus in Libra (0° to 15°); Saturn in Aquarius (0° to 20°).[7] The effect of *mooltrikona* is similar to that of exaltation: it strengthens a planet's power to do good, though it is not as strong as exaltation. The rulers of the signs which are second, fourth, fifth, eighth, ninth and twelfth from the *mooltrikona* sign of the planets will be friendly, otherwise the rulers of signs will be enemies. If planets rule more than one sign, and they have a friendly as well as an unfriendly relationship, they become neutral.

The strength of a planet's energies decreases when it moves from exaltation through *mooltrikona* to debilitation, and increases in the opposite direction, rather like the waxing and waning of the moon. If planets are in exaltation, *mooltrikona* or their own signs in a birthchart, it shows considerable maturity as the self passes through its different reincarnations in the cycle of birth and death. It is possible to work out their relative strengths, both positive and negative, depending on whether the planets are exalted or debilitated, in positive or negative relationships.

Although the diurnal motion of the planets never alters its direction (from East to West for an observer on earth), the proper motion (the apparent movement of the planets through the signs of the zodiac from West to East) does change. Apart from the sun and the moon, all the planets appear to slow down and then move backwards before speeding up and travelling forward through the constellations. This is technically known as retrogression or retrograde motion. Strictly speaking, this retrograde motion is an illusion viewed from earth because of the planets' elliptical movement. Nevertheless, Indian astrologers, like their Western counterparts, believe that planets in retrogression have a strong symbolic significance. Their normal exaltations and debilitations are also reversed. The axis of Rahu and Ketu always travels in a retrograde direction.

If this is not enough, there are ten states known as *avasthas* which planets turn into when occupying certain positions in signs and Houses. If in exaltation (*deeptha*), wealth and good offspring will come; if in its own House (*swastha*), fame and happiness will follow; and if in a friendly House (*muditha*), one can expect good temper and a good spouse. When a planet is in auspicious divisions (*santha*) strength, courage and happiness appear. Retrogression (*sakta*) will also bring courage, wealth and reputation.

On the other hand, if the planet is in the last quarter of a sign (*peedya*), evil will result. If in an unfriendly House (*deena*), expect worry and sickness. When in debilitation (*khala*), losses and quarrels take place. When in acceleration (*bheetha*), losses and mean habits result. And when planets are very close to the sun and become lost from view because of the glare, a condition known as combustion in the West, disease, disgrace and loss of children will not be far away. In Sanskrit, they are said to be in a state of *astam* which means 'having set'.

As in the West, aspects have an important bearing on an Indian horoscope, in that the position of any planet in a chart has a particular effect on planets in other parts of the chart. Unlike Western astrology, however, the aspect is to a sign as a whole and not just to one section of it. Venus at 14° Aries is opposite and aspecting the entire sign of Libra, and will aspect any planets anywhere in the House occupied by

Libra. In general, a planet will only make aspects with the signs that lie forward around the zodiacal circle from the sign it occupies, as Venus in Aries aspects Libra in the above example. All planets cast a one hundred per cent aspect or 'full sight' on the seventh sign away from them (counting the House where the planet is placed as the first).[8]

Aspects can be good or bad depending on the relation between the aspecting and aspected body. All Houses have an aspecting value of twenty-five per cent, the fifth and the ninth Houses (trines aspects in Western astrology), fifty per cent; the fourth and eighth Houses, seventy per cent (a square aspect).

A special aspect occurs when planets are in conjunction, that is, when two or more planets are located in the same sign of the zodiac. The result will depend on whether the planets are friends or enemies. If two planets are within one degree of each other (known as *yudh bala*) a state of war is declared, and the planet at the lower degree will win, absorbing the energy of the defeated for its own ends. The moon, however, escapes this battle.

Saturn, Jupiter and Mars have special aspects. Saturn powerfully aspects the third and tenth Houses; Jupiter, the fifth and ninth Houses; and Mars, the fourth and eighth Houses. It is good when benefics aspect each other. A planet aspecting its own House, whether by the seventh House aspect or special aspect, will enhance its influence. The opposition (seventh House) aspect becomes very good when it is caused by Jupiter and the moon. This opposition aspect is capable of producing good or bad results, as is conjunction, depending on the nature of the planets involved.

It is also worth remembering that each planet is an indicator or *karaka* of a particular relationship or activity. The sun is the *karaka* of father; the moon, of mother; Mars, of brother; Mercury, of profession; Jupiter, of children; Venus, of wife or husband; Saturn, of longevity; Rahu, of maternal relations; and finally Ketu, of paternal relations.

Yogas and Dashas

A unique element in Indian astrology is the importance given to certain combinations of planets known as *yogas* (meaning 'union'). By enhancing or hindering our path through life, they reveal the development of our personality and soul. Not everyone will have them in their horoscopes. The most sought after are the extremely rare *panchamaha-purusha yogas* – *panch* means 'five', *mahapurushas* means 'exalted persons'. They are formed when the five planets Mars, Mercury, Jupiter, Venus and Saturn are in their own signs or in exaltation in *kendra* Houses (the first, fourth, seventh and tenth). If they are in conjunction with Rahu or Ketu, they become very powerful, but also unpredictable.

Raja Yoga is a favourable combination of the fifth and ninth rulers with the rulers of the *kendras*. *Raja* means 'king'; a person with a *raja yoga* is likely to be very successful. Its effect can, however, be weakened or cancelled. A *Kal Sarpa Yoga* is created when all the planets in a horoscope fall between Rahu and Ketu. In this case, it does not indicate either success or failure, but struggle with strong karmic forces from the past. There are many other yogas which complicate and enrich the reading of a horoscope.[9]

Another element unique to Indian astrology is the *dashas*. *Dasha* means 'direction'. Different planets are said to 'rule' different periods of our lives which are known as *dashas*. The system introduces a time dimension into the charts and predicts events in your life. The *dashas* run consecutively, but their periods are not of equal length. The sun governs for six years; the moon for ten; Mars, seven; Rahu, eighteen; Jupiter, sixteen; Saturn, nineteen; Mercury, seventeen; Ketu, seven; and Venus, twenty. The complete cycle takes 120 years, the supposed natural life-span of a person at the time of the *Vedas* when the system was elaborated. If we are born during a Rahu *dasha*, the following *dashas* will obviously last a long time. There are even sub-*dashas*, and sub-sub *dashas* which highlight shorter periods. At any given moment, there are usually three planets affecting our lives, and their influence will depend on their sign, aspect and the House in which they are placed.

While the birthchart highlights certain elements of our karma and character, the *dasha* system shows when they will come into prominence in your life. The first *dasha* in the 120-year cycle is decided by the position of the moon at birth. To calculate the *dasha* pattern it is necessary to discover which *dasha* period you are born into.[10] The first is the most important *dasha* to examine, since it indicates what is in store later in life.

Transits (*gocharas*) are always considered in relation to *dashas*. The horoscope, of course, shows the position of planets at the moment of birth, but they are continually circling the zodiac throughout one's life and will interact with the birthchart. Most transits are considered from the position of the moon. There are brief transits from the fast-moving planets like the sun, moon, Mercury, Mars and Venus, which can bring fleeting issues into focus. The slower-moving planets, Jupiter and Saturn, will have deeper and more far-reaching effects, the former bringing good luck and opportunity, the latter struggle and challenge. The moon, the fastest planet, takes two and a half days to pass through one zodiacal sign and twenty-seven days to pass through the whole zodiac; Saturn takes two and a half years and twenty-nine years and ten months respectively. A transit by any planet lasts from the moment it enters a sign, to the moment it leaves it. As a planet occupies different Houses it will highlight different areas of your life. The moon is the most watched transit: few people in India will begin a new project when the moon is on the wane and many will adjust their lives to its monthly rhythm.

15

Lunar Mansions

WHEREAS WESTERN ASTROLOGY makes great play of our 'sun sign' (the place of the sun at our birth in a particular sign of the zodiac), Indian astrologers, like the Chinese, pay special attention to 'lunar mansions' (the place of the moon in a particular constellation). Since ancient times, Indian religious rituals have been carried out on certain days of the lunar month, especially after the new or full moon.

It was the sun's annual movement around the ecliptic that inspired early Indian astrologers to use the twelve constellations (signs) of the zodiac and twelve Houses as well as the twelve time units of the day. The moon circles the ecliptic in a month. Following the course of the moon through the stars, early Indian astrologers isolated twenty-seven or twenty-eight constellations which they called *nakshatras* or 'lunar mansions'. These are similar to the Chinese *sieu*, first mentioned in the third century BC, but they may in fact be even older and possibly their original source. The earliest surviving Indian astrological text, written by Lagadha around 400 BC, gives rules for calculating the positions of the sun and moon in terms of the *nakshatras*.

Naksha means 'to approach', *tra* means 'on guard' and the whole word originally meant 'a star'. The first known reference to the complete set of twenty-eight *nakshatras* comes in a passage in the *Atharva Veda* which begins rhapsodically: 'Marvellous all together, and brilliant in the sky are the swift serpents of the firmament! Desiring the friendship of the twenty-eight, I worship in my song the sky and the days.'[2] Each *nakshatra* is associated with a particular star, generally the brightest in its constellation, considered to be a deity keeping watch over human life. They are described as the moon's brides.

Early authorities used twenty-eight constellations for the lunar mansions, no doubt mirroring the fact there are four weeks of seven days in a month which makes twenty-eight days. The standard twenty-seven *nakshatras* used nowadays divide more conveniently into the 360° of the zodiac, creating an arc of 13° 20′ for each *nakshatra*. The rulership of the twenty-seven *nakshatras* can also be evenly distributed among the nine *grahas* or planets. And it is closer to the lunar month in which the moon takes twenty-seven days, seven hours, forty-three minutes and eleven and a half seconds to come back to 0° Aries, from whence it began its journey around the circle of the zodiac. Finally, twenty-seven divisions of the lunar mansions fit in with the *navamsha* (ninth-sign) of the *vargas,* known in the West as the 'subdecanate', by reconciling the twelve divisions of the zodiac with the twenty-seven divisions of the lunar mansions. The 108 *navamshas* correspond to the signs of the zodiac, repeated nine times over.

A traditional Indian calendar followed the *nakshatra* divisions of the month. In the *Mahabharata*, for example, a man says: 'I went out with the moon at the Pushya and have returned with the moon at the Sravana.'[3] Pushya here is the sixth constellation counting from the Pleiades and its principal stars are Gamma, Delta and Theta Cancri. Sravana is the twenty-first, marked by the stars Beta and Gamma Aquilae. This means that the man was away for just over half a sidereal month – that is, the period of time taken by the moon to make one complete revolution around the earth, measured by two successive conjunctions with a particular star.

The basic unit of the Indian calendar is the lunar month, measured by the orbit of the moon around the earth. An intercalary month, however, is added when necessary to stop the calendar moving too far away from the solar year. The months have names taken from the *nakshatras,* in which the moon is full. For most Hindus in India, the month begins with the bright half, while for Buddhists the dark half comes first and the full moon marks the main festivals. At present, the lunar year begins with Chitra, while the solar year opens with Vishakha. Hindus say that the present Age of Kali began at the New moon in Phalguna (the two Phalgunis) in 3102 BC when all the seven planets were in conjunction. The appeal of the Indian lunar-solar calendar is that the measurement of time is linked to observed changes in the heavens. When we see the full moon in the Pleiades, for instance, we know we are in the lunar mansion of Krittika.

To complicate matters further, Indian astrologers sometimes use a calendar based on a lunar month of 30 days, known as *tithis.* This is to coincide the lunar calendar with the solar calendar: the moon circles the ecliptic in twenty-seven and a half days, but since the sun appears to have moved, the moon requires another two and a half days to catch up with it to produce the full moon, which results from the sun being reflected on its surface. A lunar day is thus the time it takes for the moon to traverse one *tithi* of one *nakshatra*, while a solar day is the time between one sunrise and the next. There also twenty-seven solar-lunar *yogas* (combinations) derived from the positions of the sun and moon relative to one another. They are calculated by adding together the degrees of their positions.

On examining a natal chart, most Indian astrologers consider the nature of the *nakshatra* occupied by the Ascendant, since it is considered to be the basis of an individual's character. Next, they will consider the *nakshatra* occupied by the moon, as it stands for mental and emotional tendencies. *Nakshatras* are also used in transits, by tracing the subtle relationships between the *nakshatra* of one's birth and the other *nakshatras* in the monthly cycle.[3] Modern Indian astrologers often draw up a moon chart, called a *candralagna*, to trace the development of a woman's personality profile. Since most marriages in India are still arranged, moon charts are particularly referred to in synastry charts to see if a proposed couple are compatible. Finally, they are employed in electional astrology in order to find out the most auspicious day for a particular ritual or event, such as a marriage or moving house.

In early times, it seems that the mansions were numbered from Krittika, the Pleiades, but when the zodiac system was introduced they were renumbered so that Krittika became the third and Ashvini the first mansion.[4] The *nakshatras* still have a close link with the stars.

The lunar mansions are also used to determine the nature of different periods in life known as *dashas*. The nine planets are said to rule three *nakshatras* each.

Each of the twenty-seven *nakshatras* embodies its own rich tapestry of symbolism and mythology, independent of those of the signs and planets.[5] They represent the journey of the soul through life and run as follows. I have tried to give their essential qualities.

1 My moon sits in *Ashwini* (0°–13° 20′ Aries)

> I am the horse's head
> My gods are the Ashwini Kumaras, the miracle healers,
> I am ruled by Ketu.
> I kick up my hooves
> I am full of myself
> I am intelligent
> I accept.

2 My moon sits in *Bharani* (13° 20′–26° 40′ Aries)

> I am the vagina
> My god is Yam, the death dealer,
> I am ruled by Venus.
> I am healthy and happy
> I grow in darkness
> I give birth
> I succeed.

3 My moon sits in *Krittika* (26° 40′ Aries–10° Taurus)

> I am the razor
> My goddess is Agni, the fiery one,
> I am ruled by the sun.
> I cut through hard and soft
> I am golden
> I am known
> I catch fire.

4 My moon sits in *Rohini* (10°–23° 20′ Taurus)

> I am the chariot
> My deity is Brahma, the world creator,
> I am ruled by the moon.
> I strive towards perfection
> I am passionate
> I am red
> I move.

5 My moon sits in *Mrigasira* (23° 20′ Taurus–6° 20′ Gemini)

> I am the deer's head
> My deity is Soma, the moon god,
> I am ruled by Mars.
> I seek experience
> I am courageous
> I am shrewd
> I overcome.

6 My moon sits in *Ardra* (6° 40'–20° Gemini)

I am the jewel
My deity is Rudra, the destroyer,
I am ruled by Rahu.
I expand my mind
I absorb energy
I am green
I am proud.

7 My moon sits in *Punarvasu* (20° Gemini–3° 20' Cancer)

I am the bow
My deity is Aditi, the infinite woman,
I am ruled by Jupiter.
I bring heaven to earth
I teach the way
I aim straight
I shine.

8 My moon sits in *Pushya* (3° 20'–16° 40' Cancer)

I am the flower, the arrow and the circle
My deities are Brihaspati, the adviser to the gods,
I am ruled by Saturn.
I am complete in myself
I expand and contract
I am pure and holy
I grow.

9 My moon sits in *Ashlesha* (16° 40' Cancer–0° Leo)

I am the serpent
My deities are the Nagas, the snakes,
I am ruled by Mercury.
I kill and heal
I shed my skin
I struggle
I see far.

10 My moon sits in *Magha* (0°–13° 20′ Leo)

    I am the house and the palanguin
    My deity is Pitris, the forefather
    I am ruled by Ketu.
    I am mighty and great
    I am bountiful
    I am idealistic
    I persevere.

11 My moon sits in *Purva Phalguni* (13° 20′–26° 40′ Leo)

    I am the bed and the fireplace
    My deity is Bhaga, the lucky one,
    I am ruled by Venus.
    I am rich and happy
    I speak well
    I bring gifts
    I wander.

12 My moon sits in *Uttara Phalguni* (26° 40′ Leo–10° Virgo)

    I am the four legs of the cot
    My deity is Aryaman, the leader,
    I am ruled by the sun.
    I stand on the earth
    I am lucky
    I am erect
    I create.

13 My moon sits in *Hasta* (10°–23 20′ Virgo)

    I am the palm of the hand
    My deity is Savitar, the sun god,
    I am ruled by the moon.
    I am the five elements
    I am the twelve signs
    I hold my destiny
    I stride out.

14 My moon sits in *Chitra* (23° 20′ Virgo–6° 40′ Libra)

> I am the pearl
> My deity is Tvashtar, the heavenly architect,
> I am ruled by Mars.
> I cut through the illusion
> I break the shell
> I attract others
> I transform.

15 My moon sits in *Swati* (6° 40′–20° Libra)

> I am coral
> My deity is Vayu, the god of wind,
> I am ruled by Rahu.
> I reproduce myself
> I acquire wealth
> I breathe deep
> I balance.

16 My moon sits in *Vishakha* (20° Libra–3° 20′ Scorpio)

> I am the potter's wheel and the archway
> My deities are Indra, the god of gods, Agni, the god of fire
> I am ruled by Jupiter.
> I am on the threshold
> I am clever with words
> I turn on my centre
> I look up.

17 My moon sits in *Anuradha* (3° 20′–16° 40′ Scorpio)

> I am the lotus
> My deity is Mitra, the god of light,
> I am ruled by Saturn.
> I blossom in mud
> I reach for the sun
> I unite opposites
> I am reborn.

18 My moon sits in *Jyeshta* (16° 40′ Scorpio–0° Sagittarius)

I am the umbrella and the earring
My deity is Indra, the god of gods,
I am ruled by Mercury.
I unite heaven and earth
I know where to go
I am content
I flow.

19 My moon sits in *Mula* (0°–13° 20′ Sagittarius)

I am the tail of the lion and the elephant's goad
My deity is Nritta, the goddess of death,
I am ruled by Ketu.
I go to the root of things
I show my anger
I seek power
I enjoy.

20 My moon sits in *Purvashadha* (13° 20′–26° 40′ Sagittarius)

I am the fan and the winnowing basket
My deity is Apas, the god of water,
I am ruled by Venus.
I am wise and invincible
I change fast
I aim high
I cleanse.

21 My moon sits in *Uttarashadha* (26° 40′ Sagittarius–10°
    Capricorn)

I am the elephant's trunk
My deities are the Vishwedevas, the universal gods,
I am ruled by the sun.
I am a hard resting place
I have good friends
I know myself
I am modest.

22 My moon sits in *Shravana* (10°–23° 20′ Capricorn)

I am the ear and the arrow
My deity is Vishnu, the preserver of the universe,
I am ruled by the moon.
I see clearly
I sit quietly
I listen.

23 My Moon sits in *Dhanishta* (23° 20′ Capricorn – 6° 40′
    Aquarius)

I am the drum
My deities are the eight Vasus, the gods of the sun,
I am ruled by Mars.
I am rich and generous
I am empty within
I am courageous
I fight.

24 My moon sits in *Shatabhishak* (6° 40′–20° Aquarius)

I am a horse and a thousand-petalled flower
My deity is Varuna, the god of the ocean,
I am ruled by Rahu.
I am formidable
I am illuminated
I dive deep
I flower.

25 My moon sits in *Purva Bhadra* (20° Aquarius–3° 20′ Pisces)

I am the sword
My deity is Aja Ekapada, the one-footed Goat,
I am ruled by Jupiter.
I overcome obstacles
I attack and defend
I am blessed
I sow.

26 My moon sits in *Uttara Bhadra* (3° 20′–16° 40′ Pisces)

I am the twins
My deity is Ahir Budhyana, the god of water,
I am ruled by Saturn.
I create in darkness
I seek the universal
I support others
I let go.

27 My moon sits in *Revati* (16° 40′–30° Pisces)

I am the fish
My deity is Pushan, the sun god,
I am ruled by Mercury.
I perceive truth
I am the end
I give birth
I transcend.

I found the most interesting *nakshatra* to be *Hasta,* the symbol of which is the palm of the hand. Palmistry is often used in connection with astrology to refine an interpretation. For Indians, hands are full of symbolism. The right and left hands are male and female energies, as well as positive and negative forces throughout the universe. The hand mirrors the solar system. The joints on the four fingers represent the twelve zodiac signs. The joints of the thumbs and fingers of both hands show the thirty days of the solar month and the thirty *tithis* of the lunar month.

That is not all. The fingers and thumb of one hand symbolize the five elements (water, earth, sky, air and fire) and the five senses (sight, hearing, taste, smell and touch). The middle finger is the finger of destiny, used in *pranayama* yoga to regulate the breath of life. The four fingers are also the four directions of the compass – North, South, East and West. Above all, they represent the four great motivations of Indian spiritual life (*artha, kama, dharma* and *moksha*) and the ultimate goal of all true Indian astrology – the path to enlightenment.

16

Yogastrology

WHILE VISITING VARANASI, I met an astrologer who not only clarified the spiritual dimension of Indian astrology, but also demonstrated how its principles are put into practice. Swami Yogi Prakash lived in Varanasi's Kamachha district, down by the *ghats*. His card had an image of a naked man meditating on a lotus flower, with the uncoiling serpent of Kundalini energy rising from his groin to his head. The symbols of the planets stretched down either arm forming a triangle. Swami Yogi Prakash described himself as 'Astrologer, Yoga Expert, Tantrist, Counsellor, Healer and Naturopath'. His business, as his card declared, was 'Yogastrology'.

Swami Yogi Prakash lived in two simple rooms on the third floor of a half-built apartment block. A young boy opened the door and asked me to take off my shoes. His master was a medium-sized, middle-aged, slightly plump man with a long black beard and flowing black hair beginning to recede at the temples. The flat was furnished simply, with a bed and low table. The only luxury was a large black television in a recess. Behind a curtain was an adjoining meditation room with an ornate shrine to Shiva, the third god of the Hindu Trinity, the Destroyer, who carries a trident to chase away evil spirits.

After obtaining a Ph.D. in philosophy, Swami Yogi Prakash told me, he had abandoned the academic life for the spiritual. At the age of eighteen he had had a revelation which changed his life and now he devoted his whole time seeking enlightenment. His own guru was Swami Naryab Tirth who lived in the Himalayas where some holy men have allegedly lived to 200 years.

Swami Yogi Prakash was warm and jolly, but could quickly turn serious. He certainly seemed to fit the description by Varahamihira (who died in 587) of the ideal astrologer:

> An astrologer ought to be of good family, friendly in his
> appearance, and fashionable in his dress; veracious and not
> malignant. He must have well-proportioned, compact and full
> limbs, no bodily defect, and be a fine man ... further, that he is
> regular in worshipping the gods, in his observances and fasts; that
> he is able to raise the prestige of science by the wonderful
> perfection of his branch of study, and to solve satisfactorily any
> questions, except in cases where supernatural agencies baffle
> human calculation; finally, that he knows both text and meaning
> of the works on mathematical astronomy, natural astrology, and
> horoscopy.[1]

My astrologer sat cross-legged on a wooden board behind a low table
which had on it a small portrait of Lord Rama, mandalas and yantras,
symbols used for meditation.

'You should not sit directly on the ground,' he observed. 'You
should not earth your *prana* too much, but keep it within. If you direct
your *prana* inward, you enter the kingdom of God which is within
you.'

I asked him about the best way to achieve spiritual realization, the
ultimate goal of all Indian astrology.

'There are two ways towards enlightenment and salvation. One is to
negate, negate, negate. The other is to accept, accept, accept. The Vedic
tradition negates, the Tantric accepts. It accepts immanent phenomena
and what you are as a form of the divine. Tantra embraces the whole
world.'

'And the body? Is that considered evil?'

'The body is not an end but a means. Why did God give you a body?
The body is only a staircase to uplift you to consciousness.'

'How is that possible?'

'Tantra believes in a supreme cosmic energy hidden in man in a
certain form known as Kundalini. It is represented as a female serpent
with its mouth pointing downwards to the junction of the spinal cord.
Through certain disciplines, by the grace of a guru or a deity, the cosmic
energy can be awakened and pass up the spinal cord through the seven
chakras to the crown of the head. As it passes, it purifies. It enables you
to cross the border of nature, to free yourself from the empirical world,
to reach the kingdom of heaven.'

'Are you transformed in the process?'

'Of course. When you go into the Ultimate, your inner being is transformed. Your spiritual, astral body is purified. You leave your physical, causal body. When your destiny is wiped out, you have *samadhi*, enlightenment.'

'Can it take a long time?'

'Where there's a will, there's a way! You need the intensity of will to reach consciousness. I pour my whole energy into realizing myself. Yoga is a very practical path. The chakras can always be purified. Although I have a home life and have consciousness of the world I am not attached to them. If you surrender your life to the divine, you will never live in vain.'

'Does your horoscope determine the length of your life?'

'At birth your span of life is given you, but you can decide how to use it. If you use your breath in the proper way you can prolong your life and decide when to die. It's like a game of football. The goal is a hollow space like your breath. You can decide when to hit your body into the goal . . .

'You can even invert the rhythm of your body and cross the boundary of death,' Swami Yogi Prakash continued. 'In *samadhi*, the body is stopped but does not decay. Not everyone can do it.'

'How can you do this?'

'There are three ways to attain *samadhi* and have a glimpse of the Lord – through mantras, meditation and medicine. By repeating mantras, you pray without ceasing so as not to forget the Lord. In meditation, you direct the flow of energy within you. In karma yoga, your consciousness is at one with the Lord.'

I still found it difficult to square the idea of free will and the idea of being born with a predetermined number of breaths in your life.

'Can you escape determinism?' I asked. 'Your life then is not fixed at birth by your horoscope?'

'It's something like TV,' said Swami Yogi Prakash, smiling warmly, pointing to the inert black box in a recess above his head. 'When we come into the world of phenomena, it's just like a script of someone's life which has been written and filmed. But you can jump out of the script. You can escape this circle of dependence, you can be free of *sansara*, the bondage of rebirth, by purifying your energy and reaching cosmic consciousness.'

'What about the future? What do you foresee in the future?'

'A very harmful time is coming for mankind,' Swami Yogi Prakash prophesied. 'It's coming soon, in ten or fifteen years. We are out of balance; women are being used and men are treated like things. There's a growing lust for money and lust for sex.'

'Will it mean the end of the world?'

'The world is not going to end but about two thirds of it will go. Then there will be a new beginning. Have faith!'

Swami Yogi Prakash was very much a guru of the modern India, knowledgeable about Western as well as Indian philosophy and religion, ready to tailor his ancient wisdom to suit the needs of his Western seekers.

Drawing up the Chart

My travelling companion Elizabeth was keen to have her horoscope taken and gave Swami Yogi Prakash her date and time of birth – 20 July 1950 at 22.00 hours. We returned the next day. He had converted her time of birth from Western synodic time to Indian sidereal time, from 22.00 to 12.32, taking into account the effect of *Ayanamsha* or Precessional Distance.

Most Indian astrologers still do not use computers and make lengthy calculations. The final horoscope presents the results in the form of a chart of the planets as 'tied down' by the Ascendant or *lagna*. Whereas Western astrology gives pre-eminence to the sun sign, *Jyotish* believes that the position of the Ascendant gives the greatest insight into an individual's life.

Two different forms of chart are used in the North and South of India. Horoscopes in the West are usually circular in form, but in India they are square. The Northern form, as practised by Prakash, uses triangles and diamonds within a square, and the Houses do not move. Beginning with the *lagna* in the first House in the top diamond, the Ascendant signs of the zodiac move round anti-clockwise. The twelve signs superimposed on each of the twelve Houses will therefore vary according to the *lagna* at the birth time and birthplace. The following is the chart for Elizabeth:

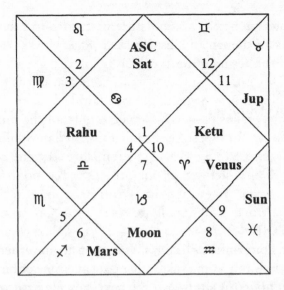

In the above chart, the number indicates the House. The Ascendant is placed in the first House. The planets at Elizabeth's birth are distributed in the appropriate signs. Venus and Ketu, for instance, occupy the tenth House and first sign (Aries).

In South India, the signs in the chart are fixed and always represented by the same squares. The Ascendant sign is usually marked with a diagonal line (or Lg, standing for *lagna*) where the first House begins and the rest of the Houses run on in a clockwise direction. It follows that Aries is in the tenth House as in the Northern form.

♓︎ 9	♈︎ 10	♉︎ 11	♊︎ 12
♒︎ 8			♋︎ 1 Lg
♑︎ 7			♌︎ 2
♐︎ 6	♏︎ 5	♎︎ 4	♍︎ 3

Unlike a Western chart, few details are placed on Indian charts. The information is listed by the side and the astrologer works out the aspects according to the rules mentioned earlier.

Interpreting the Horoscope

When it came to interpreting Elizabeth's horoscope, Swami Yogi Prakash was quite happy for me to remain and take notes of the consultation. He first stressed the importance of the moon in her chart: it not only ruled the Ascendant sign Capricorn, but also occupied the seventh House, which traditionally refers to one's spouse and death.

'The total effect of the moon,' he said, 'is to make you happy on a moonlit night. During the two days before the full moon you are joyous. It is the principle of the moon to change: you like activity and want change in your life. You like to travel across the sea, so many times. You should live on a bank of a pond or near water, not on the first or second floor of a house.'

All this was surprisingly true: Elizabeth lived near a large river and had begun long-distance sailing. She also liked travel and change.

'You attract the opposite sex like anything,' he went on. 'You like romance – romance where your emotions are enriched rather than just sexual love. The emotional for you is more important than the passionate.'

Playfully tugging her long hair, Prakash joked: 'You'll never be devoid of a partner! It is your destiny not to stay with one partner. In the East, sexual indulgence only takes place within marriage, but I know it is different in the West. Your first partnership ended in disaster. Mars is a low planet in your chart. Saturn in your first House delays the process but you will eventually meet a person who will stay in your life – your seventh husband! You have lots of friends.'

I wondered whether I was indeed the seventh love of her life . . .

Prakash then turned to the question of health. Examining Elizabeth's hand with a magnifying glass, he said: 'You have a weakness in the bowels. You should be careful with operations.'

Looking at her nails carefully, he added: 'You should not exhaust yourself. You have a nervous weakness, both mentally and physically.'

There was good news about her work prospects: 'You'll never be devoid of a job. You'll work in service, not as a freelancer.'

It was true that Elizabeth had spent most of her life as a lecturer and now had a permanent post if she wanted it. Turning to the future, he declared: 'With the sun in the ninth House, and a very good aspect between the fifth and the ninth Houses, your future is bright like the sun. You should practise *sadhana* – meditation and worship. You should be very faithful and virtuous for the forthcoming life. You should practice *bakti* yoga – devotion – using your emotions for romance for the divine. You have a hidden sign known as the "mystic cross" which shows your hidden capacity and potentiality to develop your mystical qualities.'

In his summing up, Prakash said again: 'Your future is bright. You will never be devoid of money. You have good matching between sun and moon. You can develop the faculty of imagination to make dreams come true!'

He handed over to Elizabeth a piece of paper headed with his symbol of the meditating yogi surrounded by symbols of the planets. It contained a drawing of her chart with two suggestions. The first was to wear white and a pearl of four carats in a silver ring on her left hand's ring finger. The second was to practise deep yogic relaxation daily for some time.

On his prompting, Elizabeth and I meditated in the small adjoining room, before a shrine dedicated to Shiva. When we left, Swami Yogi Prakash embraced us both warmly at the end of the corridor of his half-built apartment block, raising his voice above the noise of the building site and of the nearby bustling street. It was an emotional moment. We both felt we had met a very special person. I bought Elizabeth the ring. The next time we saw Swami Yogi Prakash was on British television explaining to millions the meaning of the great Kumbh Mela festival.

17

Crisis and Salvation

I DID NOT HAVE a horoscope done in India, so on my return to England, I decided to contact Komilla Sutton, co-founder and Chair of the British Association for Vedic Astrology, and the author of *The Essentials of Vedic Astrology*, *Vedic Love Signs* and *The Lunar Nodes*. I met her in her home in Hampshire in Southern England. She was a woman in her forties dressed in a dark green sari with a red spot between her eyes. She had a small gold necklace of the elephant-headed Ganesh around her neck and a large statue of Ganesh in her sitting room – the Hindu god of astrology, obstacles and thresholds.

Born in Delhi, Komilla had been an actress for twelve years in 'Bollywood', the Indian equivalent of Hollywood based in Bombay (now Mumbai). She divided her time between India and England and travelled the world as a lecturer and consultant on Vedic astrology.

In the quiet backwater of her suburban home, wafted by incense, she explained to me how astrology was still very much part of everyday life in India and that many families had their own astrologer. People often consulted an astrologer when confronted with a problem. Many had their chart updated every year – from birthday to birthday – to see what might be in store for them.

In the villages of rural India, the astrologer had long been highly respected as a wise man. He would give advice and expect no payment, although this was changing now. The knowledge was passed down orally from generation to generation. Only recently were women becoming astrologers.

'Astrology,' Komilla went on, 'is known as the Eye of the *Vedas*. It is related to everything. You need to have knowledge of the stars and the planetary movements to understand the *Vedas*, Ayurveda, and even dance in India.'

I asked here what she thought was the main differences between Indian and Western astrology.

'The main difference is that being a Vedic astrologer is a complete vocation. I totally respect my work and do not work against my system of belief. Vedic astrology is not just a hobby or a system of interests as astrology is in the West.'

'What are its main concerns?'

'Vedic astrology is concerned firstly with defining your purpose in life and secondly with how the timing of your birth affects you and how you can fulfil your purpose in the best possible way. It has a great profoundness and responsibility.'

Usually, she observed, people came to her with a particular question. 'The fact that you came today at two o'clock is very interesting. You come as Jupiter is rising in the sky, and Jupiter is about books, knowledge and wisdom!'

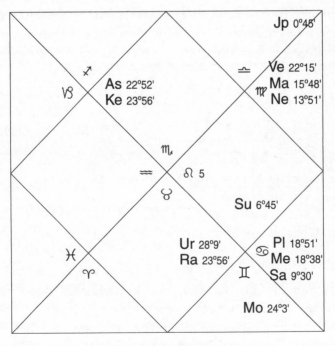

Rashi Chart
Peter Marshall
23/8/1946 Bognor Regis, England
0°41' 0''W 50°47' 0''N, Friday
Time 16h 0m 0s BST
Ayanamsha 23° 6'27'', Lahiri system

She called up my chart on a laptop in front of her. Rather than using the tropical zodiac of Western astrology, which shows the relationship of the earth to the sun, the Vedic computer program used the sidereal zodiac, which relates the planets to a backdrop of the stars. This has important implications for your sun sign and for your chart as a whole. As we have seen, because of the complex phenomenon known as the precession of the equinoxes, the equinox point in relation to the stars slowly moves backwards from East to West. The tropical and sidereal zodiacs overlapped in AD 285 but since then they have gradually grown apart. The longitudinal difference, known as *ayanamsha*, now means that according to the Lahiri system used by Komilla, the first degree of Aries in Western astrology is about 7° Pisces in Vedic astrology. Thus while Western astrologers place my date of birth of 23 August at the end of Leo, or sometimes even at the beginning of Virgo, Vedic astrologers place it firmly in Leo. Since Vedic astrology takes the precession of the equinoxes into account, its chart reflects more accurately the actual position of the planets in the sky than in Western astrology.

Glancing at her laptop, Komilla began her interpretation: 'You know, you have a very, very interesting chart. You have Scorpio rising and also an unusual situation known as a *Kal Sarpa Yoga*. The way your moon nodes are situated is extremely profound. All your planets are on one side of the nodal axis. The moon nodes Rahu and Ketu are very important in Vedic astrology and represent karma and the struggle to find our true selves. "*Kal*" means time and "*Sarpa*" means snake. It's almost as if a snake has entwined itself around you in your life. Usually a snake is a symbol of past-life memories and past-life issues.'

This sounded ominous but at least I was not alone – Nelson Mandela, Paul McCartney and Harrison Ford all have a *Kal Sarpa Yoga* in their charts!

'When you have this *yoga*', Komilla continued, 'it is a kind of block to part of your life. In your early age, half your life was empty. You must have faced rejection from an early age.'

This struck a bell. I took the rejection to be the fact that my father had left my mother when I was less than two years old and never contacted me afterwards.

'Until you found your spiritual self in your forties,' Komilla went on, 'you felt a lot of inner rejection.'

Perhaps, although I did not experience it that way. But there were some positive elements: 'With your Ascendant in Scorpio, you're a great idealist. One lucky point in your chart is that both the nodes are exalted which indicates a search for *moksha*, salvation. When you were born at 16.00 hours, Ketu was also rising above the Eastern horizon – as Jupiter is rising now – which creates a kind of mystical energy, although when you're a young person, you cannot understand it.'

That certainly was true in my case.

'Specifically,' Komilla went on, peering at my chart on her screen, 'I think the nineties was one of the most profound times in your life. This was the time of your Ketu *dasha*. It would have churned up your emotions but also enabled you to find out who you are and what you are looking for in life.'

Again this sounded right. I had separated from my wife in the early nineties and had gone through a long and difficult period of soul-searching and readjustment, during which time I had taken a more spiritual path. An off-shoot of this was my researches into alchemy and astrology.

'The chart suggests to me that relationships are important to you, but you can be too much of perfectionist. You want idealism, *moksha*, even from love!'

It seems that a big shift was underway in my life. From the year 2000 and for the following twenty years, I would be under the sway of Venus. Venus would be ruling my seventh House, which is the House of personal relationships.

'Before 2000, you could have given up everything,' Komilla suggested, 'but since then you have developed a new relationship. For the first time in your life you have found the right partner!'

It was true that from that date I had planned a new life with Elizabeth. But it would not be all sweetness and light. There were challenges ahead. My main learning curve, it seemed, would be about relationships.

Komilla went on: 'In your chart you have a Mars-Venus conjunction which takes place in the sign of Virgo. In Vedic astrology, Virgo is very idealistic – Virgo is the virgin – which suggests you want a perfect relationship. You have Rahu in the seventh House which is also a search for perfection. But there is a definite possibility of multiple partners, even now. It is a big problem for you to be committed!'

This had certainly been the case in the past, but I thought I had by now become a reformed character.

'You need a partner who understands your need to travel and be

there for you, whatever you're doing. You're a traveller by nature: you
moon *nakshatra* is *Punarvasu* (in Gemini) which means another home.
You have aspirations to travel on different levels of consciousness and
different levels of society. You like to be at home but also to go away.
If you have a very possessive partner, you'll find it difficult to handle.
You need a partner similar to you. Your whole chart says to me that
your relationships will be your greatest challenge until 2020. Sexuality
is very much part of you; your Ascendant is in Scorpio which is a sign
of sexuality. You'll have to come to terms with it. The good news is that
it will be possible for you to find happiness.'

And what would happen after 2020 when my Venus *dasha* would
end?

'After that the sun is very powerful for you at seventy-four. What
follows is good, an upward-spiralling of reaching aspirations, of
achieving what you want to achieve.'

This was long-term; the next two years would be crucial. I was
entering a period known as *sade sati*, a period when Saturn was trans-
itting over my moon. Its effect was already making itself felt and would
culminate the following July. It occurs about three times in a normal
life, about every twenty-four years.

'Usually it suggests some major change or transformation, particularly in the way you think,' Komilla explained, 'but I normally advise
my clients that it is a time not to make decisions! There is a huge
pressure to change everything suddenly. But if they do make impulsive
decisions, like giving up their job or moving house, they usually regret
it on the other side!'

'Can it be dangerous?'

'There's no need to be afraid or worried. *Sade sati* is like a
weather-warning. It's a problematic astrological situation but if you're
aware of it, it makes it easier to deal with. Just be very conscious of
your choices. Saturn is the slowest-moving planet and stands for
pressure and stress while the moon is the fastest moving-planet. When
they touch each other, the mind can get very agitated and there can be
sudden change.'

'I would have thought that a spiritually developed person would be
able to counteract the influence of the stars and remain calm in all
circumstances.'

'I don't think so. The stars influence you, you have free will, but
destiny – the result of your past karma – can intervene when you think

you're carefully planning your life. Whatever you have done in the past, you have to deal with it now, and whatever you do now will reflect on what will happen in the future. Your free will is your ability to face the transits but your destiny makes itself felt when you do something impulsive and create huge problems for yourself! For example, I'm one hundred per cent sure that next July is going to be tough for you – that's technically precise – but you can improve the situation by eighty per cent, depending on how you meet the challenge. Doing yoga or meditation can help a lot.'

'Could you explain a bit more what you mean by karma?'

'Your karma consists of the choices you made in past lives, but the moment the umbilical chord gets cut, the memory of the choices gets lost. Your karma is a set of subconscious memories of your own past actions. In Indian philosophy, karma is nothing but your own responsibility. You can't blame your mother and father or XYZ. You acted in a particular way in the past and you have to deal with it in this lifetime. Once you become aware of your karma, you can learn how to deal with it. If you deal with it with wisdom, you will have minimum pain; if you act impulsively, you'll just repeat old patterns. Only you can make the choice.'

'Can you advise people what they should do then?'

'I can give guidance but at the end of the day you must make your own choices. I can only tell you the timing and what the stars say but I don't take responsibility for giving a good prediction or not. In the end, it's your responsibility. It's just like being given a map and you can fill in the colours yourself.'

'Do you sometimes get it wrong?'

'The timing is always right but the response in not always clear. The intense planetary situation in early March 2003, for example, suggested war in the Middle East, but the situation can ignite in different ways. Instead of war breaking out, we saw peace protests throughout the world.'

Whatever the intensity of my approaching *sade sati*, Komilla insisted that I should at least not give up writing: 'With Ketu in the Ascendant, you have intuitive knowledge and when you write on your subject you can be very intuitive. Your writing can only get better.'

Having dealt with my past life, relationships and work, Komilla then turned to one of the favourite themes of Indian and all astrology: finances.

I was pleased, but not entirely convinced, to hear her say: 'Money is not a problem in your chart. You've got a lot of luck with money. You seem to have a talent for making money when it's necessary. Your chart suggests that you're good with money.'

'I'm not sure my bank would agree!'

'You may pretend you're not good with money, but you really are! You can't lie to an astrologer! Financially, it's going to be good for you.'

I finally asked Komilla what was the overall nature of my chart. Was it a good one?

'You have a chart,' she paused, trying to find the right word, 'which is very karmic.'

'Is that a polite way of saying that it indicates a lot of problems?'

'You have a lot of potential, but you haven't realized your potential yet because of your *Kal Sarpa Yoga*. At the time of your birth, your sun was in its own House in the tenth which is a very powerful position. When you were born at four o'clock, the sun was also at the Midheaven so it was really powerful. It gives you a great career. You have to be successful!'

So the prospects were good after all. I should be careful in my relationships and things were going to get intense soon, but in the long term, I shouldn't worry about my work or finances. Indeed, happiness was possible.

Towards the end of our conversation, Komilla stressed the spiritual nature of Vedic astrology. According to the *Vedas*, she explained, there is a Universal Soul (literally the 'womb of the deer' in Sanskrit) from which emerges the World Soul connected to time, which in turn gives rise to the individual soul (*atman*). Since we are connected to the World Soul and the Universal Soul, if a person decides to make a difference, he or she can make a big difference to the universe as a whole.

'When does the soul enter the body?' I asked her. 'Some say it is at the time of conception.'

'Certainly some people in India consult astrologers to decide on the right moment for conception but I believe the soul enters the body with the first breath and first cry. Before birth a soul may enter the womb, but it may not stay, as in the case of an abortion. Each soul is responsible for choosing its own body.'

I still had some outstanding questions about Indian astrology. I asked whether she thought astrology was an art or a science.

'It's a science,' Komilla insisted. 'It's so technical and precise. I can know where the planets are going to be in a hundred years or in 10,000 years. But there's always an art in analyzing the situation. It's like weather prediction.'

'An inexact science?'

'Yes. The knowledge is perfect, but the interpretation is inexact. At the end of the day, an astrologer's life should be perfect, with a calm mind and totally detached, but we all have human errors.'

'Can you tell me when I will die?'

'I don't want to see it and let you know. It's like playing with God. In India, though, people will give you ten different dates!'

'How do you think the planets influence us? Is it through some kind of magnetism or stellar rays as some astrologers say?'

'I think there is magnetism there. The moon influences the earth every day; it influences animals and the tides. It's one of those things you can't understand. You can't quantify it, but I have no doubt that the influence is there. I come from a tradition which just accepts it. I have seen it in action, again and again, absolutely precise to the minute, like switching on or switching off a light.'

'Can you give me an example?'

'Last week there was an opposition which made life difficult. I could watch the process. You know the timing; you know it will finish on Saturday. Everyone feels it but only if you know astrology do you know what's actually happening.'

'And is the same is true for world events?'

'Yes. When you get a Mars-Saturn conjunction, you get fires in America or earthquakes in China. You can predict it fifty or a hundred years in advance.'

I returned to my original reason for travelling hundred of miles to see Komilla and asked her: 'How can Indian astrology help you understand yourself?'

'Astrology helps you understand the influences you bring from previous lives crystallized in the chart.'

'Is the chart a map of the psyche, as some astrologers have called it?'

'Yes. The map of your life shows your restrictions.'

'And possibilities . . .?'

'Each chart shows the negatives and positives of each soul. But the possibilities are infinite. That is the Kundalini, the latent power within you which sleeps like a coiled snake. If you understand your own power, you can go in a different direction. You can go against the grain like a snake spiralling upwards out of its coil!'

Part Three

Mysteries of the Desert:
Mesopotamia and Egypt

18

By the Waters of Babylon

All mankind rejoice in you, Shamash, all the world longs for
your light . . .

HYMN OF NINEVEH

L OOKING ACROSS THE lone and barren deserts of Iraq, between the
Tigris and the Euphrates, immense weathered mounds rise against
the deep blue skyline. They are all that remains of the magnificent cities,
temples and palaces of several great civilizations which flourished in
Mesopotamia in a green and fertile land, watered by a complex system
of irrigation. Around 6,000 years ago, their peoples began building the
splendid cities of Ur, Uruk, Babylon and others. In their stellar religion
lie the origins of Western astrology.

It is only recently that we have begun to appreciate the glories of the
ancient civilizations of Mesopotamia and much more no doubt lies
buried below the sands of Iraq. In 1835, on a sheer cliff face in the
mountains of Behistun in Persia (present day Iran), an English diplomat
called Henry Crewicke Rawlinson discovered a huge inscription carved
in three unknown languages. The script used was carved into a carefully
prepared surface in triangular-shaped characters, now called cuneiform,
from the Latin *cuneus*, meaning wedge. It was the Mesopotamian
equivalent of the Rosetta Stone, the key to deciphering the Egyptian
hieroglyphs. Rawlinson learned that the scripts were written in Persian,
Elamite and Akkadian and that they had been carved by order of the
Persian King Darius who reigned in the fifth century BC.

Seven years after Rawlinson's discovery, the French Consul, Paul-
Emile Bota, began digging into a huge mound at Mosul, on the other
side of the Tigris river. It is now known that he had discovered Nineveh,

the ancient capital of Assyria. In the scramble for antiquities which followed, the lion's share went to the British Museum, which now holds more than 130,000 cuneiform tablets. Some 2,500 tablets and fragments from Nineveh in the Kuyunjik collection are of astrological interest.

Mesopotamia, the region between the lower and middle regions of the Tigris and Euphrates, was, in fact, the site of even earlier cults. At Jarmo, in the foothills of the Zagros mountains on the border of Iraq and Iran, remains have been found which have been carbon-dated to around 6750 BC. They show that the neolithic community had a well-developed religion with small clay statuettes of pregnant women in large numbers. These fertility goddesses may well have been associated with the planet Venus or the moon.

The first great civilization of Mesopotamia was Sumer. Its empire was established in the fourth millennium BC and reached its peak 1,000 years later. Excavations at the Sumerian city of Eridu have revealed that beneath a stepped pyramid, known as a ziggurat, which dates from 2100 BC, lie the remains of seventeen earlier temples, all built one on top of another. Some of the stepped temples reached a height of 300 feet. From their summit, they would have given a superb view of the night sky. Made of mud brick, they have now crumbled away, but the beliefs that inspired them live on in a disguised form in modern astrology.

Where the first Sumerian civilization came from remains a deep mystery. Since it suddenly developed a complex religion, monumental architecture and an intricate form of writing, many commentators have suggested that the founders came from a foreign land which had been overwhelmed by some catastrophe.[1] The Sumerians themselves recorded that they came from the island of Dilmun, where dwelt the descendants of the kings who lived 'before the flood'.[2] *The Epic of Gilgamesh*, which dates from the third millennium BC, gives a remarkable description of a flood which may well have inspired the Old Testament account. Clearly echoing the story of Noah, Utnapishtim 'the Faraway' tells Gilgamesh that the gods sent the flood to wipe out mankind, but he was able to escape with his family in a boat which came to rest on a mountain top. 'For six days and six nights the winds blew, torrent and tempest and flood overwhelmed the world, tempest and flood raged together like warring hosts. When the seventh day dawned the storm from the south subsided, the sea grew calm, the flood was stilled; I looked at the face of the world and there was silence, all mankind was turned to clay.'[3]

The invasion of central Mesopotamia by a Semitic people, probably from Arabia, saw the rise of the Akkadian civilization, which lasted from 2360 to 2180 BC. Although they spoke a different tongue, they continued to use the Sumerian script. This was followed by the rise of Babylonia in Southern Mesopotamia, whose great empire lasted from 2200 to 538 BC, when it was conquered by the Persians led by king Cyrus.

Around 3,000 years ago, the Empire of Assyria also developed in northern Mesopotamia. It reached its peak around 700 BC when it stretched from Egypt to the Persian Gulf. Its greatest city was Nineveh. Its people adopted the Semitic dialect of Akkadia and continued to write in Sumerian script. In 612 BC it was destroyed by the second Babylonian empire, whose most notorious emperor was Nebuchadnezzar. According to the Book of Daniel, dating from around 150 BC, the prophet Daniel served as an astrologer under Nebuchadnezzar as well as the Persian conqueror Cyrus. The region gradually went into decline after Alexander the Great finally seized Babylon in 331 BC.

Over 4,000 years, each of these great civilizations contributed to the growth of astrology. Modern Western astrology finds its roots in a blend of Mesopotamian, Egyptian and Greek culture.

Ancient Texts and Cosmology

The Western legacy from Mesopotamia is enormous. The Babylonian 'sexagesimal' mathematical system gave rise to the twelve-hour day, although this was later replaced by the Egyptian twenty-four-hour day. We still divide our hours and minutes into units of sixty because the Mesopotamians did. We have inherited the concept of the 'Great Year' lasting 432,000 years from Assyrian times, a concept which is behind the coming 'Age of Aquarius'.

Thanks to the Mesopotamians, we have the stories of Abraham and Sarah, of Isaac and Rebecca, of Nimrod the hunter, of the tower of Babel and the Book of Daniel. The equal-armed cross was probably a symbol of the Mesopotamian sun god, Shamash. Even the creation story, as well as the great flood in the Old Testament, find echoes in Mesopotamian literature, which predates the Hebrew scribes by a thousand years. The opening chapters of Genesis recall directly the

Sumerian account in a poem of seven tablets called *Enuma Elish* ('When on high . . .), a collection of earlier texts compiled around the turn of the second millennium BC. There are other hints of Biblical inspiration. The ancient Sumerian word for the open pasture land of lower Mesopotamia was Eden. And then there are the intriguing statuettes found in the area of Lake Van of a woman and snake looking at each other, forming one body in the shape of a crescent moon. Could they represent the temptation of Eve?[4]

The world's oldest known astrological text *Enuma Anu Enlil* was discovered, at Nineveh, in the famous library of the royal palace of King Ashurbanipal, who ruled from 668 BC. Now kept in a drawer in the British Museum, it consists of a thick clay tablet, rounded at the sides, with perfectly preserved cuneiform script. It is a copy of a much earlier compilation of omens drawn from the movements of Venus which were first written during the reign of the Babylonian King Ammisaduqa who ruled from 1646 to 1626 BC. The 'Venus Tablet', as it is called, demonstrates that astrology was already a well-developed system and discipline by the first dynasty of Babylon. One entry records: 'In month XI, fifteenth day, Venus disappeared in the West. Three days it stayed away, then on the eighteenth day it became visible in the East. Springs will open and Adad will bring his rain and Ea his floods. Messages of reconciliation will be sent from King to King.'[5] The tablet also contains the first recorded systematic observations of planetary movements.

An even earlier fragmentary text, dating from the time of King Sargon of Akkad who ruled from 2334 to 2279 BC, has been found. It tantalizingly states: 'When the planet Venus . . . an omen of Sargon, of the King and of the four quarters. . .When the planet Venus . . . so it is an omen of Sargon . . .'[6] Clearly Venus was considered the most prominent planet at this time.

The entire astrological series of the *Enuma Anu Enlil* is estimated to have contained some 7,000 omens. Individual tablets existed for the sun, moon, Mars, Jupiter, Venus, Mercury and Saturn. It clearly had a widespread circulation for traces of the work have been found as far afield as eastern Turkey.

The astrology of the *Enuma Anu Enlil* is still rather rudimentary. The constellations are employed as reference points from which the daily movement of the moon and planets could be charted. Although the twelve constellations which came to form the zodiac straddling the ecliptic are used, the zodiac itself does not yet seem to have been fixed.

While planets are seen in conjunction or in opposition, described simply as being close or far apart, aspects between the planets are not mentioned. The work is entirely concerned with mundane astrology – the destiny of the body politic. There is no mention of the Ascendant which came to be so central to astrology in classical and modern times.

Early Mesopotamian cosmology was fundamentally the same as in Genesis 1:6–10. The universe is described as being contained between two sheets of water, below and above the earth. The water above the earth is supported by a great dome across which the planets and stars travel in their daily and annual voyages.

The name *Enuma Anu Enlil* comes from the opening line, 'When the Gods Anu and Enlil . . .'. Anu was the god of heaven, and Enlil, the god of earth. They were considered to be of equal importance and two interrelated parts of one realm. Omens, messages from the gods, could just as easily be drawn from events upon the earth as those in the heavens. Indeed, there was a long tradition in Mesopotamia of reading omens from the entrails of sacrificed animals. As one manual for diviners and astrologers puts it: 'The signs in the sky, just as those on the earth, give us signals.'

The Mesopotamians believed that humans were partly divine, born of the same substance as the gods, but their principal task was to serve the gods. The sky at night, with its stars and planets, was seen as the *Shitir Shame* – the 'book of heaven' – containing the commands of the gods.

As we have seen, the earliest kind of religion in Mesopotamia probably involved the worship of fertility gods and goddesses. By the turn of the second millennium BC, the gods were not only worshipped but were also being asked to intervene in terrestrial events. It was not long before the idea of a personal god evolved: the first text expressing such an idea dates from 2600 BC. No doubt this notion was a prerequisite of astrology since the astrologers tried to change the course of things to come as forecast by the omens they saw in the sky.

Unlike the Israelites who saw history in linear terms as moving towards a goal, the Mesopotamians saw history as moving in endless cycles over vast spans of time. The past and the future continuously flowed into the present. There was no end to history, only endless repetition. Likewise, good and evil ebbed and flowed together. As a result, it is not surprising that they thought that humans could negotiate with the gods about the direction of the future. Fate (*shimtu*) was not therefore fixed or predetermined. The omens were simply signs or warnings of what was possible; they were not inescapable certainties.

It was possible, for instance, to divert the evil which was about to happen through rituals known as *namburbi*. Such a ritual involved finding a special site, purifying oneself, offering food and drink to the gods, praying and then finally symbolically 'undoing' the threatened evil by unravelling a plant, or smashing a small pot. Not only was this magical principle of sympathetic action one of the foundations of astrology, but such rituals were undoubtedly used to counter negative astrological predictions.

Observers of the Light

According to the Sumerian story of creation, in the beginning was the primeval sea from which was born the cosmic mountain which consisted of heaven (Anu) and the earth (Enlil). At this stage, the world was still in darkness and the sky was without stars, so Enlil begot the moon (Sin) who sailed in a boat bringing light to the lapus lazili (heavens). The moon in turn begot the sun (Shamash) and Venus (Ishtar).

Just as ancient Indian astrology was called *Jyotish,* the Lord of Light, so light was central to the Mesopotamian religion. The sun above all symbolized the divine light. In the great Mesopotamian epic, Gilgamesh says to the sun god, Shamash: 'Let mine eyes see the sun that I may be sated with light. Banished afar is the darkness, if the light is sufficient. May he who has died the death see the light of the sun.'[7]

The hymns from Nineveh further describe his qualities: 'All mankind rejoice in you, O Shamash, all the world long for your light.'[8] The god is all-knowing and just. He determines the decisions of heaven and earth. It is a view which has held sway for millennia in the Middle East: the sun is still called *shams* in Arabic.

The Semitic Akkadians considered the moon and Venus to be male, and the sun as male, but the other Mesopotamian civilizations gave them the same genders as in the West today. Ishtar is a lovely goddess who dwells in the planet Venus. A hymn from about 1600 BC declares: 'Reverence the queen of women, the greatest of all the gods; she is clothed with delight and with love, she is full of ardour, enchantment, and voluptuous joy, in her lips she is sweet, in her mouth is Life, when she is present felicity is greatest; how glorious she looks, the veils thrown over her head, her lovely form, her brilliant eyes."[9] However, as a queen of heaven, she is also the goddess of war and sorrow. Like the Indian goddess Kali, she is worshipped as well as feared.

It was the role of the astrologers and diviners, who formed a fraternity and were known as *tupsharru* (scribes), to interpret the celestial omens. It would seem that by the end of the second millennium BC the Mesopotamian astrologers had discovered the long-term movements of the sun, moon, planets and the stars. They plotted the planets against the fixed stars or constellations. They also measured stellar distance by 'fingers' or 'cubits'.[10] Time was measured by an *Abkallu shikla*, probably some kind of water clock. Astrolabes were slowly improved.

Ancient Telescopes

Although it is often assumed that the skies of the Middle East are always crystal clear, in reality the observation of the stars and planets was not always easy. Not only were the night skies sometimes obscured by clouds and dust storms, but the natural limitations of the naked eye made distant stars appear dim. However, despite the common assumption that Galileo was the first to develop a telescope, it is just possible that Mesopotamian astrologers used lenses to see the stars and planets.

In 1849 the diplomat Austen Henry Layard made an extraordinary find in the throne room of the North-West Palace of the ancient Assyrian capital of Kalhu (more commonly called Nimrud). Beneath a heap of fragments of beautiful opaque glass he discovered 'a rock-crystal lens, with opposite and plane faces'. It had the name Sargon on it, with his title King of Assyria in cuneiform characters and a figure of a lion. Layard asserted: 'Its properties could scarcely have been unknown to the Assyrians, and we have consequently the earliest specimen of a magnifying and burning glass.'

The lens is now in the British Museum, classified as object number 12091 in the Department of Western Asiatic Antiquities. Layard mistakenly thought he had discovered it in Nineveh and the lens is sometimes called the Nineveh lens. Its shape is that of a plano-convex lens, that is to say, it is flat on one side and bulging outwards on the other. It was not an unusual shape, for plano-convex bricks had long been used in the construction of fortifications in Mesopotamia. It measures 6.2cm long, 3.43cm wide, with a maximum thickness of

6.2mm. It would seem that it was made for Sargon II who ruled from 722 to 705 BC.

Although now deteriorated, the lens was clearly carefully polished. Robert Temple, who has made a careful study of it, observes: 'In its original condition it would have been perfectly clear and transparent with no flaws. It was made from a highly superior piece of quartz, evidently selected in the hope that it contained no "ghostly flawing", and finally polished when this was confirmed, after cutting.' He concludes that it was not really effective as a burning lens, but could have been used as a magnifying lens (from a certain position it has magnification of 2X) to correct for astigmatism. It could well have been a mounted monocle for King Sargon or his scribe.[12]

If the ancient Assyrian astronomers knew how to select and cut such lenses, it is not impossible that they made crystal lenses to magnify the celestial bodies in the night sky. It is becoming increasingly clear that the ancients were far more technically advanced than most historians are willing to admit. It is still an unresolved question whether the ancient Chinese and the Greeks observed the Galilean moons of Jupiter and the rings of Saturn. If they did, and there is some evidence to suggest that they were able to, it would not have been possible without the help of some form of telescope.[13]

The Constellations and the Zodiac

The sum of astronomical knowledge in Mesopotamia was contained in a two-tablet compilation known as *mul.Apin* which was found in the library of Ashurbanipal at Nineveh. The name means Plough Star and refers to the constellation Triangulum, which lies between Aries and Andromeda. The astronomical knowledge dated from 1000 BC although the earliest copy of the work dates from 687 BC. It is said to be the first known star catalogue.[14] From the same period, Assyrian and Babylonian astrologers began keeping 'diaries' of celestial and political events, such as battles, deaths and treaties.

Based on centuries of careful observations, the *mul.Apin* contains a list of fixed stars divided into those of the paths of Ea, Anu and Enlil (the gods of water, heaven and earth), the dates when the thirty-six fixed stars and constellations rise in the morning, the planetary periods, the seasons, equinoxes and solstices, tables of the period of the moon's visibility, rules for intercalation, gnomon tables detailing the shadow lengths of the sun, as well as weights of water for their clocks.

Eighteen constellations along the 'path of the moon' are mentioned in the *mul.Apin* which contain most of the signs of the modern zodiac: the Bull of Heaven (Taurus), the Lion (Leo), the Balance (Libra), the Scorpion (Scorpio), the Goat-fish (Capricorn) and the Tails (Pisces), the Furrow (Virgo), the Hireling (Aries) and the Great Twins (Gemini). The figure of Sagittarius (called PA.BIL.SAG) is uncertain. Aquarius (known as GU.LA) was probably a giant. While nine of the signs of the zodiac would seem to have a definite Babylonian origin, the evidence for Aquarius and Gemini is less convincing, although the Great Twins may well be based on the friends Enkidu and Gilgamesh who appear in the great early Sumerian epic. The most striking absence is the Ram for Aries which may have come from Egypt after the invasion lead by the Babylonian King Esarhaddon in the seventh century BC.[15]

The astrological content of the *mul.Apin* extends to some omens drawn from comets and fixed stars. Of particular interest is a list of all the stars in eighteen constellations in the 'path of the moon' as it moves through the sky. The 'moon's path' is a zodiacal belt 12° wide within which the sun, moon and planets all move. It seems that the number of constellations gradually fell to twelve – the same twelve which eventually became the twelve signs of the zodiac.[16] And it was not long before the notion of the ecliptic – the centre of the belt – was formulated to mark the apparent path of the sun.

How did these astrologers apply their increasingly sophisticated knowledge? Their reports to the kings conveyed information about observations of the celestial bodies as well as interpretations of their import. For instance, one message sent to King Esarhaddon in 699 BC states: 'When the planet Mars comes out from the constellation of Scorpio, turns and re-enters Scorpio, its interpretation is thus . . . do not neglect your guard; the king should not go outdoors on an evil day.'

Again, on 30 July 666 BC, the astrologer Akkullanu wrote to King Ashurbanipal: 'If the planet Jupiter is present in the eclipse, all is well with the king, a noble dignitary will die in his stead.' Did the king pay attention to this? A full month had not yet passed before his chief judge was dead.'[17] However, these messages demonstrate that astrology was still fundamentally mundane and was only concerned with the king, not as an individual, but as an embodiment of the nation. From 652 BC, the court astrologers recorded monthly summaries of planetary movements, known as 'diaries', for the kings.

From Mundane to Natal Astrology

It was the invasion of the Persians in 539 BC which finally triggered the invention of the regular zodiac and the birthchart. They also introduced more advanced mathematics into astrology. Among other things, the Persian leader Cyrus freed the Jewish exiles who had been brought to Babylon as captives by Nebuchadnezzar forty-seven years earlier – an act which earned the tyrant and his city a notorious reputation in the Old Testament.

Under Persian rule, the theory of astrology became more systematic and the practice more disciplined. The calendar was refined. The extra 'intercalary' month, added to the twelve lunar months of the year to bring it in line with the seasons, was applied on a regular rather than an arbitrary basis. This showed a greater understanding of celestial cycles. The 'synodic' period of the planets was also discovered, that is, the period between consecutive conjunctions of a planet with the sun as seen from the earth. The 'sidereal' period too was understood, that is, the length of time taken by a planet to pass through the twelve signs of the zodiac and return to its starting point.[18] This enabled the astrologers to formulate the larger planetary periods which formed the basis for predictions. The period for Saturn, for instance, was fifty-nine years. It was made up of two sidereal periods (each twenty-nine and a half years) or fifty-seven synodic periods.

During the period of Persian rule, the planets were placed in the twelve signs of the zodiac rather than the zodiacal constellations. This made it easier to calculate the future movements of the sun, as there are clearly no fixed stars visible during the day against which to track its path.

The signs of the zodiac were also divided mathematically into equal lengths. Their names were derived from the names of the actual zodiacal constellations. Initially this led to some confusion as to whether it was the constellations or signs that were actually being referred to. The first known mention of the signs of the zodiac comes in a Babylonian moon text which dates from 475 BC.[19] We can therefore confidently say that the signs of the zodiac were firmly established 2,500 years ago. The first known use of zodiacal degrees in a horoscope dates from 263 BC.[20]

Finally, this period brought a major shift from mundane astrology to natal astrology, from predicting the fate of the nation to the charting of an individual life. The move to natal astrology may have been encouraged by the introduction of the Persian religion of Zoroastrianism with its concept of an individual immortal soul that can choose between good and evil. Among the Zoroastrian esoteric mysteries was the doctrine of the harmony of the spheres – a doctrine which certainly inspired Pythagoras and Plato after him.

The first known birthchart from Babylon dates from 410 BC, probably 29 April. It states that an individual was born at that date and describes the signs within which the moon and the planets were to be found: 'At that time the moon was below the horn of Scorpio, Jupiter in Pisces, Venus in Taurus, Saturn in Cancer, Mars in Gemini. Mercury, which had set [for the last time], was [still] in[visible].'[21]

A later chart from Uruk, probably dating from 4 April 263 BC during the period of Greek domination, further gives the degrees of the sign within which the planets were placed: 'Year 48 of the Seleucid Era, month Adar, the child was born. That day the sun was 13° 30' Aries, the moon in 10° Aquarius, Jupiter at the beginning of Leo, Venus with the sun, Mercury with the sun, Saturn in Cancer, Mars at the end of Cancer.' This fascinating text further makes certain predictions based on the position of the planets: 'He will be lacking in wealth . . . His food will not suffice for his hunger. The wealth which he had in his youth will not remain. The thirty-sixth year he will have wealth. His days will be long in number.'[22] The document already shows the concern with riches and longevity which was to become a dominant theme in Western astrology.

After the defeat of the Persian army by Alexander the Great in 331 BC, thousands of Greeks settled in Babylon and came under the influence of the local astrologers who were known as 'Chaldeans' (originally referring to the people of the last dynasty in Babylon before the conquest of Cyrus of Persia). Two astrologers residing in Babylon were mentioned later by the Greeks as Cidenas (Kidinnu) and Naburianos (Nab-rimannu). Other schools flourished in Uruk and Borsippa. A great number of astrological 'diaries' exist from the period after the conquest of Mesopotamia as well as text ephemerides (the oldest dates from 307 BC).[23] The Greek concern with the individual is reflected by the growing number of horoscopes from the period.

The last known horoscope written in Sumerian cuneiform script dates from 68 BC. The first known Greek horoscope dates from 61 BC.

The latter was to commemorate the coronation of the Mesopotamian Greek ruler Antiochus I of Commagene and was carved on the cliff face at the summit of Nimrud Dagh.

A tablet found at Uruk, attributed to the Seleucid period, resembles a modern astrological 'cook book' and lists predictions for a systematic combination of planets. One suggests: 'If a child is born when Jupiter comes forth and Venus has set, it will go excellently with that man; his wife will leave.' Obviously, the interpretation is from the man's point of view and shows a preoccupation with his marriage. Another interpretation states: 'If a child is born when Venus comes forth and Jupiter has set, his wife will be stronger than he.'[24] But while the text deals with oppositions, it does not consider other aspects between the planets such as conjunctions, trines, squares or sextiles. There is also no mention of the Ascendant.

The first known example of the Ascendant used in a birthchart comes in 4 BC, just after the Saturn-Jupiter conjunction of 7 BC which probably coincided with the birth of Christ.[25]

Over a span of 4,000 years, astrology in Mesopotamia had clearly come a long way. At first, it had been entirely directed towards mundane astrology. Omens in the sky pointed to the 'fate' of the nation. Since the king was considered to have his mandate from heaven, the movement of celestial bodies, particularly the eclipses, had a direct bearing on him and the nation he embodied. But while the future was in the lap of the gods, it was not predestined or 'fated'. It could be changed – negotiated – by certain rituals and ceremonies.

It was also the role of court astrologers to observe the phases of the waxing and waning moon to establish a calendar for rituals and ceremonies, as well as for the timing of the sowing and harvesting of the agricultural year. The appearance of the new moon was an essential 'peg' for the lunar calendar.

After the Persian conquest, the twelve signs of the zodiac were finally established and the birthchart introduced. With the spread of Hellenistic culture from Greece, the birthchart gained in importance and astrology itself became more secular and democratic. Astrologers were no longer priests with courtly functions, but philosophers who tried to understand the structure of the universe and to interpret the effect of the heavens on the lives of individuals on earth.

19

Let There Be Light

*Darkness was upon the face of the deep. And the Spirit of God moved upon the face of the waters. And God said,
'Let there be light.'*

GENESIS

BABYLON WAS MORE or less a square city in plan and at its centre was the temple of Marduk, called Esagila. The most conspicuous feature in the city was the temple, a square tower of seven diminishing storeys. It symbolized the Sacred Mountain, the dwelling place of the gods. It formed a cosmic axis, a vertical bond between heaven and earth, and a horizontal bond between the lands of the Babylonian Empire. Its seven levels represented the planes of existence, the stages of enlightenment and the seven planets.[1]

The Sumerians had a complex mythology centred on the planets which they worshipped as the dwellings of the gods. When the Semitic Akkadian people from Southern Arabia invaded Mesopotamia around 3000 BC, they placed at the head of the Sumerian pantheon of gods their trinity of Sin (the moon), Shamash (the sun) and Ishtar (Venus). In keeping with their stellar religion, celestial symbols were carved above the heads of many statues of the kings: the crescent for Sin, the equal-armed cross for Shamash, and the eight-pointed star for Ishtar.

The moon

Reflecting the ancient belief expressed in Genesis that light emerged from darkness, the male moon god (Nanna for the Sumerians and Sin for the Akkadians) begot the divine twins: the sun and Venus. The moon – 'old blue beard' – was the most important of all the celestial bodies, the king of the gods. As the ruler of time, he directed the course of events on earth. The exact symbolism of the moon varied over time, but by the reign of Ashurbanipal in the seventh century BC, he was revered for the depth of his wisdom. He was called 'Father, the source of all things' and 'Lord who determines the destiny of Heaven and Earth'.[2] Only later did the moon become a mother goddess, probably under the influence of the Egyptians who revered her as Isis, and the Greeks who worshipped her as Selene.

Of the sixty-eight or seventy tablets of the astrological series *Enuma Anu Enlil*, the first twenty-two are dedicated to lunar omens. Their interpretations were not always consistent. With the calendar based on the rhythm of the moon, a 'correct' day was usually considered to be the first, seventh, fourteenth or twenty-eighth of the lunar month. The fourfold division of the lunar month gave rise to a system of sacred days, each coming at the end of a week of seven days, with an additional one on the nineteenth. The fourteenth day was considered the most important – the time of the full moon – when much rejoicing, worship and prayer took place. Its name was *Shabbatu*; from this derived the Hebrew word *Shabbat* and the English word Sabbath. The Sabbath eventually began as the four quarter-days of the moon, and from King Hammurabi's reign (1728–1686 BC) all work was forbidden on the seventh, fourteenth, twenty-first and twenty-eighth days of the lunar month. The week and month began on the evening of the appearance of the sickle moon.

The name for Mount Sinai, where the Golden Calf was worshipped and where Moses received the stone tablets of the law from an angry male god, also probably comes from the name of the Mesopotamian moon god Sin.

If the sun and the moon, who ordered the course of agriculture and fertility, were seen together on a correct day, then the effect was considered by the court astrologers to be beneficial. It was held that they met at the beginning of each year in order to determine the fates of the dwellers on earth. The appearance of the new moon on the fourteenth of the month was a sign of harmony in heaven which augured harmony on earth. On the other hand, 'When the moon appears out of its expected time, the market will be low . . . a strong enemy will overcome the land.'[3] The 'halo' of the moon was also considered important. Reversing the modern interpretation, if Saturn fell within it, then peace would come to the kingdom; if Jupiter, the opposite would occur. The appearance of Cancer in the halo would portend evil. Symbolic meaning was also attributed to the moon's colour and elevation, brightness or dimness, and to the direction of its horns.

As with many ancient peoples, the most threatening event in Mesopotamian astrology was undoubtedly an eclipse, whether solar or lunar. Almost forty per cent of the *Enuma Anu Enlil* series was devoted to them. Eclipses were thought to bring harm to the earth, making pregnant women miscarry, the land go to ruin and the king die. The tradition still holds in modern astrology. Only on a few days in the year would an eclipse not bring a catastrophe: a 'red' eclipse (when the sunlight from the earth's atmosphere is reflected on to the moon) would bring prosperity for all the people.

The sun

While the moon god Sin was the father of time, Shamash, the sun god, was the judge of heaven and earth. Originally the sun god was female, but after the invasion of the Akkadians, it became male. He ruled over the living and the dead; his titles included 'determiner of fates' and 'architect of the cosmic designs'.[4] Although the kings identified with the sun, there are only a small number of references to the luminary in published reports, which suggests that it played a minor role in Mesopotamian mythology. Indeed, it is sometimes confused in the texts with Saturn: the historian Diodorus of Sicily observed that for the Babylonians Saturn was 'the star of the sun'.[5]

As the 'sun of the people', the king was particularly fearful of a solar eclipse. The usual *namburbi* rituals were not considered strong enough to countervail its evil influence and it seems that a 'substitute' king was chosen during the event who was ritually sacrificed with his proxy queen after one hundred days. His throne would be burnt when he 'went to his fate'. To complete the purification of the land, six paired wooden statues would be buried at strategic points in the royal palace, with the words carved on the left hip of each: 'Depart, evil. Enter, good.'[6]

Venus

Of the Mesopotamian trinity, Ishtar (Venus) is the most well-known. Her ancestry is intricate and her cult complex, changing like her sex over the millennia. The Sumerians originally considered Venus female and called her Inanna – from which comes the name Jenny. The invading Akkadians on the other hand associated Venus with their male god Attar, whose name eventually became Ishtar. For a while, the planet was considered both male and female: a tablet dating from the reign of Ashurbanipal declares that Ishtar the 'morning star' is male and Ishtar the 'evening star' is female.[7] Only later was she seen as solely female.

Ishtar became the queen of heaven and, like modern-day Venus, the goddess of love, sexuality and childbirth. At the same time, she was the feared goddess of war and sorrow. Solomon in the Old Testament was condemned for celebrating her dual aspect in the Song of Songs (6:10):

> Who is this arising like the dawn
> fair as the moon,
> resplendent as the sun,
> terrible as an army with banners.

The common emblem of Ishtar in Assyria was the eight-pointed star. It may not be too fanciful to trace the symbolism of medieval eight-sided churches built by the Knights Templar to the ancient Ishtar cult. These churches were sometimes dedicated to Mary as the Black Virgin, who could have been a reincarnation of the Mesopotamian deity.[8]

The temples dedicated to Ishtar were tended by a hierarchy of priestesses. The High Priestess was often the daughter of the king. The priestesses had their own farmland. Some would also operate as temple 'prostitutes', both on a sacred and commercial basis. It would seem that Babylonian women would grant sexual favours as a way of demonstrating their devotion to Ishtar. The Greek historian Herodotus observed:

> The most disgraceful Babylonian custom is that at some point of her life every woman of the land is required to sit in a sanctuary of Aphrodite [Venus] and have sex with a strange man. It is not unknown for women who are snobbish because of their wealth, and who refuse to associate with the rest of the women there, to drive to the sanctuary in covered carts and stand there surrounded by a large retinue of attendants. The usual practice, however, is for a number of women to sit in the precinct of Aphrodite wearing a garland made of string on their heads . . . [She] is not allowed to return home until one of the strangers has thrown money into her lap and had sex with her (which happens outside the sanctuary).[9]

Rather than describing a sacred obligation for all women, Herodotus was probably referring to the life of the temple priestesses.

As for the omens drawn from the movements of the planet Venus, there are only about twenty surviving reports from the astrologers to the Assyrian kings. Since Ishtar was responsible for fertility, it is not surprising to learn that: 'If the goat-star [Venus] approaches Cancer, there will be peace and reconciliation in the country, and the gods will have mercy on the country. Empty storage bins will become full, the crops of the country will recover, the pregnant women will perfect their embryos, and the great gods will keep the sanctuaries of the country in order.'[10]

Ishtar's warlike nature is revealed in the prediction that if Venus enters the constellation of Libra, disastrous conflict will follow. Again, if Mars is in conjunction with Venus, then the king should beware: 'If, when Venus rises, Mars is seen near it, then the king's son will enter the palace and take the throne.'[11] At the same time, the presence of Venus and Jupiter in conjunction with a lunar eclipse will countervail its evil effects for the king.

While the Greeks and Romans emphasized the feminine aspect of Venus as the ruler over women, its traditional Mesopotamian qualities have filtered down the ages. Warfare is still placed under the rulership of Libra which is, in modern astrology, governed by Venus. Its association with a good harvest anticipates the modern attribution of commercial success of a nation under the rule of Venus.

Saturn

Saturn has traditionally been feared by astrologers as a symbol of repressive restrictions, a harbinger of trouble for the land and of difficult times for the individual. He is considered cold, dry and melancholic. The ancient Mesopotamians saw him in a very different light. For them, he was a conquering hero who had emerged from the primeval waters and had fought on behalf of the gods against the powers of chaos. It was Saturn who recovered the 'tablets of fate' on which the gods had written the eternal laws. These tablets had been stolen by Zu, the dragon of storms, from Enlil, the god of the earth, when he was asleep. As a result, the gods awarded Saturn the custody of the tablets and he thus became the master of destiny (*shimtu*).

In the ancient texts the sun and Saturn were often both referred to as Shamash and there is some confusion between the two. Diodorus, around 56 BC, described the planet Saturn as 'the most conspicuous' which the Babylonians called 'the star of Helius' (the sun).[12]

When the planet Saturn is called Sagush, he is associated with the god Ninurta, also known as Ninib. As a warrior god, he is brother to Mars (Nergal). Both are sometimes considered solar deities and depicted with a sun disc. Ninurta is usually represented as an eagle, often standing on a pillar and sometimes with two heads facing in opposite directions. Ninurta may well have been the sun god Sakkut (translated as Moloch in the Bible) who is attacked in the Book of Amos.[13]

The first known description of Saturn is found in the *Enuma elish,* the Babylonian creation story dating from around 1800 BC. It is called the 'star of law and order' – a view which is still held by modern astrologers who see it as a symbol of structure and limitation. Only a few reports from astrologers to the kings mention Ninurta. Three, however, stress that when a conjunction occurs between Saturn and the moon, it is a time of truth and justice: 'When a halo surrounds the moon and Saturn stands within it, they will speak truth in the land: the son will speak the truth with his father. Welfare of multitudes.'[14] Again, when Saturn stands with the moon, it is lucky for the king (who, like Saturn, is associated with the sun) and the foundation of the throne will be secure. On the other hand, if Saturn conjuncts with Mars, famine will result; while Saturn in Leo can bring three years of disruption by roaming lions and jackals.

Unlike the later gloomy interpretations by Greek and Roman astrologers, the majority of the Mesopotamian reports imply that Saturn was considered a benevolent planet, a bringer of stability and justice to the land. This positive aspect of Saturn has been recovered in recent times by astrologers influenced by Jungian depth psychology, who recognize that structure and limitation are sometimes necessary for personal growth.

Mars

As we have seen, the ancient Mesopotamian astrologers identified Mars with the god Nergal as the brother of Saturn-Ninurta. But while both were considered as solar deities, Nergal was thought to be malefic and Ninurta good. He was not only lord of the dead but of the fires of hell and the heat of summer.

In one of the earliest Sumerian myths, Nergal was present when the gods in heaven invited Ereshkigal, goddess of the underworld, to a meeting. They knew she would not come herself but send an envoy. When the envoy arrived in heaven, all the gods except Nergal got up to welcome him. The insulted Ereshkigal was beside herself with rage and demanded his life. It was eventually agreed that Nergal should descend into the underworld with fourteen companions. On his arrival, he placed them at the doors of her palace and then rushed in. He came across the envoy and killed him on the spot. He then found Ereshkigal in her throne room, seized her by the hair, and was about to cut off her head when she pleaded for her life. 'If you let me go,' she said with tears pouring down her face, 'I'll become your wife.' Moved by compassion and by her beauty, Nergal relented and they married soon after. Henceforth, they ruled over the underworld together and Nergal became god of the grave and judge of the dead.

This myth underlines Nergal's association with death and war. There are many references to Mars in this role in the Mesopotamian texts: 'When a planet and Mars stand facing each other, there will be an invasion of the enemy.' Again, 'When Mars approaches Scorpio, the prince will die by a scorpion's sting or will be captured in his palace.'[15]

Nergal was also seen as the god of plagues and fevers. Mars is still associated in modern astrology with pestilence, war and death, although since the 1930s Pluto has taken on many such attributes as ruler of the underworld. And just as Mesopotamian astrologers saw Nergal affecting the lives of cattle, so today Mars is still considered the ruler of butchers.

Jupiter

Jupiter was identified with the god Marduk to whom the great planetary temple in Babylon was dedicated. Every New Year, when the crescent moon nearest to the spring equinox first appeared, a great festival took place in Babylon over eleven days. It involved a series of rituals, each having an esoteric meaning. When the king, for instance, wore jewels on his head and roasted goats, the inner meaning was: 'He is Marduk, who carried firewood on his head and burnt the sons of Enlil and Anu in a fire.' To stress the occult nature of the rituals, a warning appeared at the end of each text: 'A secret of the great gods. May the initiate instruct the initiate. Let the uninitiated not see.'[16]

The first three days were preparatory. During the evening of the fourth, the great Mesopotamian creation myth *Enuma elish* was read by the high priest to the statue of Marduk in the temple. On the fifth day, the king was ritually humiliated before the statue by having his face slapped and his ears sharply pulled by the high priest. This was no doubt to remind him that his authority was ultimately in the lap of the god. Playing the part of Marduk, the king would then be held captive 'in the mountain' of the temple tower. A driverless chariot was then released to run out of control through the streets outside: the god had disappeared and chaos descended on the city. A white bull was sacrificed.

The next day, the sixth, Marduk's son Nabu (Mercury) arrived in the city and his statue was placed within the temple. Here the only existing tablet describing the events of the festival breaks off, but it seems from other sources that the next day Nabu rescued his father from captivity and the statues of the gods that had been brought to Babylon were assembled in the Hall of Destiny in the great temple. The liberated Marduk was elected once again king of the gods. On the ninth day, the king led a procession through the streets to attend a great banquet, celebrating his victory over the goddess of chaos Tiamat. In the evening, the king lay with a priestess in the 'room of the bed' in the temple, symbolizing the final union between the god and goddess. Order had finally been restored in heaven and on earth.

Jupiter is called the 'Star of the god Marduk' in the astrological texts. Its association with the saviour of the world meant that it was generally considered to be benefic – as Jupiter still is today. His presence would not only augur peace for the king but also bring rain and good harvests to the land. As Jupiter grew brighter, so the king became more prominent. At the planet's brightest point: 'the gods will give peace, troubles will be cleared up, and complications will be unravelled . . . the gods will receive prayers and hear supplications; the omens of the magician shall be made apparent.'[17]

There was, however, a more destructive side to Jupiter's role, particularly when it conjuncted with the moon: invasions, social unrest and even the death of the king could result. If Jupiter entered Orion, pests could destroy harvests. If it passed by Regulus (the 'Royal Star'), then the throne could be seized by an enemy. A conjunction with Mars seems to have been interpreted as a direct challenge to the king. A similar interpretation persists in modern astrology: Jupiter is the planet of expansion and increase but, badly aspected, it can mean immoderation and disharmony.

Mercury

Nabu-Mercury was the son of Marduk-Jupiter. On the eleventh day of the spring festival at Babylon, when the gods met in the Hall of Destiny to decide on the fates of the world for the coming year, he recorded their judgements. He was thus scribe to the gods and his emblem, carved on many stelae, was usually a writing desk. He was also the messenger of the gods; his name literally means 'herald'. And, like the movement of the planet, he was swift.

Little is known of the cult of Nabu. His name is first mentioned during the reign of King Hammurabi, but it was not until the turn of the first millennium that he replaced the earlier Sumerian goddess Nisaba as the deity presiding over wisdom, writing and accounts. He soon became sufficiently popular for the Babylonian kings to order a formula to be stamped upon their building bricks saying that they supported the temples of Marduk and Nabu.

One of the most important qualities of Mercury was that of rain-maker. One report to the kings observed: 'When Mercury is seen in Iyyar, a flood will come and benefit the fields and the meadow lands.' Since floods were seen as beneficial to farmers working a parched land, it is not surprising that Mercury should have been associated with a good harvest. 'When Mercury appears in Elul (heaven), there will be a heightening of the market, an increase of cereals . . . cattle will be numerous in the fields . . . Sesame and dates will prosper.'[18] What more could one wish for!

Nabu-Mercury, as the son of Marduk-Jupiter, was also associated with the crown prince. Any variation in its appearance or movement had a significance for his duties. If it was particularly bright, it was an auspicious time for the crown prince to meet the king. Thousands of years later, Mercury is still seen by modern astrologers as ruling commerce and markets, as well as writing and communication.

The centre of the Nabu-Mercury cult seems to have been in the city of Borsippa on the banks of a lake near the Euphrates, about ten miles south of Babylon. His temple, the Ezida, once housed a famous library; King Ashurbanipal sent his scribes there in search of rare tablets.

The Borsippa Ziggurat

In 1854 Henry Rawlinson, the explorer who had deciphered the cuneiform inscriptions found at Behistun, began excavations at Borsippa and revealed the ruins of the temple of Nabu.

The structure proved to be a stepped ziggurat made up of seven storeys, the first of which was 272 feet square and twenty-six feet high. As the excavation proceeded, revealing the outer wall, Rawlinson was fascinated to find that the bricks of the different levels were coloured differently: black was the colour of the first stage, red for the third and blue for the sixth. He was struck by an extraordinary coincidence – the colours, he recalled, belonged to the first, third and sixth spheres of the planetary system of the Sabeans, which were ruled by Saturn, Mars and Mercury respectively. The Sabeans had been a religious group who worshipped the stars and who had lived from the sixth to the tenth centuries AD in Harran, a city on the route from Babylonia to the Mediterranean. Confirming his hunch, Rawlinson discovered two identical cylinders in the foundations of the ziggurat which recorded 'that the Temple was dedicated to the "planets of the seven spheres"' and that it was called 'The stages of the seven spheres'.19

The seven storeys of the ziggurat were not only painted in the colours of the planets but were also associated with different metals: the lowest storey was black and lead for Saturn, then brown-red and tin for Jupiter; rose-red and iron for Mars; gold (colour and metal) for the sun; white-gold and copper for Venus; dark blue and quicksilver for Mercury; and the highest storey silver, for the moon.

The temple at Borsippa was a magnificent monument to the evolution of astrology over four millennia in Mesopotamia. It may have been buried in the sands of the desert, but the associations of the planets it embodied were to be taken up by the Egyptians and the Greeks and came to form the bedrock of Islamic and Western astrology.

20

The Image of Heaven

Do you not know, Asclepius, that Egypt is an image of heaven or, to be more precise, that everything governed and moved in heaven came down to Egypt and was transferred there? If truth were told, our land is the temple of the whole world.

HERMES TRISMEGISTUS

IT IS USUALLY ASSUMED that Egypt suddenly developed a civilization around 6,000 years ago with a complex religion, monumental architecture and a written language. Its origins, however, remain a deep mystery. That it reached its peak within a few hundred years has led some to argue that civilizers must have come from abroad with their knowledge. Professor Budge, formerly Keeper of the Egyptian and Assyrian Antiquities in the British Museum, suggested they were 'newcomers from the East'.[1] The Egyptian myths themselves support the idea of foreign civilizers, with stories of the 'Companions of Horus' coming across the sea with their sacred science to settle after a catastrophe overtook their original civilization. The memory of this no doubt inspired the myth of Atlantis, first mentioned by Plato who claimed that the Greek Solon first heard of it from an Egyptian priest.[2] Central to the sacred science they brought with them was astrology – knowledge of the movement and meaning of the stars. It undoubtedly inspired much of the architecture and art of ancient Egypt.[3]

Stellar Religion

Three hours by camel from the Great Pyramid at Giza in Egypt lies the spectacular sacred enclosure at Saqqara. It was the funerary complex of

King Zoser (2630–2611 BC) of the third Dynasty, built at the very beginning of the flowering of Egyptian civilization. Rising out of the desert under a deep-blue sky are walls of perfect symmetry, with clean and harmonious lines. The entrance is marked by a beautiful temple of utmost simplicity. So impressed were ancient visitors that over 3,000 years ago one of them observed in the world's oldest graffiti: 'It is as though heaven were within it, Re [the sun god] rising from it.'[4]

The complex is believed to be the work of Imhotep, exemplar of the universal man of genius. He was not only an architect, high priest and healer, but also a renowned astrologer. The Greeks called him Asclepius and celebrated him as the father of medicine.

The Step Pyramid was the first large-scale pyramid and still rises sixty metres high. The nearby Pyramid of Unas (2356–2323 BC) is now a pile of rubble, but as I descended into its subterranean chamber, I was astonished to find the ceiling covered with stars. The walls were carved with chaste and delicate hieroglyphs. They are known as the Pyramid Texts, the oldest known text on earth, and reveal an extraordinary body of sacred science. The meaning of the Text of Unas is multi-levelled and enigmatic, but it clearly contains many references to individuals who have travelled to the stars and returned. No less than twenty-four times, it is written: 'He is not dead, this Unas is not dead.'[5] The pharaoh is not only called a 'star of the Lower Sky' but is said to go around 'the sky like Re'.[6] Furthermore, he is to purify himself 'with the cool waters of the Circumpolar Stars'.[7]

It would seem that the pyramids of Egypt were not simply used as tombs, as has been commonly supposed, but as places of initiation. The sarcophagi found in the pyramids were not final resting places, but were used to prepare the pharaoh for the journey after death. The 'funeral rites' may well have been magical formulae to induce an out-of-body experience in which the pharaoh could ascend to the heavens and meet the gods before returning to his physical body. At the great Heb Sed Festival, the festival of the tail, the pharaoh was identified with the god Osiris who guides humanity through the three great stages of life, death and rebirth. During the ceremony, 'clad in the funeral costume of Osiris, with the tight-fitting garment clinging to him like a shroud, Pharaoh is conducted to the tomb; and from it he returns rejuvenated and reborn like Osiris emerging from the dead'.[8] The boats found buried near the pyramids were no doubt symbolic solar barques used for astral travel across the heavens.

The Pyramid Texts are the original source for the celebrated Egyptian Book of the Dead. The book is a guide for the journey beyond the grave, which passes through the Underworld to the realm of new life in the divine presence of Osiris. The chapters were intended to help the deceased overcome his foes in the Underworld, to draw on the help of friendly beings, and eventually to roam at will, whether sailing on the 'Boat of a Million Years' with Re or visiting any other imaginable realm of joy. Most Egyptian texts imply that the realized individual would be resurrected after death and become a star. Regenerated, he or she would be able to accompany the gods in the heavens in their eternal round of maintaining the order and flow of the universe. This could only be possible if the mummified body remained undisturbed and intact in its tomb.

Egyptian civilization was entirely based around religion. The pharaoh had supreme power on earth and was considered divine. Similarly, all humans contained a divine spark and could become godlike. The pharaoh represented the spiritual destiny of all humanity, being associated with the mortal god Osiris in his journey through the Underworld, transforming body into spirit, and rising with Horus in the form of the eternal sun god Re.

Religion entered every aspect of everyday life. Building, sowing, brewing, cooking, making love and playing games were all sacred acts. They symbolized the creative process of transforming nature and human nature into a more spiritual form. Herodotus records that the Egyptians were 'exceedingly religious, more so than any other people in the world'.[9]

The Egyptians expressed their religion and philosophy through symbolism and myth, art and architecture. Although they recognized many gods, their religion was essentially monotheistic. The universe was held to be the deliberate act of creation of the supreme god Atum. It was alive and infused with spirit. The gods or *neterw* responsible for its order were personifications of cosmic forces and aspects of the supreme god. Animals were not worshipped as such, but rather as manifestations of certain divine principles and functions.

The world view of the ancient Egyptians was the same as that of all later astrologers. It assumed that the universe was infused with soul – the *anima mundi*. They perceived an underlying unity in the rich diversity of the world: All is One and One is All. It was a fundamental belief of the ancient Egyptians that all phenomena were interrelated by sympathetic energies. They called the magical power that pervaded the universe *heka*. The sun was the most visible source of *heka*, but the moon, the planets and the stars all emanated it. When the Pharaoh Akhenaten (1353–1335 BC) tried to create a monotheistic religion of sun worship, his artists depicted him with outstretched arms receiving the magical rays of the sun.

Stepping-stone to Eternity

The Egyptians saw life on earth as a temporary abode, as a stepping-stone to eternity. Just as they believed that the souls of the living came from the stars, so they looked forward to returning to the stars. Indeed, the Egyptian hieroglyph for 'star' also means 'soul'. Even the Muslim *fellahin* farmers in Egypt today say the stars above are the souls of the dead.

From the earliest times the Pyramid Texts (inscribed between 2400 and 2200 BC) declared for the dead pharaoh: 'I fly from you, O men; I am not for the earth, I am for the sky.'[10] Again, the priests exhorted the soul of the deceased: 'Arise, remove your earth, shake off your dust, raise yourself, that you may travel in company with the spirits . . . Cross the sky . . . Make your abode in the Field of Offerings among the Imperishable Stars, the followers of Osiris.'[11] The most beautiful illustration of this belief comes in the second golden shrine of Tutankhamen (1333–1323 BC). Carved in gold, a row of human figures stands opposite the human-headed benu bird (symbol of the soul). Rays from the forehead of each figure stream towards an individual star, thereby linking their consciousness to the heavens. As countless hieroglyphs marvellously demonstrate, it was the hope of all Egyptians that after death they would sail with the sun god Re on his 'Boat of a Million Years' across the sky.

Heaven and earth were not considered separate but part of a larger whole. According to the Egyptian creation myth, in the beginning there were the primeval waters (Nun) from which emerged the first island. In an act of self-creation, Atum masturbated himself out of Nun. He then spat out the twins Shu (air) and Tefnut (associated with moisture) who in turn produced Geb (the Earth) and Nut (the Sky). Reversing the usual genders, Geb in Egyptian mythology is male and Nut is female; they are beautifully depicted on the ceilings of temples and tombs as a man lying on his back with an erect penis, overarched by a black woman whose limbs form the four pillars of the sky. Her back is studded with the golden stars of the firmament, across which the sun god Re travels in his solar boat from sunrise to sunset. She was said to swallow him at the end of the day and give birth to him each morning. The Valley of the Duat – the Underworld – was in her body. Nut and Geb, heaven and earth, were held apart by Shu, god of space. However, their union gave birth to the central figures in the Egyptian pantheon: Osiris and Set, Isis and Nephthys. Horus was the son of Osiris and Isis.

The Great Pyramid

One afternoon in winter I climbed the Great Pyramid at Giza near Cairo. It is now strictly forbidden, but I obtained special permission from the Director of Antiquities. Pulling myself up from one great block to another – the smooth facing stone has long disappeared – it took me about half an hour to reach the summit which is about 138 metres high. The top part of the pyramid has also gone, and I stood on a platform about six metres square. It seemed that I was on top of the world.

According to my compass, the four sides of the pyramid were exactly orientated to the four cardinal points. Across the desert, I could just make out the ruined pyramids of Saqqara to the South-East. Not far from me stretched the back and head of the Sphinx, eternally facing the rising sun. To the South-West I saw the other two pyramids at Giza and recalled the hypothesis that the three together mirror the three stars of Orion's belt, the cosmic man forever striding across the heavens.[12] The meandering Nile too was an earthly counterpart of the Milky Way. It illustrated perfectly the ancient astrological principle: 'as above, so below.'

The Great Pyramid beautifully embodies the stellar religion of ancient Egypt. Its shafts, long thought to be air vents, have recently been shown to have been aligned with particularly appropriate stars around 2500 BC. In the Queen's chamber, the southern shaft is orientated towards Sirius, the brightest star in the heavens, which was identified with Isis, the consort of the supreme god Osiris. The Northern shaft is in line with the star Beta of Ursa Minor (Little Bear), which was associated with the immortality of the soul. In the King's chamber, the Southern shaft was aimed at the brightest star of Orion's belt (Zeta Orionis), associated with Osiris, while the northern shaft was pointed to the ancient Pole Star (Alpha Draconis).[13] Laid in the Great Pyramid in an elaborate ritual before being buried, the dead pharaoh could thus re-enact the union of Osiris and Isis in a great cosmic orgasm.

Linking the Queen's chamber to the King's chamber is the steep polished slope of what is now called the Grand Gallery. It looks like the vault of a very narrow cathedral, with very smooth sides containing mysterious slots at different intervals. Before the final completion of the pyramid, when it was still open to the sky, it could well have provided a wonderful observatory for the Egyptian astrologers. The sharp top edges of the corbelled walls would have provided perfect markers to record precisely the transits of the stars as they passed overhead. The mysterious slots could have been used to hold in place viewing platforms for the astrologers. Such a gallery would seem to serve no other purpose.[14] Certainly the fourth-century Alexandrian philosopher Proclus thought so. The modern astronomer Eugene Antoniadi has also calculated that eighty per cent of the night sky could have been observed from the Grand Gallery. No doubt aware of an ancient tradition, the Arabs often depicted Egyptian astrologers on the roof of the pyramid surveying the stars.

The Great Pyramid is perfectly positioned as a celestial observatory. It is placed on latitude 30° North, one third of the distance from the Equator to the North Pole. It also observes true North more accurately than the meridian building of the Greenwich Observatory in London. Its exact location could only have been chosen by master astronomers – astrologers observing the transits of the stars for thousands of years. It comes as no surprise to learn that the name of King Semerkhet of the First Dynasty means 'the man with the astronomer's staff'.[15]

The sighting instrument called the *merkhet* was used to observe the stars and for aligning the axis of temples with the stars. Water clocks were also used during the night, especially when the stars were not visible. The hours of the day were determined by simple shadow clocks. The gold or electrum-tipped obelisks of Egypt could also have been used as giant gnomons, calculating the solstices and equinoxes by the shadow cast on the ground.

Another fascinating aspect of the Great Pyramid is that its builders appeared to have viewed the earth as a sphere. From the top of the pyramid, I realized that at the summit one could continue to see the setting sun on the Western horizon, although it had already disappeared for my partner on the ground below. This was because of the curvature of the earth's surface. Although the Greeks are usually considered to have been the first to view the earth as a sphere, it would have been a short

South Polar Star of Longevity. In ancient Chinese astrology, the god of the Pole Star of the South was thought to determine the length of a person's life.

The Temple of Heaven, Tiantan Park, Beijing,
where the Emperor would come each year to pray for good harvests.
A masterpiece of Ming architecture, it is one of the world's greatest astrological
buildings, representing the Four Pillars of Destiny of Chinese astrology.

Detail on the Temple of Heaven.
Rubbed by passers-by for good luck, the dragon represents male yang energy
and is one of the twelve animal signs of the Chinese zodiac.

Carving of Ganesh, the Hindu god of astrology, obstacles and thresholds.
Tenth century, Lakshman Temple, Khajuraho, India.

The Hindu sun god Surya riding on the back of the constellation of Leo, made from a wonderful interweaving of people and animals. Indian miniature, c. seventeenth century.

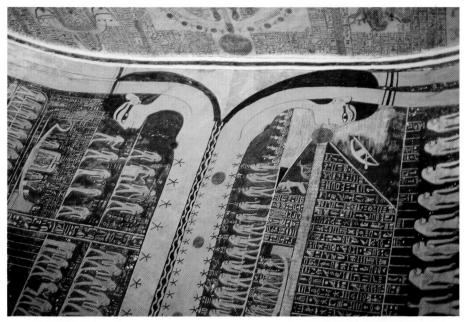

Nut, Egyptian goddess of the heavens, twice depicted as the night and
day skies. After the sun passes along her body during the night, Nut gives birth
to it through her mouth. Ceiling of the burial chamber of Ramesses VI,
twentieth dynasty (1151–1143 BC), Valley of the Kings, Luxor.

Egyptian queen Nefertiti, wife of Akhenaton,
making an offering to the sun god Re in his guise as the solar disk Aten.
Limestone tablet, eighteenth dynasty (1353–1335 BC).

Lion-headed god of the astrological cult of Mithras, with signs of the zodiac carved on his body. The seven planetary spheres corresponded to the seven grades of initiation while the snake was a symbol of rebirth. Mithraism flourished in the late Roman Empire.

The medieval world view based on Ptolemy,
with the earth at the centre and the planets revolving around it.
The system is still used symbolically by modern astrologers.

Medieval horoscopes, from the 'Heidelberg Book of Fate'.

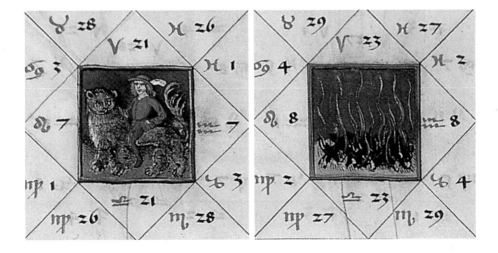

Medieval clock, made in 1410, on the Old Town Hall, Prague.
The astronomical face above represents the Ptolemaic system, with the sun
moving along the ecliptic. The face below, repainted in the nineteenth century,
contains a calendar of the months and the signs of the zodiac.

step for the builders of the pyramids to reach the same conclusion, since they held the cosmos to be shaped like a curve.

Moreover, the mathematical proportions of the four triangular surfaces of the Great Pyramid provide a scaled projection – as in map-making – of the Northern Hemisphere. The apex represents the North Pole and the perimeter the Equator. The scale is said to be 1:43,200 which represents 86,400 seconds in twenty-four hours.[16] If this seems fanciful, the Greek philosopher Agatharchides of Cnidus, who served as guardian to the pharaoh in the second century BC, asserted the same theory.

It is interesting to note that the ratio of the Great Pyramid to the earth is a multiple of seventy-two. Due to the complex celestial pheno-menon known as the 'precession of the equinoxes', the position of the stars appears to go backwards – precesses – in relation to the sun. The rate of precession is one degree every seventy-two years, thereby completing a circle of 360° in 25,920 years. The most significant astrological impli-cation of precession is that the signs of the zodiac rotate anti-clockwise in relation to the rising point of the sun on the spring equinox (known as the first point of Aries). At a rate of one degree every seventy-two years it takes 2,160 years to move across a sign of the zodiac (72 × 30). Just before the beginning of the first millennium, the vernal equinox fell in 0° Aries; it is now in 7° Pisces.

The phenomenon of precession also gave rise to the notion of astrological ages or Great Years which span 2,160 years. We are now leaving the Age of Pisces which began before the birth of Christ and entering the Age of Aquarius.

As a model of the earth, the Great Pyramid would seem not only to reveal the mathematical laws of the universe, but also to encode evidence which suggests that the ancient Egyptians knew about the precession of the equinoxes. Observing the stars for millennia, the Egyptian astrologers must have realized that their Pole Star shifted its position, particularly as they paid great attention to the circumpolar stars. Due to the earth wobbling slightly on its axis like a top, the poles make a small circle in space. This means that the position of the Pole Star gradually changes and then returns to its original place over a period of 25,868 years. The *djed* column, depicted in countless papyri, temples and tombs, may well have been a symbol of the axis on which the earth turns.[17]

It would seem that not only Egypt and Mesopotamia, but also other ancient civilizations had understood the precession of the equinoxes long before the Greeks, who are usually credited with the discovery. Herther von Dechend and Giorgio de Santillana have argued in their remarkable book *Hamlet's Mill* that a body of astronomical knowledge recorded in myths was in existence at least '6,000 years before Virgil' (that is, around 6000 BC). Surprised at first by its antiquity, they suggested that its source must have been in 'some almost unbelievable ancestor civilization' that 'first dared to understand the world as created according to number, measure and weight'.[18] In their view, accurate values for the precession of the equinoxes were given the form of particular numbers in myths, making up a kind of coded message of ancient wisdom.

Heavenly Observations

Given the central importance of the sun in their religion, it is not surprising that the Egyptian astrologer-priests should have been fascinated by the path of the sun – the 'path of Re' – as it returned to its original position every spring equinox to mark the completion of the solar year. If they had kept records from the earliest times – and there is no reason to suspect they did not – then they would have been able to predict the gradual rotation of the twelve constellations of the zodiac to the point where the sun rises on the spring equinox. This would have confirmed their sense of cosmic harmony and also provided a perfect example of eternal recurrence and the rebirth of the soul.

Not only did the Great Pyramid make a superb observatory, but it also worked as a huge sundial. Its base is aligned perfectly to the four directions. Its shadow to the North and its reflected sunlight to the South mark the equinoxes and solstices with great accuracy. As such, it could have been used as an almanac, especially if the immense jointed paving stones stretching out from its base were used as markers. Unfortunately a few metres from the pyramid the great stones have been taken away, no doubt as building material. The astronomer Sir Norman Lockyer in his book *The Dawn of Astronomy* supported the above hypothesis, although it cannot be proved today.

On the East bank of the Nile, 4° longitude further South of the Great Pyramid, lies the great solar temple of Amon-Re at Karnak, one of the finest works of architecture ever raised by human hands. Lockyer called it 'beyond questions the most majestic ruin in the world.'[19] The temple forms a gigantic telescope tube some 500 metres long. Its central axis is aligned with the setting of the sun on the summer solstice, an obvious orientation for the priests who worshipped the sun god Re. The timing of the flashing of the sun's rays into the inner sanctuary could therefore be used to determine the exact length of the solar year. Lockyer was the first to recognize this fact in recent times.

Again, the temple of Ramesses II at Abu Simbel on the edge of the Nubian desert was so designed that twice a year on the equinoxes the rising sun sent a shaft of light through the open door. It shone down the dark corridor of the Hypostyle Hall to illuminate the sanctuary fifty-five metres within the living rock face.

In reality, the annual path of the sun is not fixed but changes almost imperceptibly over long periods of time. This is not due to the precession of the equinoxes, but due to the tilt of the earth's axis in relation to the plane of its orbit around the sun. The phenomenon is called the 'obliquity cycle' which takes more than 40,000 years to complete. This means that ancient temples today will not be aligned to the celestial bodies as they were when they were built. By working out the present slight misalignment, it is possible to calculate the date the temple would have been originally surveyed. In the case of Karnak, Lockyer came up with the date 3700 BC, 1,000 years earlier than is usually assumed.[20]

If a temple could be used as a telescope, this raises the question whether the ancient Egyptians actually invented the telescope to observe the movements of the starry firmament. Although it is usual to assume that it was not invented until Galileo in the seventeenth century, we have already seen that the Mesopotamians may have invented it. There is some evidence to suggest that the Egyptians may have done likewise. I can well remember when I first visited the Egyptian Museum in Cairo being struck by the wooden statue of a striding man with a staff and startling lifelike eyes. Found at Saqqara, the character is known as Sheik el balad (the village headman), but in fact he was Ka-aper, a Fifth Dynasty chief priest (c.2470 BC) responsible for reciting prayers for the deceased. The rims of his eyes are made from copper, the white from opaque quartz and the cornea from transparent rock crystal. I soon realized that many other statues had similar rock crystal eyes.

In his study of ancient optics, *The Crystal Sun*, Robert Temple argues that the Egyptians possessed high-precision optical instruments. The planning of the pyramids would have been impossible without optical surveying instruments. The Old Kingdom crystal lenses prove that the technology existed for the Egyptians to invent telescopes; indeed, some of the finest quality lenses ever made before 1900 AD date from around 2600 BC in Egypt.[21]

The *Udjat* Eye

A remarkable image from ancient Egypt depicts the ibis-headed wisdom god Thoth holding up the 'Eye of Horus', known as the *udjat* eye. Of Horus' two eyes, the right eye is the symbol of the sun (the 'Eye of Re') and the left, of the moon (the 'Eye of Thoth'). During their titanic struggle, Seth tore out the left eye of his nephew Horus which was eventually restored by Thoth. Could this key event in Egyptian mythology represent a lunar eclipse?

The *udjat* eye has a remarkable mathematical ratio which states the universal constant known as the 'Comma of Pythagoras,' which the Egyptians seem to have called 'the little gap'. It is a number which Robert Temple calls the greatest secret of the ancient Egyptians, without which the riddles of Egyptian mythology cannot be solved. The sacred number, thought to be built into the deep structures of the universe, is 1.0136. The formula enabled the Egyptians to calculate the extra 5.2424 days to add to the 'ideal' year of 360 days.[22]

Another early myth about Thoth and the 'eye of Re' may well reflect the importance given by the ancient Egyptians to solar eclipses. As in Genesis, the myth relates that human beings rebelled against their creator and committed evil deeds. Enraged, Re sent his own eye in the form of the goddess Hathor to wreak vengeance. But even the eye of Re rebelled against the sun god and had to be brought back by Thoth. On its return, it too was enraged to find that Re had replaced it with another eye (the moon). Thoth, however, managed to pacify it and Re found a place for it in his face.[23] The sun and moon returned to their rightful places in the heavens and order was restored on earth.

21

The Return of the Phoenix

Egypt has recorded and kept eternally the wisdom of the old times. The walls of its temples are covered with inscriptions and the priests have always under their own eyes that divine heritage.

PLATO

THE EGYPTIAN WISDOM god Thoth, known to the Greeks as Hermes and to the Romans as Mercury, became the founding father of astrology and alchemy. Hermes gave his name to the Hermetic tradition of occult knowledge, while in modern astrology Mercury is still associated with communication and creativity.

Thoth was said to be born of the sun god Re. An ancient passage declares: 'I am Thoth, the eldest son of Re . . . I descended to the earth with the secrets of "what belongs to the horizon".'[1] Thoth uttered the words commanded by Re to create the world and was the creator and regulator of the laws of cosmic harmony. He surveyed the heavens, and the stability of the universe depended on his knowledge of celestial mathematics. As a moon god, he delineated the seasons and regulated time. He was the navigator on Re's solar boat and he plotted the course of each day. He was responsible for the immortality of the soul and lit the way through the Underworld. Thoth was indeed the bearer of powerful secrets.

In the Egyptian Book of the Dead, he declares: 'I am Thoth . . . the guide of heaven, and earth, and the underworld, and the creator of life of [all] nations and peoples. I gave air unto him that was in the hidden places by means of the might of the magical words of my utterance.'[2]

As the inventor of writing and the fount of wisdom, he is said to have written the now lost Book of Thoth. Some sources claim that it had only two pages; others that it consisted of forty-two books covering the whole gamut of Egyptian sacred science, including the history of the world, religion, music, medicine and astrology.

The Constellations

What did the Egyptian astrologer-priests see in their observatories with the benefit of their advanced astronomical instruments? The sun and the moon undoubtedly played a central role in their mythology, symbolized by the gods Re and Thoth. Re remained the supreme god throughout the history of Egyptian civilization. During his reign, Akhenaten even tried to make the worship of Aten, the sun disc, a monotheistic cult, although this practice died with him. The chief site of the worship of Re was On, called Heliopolis (City of the Sun) by the Greeks.

In the available literature which has come down to us there are many references to the planets ('the stars that never rest'). Prominent among them are Venus ('the morning star' and 'evening star'); Saturn ('Horus, the Bull'); Mars ('the red Horus'); and possibly Mercury. Horus, the mortal god, son of Osiris and Isis, avenged his father's dismemberment by his brother Set. Since Horus is a hero of Egyptian mythology, it is unlikely that they considered Mars a malefic planet.

As early as the Old Kingdom, the Egyptians had already arranged the stars into patterns representing figures from their mythology. As they believed, so they saw. They projected into the night sky their gods which were inspired by the creatures living around them along the Nile, such as the crocodile, hippopotamus, serpent, lion and hawk. Others were more anthropomorphic, such as Orion, a striding man forever looking over his shoulder. Like Isis, Hathor, to whom the temple at Dendera is dedicated, was identified with Sirius. Osiris was associated with 'Orion who treads his Two Lands, who navigates in front of the stars of the sky'.[3] The Lion, with its exact number of nineteen stars recorded by the Greek astronomers Erastostenes and Hipparchus, is found in the ceiling in the Ramesseum, the mortuary temple of Ramesses II, in Luxor, built in the thirteenth century BC.

The Egyptians were profoundly impressed by the eternal circuit of the stars around a point in the Northern sky – the Pole Star. They took it to be the node of the universe which they called 'that place' or the 'great city'. Since the High God was the regulator of the universe, and the universe revolved around the Pole Star, then this had to be his dwelling place. In the Pyramid Texts, it is written:

> I know his name, Eternity is his name,
> 'Eternity, the master of years' is his name,
> exalted over the vault of the sky,
> bringing the sun to life every day.[4]

The celestial pole was sometimes seen as a tree with the circumpolar stars, which contained souls, perched on its branches. The latter were particularly revered and known as 'the never-vanishing ones' and the 'imperishable stars'.

We are fortunate enough to have a chart of the heavens still extant, which shows the positions of the principal stars as seen from Memphis around 3500 BC. It makes it possible to identify some of the constellations in other ancient Egyptian star maps. The Great Bear (the so-called Plough), which at that time rotated conspicuously around the Pole, was named the 'ox-leg'; the Bedouin of the Sahara still call it 'the leg'. Other groups of stars which can be identified are: Bootes (as a crocodile and a hippopotamus); Cygnus (a man with outstretched arms); Orion (a striding man looking back over his shoulder); Cassiopeia (another figure with extended arms); Draco and the Pleiades (possibly as an egg) and the Hyades (a 'V' shaped group). The constellations Scorpio, Aries and probably Leo, which all became part of the modern zodiac, were also observed in the night sky.[5]

With special permission from the Director of Antiquities, I was able to visit the tomb of Seti I in the Valley of the Kings on the West Bank near Luxor. There in the darkness of a chamber, deep below the earth's surface, the light of my torch illuminated a wonderful vista of the constellations of the night sky. A hippo with a crocodile riding on its back represented Draco. The hippo rested one of its forefeet on a thigh (or 'ox-leg') symbolizing the Great Bear. A line of stars outlined the figure of a lion, almost certainly the constellation of Leo, which faced a standing man (probably Orion) above whom stood a bull (possibly Taurus). In that Stygian darkness deep below the Earth's surface, I was enthralled by the bright splendours of the night sky.

Egyptian Calendars

When Julius Caesar decided to give the Romans a new calendar, he wisely chose an Egyptian from Alexandria to draw it up. Darius I, the Persian conqueror of Egypt had done the same in 488 BC. The Egyptians had the only reliable calendar in the ancient world. Unlike the inferior Gregorian calendar which is used today in the West, it had no leap years.

According to Diodorus of Sicily, 'At the tomb of Ozymandias (Ramesses II) in Thebes (Luxor), there is a golden circle on the terrace, 365 cubits in circumference, which is divided into 365 parts, each part being a day of the year, and nearby is written the natural rising and setting of the stars with the predictions which Egyptian astrology draws from them.'[6]

In the temple at Abu-Simbel, carved out of the living rock in the Nubian desert, the date of the battle of Thotmes ll is recorded as 'Year 23, first month of the third season, 221st day, the day of the festival of the new moon'. In fact, the Egyptians drew on their astronomical knowledge to draw up three separate calendars: the lunar calendar, the 'Wandering Calendar' and the exceptionally accurate Sothic calendar. Unlike the Mesopotamians, the Egyptians counted their lunar month from the invisibility of the moon rather than the appearance of the new crescent. Since the most practical purpose of the calendar was for agriculture, the lunar month consisted of twenty-nine or thirty days alternatively to keep it in tune with the passing seasons as defined by the annual movement of the sun above and below the Equator. While the Egyptian calendar lost only one day in four years and about a fortnight in a lifetime, the present Muslim lunar calendar, which allows no extra days, gradually rotates through the seasons and loses about eleven days each year.

The 'Wandering Calendar' was a moving civil calendar (hence its name) of 360 days and five additional days. It was principally used by the temple priests for festivals and ceremonies. The five extra days were considered to be the birthdays of the gods.

The most accurate calendar of all was the Sothic calendar of 365 and a quarter days. It was founded on the heliacal rising of the star Sirius (known to the Greeks as Sothis) on the Eastern horizon just before dawn. By an extraordinary coincidence, the appearance of the brightest star in the heavens anticipated the rising of the Nile and the annual flood on which the entire civilization of Egypt was dependent. The Egyptian New Year thus began when Sirius was first seen about forty-two minutes before sunrise, appearing for a minute or two before its light was dimmed by the coming of dawn. This timing of the year was known to have been used officially from the Twelfth Dynasty (1991–1783 BC). Sirius now first appears in August.

Sirius was important not only because it anticipated the annual flooding of the Nile, but also because it was a symbol of Osiris, the most important god after Re in the Egyptian pantheon. Sirius was often called the 'Great Provider'. Its sixty-year cycle comes close to the Jupiter-Saturn cycle which is still thought to augur great changes. There is some evidence to suggest that the Egyptians thought that Sirius was a 'greater sun' around which our own sun and solar system orbit.

Sirius and the Phoenix

The heliacal rising of Sirius is the probable source of the legend of the phoenix, the fabulous bird that returns at the end of its life to its birthplace in the 'Arabian Desert' between the Nile and the sea. Here it builds a fire and burns itself to death, only to rise again from its ashes. As such, the phoenix is taken to be one of the oldest symbols of rebirth and renewal.

Usually depicted as a grey heron, the *benu* bird is the ancient Egyptian phoenix. It was said to have appeared at the moment of creation perched on a pillar on the Primeval Mound, the first island in the Primeval Waters. It represented the soul of the deceased and was often depicted carrying the ankh cross, symbol of rebirth.

There is also an astrological level of meaning to the legend. The phoenix is born in the Arabian Desert because the sun rises on the Eastern horizon of Egypt. The fire in which it dies is the light of dawn. The span of its life is said to be 1,460 years, that is, four times 365. At Heliopolis, this long-range 'New Year' was known as 'the Return of the Phoenix'.[7] Heliopolis – the 'City of the Sun' – had for thousands of years been a centre of astronomical and astrological science, so much so that the High Priest was called 'Chief of the Astronomers'.[8]

The figure 1,460 is significant. The Wandering Calendar gradually moved in relation to the fixed Sothic year, taking 1,460 years to complete a cycle. The coincidence of the two calendars was called the 'New Year', and probably occurred on 4240 BC, 2780 BC and 1320 BC. Since the Pyramid Texts of the Fifth Dynasty (c.2500 BC) frequently mention the inauguration of the 'New Year', it implies that the establishment of the calendar occurred earlier and points to the year 4240 BC when it is thought that Upper and Lower Egypt were united into one nation. Of course, all this knowledge could not have been acquired without a long history of accurate observation of the stars.[9] Once again, a study of Egyptian astrology suggests a much earlier date for the development of Egyptian civilization than most Egyptologists are willing to admit.

The Egyptians divided the year into three seasons of four months each, which were defined by the rhythm of the Nile: the dry season, the inundation (marking the New Year) and the period of germination. Seth was associated with the dry season, as Isis was with the flood season. Each day was divided into twenty-four hours, twelve hours of light and twelve hours of darkness. The royal tombs of the Twentieth Dynasty (from 1196 BC) have star-tables painted on the ceilings which show hour-by-hour the position of the principal stars in two-week periods. They are similar to modern astronomers' observations for stars crossing the meridian. As we have seen, months were designated in two ways: the lunar month of twenty-nine or thirty days, and the Sothic month which was defined by the periodic return of the heliacal rising of Sirius.

The religious feasts were celebrated according to the different calendars. An inscription on the tomb of the pious Khnumhotep, an administrator under Senwosret II (1897–1878 BC), at Beni Hassan gives a sense of the intermingling of the calendars:

> I decreed the offerings [food] at every feast of the necropolis, at the feast of the beginning of the year [the first new moon], at the feast of the opening of the year [the rising of Sirius], the feast of the long year, the feast of the short year [alternative lunar years], the feast of the last day, the great feast, the feast of the great heat, the feast of the little heat, the feast of the five days added to the year [the birthdays of the gods], at the feast of the sand-throwing, at the twelve monthly feasts, at the twelve half-monthly feasts, at every feast of the living and of the blessed dead.[10]

Having three calendars posed no problems. Indeed, three calendars are in general use in Egypt today – the official Muslim lunar calendar for religious observances, the Coptic (after the ancient Egyptian) for agricultural purposes, and the Gregorian calendar imported from Europe, for business and international affairs. An almanac can be bought which shows the relation between the three.

The Decans

The ancient Egyptians' preoccupation with the heavens is clearly visible in the magnificent tomb of Ramesses VI (1151–1143 BC), set in the rock escarpment of the desert on the west bank of the Nile at Luxor. Over the tomb entrance a stylized mountain with the sky above represents earth and heaven. On the left is a solar disk containing the scarab Khefri (symbol of rebirth) and the ram-headed solar deity (reflecting the Age of Aries). On the ceilings of the long corridor are depicted the sky goddess Nut, solar barges and scenes from the Book of the Day and the Night.

There, deep within the earth in the Sarcophagus Hall, which would have once housed the tomb of the pharaoh, I came across a spectacular mural in which Nut is stretched twice across the whole length of the high ceiling, surrounded by the morning and evening stars. In the small room at the end of the tomb, facing West, are figures representing the 'decan' stars worshipping the solar barque which would take the deceased and sail with Re across the skies.

What are these 'decans' which later astrologers associated with the 'Egyptian system' of astrology? They consist of groups of stars or a conspicuous star within a wide equatorial belt rising at particular 'hours of the night' during a period of ten days ('decan' is Greek for ten). Thirty-six of them make up a year. The heliacal rising of a constellation star on the Eastern horizon marked the beginning of each decan; they began with Sirius, known as the 'mistress of the year'. Since they were based on a cycle of 360 days, they fell at different periods down the years so it was necessary to draw up tables to show how they shifted through the seasons. The system can be traced back to at least the Third Dynasty (c. 2800 BC) and would have required a long period of earlier observations.

As the first chapter of Genesis (1:14) puts it: 'the lights of the firmament' can be used as 'signs for seasons, for days and for years'. Very early on, the Egyptian astrologers would have noticed that a given star would rise, culminate and then set about four minutes earlier every day. This is because the earth does not quite complete an entire rotation on its axis every twenty-four hours. The four-minute difference is therefore the daily difference between solar and sidereal time. It adds up to two hours every month. The phenomenon was known as the 'forward-wandering' of the stars.[11]

By the second millennium BC, and probably much earlier, the Egyptians had selected thirty-six 'decan' stars from the patterns of constellations they had already discerned in the sky. Their rising, culmination and setting were used to work out the approximate date of the year as well as the hour of the night.

The Egyptians believed that star maps could be used by the souls of the dead as well as the living. The coffin lid of a sarcophagus at Assiyut, dating back to around 2050 BC, works as a star calendar and star clock by depicting images to represent the circumpolar constellations and the series of the thirty-six decan stars. The method is still in use today: modern nautical almanacs have large series of 'ten-day' stars and smaller number of circumpolar stars which a navigator can use to calculate the date or hour.

The decans often take on the names of presiding gods and represent different principles of the cosmos. This could well be the source of Plato's doctrine that each sign has its ruling god, and the later astrological claim that each sign has a ruling planet.

The rise of the decans during the night was used to divide the time of darkness into hours. In summer, at the time of the heliacal rising of Sirius, twelve were observed to rise before dawn, and so the night hours were divided into twelve. Although decimal counting was the general rule, an hour of twilight was added at the beginning and again at the end of the day to the ten full daylight hours to give twelve in all. Because the length of hours varied at different times of year, the astrologers took the equal hours at the equinoxes, when night and day are the same length, as the standard – hence our twenty-four hour clock.

In the tombs of the Ramesside Dynasty (1194–1070 BC), the calendars based on the decan stars were supplemented by a series of twenty-four tables of hour stars dividing the nights of each of the twenty-four fortnights of the year into twelve seasonal hours of various lengths. These hour stars originally served as markers to track the movement of the moon.

The Egyptian decans were enthusiastically taken up by astrologers in ancient Rome who divided each sign of the zodiac into three segments of 10°. The sky was thus divided into thirty-six decans. The Roman astrologer Firmicus Maternus quoted a passage from the Egyptian text-book of Nechepso and Petosiris: 'In each sign there are three decans which occupy certain degrees and leave others void . . . So whoever has in his horoscope the sun and moon and five planets in full degrees will be like a god and raised to the height of majesty.' Sadly, the Egyptian astrologers added: 'But this can never happen.'[12] Nevertheless, the more planets one has in full degrees on a horoscope, the more fortunate one will be.

The Roman astrologer Manilius allotted the decans to the signs of the zodiac in their traditional order. Another system gave them ruling planets, beginning with Mars for the first decanate of Aries and continuing in the 'Chaldean Order' until Mars ruled the first decanate of Pisces. The fifth-century Hermetic writer Stobaeus describes how the decans 'sow upon the earth the seeds of certain forces, some salutary and others most pernicious, which the many call daemons.'[13] During the Renaissance, the Italian Jesuit Egyptophile Athanasius Kircher drew up a list, adding some Greek and Persian deities to the Egyptian ones representing the decans.[14] As late as the seventeenth century, the English astrologer William Lilly was using the so-called 'Egyptian system'.

There are very few surviving written sources on Egyptian astrology. Why should this be so? As in every field of knowledge, the Egyptians kept their underlying principles secret and only expressed them symbolically in their architecture and art. Moreover, they passed down their knowledge orally from master to initiate. Secrecy was maintained so that the knowledge would not get into the wrong hands. The Greek philosopher Pythagoras reputedly had to wait twenty years before he was admitted into the Egyptian temples.

According to spell 144 of the Book of the Dead, the astrologer is watchful of the position of the stars in the sky: 'He consults the books of astrology in silence and in secret. They are accessible in fact, only to those who have been initiated for many years.'[15] Astrology thus remained a sacred science of the temple which could only be managed by responsible and knowledgeable priests.

At present, we do not know the full details of ancient Egyptian astrology. We are left with only fragments. So far no personal horoscopes of individuals prior to the first century AD have been found in Egypt. The ancient Egyptian astrologers, however, were undoubtedly involved in what might be called 'macro-astrology' – that is, astrology used to calculate the right times for the 'birth' of temples and the auspicious timing of the rituals and ceremonies which took place within them. Like so much of Egyptian civilization, its secrets still remain hidden beneath the sands.

22

The Horoscope of Eternity

There is perhaps no land where the order and movement of the stars are observed so exactly as in Egypt. They have kept records in which these observations have been written down for an incredible number of years. Here one finds information on the relation of each planet to the birth of animals and on the good or bad influence of each star.

DIODORUS SICILUS

A REMARKABLE COINCIDENCE OF stars and planets occurred in 2767 BC during the reign of the pharaoh Zoser who built the temple and pyramid at Saqqara. The date was the summer solstice. A close conjunction of four planets, all within 7° of each other, rose on the Eastern horizon at the same time as Sirius – a conjunction which may never have occurred again. It was seen as a day of perfect harmony and was recorded in a celestial diagram called 'The Horoscope of Eternity', possibly the world's first horoscope.[1] Indeed, all later Egyptian horoscope charts are diagrams of the heliacal rising of Sirius.

A standard star map of the event was often inscribed into tombs to help the deceased navigate their way through the heavens. At its centre, Sirius was usually represented standing in a boat as the figure of Isis. Orion represented as Osiris appears to her right as a pharaoh running. To the left of Sirius are the planets Saturn, Jupiter and Mars, then two turtles (possibly the two Aselli stars in the constellations of Cancer). After five 'metadecans' comes Mercury. A large heron, the *benu* bird of Osiris and by implication Osiris himself, represents Venus. The planets were often identified with Horus, the ferry man of the sky, who 'ascends to heaven among the imperishable stars, his sister is Sothis [Sirius], his guide the Morning Star [Venus].'[2]

These astronomical diagrams with stars and planets may truly be called horoscopes since they were observed celestial moments. Although nothing was predicted from them, each was held to be a representation of the moment of a sacred marriage between Sirius (Isis) and Venus (Osiris). When they rose simultaneously every eight years, it symbolized beautifully the eternal link between heaven and earth.

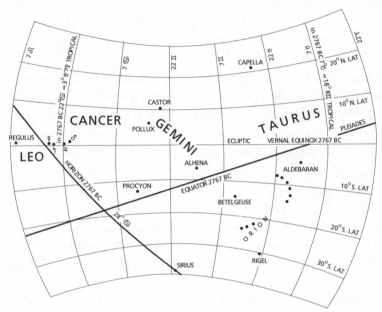

The Original 'Horoscope of Eternity' 2767 BC

Dendera and the Zodiac

In the desert at Dendera, thirty miles north of Luxor, there is a late temple which vividly illustrates the extent of Egyptian astrological knowledge, gathered over more than 4,000 years. At the entrance to the temple there are four identical rows of huge columns with the heads of the goddess Hathor, the goddess of love and fertility, who was associated with the night sky. She is often depicted with a sun between two horns on top of her head. While she can have a destructive role, like the Venus (Ishtar) of Mesopotamia, Hathor is usually considered to be a patroness of healing. She was identified with Aphrodite by the Greeks.

The temple at Dendera dates from the first century BC. Built after the conquest of Egypt by Alexander the Great, it was completed in AD 17, during the reign of Roman Emperor Augustus. It was raised on the site of earlier temples and an inscription in a crypt states that it was built 'according to a plan written in ancient writing upon a goat skin scroll from the time of the Companions of Horus'.[3] The companions of Horus were the legendary demi-gods who came from afar to found Egyptian civilization.

Another inscription declares that during a founding ceremony which took place around 300 BC, the pharaoh aligned the temple to the star *alpha Ursae Majoris* of the Great Bear: 'the living god, the magnificent son of Asti [a name of Thoth], nourished by the sublime goddess in the temple, the sovereign of the country, stretches the rope in joy. With his glance towards the *ak* of the Bull's Thigh constellation, he established the temple-house of the mistress of Dendera, as took place before . . . I establish the corners of the temple of Her Majesty.'[4]

Dendera is renowned for its astrological elements: the whole temple is covered with coloured reliefs which present a rich tapestry of astrological figures. The first aisle of the high ceiling in the vestibule with its twenty-four enormous pillars depicts the phases of the moon and the course of the sun during the twelve hours of the day. Along the second aisle are the deities of the stars and the hours of the day and the night. In the third, the figure of Nut, the sky goddess, is spread over the signs of the zodiac and some of the fixed stars and constellations. This is the so-called 'Square Zodiac of Dendera'.

It is oblong in shape, eighteen metres long, while each half is six metres wide. It has two registers. The upper register shows the signs of the zodiac and various constellations, the planets and the hours of the day (each drawn as a woman with a star over her head). Leo leads off Northwards on the Western side of the ceiling. Opposite the leg of the sky goddess Nut (who is dressed in a design of ripples), the sign of Cancer as the Crab stands out in pride of place. The rest of the signs of the zodiac follow in the usual order: Leo, Virgo, Libra and so on. The lower register depicts the decans and human and animal-headed figures in boats sailing across the night sky.

I was struck by the fact that the sign of the Crab was given such prominence. The astrologer-priests, keepers of the sacred science, knew exactly what they were doing when they instructed their artists to place it there. Why should this be so? Does it imply that Egyptian civilization began under the sign of Cancer? Because of the precession of the equinoxes, the vernal equinox precesses a fraction of a degree against the band of the zodiac each year. When the vernal equinox last rose under the sign of Cancer it was between 10,000 and 8,000 BC. This would date the rise of Egyptian civilization far earlier than the orthodox view. On the other hand, a simpler explanation of the prominence given to Cancer is that the New Year began on 19 July at the heliacal rising of Sirius within the sign of Cancer.[5]

The dark and airless crypts of the temple had a ceremonial and symbolic meaning: the statue of the *ba* soul of Hathor was kept there until the New Year, when she was brought out of the primeval darkness and carried up to the golden light of the temple rooftop, so that at dawn she was reunited with the beams of her father Re.

The little New Year Chapel gives onto an open courtyard. On the ceiling, there is a huge woman bending at the waist among the stars. She is Nut, the sky goddess, giving birth to the sun whose rays spread out from the region of her womb to illuminate the face of Hathor. It is a wonderful depiction of stellar energy.

The staircase up to the roof of the temple is square with a slight incline and turns at right angles. It is lit by thin apertures, little more than slits, with waving lines carved into the stones depicting the streaming rays of the sun. From the flat rooftop of the temple there is a spectacular view across the alluvial plain of the Nile. In a chapel in the North-Eastern corner of the roof, dedicated to the 'Sprouting of the Seed' and the 'Resurrection of Osiris', is a replica of the famous Dendera zodiac – the original is now in the Louvre museum in Paris.

The Dendera zodiac is the only extant circular zodiac to have been discovered in Egypt. An earlier example was apparently made in 221 BC during the reign of Ptolemy III but this has been lost. The circular zodiac is similar to those developed by the Babylonians and the Greeks, except that the symbols are Egyptian. In the centre are personifications of the circumpolar stars: Draco is an erect hippo, the bull's leg is the Great Bear and the jackal Anubis is the Little Bear. Sirius is represented as a cow lying in a boat, while Orion appears under the hoofs of the Bull (Taurus). The vernal equinox is shown by the baboon of Thoth following the Ram (Aries).

Cancer again has a pivotal role: the round-bodied crab is just off-centre, immediately above the lion's head (Leo) . The other signs of the zodiac run in a counter-clockwise direction. A goddess holds the lion by the tail, and behind her Virgo is depicted as Isis with an ear of corn. Being further South, Scorpio, Sagittarius and Capricorn lie near the outer circle which has thirty-six curious figures representing the decan stars. A hawk on top of a papyrus column marks the summer solstice and is in line with the axis of the temple.

Another intriguing detail of the zodiac is the positioning of four female figures whose upstretched arms hold the circle of the zodiac. They would seem to represent opposing signs and the most important constellations in which the sun rises at the two equinoxes and at the two solstices. In ancient myths, the twinned pair of constellations were often personified as 'keepers' or 'bearers' of the sky.

Taking into account the precession of the equinoxes, with the spring equinox now in Pisces, the four sky-bearing constellations are Pisces, Virgo, Gemini and Sagittarius. Around 700 BC, they would have been Aries, Libra, Cancer and Capricorn, but for the signs of the zodiac to have been meaningful at this time, the celestial observations necessary to identify them would have had to go back to around 6000 BC.[6]

If we apply this understanding to the Dendera circular zodiac, we come up with some surprising conclusions. The four sky-bearing female figures are opposite the signs of Leo-Aquarius and Taurus-Scorpio. This configuration seems to indicate it was during to the Age of Taurus, which lasted approximately from 4380 BC to 2200 BC, that the original foundations of the temple were laid down.

All this raises the obvious question: 'Did the Egyptians invent the modern zodiac?' Most commentators give a resounding 'no'. The existing zodiac used by astrologers is usually taken to be the product of a confluence of influences from Mesopotamian and Egyptian astrology.[7] Some Egyptologists even claim the twelve signs were entirely a Greek invention.[8] The traditional view is that, after the conquest of Mesopotamia and Egypt by Alexander the Great in the fourth century BC, Mesopotamian and Greek astrological ideas were grafted by the Egyptians on to their older astrology.

Mesopotamian ideas were undoubtedly brought by the Assyrians who invaded Egypt in 671 and 664 BC, and by the Persians who conquered Egypt in 525 BC. What is certain is that by the third century BC, the Egyptians had developed the planetary sequence know as the 'Chaldean Order' which held sway in Europe until the Scientific Revolution in the seventeenth century. It places the planets in an order relating to their apparent motion and supposed distance as viewed from the earth. The nearest and swiftest is the moon, the slowest and the furthest is Saturn; in between, in descending order, are Mercury, Venus, the sun, Mars and Jupiter.

Nevertheless, there are some remarkable indicators in their architecture and art which suggests the ancient Egyptians knew of the precession of the equinoxes and used the signs of the zodiac to describe the ages of the Great Year. In the art of the Old Kingdom from around 4240 BC, the bull (Mentu) is the predominant motif, representing the Age of Taurus. After 2100 BC, which marks the beginning of the Age of Aries, the ram becomes associated with the sun god Amon. It is impossible to miss the colossal statue of the ram in the forecourt of the temple of Amon-Re at Karnak.[9] Then, just before the birth of Christ, the fish representing the Age of Pisces, makes an appearance. Indeed, the symbol of Christ in Graeco-Roman Egypt was the fish.

Although it cannot be proved that the ancient Egyptians developed *all* the signs of the zodiac, their astrologers certainly saw similar patterns in the sky. Using constellations of stars as markers to trace the movement of the moon through its monthly cycle, they probably traced out the lion shape of Leo, saw the twins of Gemini, paid particular attention to the ram of Aries, and imagined two turtles in Cancer. They also probably had constellations which resembled fish and water-pots, thereby contributing to the signs of Pisces and Aquarius in the conventional zodiac. In sum, it is almost certain that Aries was originally an Egyptian constellation, as was possibly Gemini, and as were probably Aquarius, Pisces and Leo.[10] The final zodiac as we know it is thus a product of a confluence of influences from both Egypt and Mesopotamia.

Some interpreters have gone even further. Assuming that the ancient Egyptians had already established the signs of the zodiac 5,000 years ago, the Egyptologist and esoteric thinker Schwaller de Lubicz argued that the ground plan of the Temple of Luxor, the Parthenon of Egypt, resembles the figure of a man with each part of his body associated with a particular sign of the zodiac. If a human skeleton is superimposed on the general plan of the temple, the head is located exactly in the sanctuaries of the covered temple. As such, it is an expression in stone of the celestial nature of man. Its esoteric symbolism reveals that 'Man is the microcosm', a small world mirroring the macrocosm of the universe.[11]

The Temple of Horus at Edfu

The best preserved ancient temple so far discovered in the world is at Edfu. Most Egyptian temples are orientated East-West, but Edfu is unusual in that it faces South. It was probably linked with Dendera which faces North. They thus face each other and, although separated by 140 kilometres, they clearly share certain myths, rituals and astrological themes. While again founded on the site of earlier temples – some portions of the Western enclosure wall date from the Old Kingdom – work on the existing building was begun in 237 BC and finished in 57 BC. The temple shows that at the end of thousands of years of civilization, the Egyptian architects, priests and craftsmen had lost neither their skills nor their beliefs.

The temple is dedicated to Horus, the falcon-headed god, who symbolizes the different aspects of resurrection. He is represented by two imperious granite statues of a crowned falcon that stand at the entrance to the Great Court. The falcon aptly expresses the doctrine of resurrection: it strikes in silence and carries away its prey into the eye of the sun, the eye of Re himself.

In the founding myth of Egyptian civilization, Horus is the son of Isis and Osiris. As the avenger of his father (who was dismembered by his uncle Set), he is known as Horus Behdety, who flew up to heaven in the form of a winged disk. Equated with the sun-god Apollo by the Greeks, Horus is the Greek name for the Egyptian Heru which means 'He who is Above'.

As at Dendera, the vestibule has a dozen huge pillars, which give way to the Hypostyle Hall which contains a dozen smaller ones. This leads in turn through two antechambers to the inner sanctuary, which almost certainly contained a golden effigy of Horus.

An inscription at Edfu states that the orientation of the temple 'lay from Orion in the South to the Great Bear in the North'. This may well be the place in the heavens known as the Duat-N-Ba, literally the 'Netherworld of the Soul'.[12] Astrological themes run throughout the whole temple. The ceiling of the vestibule is full of astrological signs, which unfortunately are now too blackened by smoke to decipher. Nevertheless, on the starry ceiling of a kiosk devoted to Nut, the sky goddess, I could make out all the signs of the zodiac.

By far the most interesting aspect of the temple, for me, were two small chapels, hardly two metres by two metres, attached to the inner wall of the vestibule. On the Western side the pharaoh is blessed by Horus and Thoth, the ibis-headed god of wisdom and the patron of later astrologers and alchemists. On the Eastern side a small room known as the 'Chamber of Writings' housed a library which once contained many works on astrology. We know it was a library because it has a card catalogue inscribed in hieroglyphs upon the wall. It mentions twenty-two works, which include a work called 'Horoscope of the hour' as well as the following: '9 Book of knowing the return to their stations of the sun and the moon. 10 Book which regulates the return of the stars. 11 Detailed account of all places and knowledge of what is in them. 12 All the reckonings of the rising of His Majesty Horus [Saturn or Mars?] in the retinue of thy [Re] House in thy festivals.'[13]

Five centuries later, the Christian father Clement of Alexandria drew up a list of the thirty-six books containing the 'entire philosophy of the Egyptians' and six volumes on their science. The last four works mentioned at Edfu are very close to the four books dealing with the stars mentioned by Clement: 'one regarding moving stars, the other about the conjunction of the sun and the moon, the other two respecting their risings, confided to the Astronomer whose symbols are a clock and a palm branch.' Other books entrusted to the Scribe are also noteworthy:

Eight books dealing with knowledge of what are called hiero-glyphics and including cosmography, geography, the positions of the sun and the moon, the phases of the five planets, the chorography [mapping the regions] of Egypt, the charting of the Nile and its phenomena, a description of the equipment of the temples and of the places consecrated to them and information regarding the measure of all that is used in the sacred rites.

Clement claims that all these books were kept in a chamber of a temple as 'a priceless treasure, a gift to the human race from Thoth, master of all science'.[14]

The two book lists are close enough to show that the tradition of sacred astrology continued at a time when the practice of the ancient Egyptian religion was in serious decline. Complete versions of the works have been lost but fragments undoubtedly survive in the so-called Hermetic writings, named after Hermes, the Greek name for the Egyptian wisdom god Thoth.

At Edfu there are some remarkable 'Building Texts' inscribed on the walls of the temple around 200 BC. At first sight they would appear to be little more than a history of the temple and a description of its chambers, but they imply that the temple was a continuation of a mythical temple that was built at the beginning of the world when the Primeval Mound emerged from the Primeval Waters. An inscription declares that the temple was built according to a plan which 'fell from heaven'.[15]

The 'Building Texts' are probably fragments of a much older and more complete literature of cosmology. They refer repeatedly to the *Zep Tepi,* the 'First Time', a remote golden age when the demi-gods known as the 'Companions of Horus' reigned in Egypt.

These Seven Sages followed the path of Horus, that is, the solar way of Re. They were thought to be superior beings of divine origin who produced the race of pharaohs and who brought sacred science to the people living along the Nile. They are the 'Lords of Light', mentioned in a text at Edfu, who escaped from the 'Homeland of the Primeval Ones' when their island was destroyed in a flood; they were 'the Senior Ones' who 'illumined this land [Egypt] when they came forth unitedly'.[16] This implies that Egyptian civilization did not evolve; it was a legacy from an earlier people. If this were the case, it would explain why Egyptian civilization was complete from the beginning: its astrology, its mathematics, its myths and its hieroglyphs.

The introduction to the 'Building Texts' says it is a 'Copy of the writings which Thoth made according to the words of the Sages'.[17] Since the astrologers and alchemists traced their knowledge back to Thoth, and Thoth wrote down the teachings of the Seven Sages, this sacred book may well be the fountainhead of Egyptian astrology.

There are some fascinating echoes of other traditions in all this. The Primeval Mound recalls the mountain in the flood stories of the Epic of Gilgamesh and the Bible. In Babylonian tradition, there were 'Seven Sages' who lived before the Flood, built the walls of the sacred city of Uruk and brought with them a knowledge of astrology. Again in the Indian tradition, Seven Sages (*Rishis*) are said to have survived the Deluge in order to pass down to later generations the wisdom of the antediluvian world, which included astrology.[18] And in China, there is the Taoist tradition of the 'Sons of Reflected Light' who came across the sea with their knowledge. There seems to be much more than a coincidence at work here. Myths passed down orally often contain disguised elements of historical truth.

It may indeed be the case that the ultimate origins of astrology are to be found in a lost civilization – known to the Greeks as Atlantis – which underwent a terrible catastrophe. Some survivors may well have escaped with their sacred science and scattered across the tropical world China, India, Mesopotamia and Egypt. There they became the founding fathers of new civilizations which all developed their own traditions of astrology.

The Discoveries of the Egyptians

What then was the overall contribution of the Egyptians to astrology? The historian Diodorus of Sicily, writing around 59 BC, claimed that the Egyptians had invented astrology and that the Babylonians were Egyptian colonists who had taken astrology to Mesopotamia.[19] While the latter claim seems confused and unlikely, the modern scholar Rupert Gleadow in his work *The Origin of the Zodiac* claims that: 'the first notion of astrology as we know it was begotten on Babylon by Egypt between the seventh and fifth centuries BC, and the zodiac itself, as a calendrical device, was a similar origin, but may be a little older.'[20] On the other hand, the conventional view among Egyptologists today is that astrology developed late in the first millennium BC in Egypt from a fusion of Greek science with Egyptian and Mesopotamian 'star lore'.[21]

It is certainly *not* the case that astrology was a 'fairly late arrival in Egypt' and that the Egyptians 'never developed their own astrology'.[22] From the earliest times ancient Egyptian astrology was a central part of their sacred science which they expressed in a symbolic form in their art and architecture. While no doubt there was some late cross-fertilization, in my view both Egypt and Mesopotamia may have inherited their astrology as a central strand of sacred science from an earlier lost civilization.

Writing around 460 BC, Herodotus mentioned certain 'discoveries' of the Egyptians: 'Every month and every day is sacred to a particular deity, and the day of a person's birth determines what will happen to him, how he will die, and what kind of person he will be. This is something Greek poets have made use of.'[23] While Mesopotamians were fascinated by omens in the sky, believing that events in the heavens foretold events on earth, the Egyptians were chiefly interested in the stars to learn how the soul could ascend to heaven and join the solar boat of Re. But they also believed in lucky and unlucky days, and that each hour of the day or night had its guardian god or tutelary spirit. It is not surprising that some hours, and later some ruling gods and groups of stars, should be considered more auspicious than others.

The earliest surviving Egyptian horoscope was written in the first century AD in Coptic and discovered in Alexandria. Even at this late date, the technique of prediction was still unsettled. Nevertheless, there can be no doubt that the Egyptians recognized the intimate and powerful correspondence between events in heaven and happenings on earth. Every Egyptian, male and female, believed that they were a microcosm of the universe, descended from the stars to which they were destined to return.

Part Four

Shooting Stars:
Greek, Roman and
Islamic Empires

23

The Harmony of the Spheres

When Orion and Sirius shall have reached mid-heaven and Arturus shall rise with Dawn, then, oh Perses, gather your grapes.

HESIOD

MANY EARLIER EUROPEAN scholars glorified the Greeks as cool rationalists, forgetting their deep indebtedness to Mesopotamia and Egypt and the Orphic mysteries. Typical of this attitude is F. Cumont who declared that: 'It is to their everlasting honour that, amid the tangle of precise observations and superstitious fancies which made up the priestly lore of the East, they [the Greeks] discovered and utilised the serious elements, while neglecting the rubbish.'[1] Indeed, in the traditional view, the adoption by the Greeks of the Eastern practice of astrology in the third century BC was seen as symptomatic of their decline from the greatness of the Golden Age.[2] In reality, there is growing evidence to suggest that classical Greece of the fifth and the fourth centuries BC knew about and appreciated the astrology practised in the Near East and North Africa. In *The Origin of the Zodiac* Gleadow argues persuasively that 'Astrology as an effective technique arrived in Greece at the latter half of the fourth century BC.'[3]

From their first contacts with the Egyptians, the Greeks were deeply impressed by their civilization. Clement of Alexandria claimed that the Greek philosophers borrowed a great deal from Egypt and that Homer, Thales, Pythagoras and Plato all received instruction from the Egyptian temples. By the fifth century BC the ancient Egyptian belief that the souls of the dead connect with stars was well established in Greece.[4] Mesopotamian influence had reached Greece even earlier. The poet Hesiod's *Theogony*, dating from the eighth century BC, contains Greek versions of Babylonian myths, and the Greeks translated Babylonian star names as early as the sixth century BC. After the Persian invasions of Greece in the first quarter of the fifth century, cultural contacts between the two peoples continued, filtering Indian, Babylonian and Egyptian ideas. In a fragment from a history of Persia, dating from the late fifth century BC, Ctesias expresses his admiration for the amazing accuracy with which a 'Chaldean' priest, expert in 'astrology and divination', could predict the future.[5]

These new influences fell on fertile ground. The Greeks had long been interested in omens derived from celestial events; their first great writer, Homer (c.800 BC), gives many examples in his *Odyssey* and *The Iliad*. He mentions the constellations of the Pleiades, Hyades and Orion which mark the onset of winter. Early Greeks also took a keen interest in the movement of celestial bodies as indicators of changes on earth.

In his *Works and Days*, written before 750 BC, Hesiod described the 'starry heaven' (*ouranos*) as the 'ever-secure home of the gods'. He drew up the days which were most auspicious for different farming activities, defining them by the rising and setting of certain stars. Pruning, for example, should start at the beginning of spring 'when sixty days of winter have passed after the solstice, then Arcturus leaves Ocean's holy stream [the Milky Way], the first to shine out in the twilight.'[6] And the time for harvest? 'When Orion and Sirius shall have reached mid-heaven and Arturus shall rise with Dawn, then, oh Perses, gather your grapes and bring them home.'[7] In the same spirit, he also suggested that there are right times for important social activities, such as getting married.

The Greek Philosophers

Many Western astrological beliefs, especially about the nature of the cosmos, can be traced back to the early Greek philosophers. In the past there has been a Eurocentric prejudice in thinking that Western astrology originated in Greece. Indeed, the historian of science O. Neugebauer categorically stated that 'the main structure of astrological theory is undoubtedly Hellenistic' while the classical scholar Jim Tester declared that astrology is 'a fairly recent and largely Greek creation'.[8] The Greeks themselves, however, repeatedly acknowledged earlier sources in Asia Minor, the Middle East and North Africa.

Thales of Miletus (c.630–546 BC), regarded as the first philosopher in Western history, is said to have fallen down a well while walking along and gazing up at the stars. He was rescued, so the story goes, by a pretty servant girl. However, he is usually remembered as the founder of the Ionian school of philosophy (based in Miletus on the Aegean coast of present-day Turkey) and the father of Greek astronomy. As a materialist, Thales rejected the mythology so beloved by Homer as a source of knowledge, and insisted on the careful observation of natural phenomena. He induced that not only the contents of the well he fell into, but everything in the universe, is made from water. Applying his astronomical knowledge to good astrological effect, he is said to have predicted an eclipse, probably in 585 BC, which prevented a war between the Medes, a people from a mountainous country South-West of the Caspian Sea, and the Lydians, who lived in Asia Minor, present-day Turkey.

Anaximander (b.610 BC) was another Ionian philosopher who argued that the heavens consisted of separate spheres through which the planets travelled on their eternal round – an astrological view which continued down to the Scientific Revolution of the seventeenth century. He described the universe as being contained within the rim of a huge wheel filled with fire, and the stars and the planets as sparks of fire seen through holes in the rim. Anaximander first introduced the notion of eternal recurrence – the 'Law of Return of All Things' – which was to become a key concept in Western astrology. Turning his eyes from heaven to earth, Anaximander also made the first known map of the world.

The Ionian philosopher Anaximenes (c.550 BC) further believed that the stars were like nails attached to crystalline spheres which rotated around the Earth rather like a hat on a head, a belief which held sway to the seventeenth century. The central astrological notion of the microcosm and macrocosm – 'as above, so below' – is often traced back to his work but, as we have seen, it was a view held much earlier by the Mesopotamians and Egyptians. He is also remembered for observing the obliquity of the ecliptic, which again was almost certainly known by the Egyptians.

While the Ionian school of philosophy tended to be materialistic and mechanical, the Greek colony in Southern Italy at Elea produced a much more mystical band of philosophers. The difference between their 'scientific' and 'intuitive' approaches to the heavens still divides modern astrologers. Stressing the importance of Being, the Eleans believed that physical change is illusionary. Xenophanes of Colophon (c.580–472 BC),

Elea's most prominent thinker, maintained that the universe is a unity (as its name implies) created and guided by a single intelligence: All is One and One is All. Rejecting the gods of Homer and Hesiod, he nevertheless insisted: 'One god, greatest among gods and men, not like to immortals at all either in body or in thought. As a whole he sees, as a whole thinks, as a whole hears.' The one god gives life and energy to the creation: 'But without toil, by the power of his mind, he causes everything to vibrate.'[9]

On the other hand, Heraclitus of Ephesus (c. 500 BC), like the ancient Chinese Taoists, emphasized the importance of Becoming. Everything changes; nothing remains the same: you cannot put your toe in the same river twice. At the same time, he thought that change occurred through the reconciliation of opposites, a view at the heart of the astrological notion of positive and negative signs of the zodiac. Yet for all the continuous flux of life, there was unity in the diversity of the world: 'Listening not to me but to the *logos*, it is wise to agree that all things are one'.[10]

While these early Greek thinkers began to lay the philosophical foundations for later Western astrology and astronomy, there is little evidence to suggest that they had at this stage developed it into a system of the kind used in Mesopotamia and Egypt. However, during the fifth century BC, the Greeks began to take note of Mesopotamian and Egyptian astrology. The Persians, who had conquered Mesopotamia and Egypt, reached the Aegean coast of Ionia by 546 BC, bringing with them their own ideas, and those of their conquered peoples.

Pythagoras and the Pythagoreans

The most influential Greek philosopher to be exposed to these new influences was Pythagoras of Samos. Born around 558 BC, he was educated in the Ionian school and as a young man knew both Thales and Anaximander. At the age of twenty, he is said to have travelled to Egypt where he remained for about twenty-five years, studying with the temple priests. He was then captured by the Persians and taken as a captive to Babylon. There he was taught by a Zoroastrian priest, Zaratas, and initiated into the esoteric doctrines of his religion, which included the idea of the transmigration of the soul. Finally, convinced that numbers were the key to understanding the universe, he gave mathematical values for the relationships between the celestial bodies.

It was probably in Babylon that Pythagoras first became acquainted with the concept of the 'harmony of the spheres'. Appealing to his mystical love of mathematics, this concept assumes that the distances between the planetary spheres have the ratios of simple whole numbers and mirror the intervals of the musical scale. The notes of the seven planets thus create a chord as they turn in the heavens – music which in our gross state on earth we are unable to hear. It may also have been in Babylon that Pythagoras picked up the idea that the earth was a sphere.

Around 518 BC, Pythagoras returned to his home on Samos and two years later settled in the Greek colony at Croton in Southern Italy. Here he attracted disciples who formed a brotherhood organized on stern moral principles. They abstained from eating meat (to avoid suffering) and beans (which excite the passions), took a mixture of wine and opium (to reach transcendental states), grew their hair and nails (rejecting artificial fashion), and held all their goods in common (practising brotherly love). Adopting a strict code of secrecy, they did not teach their doctrines outside their sect. They combined a love of mathematics with a mystical vision of the Absolute.

The Pythagoreans developed Anaximander's doctrine of eternal recurrence, by declaring that everything would come back in the same numerical order. Since time is measured by the movement of the planets, then the same time recurs by virtue of the same celestial movements recurring. When all the planets return to a similar position in relation to the fixed stars, the Great Year is completed – a view held by the ancient Mesopotamians and Egyptians.

It has been argued that 'the tenets of Pythagoreanism have always been at the roots of astrological theory'.[10] Indeed, Pythagoras' major contribution to astrology is that the universe can be explained through numbers. In his scheme of sacred numerology, each number is also symbolic: one, for instance, stands for unity, two for duality, and so on. Mythology and mathematics are aspects of the same indivisible reality. In Western astrology, the convention that the fourth 'House' represents home is due to the fact that the Pythagoreans considered four to be the number of structure. Their influence in the West has been profound and enduring: in the seventeenth century, Galileo believed that the universe was reducible to number and Kepler based his theories of planetary motion on Pythagorean geometry.

Philolaus of Croton (c.470–390 BC), a pupil of Pythagoras, also had a lasting influence on Western astrology and astronomy. According to ancient authorities, his work offers the earliest firm piece of evidence about astrology in Classical Greece. He knew about the twelvefold division of the zodiac around 430 BC. He also dedicated the angles of certain geometrical figures to certain gods. According to the fifth century Neoplatonist philosopher Proclus, he said that the 'angle of the triangle' was sacred to four male gods, while the 'angle of the square' was sacred to female deities. This would seem to be truly astrological, for four triangles can be inscribed with the twelve signs of the zodiac (one for each element) and three squares (one for each quality).[11]

Philolaus argued that the earth and all the planets, including the sun, orbited a central fire which he called the 'watchtower of Zeus'. This would explain why the planetary orbits, which according to the Pythagorean doctrine of universal perfection move in perfect circles, appear irregular from the earth. Apart from breaking away from a geocentric view of the universe, Philolaus was the first Greek philosopher to realize that the earth moves through space and to distinguish between the diurnal and the annual motion of the planets.

Meton, a contemporary of Philolaus, attempted to reform the calendar in Athens around 432 BC based on Babylonian models. He introduced the Great Year of nineteen years to coincide the solar and lunar cycles (nineteen solar years = 235 lunar months). Just before the Athenian state sent an expedition to attack Sicily, it is said that the *astronomos* pretended to be mad and burnt his house down so that he could plead for his son to stay in Athens. Plutarch suggests that he was prompted 'either by calculations (*logismos*) or by results of divination of some kind' – almost certainly the result of astrological predictions.[12]

The most influential Pythagorean philosopher was Empedocles (c.495–430 BC) who came from Agrigentum in Sicily. It was he who popularized the doctrine of the four elements which lies at the heart of ancient and medieval medicine and modern astrology. Earlier Greek philosophers had argued that the physical universe is made of one fundamental element – Thales, for instance, opted for water; Heraclitus for fire. Empedocles, however, maintained that all things, including humans, are composed of four elements – earth, fire, air and water. They are in a permanent state of flux, combining with each other in different ways to give the vast diversity of the universe. Empedocles used the analogy of painting to explain how the many can come from the few: 'As painters decorating temple offerings take in their hands pigments of various colours, and after fitting them in close combination

– more of some and less of others – produce from them shapes resembling all things.'[13]

Astrologers later developed Empedocles' theory of the four elements and associated them with the different signs of the zodiac, planets and Houses:

Element	Signs	Planets	Houses
Air	Gemini, Libra, Aquarius	Mercury, Uranus	Third, Seventh, Eleventh
Fire	Aries, Leo, Sagittarius	Sun, Mars, Jupiter	First, Fifth Ninth
Water	Cancer, Scorpio, Pisces	Moon, Venus Neptune	Fourth, Eighth Twelfth
Earth	Taurus, Virgo, Capricorn	Saturn, Pluto	Second, Sixth, Tenth

The concept of the four elements was taken up by Hippocrates (born c.460 BC) who, like Empedocles, studied at the medical school on the island of Cos. He associated the four elements with four 'humours' or conditions of the body, and argued that an imbalance between them resulted in illness. In many ways, this finds echoes in the Ayurvedic medicine of India which defines health as a balance between the elements. The four humours as bodily fluids became associated, especially in the Middles Ages, with certain psychological types: the sanguine (preponderance of blood and associated with air), the phlegmatic (phlegm/water), the choleric (yellow bile/fire) and the melancholic (black bile/earth).

Hippocrates not only originated the oath to save life that is now taken by all medical professionals, but also laid down the foundations of medical astrology, known by the Greeks as *iatromathematica*. He allegedly said that a physician without a knowledge of astrology had better call himself a fool rather than a physician. Anticipating homeopathy and 'holistic' medicine, he insisted that one should treat the whole patient and not the disease.

At some stage during the fourth and third centuries BC, the parts of the human body were allocated to the signs of the zodiac which were said to 'rule' them:

Zodiacal Sign	Parts of the Body
Aries	Head
Taurus	Throat
Gemini	Lungs, shoulders, arms, hands
Cancer	Mucous membranes
Leo	Heart, spine
Virgo	Stomach, intestines
Libra	Kidneys, loins
Scorpio	Colon
Sagittarius	Hips, thighs
Capricorn	Joints, gall bladder
Aquarius	Lower legs, ankles
Pisces	Feet

The signs were later said to rule the Houses of the natal chart in the same order, starting with Aries in the first and ending with Pisces in the twelfth.

In the diagnosis of illnesses, it was believed that if a sign ruling a particular part of the body was affected by a malefic planet or by a planet in a negative aspect, then by sympathy that part of the body would also be affected. The remedy was to increase the power of the sign by using plants, animals, stones and colours associated with it. This 'magical' approach had long been practised in India, Mesopotamia and Egypt with good results.

24

The Moving Image of Eternity

Concerning all the planets and the moon, the years, months and all the seasons, what other account shall we give than just this, that since soul or souls, good in all virtue, have turned out to be responsible for them, that these souls are gods?

PLATO

THE PHILOSOPHER DIOGENES LAERTIUS records that Socrates, the great Greek philosopher, met a Babylonian 'magus' who had come to Athens. The exotic foreigner made a number of predictions, including Socrates' violent death.[1]

Socrates left no writings but his pupil, Plato (c.429–347 BC), wrote down his master's teachings – and his own – in dialogue form. Although there is no evidence of Plato having visited Mesopotamia, he undoubtedly studied its thinking, not only mediated by Pythagoras, but also directly. He was aware of the use of astrology for divination and if Laertius' information was correct it shows that natal horoscopes were being used in Greece early in the fourth century.[2] Plato probably visited Egypt and undoubtedly had an enormous respect for the Egyptians. Using an Egyptian priest as a mouthpiece, he declared that by comparison the Greeks were 'all children'.[3] He gave these 'barbarians' (that is, non-Greeks) the greatest acclaim, calling them a 'race of philosophers'.

Plato's principal treatise on cosmology, *Timaeus* (c.365 BC), was his only work known to the West until the eleventh century. It contains the characteristically Babylonian doctrines of the transmigration of the soul and the harmony of the spheres, and also expresses the fundamental world view of Western astrology which has since undergone little change. It has been correctly argued that 'If Pythagoras laid the foundations, then Plato is the main builder of astrological theory.'[4]

Plato's Cosmology

According to Plato, this changing world on earth is a unique copy of a perfect and eternal 'living being'. The fleeting objects in this world of Becoming take their shape from the eternal and unchanging Forms or Ideas in the world of Being. The creator of the universe (the good 'framer') first created the soul. He then composed the body of the world out of the four elements – earth, air, fire and water – which form an indeterminate substance in confused motion. The creation took the form of a sphere which revolves on its axis. The creator then put 'soul in the centre and diffused it through the whole and enclosed the body in it.' The resulting creation was a 'blessed god'.[5]

For Plato and all Greeks, motion must have a cause: in the created universe the soul which moves itself is the ultimate cause of motion. The planets are no different from a new ship which remains immobile on the shore until it is pushed down into the sea. The observed regularities of the movements of the heavenly bodies must therefore be caused by the action of a divine intelligent 'world soul'. This self-moving soul is the original source of motion and keeps the heavenly bodies turning in perfect circles at perfect speeds. The sun, moon and planets are thus 'living creatures with their bodies bound by the ties of soul'.[6]

From the earliest times, the Greeks imagined the heavens as a dome. Plato considered the shape of the universe to be spherical. The earth was at the centre and the fixed stars were on the outer limit. The planets circled on rings between the two. But how was it created? Plato argued that the 'soul stuff' of the world was a kind of material that was mixed and given a mathematical structure. He described it as forming a fabric cut down into narrower strips.

There were two stages in the operation. First the material was cut into two strips which were placed cross-wise and bent round to form two circles, one inner and one outer. The outer strip Plato called the 'Circle of the Same' on which the fixed stars were lodged, and the second the 'Circle of the Different' along which the planets moved. The Circle of the Different was set at an incline to the circle of the Same, representing the difference in the angle between the axes of the ecliptic and the axis of the fixed stars. The Circle of the Same revolved from left to right and the Circle of the Different from right to left. The inner circle was split into seven unequal circles – for the sun, moon and five planets – which revolved at different speeds but were related proportionally.

Plato thus explained in a very condensed way the observed movements of the heavenly bodies from the Earth. Albeit difficult to imagine, it was beautifully illustrated by later armillary spheres.

To explain the relationship between the eternal world of Being and our changing world of time, Plato wrote that when the creator of this world saw that it was 'alive and in motion, a shrine for the eternal gods, he was glad, and in his delight planned to make it still more like its pattern . . . The nature of the Living Being was eternal, and it was not possible to bestow this attribute fully on the created universe; but he determined to make it a 'moving image of eternity'.[7] Before the heavens came into being there was no time. The sun, moon and five planets were therefore created to define and preserve the measure of time on the circle of the Different. The sun gives us night and day; the moon, the month; and the sun, the year.

To explain the observation that the planets change their relative positions in their journey through the signs of the zodiac in a solar year, rather like runners in a race, Plato suggested that they possessed 'a power of motion in a contrary sense' to the sun. The varying speeds and irregularities in their movement were due to their being divine souls composed of soul and body. He is referring here to the concept of retrogression, based on the observation that at certain periods the outer planets seem to move backwards in relationship to the inner ones.

The wandering movement of the planets (planet in Greek means 'wanderer') was well known to the Pythagoreans, who analysed it into a combination of two or more actual movements. It was carried still further by Eudoxus of Cnidos, a fellow member of Plato's Academy, who explained it in terms of concentric spheres. The notion was adopted by Aristotle and later developed by Ptolemy and remained the foundation of astronomy until Copernicus in the seventeenth century. It continues to form the basis of astrology today.

The theory of the Great Year was also spelled out by Plato. This is the period of time that it takes the sun, moon and the five wandering planets (Mercury, Venus, Mars, Jupiter and Saturn) to rotate completely and return all together to a similar position in relation to the background of fixed stars. The Egyptians had been aware of the precession of the planets and put the span of time at 26,000 years. Hindu writings reported 12,000 years. Plato did not give a figure but observed that 'time in a way *is* their wanderings'. He recognized that it was possible 'to perceive that the perfect temporal number and the perfect year are complete when all eight orbits have reached their total revolutions relative to each other, measured by the regularly moving orbit of the Same.'[8]

In his famous discussion of Atlantis in *Timaeus*, Plato referred to the ancient records of the Egyptians, as reported to Solon, which mention recurring large-scale devastations. They could be interpreted, Plato suggested, as floods in the winter of the Great Year and as conflagrations in its summer. They do not come as a form of divine retribution but as a result of the configurations of the planets in the heavens which have unavoidable consequences on earth. This, of course, could explain the Flood mentioned in the Bible, in the Epic of Gilgamesh, in the story of Deucalion (the Greek Noah) and in many other flood myths of the world.

Plato further suggested in *The Statesman* that 'Time's arrow' could be reversed periodically: 'God himself at times assists the cosmos on its way and aids in its rotation, at others he lets it go, when its periods have reached the measure of time appropriate to it, and it goes back in the opposite direction by itself.'[9]. Even life would be reversed in this universal unravelling, with old men losing their white hair and the dead emerging from the earth.

Another assumption of astrology was given poetic expression by Plato in *Timaeus*. He said that after the creator mixed the soul of the universe, he took the same bowl in which he had fashioned first gods and then humans and animals who were not so pure and compounded the mixture. He 'divided it up into as many souls as there are stars, and allotted each soul to a star. And mounting them on their stars, as if on chariots, he showed them the nature of the universe and told them the laws of their destiny.' All souls were then combined with bodies subject to time and 'sown in its appropriate instrument of time'. When the souls visited earth they transmigrated up and down a hierarchy of lives, depending on their behaviour, but 'any one who lived well for his appointed time would return home to his native star and live an appropriately happy life.'[10] Other souls would be reincarnated until they chose to live well. This doctrine of the transmigration of the souls, which was held by the Pythagoreans, could have come from the stellar religion of Mesopotamia.

Far from condemning astrology as superstitious and muddle-headed, Plato clearly approved of the ability to forecast events from the movements of the planets in the following passage in *Timaeus*:

> But as for the circular and couple dancing of these astral deities, and their retrogressions and progressions; as for which of them come into conjunction and opposition with one another, and in what order they pass in front of one another, and at what times any of them are hidden from our sight and then reappear to frighten those who are capable of calculation and to send them signs of the future – to describe all this without visible models would be labour spent in vain.[11]

The Spindle of Necessity

At the end of *The Republic*, his work on the ideal State, Plato expresses his doctrine in the form of a myth which he used to convey religious and moral truths for which plain prose was not good enough. The myth relates how after being killed in battle the body of Er remained sound. On the twelfth day on his funeral pyre, he came to life again and described what he had seen in the other world. He had travelled with other souls to a place from which they could see a shaft of light closely resembling a rainbow which stretched from above like a pillar straight through heaven and earth.

From the middle of the light was the bond of heaven which held its whole circumference together like 'the swifter of a trireme', a piece of rope tied from stem to stern on a wooden boat that holds its hull in place.[12] A 'Spindle of Necessity' was hanging from the ends of the bond which caused all the orbits of the planets to revolve. With earth at the centre, there were eight whorls in all: the fixed stars on a sphere on the outside, then Saturn, Jupiter, Mars, Mercury, Venus, and the sun and moon. The heavenly bodies thus go around the earth in concentric rings, each of which differs in colour and breadth. The breadth and relative motion of the rims represent the distances and relative speeds of the planets. The whole revolves with a single motion, but within the movement the seven inner circles of the planets revolve slowly in the opposite direction. This is intended to explain why the sun and moon appear to move from East to West while the planets move from West to East in relation to the fixed stars.

Plato's analogy does not, however, allow for the inclination of the axis of the ecliptic in which sun, moon and planets move relative to the position of the fixed stars. However obscure and imperfect, this was Plato's attempt to give a picture of the operations of the universe, a world view adopted by later astrology.

Plato still had the signs of the zodiac ruled by gods and goddesses. However, a siren, sometimes translated as a 'daemon', stands at the top of each circle of the planets and fixed stars which form a system of eight concentric whorls. As the siren is carried round with the circle, it utters 'a note of constant pitch and the eight notes together make up a single scale'.[13] This is undoubtedly the doctrine of the 'Harmony of the Spheres' which Plato probably picked up from the Pythagoreans whom he visited in Southern Italy in 388–387 BC.

At equal distances round the Spindle of Necessity (on which are located the planets) sit three garlanded figures dressed in white, each on a throne, singing to the sirens' music. These are the three Fates, the daughters of Necessity: 'Lachesis of things past; Clotho of things present; Atropos of things to come.' Clotho helps from time to time to turn the outermost rim of the spindle, Atropos the inner rims, and Lachesis takes inner and outer rims with her left and right hand alternatively. Lachesis allots the soul the guardian it has chosen; Clotho 'the weaver' ratifies the destiny (*moira*) of the soul, while Atropos weaves the warp on to Clotho's woof and fixes the destiny. For Plato the existence of necessity – the observed regularities or laws of nature – was a sign of a rational and purposive design in the universe.

The Transmigration of Souls

From an astrological point of view, one of the most interesting aspects of Plato's myth of Er is his doctrine that the souls of the deceased, after passing through a period in the underworld or in heaven (depending on their behaviour in their previous lives), can choose their lot in their next life on earth. This doctrine would explain the importance astrologers give to the moment of conception or birth, depending on what time they think the soul enters the body. The souls have to go straight before Lachesis and an Interpreter takes a number of 'lots and patterns of life' from her lap. He then announces:

> Souls of the day, here you must begin another round of mortal life whose end is death. No Guardian Spirit will be allotted to you; you shall choose your own. And he on whom the lot falls first shall be

the first to choose the life which shall of necessity be his. Excellence knows no master; a man shall have more or less of her according to the value he sets on her. The fault lies not with God, but with the soul that makes the choice.[14]

Every conceivable pattern of life is on offer, both animal and human. The key passage for astrology is: 'There was no choice of quality of character since of necessity each soul must assume a character appropriate to its choice; but wealth and poverty, health and disease were all mixed in varying degrees in the lives to be chosen.'[15] This explains why later astrologers should place such emphasis on the natal chart in shaping a person's character and direction in life. But this is not fatalism. Plato makes the important distinction between qualities 'inborn or acquired'. Every soul is free to choose between a good life or an evil one. The middle course between extremes is recommended as the surest guide to a good life and the highest human happiness. And love is the driver of the chariot of the self, directing reason, appetites and passions.

In a discussion of what is called the 'nuptial number', Plato imagines the guardians of his ideal republic using arithmological and astrological knowledge to choose the most auspicious times for conception to ensure that the offspring produced will grow into good citizens of the State. This shows that Plato not only knew about astrological practices but actually encouraged their use.[16]

In *Phaedrus*, his dialogue on love, Plato further develops his notion of the transmigration of souls. He describes how souls travel with the gods beneath the vault of heaven. The immortal ones can even stand on the 'back of the universe' and contemplate what lies outside the heavens – absolute reality which is only apprehensible by intellect, 'the pilot of the soul'.[17] Some souls, however, lose their wings and fall to earth and become incarnated as humans. Before taking on a body each soul can choose its lot according to its own pleasure: some choose to be tyrants, warriors, financiers, doctors, soothsayers, poets, artisans or farmers. But all have had a glimpse of the 'plane of truth and beauty' and can recollect the things which their souls had once perceived. The person most likely to succeed and to regain his or her wings is the philosopher, the lover of wisdom. For Plato, philosophy was a process of remembering the truths to which we were exposed before being born into this world. The aids to recollection brought by philosophy thus form 'a continuous initiation into the perfect mystic vision'.[18]

The same might be said of astrology in its highest form. A similar role to the philosopher could be made for the astrologer if he or she reminds us of the divine origins of our soul and encourages us to realize our potential as rational and spiritual beings.

In *Phaedrus*, Plato presents through Socrates the soul as a winged chariot, with reason as charioteer and spirit and desire as the horses. The chariots of the gods encircle the perimeter of the sky forever, and before birth the chariots of human souls travel in their company gazing at 'what is beyond there' – the world of true being and absolute reality. The human teams, however, crash to earth and take on human lives. But even in human form it is still possible to recall the nature of true knowledge and virtue, regain one's wings and return to one's celestial origins.

Before reading *Phaedrus* and the myth of Er in *The Republic*, I was not clear why astrologers should place such emphasis on the moment of birth as a key to understanding our future personality. It seemed too deterministic. But after reading Plato, it began to make sense. What happens before our birth is as important as what comes after. Even the humanist philosopher Bertrand Russell recognized that pre-existence is as logical as an afterlife. Although not an idea familiar to Christians, it was obvious to ancient Greeks and always has been to Hindus and Buddhists.

It is the choice of our soul at the moment of birth which influences the type of character we develop. We can decide the kind of body we would like to dwell in, the kind of person we would like to be, the kind of parents to support us and the kind of society we would like to grow up in. We can choose whether we want to lead a good life or an evil one, one of wealth or poverty, wisdom or stupidity. We can try to recall the mystic vision or live a life of ignorance and forgetfulness. If this is the case, the position of the stars are signs pointing to the kind of original choice we made. If we are born under Mars and become a tyrant it is our choice. It is no good bemoaning our lot for it was chosen by us. As the Interpreter warns, the man who blames 'fate and heaven and anything but himself' should not forget that 'his misfortunes were his own fault'.[19]

Aristotle's Unmoved Mover

Plato's greatest pupil Aristotle (384–323 BC) was more sceptical than his master and made less of an impact on subsequent astrologers. He took a more biological approach and placed greater stress on the value of observation and experience as a source of knowledge. But it is somewhat misleading to say that Plato was a rationalist and Aristotle was an empiricist. Aristotle accepted the broad picture of Plato's geocentric universe with its perfect motion and planetary cycles. He continued the work of Plato's pupil Euxodus, the first to develop mathematical astronomy, who explained the irregular orbits of the planets by saying that they moved in twenty-six spheres and one sphere for the fixed stars, making twenty-seven in all. Aristotle proposed an even more complex pattern of fifty-four spheres.

Like Homer and Hesiod before him, Aristotle believed in the everlasting existence of the heavens and their movements. Movement is imperishable. But to start the whole universe and its celestial bodies rolling there must have been an unmoved mover. He considered *aither* (ether) to be in existence prior to the four elements of Empedocles; within it are the 'most divine of visible bodies', the sun, moon, planets and stars.[20] He was also fully convinced of their effect on the earth: he claimed that the annual movement of the sun and the monthly waxing and waning of the moon govern biological processes as well as the length of animate lives. They also control various inanimate physical processes on earth such as the strength of the winds.

At the same time, Aristotle placed the creator outside the universe as the unmoved mover, a god which is the first and final cause of the universe. He did not separate the soul from the body, and argued that when the body dies, the soul also dies. Indeed, the soul in his view is merely a set of capabilities manifesting life. He also rejected Plato's belief that the planets are divine intelligences. Nevertheless, the stars and planets are not random; they are alive and their activity is directed toward an end-purpose or *telos*, described as 'that which is in the best state'. The sphere of the stars, involved in the least movement, comes closest to the telos.

Aristotle was still sufficiently Pythagorean to believe that the nature of an object is contained in its form and to give central place to mathematics in understanding the universe. He gave an ingenious explanation of why we cannot hear the music of the spheres. In his view, bodies so great inevitably produce a sound by their movement as do smaller bodies on earth. Since the speeds of the stars, judged by their distances, are in ratios of musical consonances, it follows that the sound of the stars as they revolve is harmonious. He maintained that the sound is with us right from birth but there is no contrasting silence to show it up: 'for voice and silence are perceived by contrast with each other, and so all mankind is undergoing an experience like that of a coppersmith, who becomes by long habit indifferent to the din around him.'[21] The music of the harmony of the spheres is always there, only we cannot hear it in this cacophonous world.

The Blessed God

For later Aristotelians, the divine will originated beyond the fixed stars and filtered down through the planetary spheres to earth at the centre. This world view might give more room for human free will, but it also led to the disenchantment of the universe. Instead of being Plato's 'blessed god' and living organism, the universe increasingly appeared as a soulless machine. The tension between Plato's spiritual approach and Aristotle's more physical approach to the world has been reverberating ever since.

It has been said that all Western philosophy is just footnotes to Plato and Aristotle. Like all *bon mots*, this is an exaggeration, but astrologers have undoubtedly followed Plato rather than Aristotle. For those modern Aristotelian scientists who attack astrology, it is worth recalling that for Plato the world of ordinary perception was not fully real. The real world, the world of Being, contains the forms which are the objects of rational understanding and the operations of mathematics and logic. It can be perceived intuitively. On the other hand, the world of Becoming, which scientists deal with, is a corrupt and imperfect copy of the ideal. It contains all things perceived by our senses, about which no final knowledge is possible. Plato thus draws a clear distinction between a rational and empirical approach to knowledge – the one based on reasoning and intuition, the other on observation and experience. Since the senses are unreliable and this world is an illusion, the only sure guide is the intellect (in the broadest sense of the word). Whereas logic and mathematics are self-validating and ultimately based on intuition, physical science grounded in the senses can only be a 'likely story'. Astrology falls into the former category, astronomy into the latter. It is not therefore surprising that astrology is presented as the supreme science in the work *Epinomis*, intended as an appendix to Plato's *Laws* and probably written by one of his pupils.

Plato's rejection of empirical science as a sure guide to knowledge had a lasting influence on astrology and astronomy until the seventeenth century. The overall approach was first to construct a symbolic model of the universe and then make the observed movements of the celestial bodies – such as the irregular orbits of the planets – fit in with the preconceived system. Both the Arab and medieval European astronomers followed this method, keeping to the geocentric model of the universe because it appeared more rational and perfect. The more anomalies that were discovered, the more complicated their explanations became. Despite the scientific evidence to the contrary, modern astrologers continue in the Platonic tradition and believe that the cosmos with its regular movements of stars is indeed a 'blessed god'.

25

The Hellenistic World

*The lower world was seized with fear and sighed before the
extraordinary beauty and eternal stability of the things above.*

IT IS SAID THAT an astrologer was present when the Macedonian
general Alexander the Great was born in 357 BC. According to the
eighteenth-century English astrologer Ebenezer Sibly, the astrologer
Nectanebus 'besought her [Alexander's mother] not to permit the child
to be until he gave the word'.[1] Presumably his counsel was taken, for
Alexander became the most famous conqueror of the ancient world. But
it was a short-lived life and his death at thirty-three years old was
allegedly foretold by astrologers when he entered Babylon.

Alexander's conquests changed the face of the known world in the
Mediterranean and the Near East. After taking the city states of Greece
in 336 BC, Alexander went on to defeat Egypt in 331 BC, the Persian
Empire (including Mesopotamia) in 328 BC, and then fought his way
East as far as India. But by respecting local cultures and beliefs, he helped
to bring East and West closer together. The result was a considerable
cross-fertilization of ideas: while extending Greek influence to foreign
lands, his soldiers also returned home with many foreign beliefs, including
those of astrology.

Alexander himself made a dangerous march to the desert oracle of
Ammon in Sihaw in Egypt, where he declared himself to be Ammon's
divine son. Alexander's brother rebuilt the inner sanctuary of the temple
at Karnak, while the conqueror himself built an adjoining room, in
which he is depicted on reliefs making offerings to the Egyptian gods.
His general, Ptolemy, founded a dynasty which lasted until the final

defeat of Cleopatra and Anthony in 30 BC. The period witnessed a unique flowering of Hellenistic civilization which drew on the wisdom of the Egyptian temple priests and classical Greek philosophy. Alexandria, with its unique library and museum, not only became one of the greatest centres of learning in the ancient world but also a hotbed of astrology. It lasted as a dynamic, cosmopolitan city for 900 years until it fell to the invading Muslims in AD 640.

Thousands of Greeks also settled in Mesopotamia after the conquests of Alexander and came under the influence of local astrologers. Two astrologers residing in Babylon were mentioned later by the Greeks as Cidenas (Kidinnu) and Naburianos (Nab-rimannu). The fact that the Mesopotamian astrologers had become so fashionable and influential in Greece in the fourth century BC is attested by Eudoxus' alleged dismissal: 'No reliance whatever is to be placed in Chaldean astrologers when they profess a man's future from the position of the stars on the day of his birth.'[2] From the period of the Greek Seleucid rule in Mesopotamia (353 BC to 42 AD) come the earliest known representations of zodiacal figures and constellations. They depict the bull of Taurus, Virgo as a woman holding an ear of corn, Leo the Lion and Jupiter as an eight-pointed star.[3]

The Greeks adopted much of the astrology of the Chaldeans, but made many improvements. By applying their mathematics, they made it a much more systematic discipline. With their more philosophical frame of mind, the Greeks were not content simply to observe and record the movement of the celestial bodies; they also wanted to know why the planets should move in a particular way. And their concern with the individual led to a move from mundane astrology, dealing with the fate of the nation, to natal horoscopes, depicting a person's character and destiny.

An important stepping stone for the spread of Mesopotamian astrology to the West was the Greek island of Cos where Hippocrates had established his medical school. After 281 BC, the priest Berosus from Bel in Babylon established himself on the island, bringing with him the accumulated knowledge of thousands of years of astrology. His reputation for predictions grew to such an extent that the Athenians raised a statue to his honour. The Elder Pliny also says that he claimed that observations in Chaldaea (Babylon) had been carried out for 490,000 years.[4]

The first-century BC Roman writer Vitruvius, in his treatise on architecture, recognized the importance of Berosus in bringing natal astrology to Greece:

> It must be allowed that we can know what effects the twelves signs, and the sun, moon and five planets, have on the course of human life, from astrology and the calculations of the Chaldeans. For the genethlialogical art is properly theirs, by which they are able to unfold past and future events from their astronomical calculations. And many have come from that race of the Chaldaeans to leave us their discoveries, which are full of acuteness and learning. The first was Berosus, who settled on the island of Cos and taught there, and after him the learned Antipater, and then Achinapolus, who however set out his genethlialogical calculations not from the date of birth but from that of conception.[5]

The Stoics

The period immediately following Alexander's campaigns saw astrology come under the influence of Stoicism. The movement was founded by the Syrian Zeno who came to Athens in 313 BC and died in 264 BC. He set up a school in the *Stoa Poikile* (Painted Colonnade), hence the name 'Stoic'. The Stoics, who were among the greatest logicians and physicists of their times, fully integrated astrology into their system. They kept to the Platonic tradition of a spherical world-system, with the earth at the centre of the universe and the celestial bodies moving around it in circular motions. They also reaffirmed Plato's belief that the heavens revealed the divine presence and that the gods dwelt in the planets.

The cosmology of the Stoics is neither materialist nor idealist; they make no distinction between matter and spirit. God is immanent throughout the universe as *logos*. The universe is also pervaded with a form of energy which they called *pneuma* ('warm breath'), a notion similar to the Chinese *chi* and Indian *prana*. Everything in the universe works according to the same universal laws. As a result all is united by a kind of cosmic sympathy: a change in one part affects all the other parts. Minds and bodies are made of the same stuff and man is a microcosm of the macrocosm, a universe in miniature.

The teaching of the Stoics influenced astrology in several important ways. Firstly, since everything was interrelated by sympathy and governed by the same laws, it followed that what happened in heaven would inevitably affect what happened on earth and vice versa.

Secondly, the Stoics took up the ancient Mesopotamian idea of eternal recurrence based on the cyclical nature of the universe. They supposed that the Great Year would end with a cosmic conflagration (*ekypyrosis*, a 'burn-up') when the planets returned to the same point in longitude and latitude where they were when the cosmos was first formed. Phoenix-like, the fire contained within itself the four elements from which a new cosmos would be born. All would be exactly the same (one would live again although one might not have freckles the next time around). Thirdly, perhaps inspired by the new contact with different peoples in Asia, they advocated a world community based on the brotherhood of men.

The Stoics' belief that the individual could be master of his life encouraged the shift from mundane astrology to natal astrology in which the horoscope enables the individual to understand his fate and thereby help free himself from it. But how can this be the case if what happens could not have happened otherwise? A Stoic belief in universal law does not necessarily mean that we have no free choice. We can still choose to act in this way or that, or not at all. However, it does mean that if we go against Nature we will inevitably suffer disappointment, while if we act in harmony with it we shall achieve contentment. The quality of our lives is therefore in our own hands. Stoicism shares with Taoism a desire to attain an ideal state of self-sufficiency so that nothing can disturb one's peace of mind. This is best achieved by living according to Nature.

Mathematical Astronomers

In the meantime, Greek mathematical astronomy, which had begun with Euxodus in the fourth century BC, reached its zenith in the third and second centuries in the Hellenistic world. Herakleides (died 310 BC) had developed the work of Philolaus and proposed what he called the 'Egyptian' system. He still thought that the earth was at the centre of the universe, but turned on its own axis, causing the diurnal motion of the heavens. Mars, Jupiter and Saturn orbit the earth, but in order to explain the erratic orbits of Mercury and Venus, he suggested that they orbit the sun.

It was only a short step for Aristarchus (b.310 BC) to put forward the revolutionary idea that the earth and all the planets orbit the sun. The beautiful simplicity of this theory explained at a stroke the old problem of the erratic orbits of the planets. But due to the dominating influence of Plato and Aristotle, the concept of a geocentric universe held sway in Europe among most astronomers until the seventeenth-century, and continues to be the symbolic model of modern astrologers.

The last great Greek astronomer was Hipparchus (c.190–120 BC). He is remembered for inventing the co-ordinates of latitude and longitude used for mapping the skies, as well as the earth. He is also usually accredited with 'discovering' the precession of the equinoxes but, as we have seen, it seems likely that the Mesopotamians and the Egyptians had already worked this out. Nevertheless, by bringing attention to the movement of the vernal point through the constellations, he precipitated a split between the use of the sidereal zodiac based on the constellations and the tropical zodiac tied to the seasons.

While astrologers in the East continued to use the former, Arab and European astrologers were to opt for the latter. The result is that today the vernal equinox does not rise at the beginning of Aries, as it did in Hipparchus' day, but in Pisces. The last known use of the sidereal zodiac in Europe was in Constantinople in the sixth century AD.

Hermetic Writing

In the first century, Alexandria in Egypt on the shores of the Mediterranean became the astrological centre of the Hellenistic world. It was an intellectual melting pot where East met West, where Europe met Africa, and where Egyptian priests discussed religion and philosophy with Greeks, Romans, Syrians, Persians and Jews, among others. The Egyptian wisdom god Thoth was called Hermes by the Greeks, and astrologers writing in Greek deliberately cultivated a 'Hermetic' style and claimed knowledge of Hermetic writings. They saw themselves as part of a long tradition of ancient wisdom which could be traced back to the Old Kingdom of ancient Egypt.

Hermetic literature emerged during the Ptolemaic era in 'Hellenized' Egypt after the conquest of Alexander. The Ptolemies spoke Greek but adopted local customs and beliefs. The early Greek settlers who followed Alexander identified further Egyptian gods with their own, not only Thoth with Hermes but Osiris with Dionysius, Isis with Ceres, Persephone and Athene, and Horus with Apollo. They also associated Isis with Tyche, the goddess of Fortune. She did not represent implacable fate but the kind of destiny that could be altered by foreknowledge.

The earliest truly astrological texts are from Hellenistic Egypt and are written in Greek. One of most important writings – the *Salmeschiniaka* – only exists in fragments. Many more fragments are buried in twelve volumes of the *Catalogus Codicum astrologorum graecorum* (Brussels, 1898–1936). Among the literature which has survived, horoscopes are rare. The earliest horoscope preserved in a literary text deals with a birth in 72 BC while the earliest papyrus horoscope concerns a birth in 10 BC.[6]

Astrologers also drew on the writings of the legendary Egyptians Petosiris and Nechepso, who claimed to have received their knowledge from Hermes. *The Revelations of Nechepso and Petosiris* was a popular manual on astrology, probably written in Alexandria around 150 BC. Petosiris represents the prestige of the Egyptian priests; his tomb which predates 341 BC became a centre of a cult. Nechepso (663–522 BC), a king of the Twenty-sixth Dynasty, symbolizes the wisdom of the pharaohs. Their alleged works exist only in fragments and in quotations mentioned by later writers. They reveal a concern with astral omens (including the eclipses and the heliacal rising of Sirius) as well as horoscopes (with references to a method of calculating the length of life, the good and bad periods in a life based on planetary periods, and the finding of the Lord of the year). Plants and stones were associated with certain astral influences. They also claimed that the sign the moon was in at the time of conception should be the Ascendant in a nativity. According to the fourth-century astrologer Firmicus Maternus, Nechepso and Petosiris gained from Hermes the doctrine of the horoscope of the world, known as the *thema mundi*.[7]

Many astrological writings were attributed to Hermes. While these were considered by earlier scholars to be fundamentally Greek, the discovery of the *Nag Hammadi* library in Upper Egypt in 1945, which contained Hermetic and Gnostic writings, suggests that Hermetic literature was a fusion of Egyptian and Greek ways of thought. The text was in Coptic, that is, the Egyptian language written in the Greek alphabet.

The authentic voice of the Hermeticist comes through in the following passage:

> The ordering of the heavenly bodies is superior to that of our world below. It is immovable for all time, and transcends human under-standing. And so the lower world was seized with fear and sighed before the extraordinary beauty and eternal stability of the things

above . . . mysteries moved severally amidst the heavens according to fixed movements and periods of time, ordering and nourishing the lower realm through certain secret effluences.[8]

The Hermetic tradition was considered both mystical and secret. Clement of Alexandria argued that the wisdom teaching of Egypt was disguised from the profane and only revealed to the pure and worthy:

> Wherefore, in accordance with the method of concealment, the truly sacred Word, truly divine and most necessary for us, deposited in the shrine of truth, was by the Egyptians indicated by what were called among them *adyta* [the Holy of Holies], and among the Hebrews the veil. Only the consecrated – that is, those devoted to God, circumcised in the desire of the passions for the sake of love for that which is alone divine – were allowed access to the sanctuary. For Plato also thought it not lawful for 'the impure to touch the pure'. Whence the prophecies and oracles are spoken in enigmas, and the mysteries are not exhibited incontinently to all and sundry, but only after certain purifications and previous instructions.[9]

In an excerpt from the Hermetic writings, Firmicus Maternus confirms the secret of the sacred science was kept by the Egyptian temple priests: 'At the moment of my revealing the august secrets of this doctrine, secrets which the divine ancients communicated only with trepidation, and which they enveloped in profound darkness, fearful that the divine science, once brought to the light of day, would become known to the profane.'[10] Secrecy was thought necessary to prevent the powerful knowledge from being misused in the wrong hands.

What was the hidden message of the Hermetic writings which emerged in Alexandria? They offered a spiritual way to enlightenment, a method of salvation through knowledge or *gnosis*. The main writings are the *Corpus Hermeticum*, originally written in Greek, and the Latin *Asclepius* (known together as the *Hermetica*), as well as the anthology of Stobaeus. They contain both philosophical and technical material – along with magic, the technical details of astrology are seen as a suitable prelude to gnosis.

The anthology of Stobaeus especially mentions the decans and their 'sons', the 'demons' who dwell in the stars. They describe the functions of the soul in the light of its astral origins, as well the differences among embodied souls due to their astrological and elementary constitutions. The longest excerpt, the *Kore Kosmou* (Daughter of the Cosmos), asserts that 'no prophet about to raise his hands to the gods has ever ignored any of the things that are, so that philosophy and magic may nourish the soul and medicine heal the body.'[11]

What is the Hermetic teaching on astrology? It insists that 'the divine is the entire combination of cosmic influence renewed by nature'. It was not god but a craftsman created by god who fashioned the heavenly bodies: 'The mind who is god, being androgyne and existing as life and light, by speaking gave birth to a second mind, a craftsman, who, as god of fire and spirit, crafted seven governors; they encompass the sensible world in circles and their government is called fate.'[12] The 'seven governors' are of course the five planets and the two luminaries, the sun and the moon. The gods are visible in the shapes of the stars and all their constellations.

In a passage about rebirth, Hermes tells his son Tat that the 'tent' of the body was made from the zodiacal circle.[13] In another passage, the craftsman (created by the high god) is the sun and the cosmos the instrument of craftsmanship. In descending order of the Chain of Being, heaven governs the gods while 'demons' (daemons), posted by gods, govern humans. Each star has a daemon and follows its orders. The daemons would seem to act like guardian angels but they are good or evil or of a mixed nature according to their energies, for energy is the essence of a daemon and 'energies are like rays from god'.[14] The daemons have been granted authority over the earth and bring about changes for cities and nations as well as for individuals. It is the sun that organizes the troops of daemons under the regiments of the stars – the rays of the sun being a manifestation of *heka*, the magical power that energizes the universe. Their presence also explains the importance of the horoscope in determining a person's character and destiny:

> The demons on duty at the exact moment of birth, arrayed under each of the stars, take possession of each of us as we come into being and receive a soul. From moment to moment they change places, not staying in position but moving by rotation. Those that enter through the body into the two parts of the soul twist the soul about, each toward its own energy. But the rational part of the soul stands unmastered by the demons, suitable to be a receptacle for god . . . So, with our bodies as their instruments, the demons govern this earthly government. Hermes has called this government 'fate'.[15]

For me this explains beautifully the way the influence of the stars enters with our soul into our body at birth or conception (I lean towards the latter). It also shows how we can escape our destiny by using our 'rational part' – not reason as an analytical tool but reason as the sublime part of our make-up which enables us to attain salvation through gnosis.

Also celebrated in the *Hermetica* is Asclepius, whose name is given to a treatise in Latin. The original Egyptian Asclepius was Imhotep, an official of the Third Dynasty whose reputation as architect, healer and astrologer was so great that he was deified by later generations as the son of Ptah and the godson of Thoth himself. In Alexandria, a statue portrayed him in Greek costume with Thoth's sacred baboon. The Greek-speaking people of Egypt identified Imhotep with Asclepius, son of Apollo and god of healing. His attributes were the traveller's staff and the serpent of rejuvenation.

In a discussion of why mankind is one in form while each individual human is different, Hermes tells Asclepius that:

> it is impossible for any form to come to be in close similarity with another at distant points of time and latitude. The forms change as often as the hour has moments in the turning circle where the god resides whom we have called Omniform. The class persists, begetting copies of itself as often, as many and as diverse as the rotation of the world has moments. As it rotates the world changes, but the class neither changes nor rotates. Thus, the forms of each kind persist, though within the same form there are differences.[16]

The passage is obscure but full of references to Hermetic astrology. While the horoscope gives the fate of the individual, 'latitude' was thought to shape the fate of peoples or nations. Daemons who ruled the seven heavenly zones were associated with the seven geographical regions defined by latitude. The 'turning circle' is the zodiac. Its god Omniform produces the forms of humans through the thirty-six decans, three of which reside in each sign of the zodiac. The 'moments' refer to the stars ruling each of the 360° of the circle of the zodiac; no instant in time is therefore without a god presiding over it.

26

The Poetry of the Stars

*Why wonder that men comprehend heaven, when heaven exists
in their very beings and each one is in a smaller likeness the
image of God himself?*

MANILIUS

AFTER THE DEFEAT OF Cleopatra in 30 BC, Egypt became part of
the Roman Empire, but Alexandria continued as a cosmopolitan
centre of learning. The Romans respected the local culture and the
Egyptian priests continued to write in Coptic and the philosophers in
Greek. The temple of Dendera, for instance, was finally completed
under the Roman Emperor Augustus (30 BC–AD 14). As a symbol of
the continuity, a 'birth house' – a shrine dedicated to the birth of a
pharaoh – was constructed at the temple site under Nero, with reliefs
added by Trojan and Hadrian in the second century AD. The Roman
emperors clearly valued and respected the sacred science of Egypt and
wished to acknowledge it as part of their own tradition. Alexandria
remained the main centre of astrology throughout the Roman Empire
and many Roman emperors consulted Egyptian astrologers.

The signs of the zodiac regularly appeared on coffins in Roman
Egypt. In the British Museum, there is a beautiful painting of the sky
goddess Nut, surrounded by the signs of the zodiac, in the interior of the
painted wooden coffin of Soter from Thebes dating from the first
century AD. Graeco-Roman magical papyri also include lists of the type
of magic which would work best under each star sign. The energies of
individual stars continued to be linked with parts of the human body,
plants and precious stones.

The actual beginnings of astrology in Rome remain obscure, but it seems to have reached the city mainly through Greek learning from the third century BC onwards. Mesopotamian influence was also felt: Cato, writing a treatise on farming in 160 BC, warns that a good overseer should not consult Chaldeans among fortune-tellers. By 138 BC, during a period of unrest, astrology was seen as a sufficient threat for astrologers to be expelled from Rome and Roman Italy.

The historian Pliny the Elder calls the slave Manilius Antiochus the 'founder of astrology at Rome'.[1] However, it was the Greek Stoic philosophers who first made it respectable. The philosopher Posidonius (c.135–50 BC), who possessed an armillary sphere, had a decisive influence on the educated elite in favour of astrology. Probably of Syrian origin, he rationalized divination for the Roman upper classes.

Cicero (106–43 BC) attended some of the lectures of Posidonius. Although he was not persuaded, he recorded accurately the beliefs of the astrologers at the time:

> They say that the starry circle, which the Greeks call the zodiac, contains a power such that each single part of the circle moves and changes the sky in a different way according to the positions of the stars in these and neighbouring regions at any time; and they say that power is modified by the planets, either when they enter that very part of the circle containing someone's birth, or that part which possesses some familiarity or harmony with the birth-sign – they call these triangles and squares . . . They think it not only plausible but also true that howsoever the atmosphere is modified so the births of children are animated and shaped, and by this force their mentalities, habits, mind, body, action, fortune in life and experience are fashioned.[2]

In his *Republic*, Cicero developed his belief in stellar religion in a Latin version of the Platonic myth known as 'The Dream of Scipio'. 'Humans,' he declared, 'have been endowed with souls made out of everlasting fires called stars and constellations.' In his view, the way back to the 'habitation for all eternity', particularly in the constellations of the Milky Way, was through disinterested service to one's country.[3]

During the period of the Roman Republic, there were State diviners known as *haruspices* who were devoted to interpreting omens. Senators made up the college of augurs, who took omens from birds and the custodians of the books of Sibylline prophecy. Astrology, however, emerged with a flourish in the first century AD with the foundation of the Roman Empire. However, not all were impressed by the new interest in astrology. Pliny the Elder lamented: 'The most fraudulent of arts [magic] has held complete sway throughout the world for many ages . . . meeting with success [with medicine] it made a further addition of astrology, because there is nobody who is not eager to learn his destiny, or who does not believe that the truest account of it is that gained by watching the stars.'[4]

Suetonius, the chronicler of the lives of the Caesars, records prophecies made for all the emperors. He records:

> At Appollonia, Augustus and Agrippa together visited the house of Theogenes the astrologer, and climbed upstairs to his observatory; they both wished to consult him about their future careers. Agrippa went first and was prophesied such almost incredibly good fortune that Augustus expected a far less encouraging response, and felt ashamed to disclose the time of his birth. Yet when at last, after a great deal of hesitation, he grudgingly supplied the information for which both were pressing him, Theogenes rose and flung himself at his feet; and this gave Augustus so implicit a faith in the destiny that he even ventured to publish his horoscope, and struck a silver coin stamped with Capricorn, the sign under which he was born.[5]

Augustus adopted Capricorn as a personal emblem. Since it was the sign in which the sun begins to rise after the winter solstice, he presented it as a sign of a new age of peace after the Roman civil wars.

Another imperial enthusiast was Septimius Severus who drew on astrology to legitimize his rule. He had his horoscope drawn on the ceiling of the rooms in his palace, but was careful to make sure the Ascendant was placed at a different place in each room so that no one could make their own calculations, particularly about the time of his death!

Women of the Roman Empire were particularly drawn to the astrologers. The Roman satirist Juvenal (c.60–c.140 AD) offers a portrait of a frequenter of astrologers which is immediately recognizable today:

> Your wife, your Tanaquil,
> Is for ever consulting such folk. Why does her jaundice-ridden
> Mother take so long dying? When will she see off
> Her sister or her uncles? (She made all enquiries
> About you some time back.) Will her present lover

Survive her? (What greater boon could she ask of the Gods?)
Yet she at least cannot tell what Saturn's gloomy
Conjunction portends, or under which constellation
Venus is most propitious; which months bring loss, which gain.
When you meet such a woman, clutching her well-thumbed
Almanacs like a string of amber worry-beads,
Keep very clear of her. She isn't shopping around
For expert advice; she's an expert herself . . .
When she wants to go out of town, a mile even, or less,
She computes a propitious time from her tables. If she rubs
One corner of her eye, and it itches, she must never
Put ointment on it without first consulting her horoscope; if
She is ill in bed, she will only take nourishment
At such times as Petosiris, the Egyptian, may recommend.[6]

Manilius' *Astronomica*

It was during the reigns of Augustus and Tiberius that modern astrology
took on its recognizable form. The earliest known astrological treatise
is the Latin poem *Astronomica* by Manilius. Written at the beginning
of the first century AD, its five books were dedicated to Emperor
Augustus. It is enlivened with the passionate rhetoric of fatalism which
reveals the poet's Stoic beliefs. It opens by acknowledging the legacy of
the 'dusky nations' of the Babylonians and Egyptians and calls the god
of Cyllene (Mercury, the self-same Greek Hermes and the Egyptian
Thoth) the 'first founder of this great and holy science'.[7]

   In his account of the celestial phenomena, Manilius presented the
earth as a sphere composed of four elements at the centre of the universe.
The stars were fires panelling the roof of the universe, which was sacred
and pervaded with spirit, forming a harmonious whole from its diverse
parts:

> This fabric which forms the body of the boundless universe, together
> with its members composed of nature's divers elements, air and
> fire, earth and level sea, is ruled by the force of divine spirit; by
> sacred dispensation the deity brings harmony and governs with
> hidden purpose, arranging mutual bonds between all parts, so that
> each may furnish and receive another's strength and that the whole
> may stand fast in kinship despite its variety of forms.[8]

On earth, everything was continually changing, but heaven remained the same. God and 'all-controlling reason' created earthly beings from the signs of heaven. God compelled recognition of the influences of the distant stars in that they gave people their lives and destinies and each man his own character.

The Stoic in Manilius lamented the folly of human beings who spent their lives in worry, tormenting themselves with fears and senseless desires, wasting their lives in pursuit of gain: 'Everyone is the poorer for the possessions because he looks for more: none counts his blessings, but only lusts for what he lacks.' If only people would realize that they can do nothing about their fate for it is written in the stars. In true Stoic spirit, he exclaimed: 'Set free your minds, O mortals, banish your cares, and rid your lives of all this vain complaint! Fate rules the world, all things stand fixed by immutable laws, and the long ages are assigned a predestined course of events. At birth our death is sealed, and our end is consequent on our beginning.'[9]

In the first book of his *Astronomica*, Manilius describes the signs of the zodiac with a characteristic flourish:

> Resplendent in his golden face the Ram (Aries) leads the way and looks back with wonder at the backward rising of the Bull (Taurus), who with lowered face and brow summons the Twins (Gemini); these the Crab (Cancer) follows, the Lion (Leo) the Crab, and the Virgin (Virgo) the Lion. Then the Balance (Libra), having matched daylight with the length of night; draws on the Scorpion (Scorpio), ablaze with his glittering constellation, at whose tail the man with body of a horse (Sagittarius) aims with taut bow a winged shaft, ever in act to shoot. Next comes Capricorn, curled up within his cramped asterism, and after him from urn upturned the Waterman (Aquarius) pours forth the wonted stream for the Fishes (Pisces) which swim eagerly into it; and these as they bring up the rear of the signs are joined by the Ram.[10]

The second book focuses on the characteristics of the signs of the zodiac. Manilius mentions the parts of the body associated with the signs of the zodiac and how plants and stones associated with the planets can be used in cures. He also treats the so-called *dodecatemoria* (*dodeca* is Greek for twelve; *morion*, for part). They refer to the twelve parts of the 30° sign of the zodiac. Each dodecatemory consists of 2.5°, and is allocated a sign in the same order as the zodiac. In this way, interpretations become more subtle and complex. While a planet might be in the sign of Leo, its dodecatemory might be in Sagittarius, thereby deepening the analysis. Manilius considers the zodiacal dodecatemories – that is, the twelve-fold division within each sign allotted to different signs – as well as planetary dodecatemories, of which five, consisting of one degree assigned to the planets, make up every zodiacal dodecatemory.

The division of the horoscope into four points known as quadrants is also explained. These were called *cardines* in Latin. The first and most important is the point of the ecliptic (the degree or sign of the zodiac) rising above the horizon at the time in question, known in Latin as the *horoscopus* or *ascendens* and now called the Ascendant (often abbreviated to ASC). The second point, where the meridian (the arc of longitude passing through the observer's zenith) cuts the ecliptic (that is, the culmination point above his head) is the Midheaven, still known by its Latin name *Medium Coeli* (MC). The third is the setting point opposite the Ascendant, known as the *Occasus* or Descendant (DESC). And the fourth, which is directly opposite the second (where the other half of the meridian cuts the other half of the ecliptic) is still known by its Latin name *Imum Coeli* (IC).

It was probably Egyptian astrologers who inspired the division of the horoscope into quadrants. The sun is strong and young in the East, rises to its greatest power in the Midheaven, and declines into age and weakness in the West. This is the daily voyage of the sun god Re across the heavens which clearly mirrors our journey on earth. Applied to human life, it is not surprising that the first quadrant, from the ASC to the MC, should rule a person's youth; the next quarter, middle age; the third, old age; and the fourth, extreme old age and death.

It was a short step to divide further each of the quadrants, so that each cardinal point had two Houses. A particular realm of human life, such as marriage, children, work or health, was allocated to each of the eight Houses. No doubt influenced by the number of signs in the zodiac, the next move was to devise a system of twelve Houses, each having an equal space on the ecliptic. This would have been easy, since old diagrams of horoscopes were square, as they still are in India. The position of the Houses round the ecliptic was fixed – and still is – by the Ascendant. The sign of the zodiac which tallies with the House will thus depend on the time and place of the horoscope. The zodiac thus revolves within the framework of the Houses.

Manilius defines the significance of the twelve *loci* (Houses) in a way which reflects the aspects of life considered most important at the time: 1 home and property; 2 warfare and travel; 3 business and social life; 4 law; 5 marriage and friendships; 6 means and prosperity; 7 dangers; 8 class and reputation; 9 children; 10 way of life and character; 11 health and sickness; and 12 success in reaching goals.

The third book of Manilius' work addresses the twelve lots (*sortes* in Latin), the points on the birthchart which indicate particular areas of life. The most important is the Lot of Fortune (usually represented by a cross within a circle), the position of which determines the other lots. If the birth was during the day, the Lot of Fortune is calculated by measuring the degrees between the sun and the moon and then measuring off the same amount along the zodiac from the Ascendant. If by night, the procedure is reversed, counting from the moon to the sun.

The Lot of Fortune was sometimes called the 'Horoscope of the moon'. Other lots were developed, such as the Lot of Daemon, the Lot of Necessity and the Lot of Eros, but there was often considerable confusion between the lots and the Houses, with different ancient authorities giving different indications. The Lot of Fortune is the principal one to have survived.

The fourth book of Manilius' *Astronomica* describes the decans, the three-fold division of the zodiac signs allotted to different planets, which was adapted by the Greeks from the Egyptians. Manilius then gives a map of the world along with the rulers of the zodiac for each region. The last book deals with the *paranatellonta*, the stars that rise and set at the same time as the sections of the ecliptic, but North or South of them. A treatment of the planetary influences here may well have been lost. While many of the more complicated details such as the lots, dodecatemories and paranatellonta were subsequently dropped, the main elements of Manilius' work became part of mainstream astrology.

The Trickle Becomes a Stream

Another work written in the first century which has recently been discovered is by Dorotheus of Sidon. Originally in Greek verse, it was preserved in an eighth-century Arabic version made from a third-century Persian translation. It is a complete treatise on astrology, covering horary as well as natal astrology. Placing himself firmly within the Hermetic tradition, Dorotheus called himself the King of Egypt and addressed the book to his son Hermes. During his travels in Egypt and Babylon, he claimed to have gathered the best teachings of the first authorities. His fifth book is concerned with 'interrogations' (*katarchai*) which depend mostly on the Ascendant and the moon and how they are aspected. The chapter on marriage and the seven medical chapters are mostly based on the moon. If the moon is flowing from Saturn, for instance, then it indicates 'a fever that shakes him and a hidden malaise of his diet'.[11]

The trickle of astrological literature soon became a stream. Manetho, in his *Prognostics*, used Dorotheus as a source. Using his own horoscope dated 27 May AD 80, he celebrated in verse 'what Fate granted me to teach, the wisdom and beautiful poetry of the stars'.[12]

Vettius Valens brought together the new work in his *Anthologies*, which contained about 130 examples of nativities. Despite his Latin name, the author came from Antioch in Syria, probably resided in Alexandria during the second century AD and wrote in difficult Greek. He regularly mentions the 'divine Egyptians' and often refers to the work of Nechepso and Petosiris and the legendary *Book of Hermes*. Belonging to the Hermetic tradition, he implies that he is revealing mysteries and that the reader should take an oath not to reveal the secrets to the wrong people. His work proved one of the most popular ancient texts, and was much copied later, often with amendments and additions.

Valens listed the four trigons and links them with the planets and the four elements as follows:

Trigon	Planets	Element
Aries, Leo, Sagittaruis	Sun, Jupiter, Saturn	Fire
Taurus, Virgo, Capricorn	Moon, Venus, Mars	Earth
Gemini, Libra, Aquarius	Saturn, Mercury, Jupiter	Air
Cancer, Scorpio, Pisces	Mars, Venus, Moon	Water

Like Dorotheus, Valens stressed the need for secrecy: 'I adjure you, most honoured brother, and all those being initiated into this systematic art, learning of the starry bowl of heavens, and the zodiac, and the sun and moon and the five planets, and also of foreknowledge and holy Necessity, to keep all these things hidden, and not share them with the uninstructed, except those who are worthy and able to guard and receive them rightly.'[13]

It is clear from these works that by the second century AD the main outlines of astrology were already established. It was left to the Greek author Lucian of Samosata to make the clearest defence of astrology:

> If it is admitted that a horse in gallop, that birds in flying and men in walking make the stones jump or drive the little floating particles of dust by the wind of their course, why should you deny that the stars have any effect? The smallest fire sends us its emanations, and although it is not for us that the stars burn, and they care very little about warning us, why should we not receive any emanations from them? Astrology, it is true, cannot make that good which is evil. It can effect no change in the course of events, but it renders a service to those who cultivate it by announcing to them great things to come: it produces joy by anticipation at the same time that it fortifies them against evil.[14]

It was, however, the Greek writer Ptolemy, one of the most brilliant thinkers in the history of science, who brought the work of his forebears together to give a definitive account of astrology which became the foundation of the Western tradition.

27

The Ambient

To *any vision must be brought an eye*
adapted to what is to be seen.

PLOTINUS

W<small>HILE</small> <small>PLATO</small> <small>PROVIDED</small> the philosophical background of astrology, Ptolemy developed it into a system that has undergone little
subsequent change in the West. Claudius Ptolemaeus (c.100–178 AD)
was born in Ptolemais in Egypt, lived in Alexandria and wrote in Greek.
He is remembered for his *Almagest*, which is a complete exposition of
mathematical astronomy and the climax of centuries of Mesopotamian,
Egyptian and Greek cosmology. Well into the Renaissance, his name was
still pre-eminent in astronomy and geography. While firmly believing
that the earth was at the centre of the universe, he used eccentric and
epicyclical models to explain the observed erratic behaviour of the
planets.

The companion volume to the *Almagest* is the *Tetrabiblos* (Four
Books) which has been called the 'Bible of astrology'. It provided the
fundamental lines along which developed the greater part of Western
astrology. Ptomely's views on the nature of astrological causation and
the origins of human character became accepted as basic tenets. Mainstream astrology today is still as 'thoroughly Ptolemaic' as at any time
in the last two millennia.[1]

Although the *Almagest* deals with what we would now call astronomy and the *Tetrabiblos* with astrology, Ptolemy saw them as two
parts of the same enquiry. Indeed, the words *astronomia* and *astrologia*
continued to be used more or less indiscriminately well into the Middle
Ages. In the opening of *Tetrabiblos*, Ptolemy draws a distinction between

two means of prediction: 'One, which is first both in order and effective-
ness, is that whereby we apprehend the aspects of the movements of the
sun, moon, and stars in relation to each other and to the earth, as they
occur from time to time; the second is that in which by means of the
natural character of these aspects themselves we investigate the changes
which they bring about in that which they surround.'[2]

The first, of course, is what we would now call astronomy and the
second, astrology. For Ptolemy astrology was a discipline which follows
carefully developed rules, but like medicine, it was also a conjectural art
that could make mistakes because of the number of variables involved.
While there may have been many charlatan astrologers, it does not
follow that the subject itself is suspect: we do not discredit the art of
the pilot despite its many errors. At the same time, Ptolemy wanted to
approach the subject in 'a properly philosophical way'. Although it does
not possess the certainty of the 'unvarying science' of astronomy,
astrology is the sort of investigation which is 'within the bounds of
possibility, when it is evident that most events of a general nature draw
their causes from the enveloping heavens.'[3]

Ptolemy believes that an 'ambient' or ether (Aristotle's fifth element)
is suffused throughout the universe. Changes in the ambient affect the
sublunary realm made from the four elements, first fire and air, and then
earth and water. The elements explain the beneficent and malefic roles
of the planets. Hot and moist qualities are fertile and active, dry and cold
are destructive and passive. The mixture of elements also classifies them.
Moisture is a feminine quality and so Venus and the moon are feminine,
while the sun, Jupiter and Mars are dry and masculine. Mercury, being
dry and moist, is hermaphrodite.

There is a continuous celestial influence upon terrestrial events. To
provide evidence for the effect of celestial bodies on earth, Ptolemy
mentions changes in the tides, the seasons, the weather, animals and
plants. If a man can predict the weather, he asks, then, 'Why can he not,
too, with respect to an individual man, perceive the general quality of
his temperament from the ambient [celestial environment] at the time
of his birth?'[4]

Prediction by astronomical means is not only possible but also
beneficial: 'For if we look to the goods of the soul, what could be more
conducive to well-being, pleasure, and in general satisfaction than this
kind of forecast, by which we gain full view of things human and divine?'
Echoing the sentiments of the Stoics, he maintains that foreknowledge

'accustoms and calms the soul by experience of distant events as though they were present, and prepares it to greet with calm and steadiness whatever comes.'[5] It also enables us to take preventive remedies 'quite in accord with fate and nature' so that forecasted events do not occur at all, or are rendered less severe. We can therefore alleviate if not alter our fate as indicated by the stars at birth. Moreover, not all things are subject to fate; chance plays a role too.

While the first book of his *Tetrabiblos* deals with the signs, aspects and Houses, Ptolemy begins the second with general astrology as it relates to whole races, countries and cities. With his Alexandrian bias, he saw the Mediterranean as the cradle of civilization. The Greeks, being subject to Jupiter and Mercury, were lovers of liberty and learning. On the other hand, Britain, Gaul (France) and Germany, being in close familiarity with Aries and Mars, were 'fiercer, more headstrong and bestial' than the Southern Europeans. As for the Egyptians, who were familiar to Gemini and Mercury: 'they are thoughtful and intelligent and facile in all things, especially in the search for wisdom and religion; they are magicians and performers of secret mysteries and in general skilled in mathematics.'[6] Elsewhere, Ptolemy claimed that the Egyptians had entirely united medicine with astronomical prediction.

Looking at the active powers of the planets, Ptolemy observed that when Saturn gains sole dominance, it is in general the cause of destruction by cold; Jupiter produces increase in general; Mars is the cause of destruction through dryness; Venus has similar results to Jupiter but with the addition of a 'certain agreeable quality'. Mercury has the active power of whichever planet may be associated with him. In combinations one must consider not only the mixture of the planets with one another, but also their combination with the other celestial bodies that share the same nature, whether they be fixed stars or signs of the zodiac.

Although he was aware of the precession of the equinoxes, Ptolemy, like most modern astrologers in the West, worked with a fixed zodiac and not a natural one. Whichever constellation the vernal equinox is actually in, it is symbolically placed in 0° in Aries, which is taken as the beginning of the zodiacal circle. He also divided the circle into equal quadrants, defined by the Ascendant, the *Medium Coeli*, the Setting point and the *Imum Coeli*. He did not worry about the problem of the inequality of quadrants caused by the obliquity of the ecliptic and so did not mention it.

In the second book, Ptolemy treated what he calls the 'genethlia-logical art', that is to say, the prognostic art relating to the individual. He defined the art as the 'scientific observation' of the change in the 'sub-jective natures which corresponds to parallel movements of the heavenly bodies through the surrounding heavens.'[7] He insisted, however, that in all genethlialogical inquiries a more general destiny, namely that of a country of birth, should take precedence over all particular considera-tions, such as the form of the body, the 'character of the soul' and the variations of manners and customs. This was to avoid unwittingly calling the Ethiopian white or straight-haired and the Greeks 'savage of soul and untutored of mind'.[8]

In his view the general characteristics of an individual's tempera-ment were 'determined' from 'the first starting-point'. But what is this starting point? Is it the moment of conception or the moment of birth? Chronologically, it is the 'very time of conception, but potentially and accidentally the moment of birth'. If the former can be ascertained, it is 'more fitting' in determining the nature of the body and the soul, by examining the 'effective power' of the configuration of the stars at that time: 'For to the seed is given once and for all at the beginning such and such qualities by the endowment of the ambient; and even though it may change as the body subsequently grows, since by natural process it mingles with itself in the process of growth only matter which is akin to itself, thus it resembles even more closely the type of its initial quality.'[9]

The time of conception may be called 'the genesis of the human seed' and the moment of birth 'the genesis of the man'. But since it is usually difficult to calculate the former, Ptolemy accepted that one must work with the latter. Indeed, the primary concern of the third and fourth books of the *Tetrabiblos* is the horoscope of birth as the origin of human nature. The sign in which the moon is found at the moment of conception should be the Ascendant; in the case of the birth, the sun.

In general, the planets will determine the physical appearance of individuals, while Mercury indicates the 'reason and mind'. In addition, the signs which contain Mercury and the moon, the planets which dominate them, and their aspects to the sun, contribute much to the 'quality of the soul', by which he would seem to mean the mental character of a person. In a section dealing with the 'diseases of the soul' or mental disorders, he suggests that if the benefic planets Jupiter or Venus have any influence, the afflictions can be cured. With Jupiter, the disease can be cured with diet or drugs; with Venus, through oracles and with the help of the gods.

Ptolemy was the source of much of the rhetorical lists of character's traits so beloved by later astrologers. Typical is the following tirade:

> Allied with Venus in honourable positions Saturn makes his subjects haters of women, lovers of antiquity, solitary, unpleasant to meet, unambitious, hating the beautiful, envious, stern in social relations, not companionable, of fixed opinions, prophetic, given to the practice of religious rites, lovers of mysteries and initiations, performers of sacrificial rites, mystics, religious addicts, but dignified and reverent, modest, philosophical, faithful in marriage, self-controlled, calculating, cautious, quick to take offence, and easily led by jealousy to be suspicious of their wives. In positions of the opposite kind he makes them loose, lascivious, doers of base acts, undiscriminating and unclean in sexual relations, impure, deceivers of women.

In short, 'rogues who will stop at nothing'![10]

As for the 'morbid perversion of the active part of the soul', one must consider the relationship between the sun and the moon and the relation to them of Mars and Venus. If the luminaries are unattended in the masculine signs, 'males exceed in the natural, and females exceed in the unnatural quality'. If likewise either Mars or Venus, or both of them, is in a masculine sign, the males are 'adulterous, insatiate, and ready on every occasion for base and lawless acts of sexual passion, while the females are lustful for natural congresses, cast inviting glances of the eye, and are what we call *tribades* [translated as 'female perverts']; for they deal with females and perform the function of males'.[11] Men may come from Mars, and women from Venus, but these planets should be in the right signs if they are to have a 'normal' sex life.

In the case of marriage, it is necessary for men to look at the position of the moon in their genitures; for women, the position of the sun. If the moon applies to beneficent planets, men get good wives; if malefic, the opposite. If the moon applies to Saturn, 'he makes the wives hard-working and stern; Jupiter, dignified and good managers; Mars, bold and unruly; Mercury, intelligent and keen. Further, Venus with Jupiter, Saturn or Mercury makes them thrifty and affectionate to their husbands and children, but with Mars, 'easily roused to wrath, unstable, and unfeeling.' Similarly, if the sun is aspected to Saturn, women marry 'sedate, useful, industrious husbands; if Jupiter is in aspect, dignified and magnanimous; Mars, men of action, lacking in affection, and unruly; Venus, neat and handsome; Mercury, thrifty and practical; Venus with Saturn, sluggish and rather weak in sexual relations; Venus with Mars, ardent, impetuous, and adulterous; Venus with Mercury, infatuated with boys.'[12]

I was particularly interested in what Ptolemy had to say about foreign travel. To find out one must observe the position of the luminaries to the 'angles', particularly the moon (the greatest traveller in the heavens). When it is setting or declining from the angles, that is when the moon is in the seventh, third, sixth, ninth and twelfth Houses, it portends voyages abroad. If Jupiter and Venus are rulers of the Houses which govern travel, they make the journeys safe and pleasant. If Saturn and Mars control the luminaries, and particularly if they are in opposition, they will involve the subject in great dangers: 'through unfortunate voyages and shipwrecks if they are watery signs, or again through hard going and desert places; and if they are in solid signs, through falling from heights and assaults of winds.'[13]

Towards the end of the fourth book, Ptolemy makes an eloquent link between the planets and the seven ages of man, which depend on the order of the seven planets, beginning with the moon, the first sphere, and ending with Saturn, the outermost of the planetary spheres. The moon rules over the age of infancy up to the fourth year and produces the suppleness of its body. In the following ten years of childhood, Mercury begins to fashion the intelligent and logical part of the soul. Venus takes in charge the third age of youth and implants 'an impulse toward the embrace of love'. The lord of the middle sphere is the sun, the period of young manhood which lasts for nineteen years and which engrafts mastery of actions and ambition. In the fifth age of manhood, Mars assumes command for fifteen years and introduces severity and misery into life. Jupiter, sixth in order, is responsible for elderly age for a period of twelve years, bringing about the renunciation of manual labour and dangerous activity and introducing decorum, foresight and consolation. Finally, Saturn takes as his lot old age which lasts for the rest of life. Now the movements of both body and soul are cooled and worn down with age and one becomes 'dispirited, weak, easily offended, and hard to please in all situations'.[14] Such a gloomy picture anticipates Jaques' famous speech in Shakespeare's *As You Like It* about the last scene of life: 'second childishness and mere oblivion: / Sans teeth, sans eyes, sans taste, sans everything.'

Since everything is not governed solely by one malevolent or benefic planet or star and many variables are involved, Ptolemy observes that the fortune of life on earth is inevitably mixed: 'One may, for example, lose a relative and receive an inheritance, or at once be prostrated by illness and gain some dignity and promotion, or in the midst of misfortune become the father of children.'[15] Such are the vagaries of fate in this sublunary scene.

Plotinus and the World Soul

While Ptolemy laid the technical foundations of Western astrology, it was another Alexandrian who reinforced its mystical dimension. Following in the tradition of Pythagoras and Plato, the philosopher Plotinus (AD 204–70) has been called the founder of 'speculative mysticism' in the West.[16] Born in Alexandria, he eventually settled in Rome at the age of forty. According to his pupil Porphyry, Plotinus was particularly interested in the 'Persian methods and the system adopted among the Indians.'[17] He also drew on the ancient wisdom of the temples of his native land; he participated in a seance with a visiting Egyptian priest in the Temple of Isis in Rome to call down his 'spirit' which was declared to be that of a god. He was no stranger to astral travel and often experienced being 'lifted out of the body into myself; becoming external to all things and self-centred; beholding a marvellous beauty.'[18]

In Plotinus' scheme of things, from the One emerges the Divine Mind and the Universal Soul which is responsible for all life. The 'gods' and the lesser 'daimones' are expressions of the One. Humans have two souls, the higher 'intellectual soul' untouched by matter, and the 'reasoning soul', the normal nature of humankind.

Like the Stoics, Plotinus was convinced that the world is not only one, but that it is also harmonious and good. He therefore rejected the Gnostics who identified evil with matter in this sublunary world. For Plotinus, matter is ultimately a feeble shadow of Being. Man is not the centre of the universe; he *is* the universe. And since animals participate in the World Soul, Plotinus declined from eating them.

Since the Good is all-reaching, strictly speaking evil does not exist. What is commonly understood as evil is merely the half-existence of the Good in matter. Wrong-doing thus comes from bewilderment and laziness: 'wickedness is a miscalculating effort towards Intelligence [the highest principle in man].'[19] The corollary of this is that salvation is not to be strived for: we are already saved. We simply have to become aware of what we already are in our innermost nature. The mystical path is thus an ascent and a return to one's origins. We can all experience the ecstatic union of the soul with the One which is within us as a divine presence. Plotinus called this experience a 'vision':

> When you are self-gathered in the purity of your being, nothing now remaining that can shatter that inner unity, nothing from without clinging to the authentic man, when you find yourself wholly true to your essential nature, wholly that only veritable Light which is not measured by space, not narrowed to any circum-scribed form nor again diffused as a thing void of term, but ever unmeasurable as something greater than all measure and more than all quantity – when you perceive that you have grown to this, you are now become very vision: now call up all your confidence, strike forward yet a step – you need a guide no longer – strain, and see.[20]

Plotinus showed himself fully aware of the art of the astrologer. He gives the traditional interpretation of the influence of the planets:

> The star known as Jupiter includes a due measure of fire (and warmth), in this resembling the Morning-star [Venus] and there-fore seeming to be in alliance with it. In aspect with what is known as the Fiery Star [Mars], Jupiter is beneficent by virtue of the mixing of influences: in aspect with Saturn unfriendly by dint of distance. Mercury, it would seem, is (in itself) indifferent whatever stars it be in aspect with; for it adopts any and every character.[21]

Plotinus also gave supreme expression to the astrological world view which still holds sway today. The influence of the planets on the earth is brought about by cosmic sympathy: 'All things must be enchained; and the sympathy and correspondence obtaining in any one closely knit organism must exist, first, and most intensely, in the All.' The circuit of the heavens does not operate by chance but under the direction of the World Soul of the living whole of the universe. Therefore there must be 'a harmony between cause and caused . . . every several configuration within the Circuit must be accompanied by a change in the position and conditions of things subordinate to it.' Plotinus saw this happening through 'the material emanations from the living beings of the heavenly system'.[22]

It is not, however, a deterministic picture. Plotinus likened the situation to a dance. The co-ordinated limbs of a dancer move to a certain rhythm but it is the dancer's mind that decides his overall purpose. In a similar way, the stars are not the direct cause of events on earth; 'the cause is the 'co-ordinating All.' Thus all the stars are service-able to the universe 'in a harmony like that observed in the members of any one animal form.'[23] Just as the gall exists not merely for its own immediate function but for the body as a whole, so the stars exist for the overall purpose of the Divine Mind.

Contrary to the general opinion of his contemporaries, Plotinus asserted that 'the circuit of the stars indicates definite events to come but without being the causes.' Given the perfection of the universe, each star – a god of the heavenly sphere – must be 'continuously serene, happy in the good they enjoy and the Vision before them.' While not strictly speaking causes, Plotinus thought of the stars as 'letters perpetually being inscribed in the heavens'.[24] If we read the symbols aright, we can then read the future.

Taking up the metaphor of the Spindle of Necessity given in Plato's *Timaeus*, which explains how 'our personality is bound up with the stars', Plotinus argued that we are not slaves to the stars' ordering. Since we are more than a 'body ensouled', we can through the development of our mind work out our liberation from the heavenly sphere.[25] Thus while the stars announce or foreshadow the future, they do not actually cause what takes place on earth and what we make of our lives. It is a strikingly modern conception shared by many contemporary astrologers.

28

Myriogenesis

*Be modest, upright, sober, eat little, be content with a few goods,
so that the shameful love of money may not defile the glory of
this divine science.*

FIRMICUS MATERNUS

ASTROLOGY NOT ONLY became part of everyday culture but formed
an integral part of medicine, magic and several influential cults in the
Egyptian and Graeco-Roman world at the beginning of the Christian era.

Galen (c.AD 129–199) studied in Greece and Alexandria before
becoming the court-physician in the Rome of Marcus Aurelius. Inspired
by Plato and Hippocrates, his version of medical theory continued as
the principal model well into the Middle Ages. It was based on the
notion of the four humours associated with the four elements blended
in different parts of the body. For Galen, 'Astrology is the foreseeing
part of their [the physicians'] art, and if not all, but at least most of them
have accepted this part of astrology as part of medicine.'[1]

Magic was very closely intertwined with medical astrology at the
time. Flowers and stones were associated with the planets and were used
to counteract the baneful effect of a planet, or to enhance a beneficial
influence. As the following recipe illustrates, astrology and magic were
clearly part of preventive as well as curative medicine:

> A contraceptive, the only one in the world: take as many bittervetch
> seeds as you want for the number of years you want to remain
> sterile. Steep them in the menses of a menstruating woman. Let her
> steep them in her own genitals. Take a frog that is alive and throw
> the bittervetch seeds into its mouth so that the frog swallows them,
> and release the frog alive at the place where you captured him. And

take a seed of henbane, steep it in mare's milk; and take the nasal mucus of an ox, with seeds of barley, put these into a [piece of] leather skin made and attach it as an amulet during the waning of the moon [which is] in a female sign of the zodiac on a day of Saturn or Mercury. Mix in with the barley grains cerumen from the ear of a mule.[2]

The waning of the moon is linked with the decline in fertility, Saturn is associated with coldness and dryness, and Mercury represents volatility.

Magic and astrology went hand in hand outside the garden of medicine. In a procedure to divine a dream, instructions were given to use cinnabar to inscribe all the signs of the zodiac, as well as their magical names, on each leaf of a laurel-branch and then sleep on it.[3]

A magical papyrus further gives an horary astrological scheme based on the orbit of the moon through the signs of the zodiac for the auspicious timing of spells. It illustrates well the concerns of astrologers' clients at the time:

Moon in Virgo: anything is rendered obtainable. In Libra: necromancy. In Scorpio: anything inflicting evil. In Sagittarius, an invocation of invocations to the sun and the moon. In Capricorn: say whatever you wish for best results. In Aquarius: for a love charm. Pisces: for foreknowledge. In Aries: fire divination or love charm. In Taurus: incantation to a lamp. Gemini: spell for winning favour. In Cancer: phylacteries. Leo: rings or binding spells.[4]

Not only was astrology used to enhance magic, but magic could, in turn, be used as a remedy to counteract inauspicious predictions. By calling up a god in the correct manner, one could dispense with the services of an earth-bound astrologer. The god could then tell you about your star, what kind of daemon you have, your horoscope and where you may live and where you may die. Furthermore, some magicians even claimed to control the astral forces and even direct the goddess Necessity, thereby ensuring 'well-being, prosperity, glory, victory, power, sex appeal' – qualities still sought after by the grasping but not by the wise.[5]

Mithras and *Sol Invictus*

With its magical aura and roots in stellar religion, it is not surprising that towards the end of the Roman Empire astrology influenced various cults. On the Northern frontier of the great Empire, at a site on

Hadrian's Wall at Housesteads in Britain, there is a carving dedicated to Mithras, a god of light who first emerged in the Near East. In the shrine at Housesteads the signs of the zodiac are arranged in a horse-shoe shape with the top two – Cancer and Leo (associated with the moon and the sun) – separated off by Mithras' sword and torch. The whole is thought to depict his birthday. The cult may have originated with Stoic philosophers of the region of Tarsus who were not only interested in astrology but believed that each World Age would end in a conflagration.

The cult of Mithras which flourished in the second century had a strong following in the Roman army. Its beliefs remain obscure, but it seems that Mithras formed an alliance with the sun after a trial of strength and slaughtered a mysterious bull from whose body came useful plants. Mithraic rites took place in artificial caves where bulls were ritually slaughtered on altars, with the hot blood flowing over the initiates below. The Mithraic god Aion (eon, or eternity) has a lion's head, devouring all, like Time itself.

In the remains of the Mithraic temples there is much astral symbolism. The signs of the zodiac were often placed in a circle or in niches; the seven planets were depicted on the figure of Mithras; and the sun and moon were personified as statues. The Neoplatonist Porphyry observed: 'The equinoctial region they assigned to Mithras as an appropriate seat. And for this reason he bears the sword of Aries, the signs of Mars; he also rides on a bull, Taurus being assigned to Venus.'[6] The seven grades of initiation were associated with the seven planets in the following order: Mercury, Venus, Mars, Jupiter, moon, sun and Saturn. This was probably a product of conflating the days of the week with the traditional Chaldean order of planets based on their distance from the earth.

Mithras was sometimes called *Sol Invictus* (the Unconquered Sun). In a recently discovered subterranean chamber under the altar of St Peters in Rome, at the heart of Christendom, I came across a wall painting of the Egyptian gods Horus, Isis and Osiris, and another of Jesus depicted as *Sol Invictus*, with rays of sunshine coming out of his head. Possibly of Syrian origin, but helped by the Greek identification of Apollo with Helios (the Egyptian sun god Re), the cult of the sun became the State religion of Rome in AD 218 when the priest Elagabalus (named after the Syrian sun god) became emperor and declared himself the *Sol Invictus*. The god Sol had a magnificent temple built in his honour on the campus Agrippae. It was the culmination of a minor cult of Sol and Luna from the early empire. Emperor Julian, addressing a hymn to the sun, recalled how 'from my childhood I was consumed by a passionate longing for the rays of the god, and my mind was utterly absorbed from my tenderest years in his ethereal light . . . I was already taken for an astrologer when the down was still scarcely on my chin.'[7] Nero was compared to the sun god as a charioteer and thanked Sol for uncovering a conspiracy against him. Septimius Severus not only called himself *Sol Invictus* on coins, but built the temple of Septizonia which portrayed the seven planets.

The cult remained the official form of worship until Constantine converted to Christianity in AD 312. In the anti-pagan legislation which followed, astrology was associated with divination and magic, which were declared offences punishable by death. The Catholic Church banned astrology at the Ecumenical Council of Nicaea in AD 325. Constantius warned in 358: 'If any wizard . . . soothsayer, diviner . . . augur, or even astrologer . . . should be apprehended in my Retinue or in that of the Caesar, he shall not escape punishment or torture by the protection of his high rank.'[8]

Firmicus' *Mathesis*

This atmosphere of persecution no doubt impelled the astrologer Julius Firmicus Maternus, probably a senator from Sicily, to warn his fellow astrologers in 334: 'Study and pursue all the distinguishing marks of virtue . . . Be modest, upright, sober, eat little, be content with a few goods, so that the shameful love of money may not defile the glory of this divine science . . . Beware of replying to anyone about the condition of the State or the life of the Roman emperor . . . In drawing up a chart, do not show up the bad things about men too clearly.'[9]

Only the emperor, Firmicus claimed, was not subject to the course of the stars. Since he was master of the world, his destiny was governed by the judgement of the god most high. Far from being fatalistic, Firmicus argued that the celestial influences did not absolve one from personal responsibility. Indeed, we should worship the gods so that, 'reassured of the divinity of our own minds', we might resist the power of the stars.[10]

Firmicus' Latin treatise on astrology is called *Mathesis*, which means 'Learning' in Greek. In Latin, it was translated as *doctrina* and especially referred to the part dealing with 'mathematical sciences'. For

Firmicus astrology consists principally of three parts: the mathematical and astronomical calculations from which the chart is derived; secondly, the more astrological machinery, that is the aspects, decans, Houses, and the characteristics of the signs and planets; and thirdly, the interpretation of the first in the light of the second. Firmicus takes the first for granted (it was well established by his time, thanks to Ptolemy) and goes straight to the second and third parts.

Firmicus stands firmly in the Hermetic tradition. In Book III, he deals with the relationship between the microcosm and macrocosm and the *anima mundi,* the World Soul. In Book VIII, he presents the *sphaera barbarica*, the non-Greek description of the heavens. He offers what is claimed to be the 'Egyptian' pattern of constellations in order to give the effective power of the brighter stars. It is mainly concerned with the *paranatellonta,* the stars rising with the signs of the zodiac. He further claims that the legendary Egyptian astrologer Nechepso was skilled in medicine: 'by means of the decans [Nechepso] predicted all illnesses and afflictions; he knew which decan produced which illness and which decans were stronger than others. From their different nature and power he discovered the cure for all illnesses, because one nature is overcome by another, and one god by another.'[11]

One of the more intriguing aspects of Firmicus' work is what he calls *myriogenesis* (literally 'multiple generation') taken from the title of a work by 'Aesculapius' (Asclepius) who was allegedly instructed by Mercury (the Greek Hermes and the Egyptian Thoth). It expounds all birthcharts by the 'single minutes of the zodiac without adding any planet'. This would mean very careful calculations for there are sixty minutes in the 360° of the zodiac. One minute of arc equals twenty-four minutes of time so that a person's fate could be determined by the exact minute of his birth.

Firmicus offers a simplified version of the influence and meaning of each degree. One degree could be crucial in determining one's whole life. For instance, those who have their Ascendant in the first degree of Aries, 'if they are favoured by the rays of benevolent planets, will be born kings and leaders, always leading their armies successfully.' On the other hand, those who have their Ascendant in the second degree of Aries will be 'persistent thieves who always use unnecessary and extraordinary violence in their attacks; such as keep shifting their residence to places where they are not known.'[12] And if Mars affects this degree, and their Ascendant and the moon aspects it in square or opposition, their crimes will be detected and they will be punished in public.

Unless one has forecast the degrees before birth and chooses the exact moment, being induced can have important consequences – good or bad. The source for the *myriogenesis* might well have been in the Egyptian list of 360 lucky and unlucky days in the calendar.

Firmicus' work added little to Manilius and Ptolemy but it was historically important. It was one of the first works on astrology to reach the West in the eleventh century when it was widely read and discussed by Christian translators and theologians.

The Coming of Christianity

Towards its end the Roman Empire was not a hospitable place for astrology. When Porphyry published the works of his master Plotinus at the beginning of the fourth century, he turned against astrology. Furthermore when Christianity became the official religion of the Empire, the practice of astrology was outlawed. However, the Alexandrian philosopher Iamblichus came to its defence in his book *Theurgia or* the *Egyptian Mysteries*. He specifically defended astrology as a 'mathematical science' against the criticisms of Porphyry:

> When the signs of the measurement of the revolutions of the divine ones [the planets] are clearly evident before the eyes, when they indicate beforehand the eclipses of the sun and the moon, the enterings of the sun into the signs of the zodiac, and departures out of them, and the concurrent risings and settings of the moon with those of the fixed stars, the proof of actual signs is manifested agreeing with the predictions.[13]

He describes the rules of 'the art of vaticination' in respect to the time of birth in which astrologers summon the personal daemon in a prescribed form from 'the dekans and the risings of the constellations of the zodiac and likewise the stars; the sun also the moon, and from the Bears and likewise from the elements, and from the world.' In his view the 'aura or emanation from the stars' brings the daemon to us, whether we are aware of it or not.[14]

Astrology at the time was seen as part of the art of theurgy, a profound spiritual experience in which the initiate could unite with the divine. Like Firmicus, Iamblichus believed that we can ultimately escape the influence of the stars. He explains this by arguing that we have two souls, one from 'the first Mind' which partakes of the 'Power of the Creator', and the other, 'the soul under constraint', which comes from the revolution of the celestial spheres. While the latter is subject to fate, the former can rise above it.[15]

Despite the strictures of Constantine, astrology continued to be taught in Alexandria in the fifth and sixth centuries as part of the standard curriculum. Byzantium credited philosophers such as Synesius, Olympiodorus and Stephanus with works on astrology, although their actual authorship is not certain. Olympiodorus definitely taught astrology. Synesius studied science and philosophy under Hypatia, who was torn to pieces in AD 415 by a Christian mob when she was returning from lecturing at the Museum. 'With her,' E. M. Forster wrote, 'the Greece that is a spirit expired – the Greece that tried to discover truth and create beauty and that had created Alexandria.'[16] In addition, the great library of Alexandria, the greatest library of the ancient world, which had been partly destroyed during Cleopatra's last stand, was finished off during the Christian era.

The Christian attitude to astrology was ambiguous. In Genesis, there is a passage referring to God creating the stars as signs, but in general the Old Testament is hostile to astrology as it fails to leave matters to divine Providence. In the New Testament, the story of the three Magi who followed a star which augured the birth of a great king were undoubtedly astrologers from the East. Without question the story was intended to show how the old philosophy was giving way to the new dispensation. But astrology was generally seen as a serious threat to the Christian State because it was associated with pagan divination and magic. As such, it offered an alternative source of knowledge and authority.

Dogmatic critics merely dismissed the whole subject as the work of the Devil. Many Christians allowed that while stars may be signs of the future, astrologers could have no knowledge of that future. The claim that astrology could provide an independent means of knowing the future was simply not acceptable. The more thoughtful opponents focused on the issue of free will and determinism. If the stars determined the fate of humans, it was argued, then it denied the hand of God and His divine Providence. When a friend of Sidonius was strangled by his slaves, he implied that it was his interest in astrology which was the cause of his downfall: 'Death enmeshed our reckless enquirer exactly when and where foretold . . . I fear he who presumes to probe forbidden secrets sets himself beyond the pale of the Christian faith.'[17]

While recognizing its power over the imagination, the Egyptian Christian father Origen (c.185–255) had attacked astrology in his *Commentary on Genesis*, when he came to the famous passage on the creation of the stars. He insisted that the stars are merely signs and not agents, and that humans could not have accurate knowledge of them. Only God could know the future: 'our freedom is safeguarded when God knows in advance for all eternity the acts that each man is judged to have accomplished.'[18] Other Christian apologists criticized astrology on grounds which are still debated to this day. Why do large numbers of people share the same characteristics and die in similar ways when they have different horoscopes? Why do twins with the same horoscopes suffer different fates? How can the stars be said to determine the customs of different regions in the world?

At the end of the fourth century, John Chrystostom summed up the general concern and warned against consorting with astrologers: 'In the same way as murder and adultery are sins and forbidden actions, so also trust in astrology and belief in Fate are perverse . . . in truth, no doctrine is so depraved and bordering on incurable madness as the doctrine of Fate and astrology.'[19] With such withering attacks, it is not surprising that astrology was forced to retreat. By the sixth century the Church had triumphed over astrology and Sol and Luna went underground in the Christian West until the eleventh century. In the meantime, they took refuge and flourished in the expanding world of Islam.

29

The Stargazers of the Middle East

And that inverted bowl we call the Sky,
Whereunder crawlings coop't we live and die . . .
'Tis all a Chequer-board of Nights and Days
Where Destiny with Men for Pieces plays.

RUBÁIYÁT OF OMAR KHAYYÁM

THERE IS AN old story, much loved by Islamic scholars, about a young carefree servant who was sent to the market on an errand. On his return, he was in a terrible state. His master asked him what had happened and he replied: 'I have seen the Angel of Death among the crowds in the market-place; he looked at me with his piercing eyes in astonishment. Let me take one of your swiftest horses and ride to the city of Samara so that I may escape the hand of Death!' The master, knowing the power of Death, readily agreed and let him take his choice.

Later that day, the master went down to the market himself and found that the Angel of Death was still there. 'Where is your servant?' he asked. The master explained that he was no longer with him but had taken a fast horse to the city of Samara. The Angel of Death nodded knowingly and said: 'I was surprised to see him here this morning because tonight I have an appointment with him in Samara.'

The story illustrates well the workings of fate, but was the meeting written in the stars? Could the servant have avoided his fate through a conscious exercise of his free will? Could he have taken another path in life? This was a dilemma which exercised the best Islamic minds.

The Rise of Islam

When the Muslims conquered Egypt in the seventh century, they found a lingering tradition of learning and, in Alexandria, discovered works of astrology among the dispersed remnants of the great libraries of the city. They also came into contact with the Hermetic tradition which carried a residue of the ancient wisdom of the Egyptian temples.

As the Islamic Empire spread, new centres of learning in the Near and Middle East developed. The persecuted Christian Nestorians played a special part in transmitting Egyptian and Greek learning to the Arab world. They had settled in Edessa in the North of Syria from where they were expelled in 489. They then moved to Nisibis in Mesopotamia and finally settled in Judi-Shapur in Persia where there was a famous observatory. They translated works written in Greek, chiefly into Syriac, ensuring their transmission to the Islamic world.

Syria became the most dynamic of the new Islamic states, a meeting ground of different cultures and tongues. However, it was Baghdad in Iraq which, under the Abbasid caliphs from 750, became the greatest centre of learning. Sciences flourished there in the late eighth and ninth centuries, where many ancient texts were recovered and translated. Further centres developed in Islamic Spain, especially in the tenth century under Abd er-Rahman III and his successor al-Hakam II. Their court at Cordoba became the chief centre of learning in the Islamic Empire.

In the meantime, the city of Harran in North-West Mesopotamia remained a fortress of Hermetic wisdom. Although it fell to the Muslims, its pagan inhabitants, notable stargazers, did not convert to Islam any more than they had to Christianity. They adopted the name Sabians from the Qur'an as a term for a prophetic religion of the 'Book' tolerated by the Islamic mullahs. Their prophet was Hermes, whom they identified as Idris in the Qur'an and Enoch in the Bible. They held out until the eleventh century and ensured that the Hermetic tradition was kept alive and transmitted to Europe.

Islam was very accommodating to astrology. It saw no conflict between religion, philosophy and science; all could lead to *tawhid* (unity) rather than a denial of the divine. The ultimate aim of all Islamic knowledge was to free the mind from dependence on physical appearances and to prepare it for a vision of the Whole. Astrology was early accepted by the Shias and especially the Sufis. The Shia group with Sufi tendencies known as the Ikhwan al-Sufa (Brethren of Purity) wrote an influential encyclopaedia, *Rasai'l* (Epistles), which stressed the Unity of Being: 'Universal Soul is the spirit of the world. The four elements are the matter which serve as its support. The spheres and the stars are like its organs, and the minerals, plants and animals are objects which make it move.'[1]

Central to the Muslim world view was the Hermetic belief that there is a correspondence between heaven and earth and that man is a microcosm of the universe. Moreover, since the world is One, the seeker of wisdom (*hakim*) must understand all aspects of the world. Since the universe was considered to be a symbol of God, any enquiry into nature was seen as a process of divine revelation. By studying astrology, one could rediscover one's celestial nature and cosmic roots. Moreover, Islam's deterministic view of fate as the will of Allah and its stress on the need for acceptance – 'Islam' means 'surrender' – made it theoretically receptive to astrology.

Before the eighth century the Arabs had little knowledge of astronomy and astrology. They told the time at night by means of twenty-eight lunar mansions and the seasons by the heliacal risings and cosmic settings. However, astrology soon became an essential part of Islamic science. In al-Farabi's famous *Enumeration of the Sciences*, later translated into Latin as *De Scientiis*, he divided the 'science of the heavens' into 'Astrology' and 'motions and figures of the heavenly bodies'.[2] As in Greek, the same Arabic word denotes both astrology and astronomy. The subject was cultivated for a number of reasons. There were problems of chronology and of the calendar. Princes and rulers, uncertain of the future, nearly always consulted astrologers for their decisions and actions. And of course there was the overall Islamic desire for the perfection of knowledge.

The main Greek tradition came down through Ptolemy, but there was also the Indian school embodied in the *Siddhantas* translated from Sanskrit. In addition Chaldean and Persian texts were consulted, most of which have now been lost. Muslim astrologers soon made these influences their own, however, and added their own original contributions to the subject.[3]

Al-Kindi and Abu Ma'shar

The most important founder of Islamic science and philosophy, Al-Kindi (c.801–873), was strongly sympathetic to astrology. After visiting

Baghdad, he became a tutor and physician to the great patron of learning Khalif al-Ma'mun. Known to the West as 'the Philosopher of the Arabs', he established the philosophical basis for astrology and helped developed an Arabic philosophical language. Although he wrote profusely, especially on astrology and the astrolabe, many of his works have been lost. One which has survived in Latin, *De Radiis* ('On rays'), expressed the correspondence between heaven and earth in terms of 'stellar rays'. Together with the elements, they were held responsible for the diversity within the unity of the world: 'So the diversity of things in the world of the elements apparent at any time proceeds from two causes, namely the diversity of their matter (elements) and the changing operation of the stellar rays.'

Al-Kindi's belief in universal determinism was so profound that he argued: 'If it were given to anyone to comprehend the whole condition of celestial harmony, he would know fully the world of the elements with all contained therein at any place and any time'. If that were the case, one would be able to know what is caused from the cause and vice versa. Furthermore, 'whoever has acquired the knowledge of the whole condition of the celestial harmony will know the past and the present and the future.'[4]

Al-Kindi's best pupil, Abu Ma'shar, became the most famous of Muslim astrologers. He was born in 787 at Balkh in Khurasan, a city now in Northern Afghanistan. It was a great cosmopolitan centre of religion and learning, where communities of Jews, Nestorians and Manicheans rubbed shoulders with Buddhists, Hindus and Zoroastrians.

There is a story that when Abu Ma'shar was a student of a doctor at the court of Persia he was criticized in public by Al-Kindi. He was so incensed that he decided to kill his master. But when he entered his room with a dagger, the old astrologer gave him a penetrating glance and said: 'Art thou not Abu Ma'shar of Balkh? Thou shalt be the greatest astrologer of the century, but thou must renounce thy evil design. Throw away the dagger, sit down and accept my doctrine.'[5]

He adopted his master's determinism and argued that just as the doctor studies the changes in the elements, so the astrologer follows the movements of the stars to arrive at 'the causes of the elementary changes'. But where Al-Kindi was primarily a Neoplatonist, Abu Ma'shar was largely an Aristotelian in that he argued that all sublunary change is caused by motions in the heavens.

His works became the most influential in Europe where he was known as Albumasar. His *Great Introduction to Astrology*, translated by Adelard of Bath as *Introductorium*, was mainly devoted to the grammar of astrology. His *Flores Astrologiae*, translated by John of Seville, was a guide containing many useful hints and pithy aphorisms. In both, he wrestled with the issue of free will. Distinguishing between the influence of the planets and that of the fixed stars, he argued that while the former could control the details of everyday life, the latter only affected the design of things in such a slow way and on such a grand scale that they hardly influenced human destiny at all.

The Lunar Calendar

Muslim astrologers were only too well aware that to draw up a horoscope it was necessary to have accurate instruments as well as reliable tables. The latter could not be made without the former. From the Greeks, they acquired the astrolabe which enabled the projection of the observed sphere of the heavens on to a plane. It was not only used for observing heavenly bodies but also for finding the time, latitudes, heights and distances. For the horoscope, it provided accurate observations of the heavens at the moment of birth. And in a period when there were no accurate clocks or chronometers, the astrolabe could be used on a clear sky to calculate the time.

It was still necessary for the astrologer to find the Ascendant and the positions of the planets from the tables. The accuracies of the tables depended on the observational skills of the astrologers as well as the care of the copyists. The tables included important 'fixed' stars, not only because those rising with a sign of the zodiac, the paranatellonata, might be observable while the sign was invisible, but also because the Muslims used the stars associated with the signs and even with the degrees of signs in their interpretations.

Because of the precession of the equinoxes, it had long been known that the 'fixed' stars were not really immobile. Although some continued to believe that the equinoxes moved forward and backward (known as 'trepidation'), Ptolemy's view that they took 36,000 years to return to their beginning ('The Great Year') became the accepted theory of Muslim and Christian astrologers in the Middle Ages.

The Muslims, like the Indians and Jews, used a lunar calendar in which time is measured by the moon's orbit around the earth. A year consists of twelve lunar months. While the solar calendar marks the year by the equinoxes and solstices, the lunar calendar provides the month from one new moon to the next. There is no simple way of tallying the two for neither are made up of the same number of days or months. Muslims and Jews fix the number of months in a year at twelve, giving 354 days. Since this is about eleven days less than the solar year, the annual festivals gradually move backwards through the seasons, taking thirty-four lunar years (thirty-three solar ones) to complete the cycle.

The lunar year therefore progressively gets out of step with the solar year of 365 days used by Christians. However, Christians still calculate the date of Easter according to the lunar calendar. In the past the lunar month was divided into three weeks of nine days or four weeks of seven days. The former may well be behind the Roman *Nones* (nine days after the full moon) and the *Ides* (the days of the moon's light, that is around the time of the full moon).

Arabic astrology uses twenty-eight *manâzil* ('stations' or 'Houses') to track the monthly movement of the moon across the ecliptic. These lunar mansions are groups of stars or asterisms through which the moon passes in a synodic month of twenty-seven and a half days. The mansions were often used to calculate the passage of time by measuring the moon's path against the stars, rather than by the moon's phases. One would therefore say: 'My father died when the moon was in such and such a mansion' rather than 'he died three days after the third quarter'.[6] They could therefore reckon the time in a similar way to the decans and the zodiac.

No doubt because of the use of the lunar calendar in Muslim countries, the tables contained the twenty-eight mansions of the moon and its nodes. The nodes mark the point where the moon crosses the ecliptic. Like the Indians, the Muslims treated them as invisible planets.

The Muslim lunar mansions originally began with *Al Thurayya*, the 'Many Little Ones'. These are the Pleiades in the constellation of Taurus. Apart from being so striking, they were probably chosen because their position coincided with the degree of the spring equinox in the third millennium BC. This suggests a possible Mesopotamian source. Because of the precession of the equinoxes, the former twenty-seventh mansion, *Al Sharatain,* 'the Two Signs' (β and γ Arietis), became the first, beginning with the first degree Aries. The 360° circle of the ecliptic was divided into twenty-eight equal divisions.

European astrologers of the Renaissance adopted the lunar mansions of the Arabs. This seems to have been motivated by an interest in magic, for the moon had long been considered the mistress of magic. Different mansions were ascribed different properties, some positive and some negative. The Italian philosopher Giordano Bruno (1548–1600) in particular used the imagery of the Arabic lunar mansions, along with that of the Egyptian decans, to develop an elaborate art of memory.[7]

Muslim astrologers also made much use of the 'division of times' which ranged from world epochs to the stages in the life of an individual. According to Abu Ma'shar, there are four kinds of *fardarat* or periods. The 'mighty fardar' lasts for 360 solar years. The big fardar is seventy-eight years, shared out among the twelve signs, twelve for Aries down to one for Pisces. The middle fardar is seventy-five years; each is ruled by one of the nine 'planets' (the usual seven plus the lunar nodes) in the order around the zodiac of their exaltations. The order of the planets is the sun, Venus, Mercury, Saturn, Mars, Venus. The small fardar is equally seventy-five years but is divided into nine *fardariyat* and distributed to the nine planets according to the same order of exaltations.

In an uncertain world, Muslims, like most people, were concerned with questions such as 'when is the best time to begin a journey?' or 'will the outcome of my decision be good or bad?', or even 'when will I die?'. To answer them, their astrologers developed from Greek astrology the techniques of progressions, elections and transits and passed them on to the Latin West.

In a progressed chart, the elements of the chart are revolved through an angle corresponding to the period of time, from the date of birth to the date of the required prognostication. The two charts are then compared to give information about the subject for the present and future. When the enquiry concerns the length of life, the moment of birth is called the *hyleg* (the Latin form of the Arabic *haylaj*).

In the case of elections, the aim is to work out the best time to start something. This again involves rotating the beginning point – known as the radical – of the chart. The most common method among modern astrologers for measuring the time round the zodiac is to take 'a day for a year' – that is to say, on the progressed chart the same number of days ahead of the date of birth is used as years in the life of the subject. In *De Revolutionibus Nativitatum*, Abu Ma'shar wrote about the transits of the planets: 'The entry of the planets, in the revolution of the years, the radical places and the radical places of the others, have certain ineffable significations of good and evil consequences. . . One must look at the sign in which the planet was in the radical chart and treat it as the Ascendant and interpret accordingly.'[8]

The Arabian Parts

One of the most important developments of Islam was the 'fates of the Houses', the so-called Arabian Parts, which the ancient Greeks and Romans called Lots. They were thought to enhance the positions of the planets in the birthchart. The parts are positions in the zodiac produced by an equation involving three factors, one of which is usually a cusp. The Part of Fortune, represented by a square in a circle, is calculated by adding the degrees of the Ascendant to those of the moon and subtracting those of the sun from the sum. As a result the Part of Fortune is as many degrees on the zodiac from the Ascendant as the moon is from the sun. It is considered to be good fortune since it links the powers of the sun and moon and brings them down to earth through the Ascendant (the horizon).

The ancient Greeks and Egyptians originally had seven lots: Necessity, Eros, Daemon, Audacity, Nemesis, Victory and Fortune. They followed the same part as the Lot of Fortune, determining the mid-point between the Ascendant and Saturn, Venus, Mercury, the sun, Mars and Jupiter respectively. They developed more than forty of these equations. With their fondness for mathematics, Muslim astrologers at first developed ninety-seven corollary points from the seven, and then by the eleventh century had increased the number to 143. While most of the Parts are centred on the relationship of the Ascendant with planets, House cusps and nodes, some are even focused on the relationship between two Parts. It was developed into a highly sophisticated and subtle system, which enabled the astrologers to refine a birthchart, deal with hororary questions and check the indicators of the planets. However, Al Biruni, the eleventh-century astrologer and astronomer, upbraided his fellow astrologers for trying to devise a Part for every human activity since it degraded the noble art of astrology to the level of divination.

Unfortunately, the loss of texts and the complexity of the calculations meant that many of the Parts were lost to the West. Those that have survived are mainly due to the extracts from the works of Abu Ma'shar and the eleventh-century Jewish astrologer Abraham ben Neir ibn Ezra. According to the thirteenth-century Italian astrologer Guido Bonatti, the Parts were subdivided into three major categories: planetary, House and horary. The surviving method to calculate and interpret the Arabian Parts is incomplete and the procedures applied to other Parts have entirely disappeared.

Of the original 143 Parts, the best known is the Part of Fortune. Other ones include those of life, aptness, understanding, durability (including the life of a person), goods, collection (ability to accumulate wealth or recover lost goods), sorrow, brethren, love of brethren, father, inheritances and possessions, husbandry, children, female children, male children, sickness, servants (ability to order servants), slavery and bondage (whom or what a slave serves), plays (pursuit of pleasure and romance), desire and sexual attraction, sex (quality of sexual drive), discord and controversy, marriage, death, faith, journeys by water, journeys by land, honour, sudden advancement, magistery and profession, merchandise, friends and mother, private enemies, and finally the Part of the perilous and most dangerous year.[9]

By the eleventh century, the fundamental tenets of Arab astrology had been established. Astronomy and astrology were still considered to be two aspects of the same enquiry. The increasingly accurate tables based on close observation of the heavens were used by astrologers. The famous astronomer Al-Biruni was known for the accuracy of his tables, as well as for the subtlety of his astrological works. While adept at interpretations, he was keen to draw the boundaries of what was scientifically acceptable. In his *Elements of Astrology*, he divided the subject into five areas, of which the first four were: meteorology; plants; animals and humanity; the individual's life and prosperity and the individual's actions and occupations. The fifth division encompassed those areas which he rejected because they threatened to transgress its 'proper limits' by trying to solve impossible problems. As he explained, here 'the matter leaves the solid basis of the universal for one of particulars. When this boundary is passed, where the astrologer is on one side and the sorcerer on the other, you enter a field of omens and divinations which has nothing to do with astrology.'[10]

It was statements like this, as well as its superior knowledge of the heavens, which made Muslim astrology so appealing to the medieval scientists or 'natural philosophers' in the Christian West. Al-Biruni's *Elements of Astrology* became a standard text of the *Quadrivium* which covered the mathematical sciences for centuries. Even as late as the seventeenth century, the tables of Ulugh Beg, the grandson of Tamerlane, were published in Oxford. The reputation of this Muslim astronomer and astrologer was so high that he was considered one of the best in the world. When I took the 'golden road' to Samarkand (now in Uzbekistan) to visit his famous fifteenth-century observatory, all that I found of its former glory was a semi-circular pit and a small adjoining museum.

Although Western astrologers during the Middle Ages and the Renaissance did not embrace the Arabian Parts wholeheartedly, the Part of Fortune has become a regular feature in modern horoscopes. Another Muslim legacy is the 'Placidus House system' which divides the ecliptic into twelve unequal segments. Named after the seventeenth-century Italian astrologer, Placidus di Tito, it was in fact based on a set of calculations made by the eighth-century Muslim astrologer Ben Djabit.

The Emerald Tablet and Picatrix

The general metaphysical assumptions of the Muslim philosophers and scientists probably had the greatest influence on creating an atmosphere congenial to astrology in the West. The most important text to come out of Islam was the short work known as *The Emerald Tablet* attributed to Hermes Trismegistus. An Arabic version exists in the work of the alchemist Jabir which dates from at least the eighth century. It not only stressed the inextricable correspondence between heaven and earth, the microcosm of man and the macrocosm of the universe, the Many and the One, but it also prophesied that 'marvellous adaptations' would take place in the world if its import was properly understood: 'True it is, without falsehood, certain and most true. That which is above is like that which is below, and that which is below is like that which is above, to accomplish the miracles of the one thing . . . It is the father of all the works of wonder throughout the whole world.'[11]

The anonymous *Picatrix, Libro de la Magia de los Signos*, was another Muslim work which first emerged in Toledo and had a great influence during the Renaissance. It was a translation of the Arabic work *Gayat al-hakim* (The Final Aim of the Wise) attributed to the tenth-century alchemist Al-Majriti. It combined magic and astrology, offering an exotic mix of incantations from a wide variety of sources, including Egyptian, Mesopotamian, Greek and Hebrew. It also drew heavily on the astrology of the Sabeans and the philosophy of Hermes. It recommended the use of talismans to draw down the energy from the spirits of the planets and the positions of the celestial spheres: 'All sages agree that the planets exercise influence and power over the world . . . from this it follows the roots of magic are the movements of the planets.'[12] The skill of the true magician was to discover the hidden secrets of nature and to direct them to beneficial ends by channelling the virtues of superior bodies (*spiritus*) in the heavens into lower bodies (*materia*) on earth.

Jewish Astrology

The Muslims were not the only astrologers to emerge from the Middle East. The Jews developed their own version of astrology, drawing on Greek and Mesopotamian traditions, as well as Arab sources. There are many references to the Chaldeans in the Torah (the five books of the Old Testament said to have been written by Moses) and the Talmud (the central Jewish work on civil and religious law). In the first century BC there emerged from the large Jewish community in Alexandria a work called *The Treatise of Shem*. Written in Aramaic, it offered twelve chapters for each of the signs of the zodiac, with such predictions as: 'And if the year begins in Taurus: everyone whose name contains a Beth, or Yudh, or Kaph will become ill, or be wounded by an iron [weapon]. And there will be fighting. And a wind will go out from Egypt and will fill the entire earth.'[13] In Palestine and elsewhere in the Middle East, depictions of the signs of the zodiac in a central position became quite common in synagogues from the fourth century AD onwards.

Embracing attributes of both the solar and lunar schools, Jewish astrology was more spiritually-orientated than Muslim and later Western astrology. Astrologers encouraged their clients to lead a religious life in accord with *Halachah* (Jewish law). Not surprisingly, with the traditional Jewish emphasis on the family and wider community, the individual was seen very much as a social being with earthly responsibilities as well as celestial connections.

Jewish natal horoscopes are calculated according to the tropical zodiac based on the annual rotation of the sun. The Jewish calendar is a luni-solar system that applies the nineteen-year Metonic cycle developed by the Greek astronomer Meton. It is similar to Chinese and Indian calendars in that it divides the year into twelve lunar months, adding an intercalary month to coincide with the solar year of 365 days. Unlike the Chinese calendar, which begins with the second new moon after the winter solstice, the Jewish ecclesiastical year starts with the first new moon after the vernal equinox while the civil year begins with the first new moon after the autumnal equinox. The calendar dates from the traditional Jewish Year of Creation in 3761 BC.

At the same time, Jewish astrology shares the Chinese, Indian and

Western concept of 'Great Years' based on the gradual precession of the equinoxes but calls them 'Prophetic Ages'. Each lasts 2,160 years in the 25,920 year cycle. The actual timing of the Age of Aquarius remains a subject of debate among contemporary Jewish astrologers. Rabbi Joel C. Dobin argues that it took place when Jupiter and Saturn formed a conjunction in Libra on 31 December 1980, but others say that it took place at the same conjunction in 2001.[14]

The ancient Judaic terms for the signs of the zodiac correspond to the Hebrew words for the twelve constellations which, according to the Talmud, were created by God. The translation of their names and their symbols differs slightly from their Mesopotamian and Greek counterparts. In the traditional order from Aries to Pisces they are: Taleh (prince), Shor (heavenly bull), Teomin (two figures), Sarton (north gate of the sun), Ari (lion), Betulah (wife of Bel), Moznayim (chariot yoke), Akrab (stinger), Kasshat (archery bow), Gedi (ibex or goat-fish), Deli (god of the storm), and Dagim (fish).[15] Many commentators have noted clear associations between the characteristics of the twelve signs of the zodiac and the personalities of the twelve sons of Jacob as described in the Torah. Moreover, there are links made in the Torah between the zodiac signs and the six archangels Raphael, Gabriel, Michael, Haniel, Ma'admiel, Zidkiel and Zophkiel.[16]

An aspect of Jewish astrology which has passed into the popular consciousness is the connections mentioned in the Talmud between planetary influences and the days of the week. A person born on Sunday (ruled by the sun) is said to be 'wholly good or bad'; on Monday (moon), bad-tempered; on Tuesday (Mars), lecherous and rich. Born on Wednesday (Mercury), the person has a good memory and is wise; on Thursday (Jupiter), is benevolent; on Friday (Venus), is active and pious. However, the person born on Saturday (Saturn) will die on a Sabbath because he or she profaned the sanctity of the day by making the mother and midwife attend to the birth rather than their religious duties![17]

Many Jewish astrologers, living closely with their Muslim neighbours, made use of the Arabian Parts to enhance their interpretations of the horoscope. But their over-zealous use was condemned in the eleventh century by Abraham ben Meir ibn Ezra in his work *The Beginning of Wisdom* as being a form of divination and inconsistent with the spiritual aim and higher purpose of Jewish astrology. Other Talmudic scholars concurred and the Parts were eventually discarded.

The methods applied by modern Jewish astrologers for casting the horoscope are almost identical to those used by their Western counter-parts, except that many prefer to employ the Meridian House system as opposed to the more common Placidus scheme. The overall interpreta-tion, however, is more in keeping with the teachings of the Talmud and the Torah.[18]

A general emphasis on free will runs throughout Jewish astrological texts and commentaries. This is illustrated by the Jewish tradition of taking on a new name which requires a new chart for the symbolic rebirth. The name-changing ceremony probably comes from the sixth-century *Midrash Rabbah* where 'Rabbi ben Isaac commented that Abram said: "My planetary fate oppresses me and declares 'Abram cannot beget a child'." Said the Holy One, Blessed Be He to him: "Let it be even as thy words. Abram, and Sarai cannot beget, but Abraham and Sarah can beget".'[19]

Cabbala and the Tree of Life

Jewish esoteric astrology, part of the mystical Jewish tradition of the Cabbala, shares the same emphasis. Its metaphysical system is based on ten fundamental aspects of Divinity which emanate out of the original 'No thing'. The relationship between the ten Divine Attributes known as the *Sefirot* are depicted in the diagram of the Tree of Life. Each planet is associated with a *Sefarih* (Divine Attribute): the sun is at the centre linked with 'Beauty', Neptune at the top with the 'Crown' and earth at the bottom in 'Kingdom'.

In the great 'ladder of existence', or 'Chain of Being', there are four worlds in descending order. These are the eternal World of Emanation, the cosmic World of Creation, the subtle World of Formation, and the natural World of Action. The planetary influences operating in the third world affect the fourth, where we live on earth. Whereas mundane astrology is mainly concerned with the subtle or astral level of existence and its effect on the natural world, the esoteric astrology of the Cabbala deals with the whole picture.[20]

The spirit of a human being descends from the cosmic world to the natural world, taking on a spiritual body, a psychological body and finally the carnal body. The sun in the horoscope represents the psyche, the connecting point between the physical and subtle worlds. Destiny belongs to the spiritual aspect of the sun. Beyond the psyche, is the soul, beyond which is spirit.

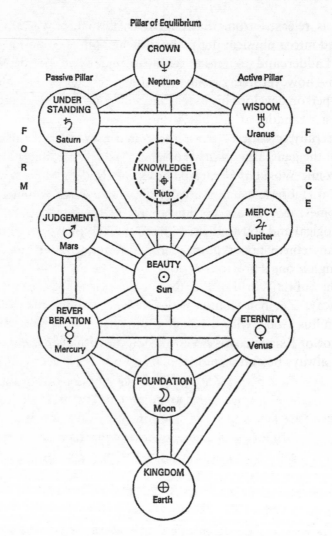

The Cabbalistic Tree of Life with the planets associated with each of the ten
Sefirah or Divine Attributes which emanate from the original 'No thing'.
This forms part of esoteric Jewish astrology.

A contemporary Cabbalistic astrologer, Warren Kenton (Zev ben
Shimon Halevi), insists that there is no such thing as a disastrous chart.
It is a 'platform' from which we begin our journey on earth. Although it
provides an 'interior pattern' which will lead to a particular lifestyle,
it is not entirely fixed. Every person has three fundamental choices: 'to
develop, just maintain what he is or go down in the quality of being,

until he is released from that chart's encapsulating form.'[21] Having descended into a physical body, the ultimate aim is to ascend again up Jacob's Ladder and to return as a realized being to the World of Creation – however many lives it may take.

As a person develops his psyche, he will begin to understand that life is not just a random affair, like a dice thrown at the moment of birth, but a carefully considered piece in a great jigsaw. Every individual life is part of the general work of Providence, which originates at the level of the cosmic World of Creation and is managed by archangels known as 'Irin' in Hebrew, usually translated in English as 'Watchers'. When death comes, it is seen according to the Cabbala as a release of the 'psychological and spiritual Trees' from the 'physical Tree'. For most it will mean rebirth up or down the evolutionary ladder of existence, depending on one's previous actions. But some exceptional beings will rise to the Subtle World of Paradise or the Spiritual World of Heaven. 'In this way,' Zev ben Shimon Halevi tells us, 'Adam, the image of the Divine, fulfils God's will to behold God, until the End of Time, when the mirror of Existence dissolves into union with the One that was, is and will always be and be not.'[22]

Part Five

The Milky Way:
Europe

30

At the Beginning of Light

Sapiens homo dominatur astris:
The wise man is master of the stars.

THOMAS AQUINAS

A T THE ENTRANCE TO Chartres Cathedral are statues representing the seven 'Liberal Arts' which were originated by the Greeks. They include the celebrated *quadrivium*, the four 'mathematical sciences' of arithmetic, geometry, music and, above all, *astronomia*. When you enter the cathedral you become aware of a huge stained glass window, rich in deep blues and reds, depicting the signs of the zodiac. Designed according to Pythagorean principles, embodying planetary energies in geometrical form, the cathedral is a marvellous and magical emblem of celestial harmony. It is a model of heaven on earth.

In 1142 Thierry of Chartres recommended the study of Ptolemy to his students. Astrology was now a central part of learning in Europe. How had this come about?

It has been argued that from the early sixth to the late twelfth century 'there was no astrology in Western Europe', and that before the twelfth century there was 'nothing more than a faint memory of a lost, illicit, art'.[1] This is not entirely the case. Certainly, astrology suffered, along with the rest of pagan learning, during the Dark Ages following the collapse of the Roman Empire, but it continued in pockets. Astrology was popular in late Roman Gaul and the first Frankish and Gothic kings probably inherited some of its practitioners. Edwin, King of Northumbria (c.616–632), the most powerful king in Saxon England, employed a Spanish astrologer called Pellitus who gave him advice in the war against the Celtic British. For the general population, however, it did virtually disappear, surviving only in the system of 'Egyptian Days' – that is, the tradition of lucky and unlucky days.

The light of learning was kept aglow in the monasteries, along with the glimmer of the former glory of astrology. The best libraries would have contained copies of Macrobius' commentary on Cicero's *Somnium Scipionis* (Dream of Scipio) (c.430) with its astrological references and view of the immortality of the soul, and the vast *Etymologiae*, by Isodore, Bishop of Seville (c.560–636), with its definition of astrology. Boethius (c.480–c.524), whose *Consolation of Philosophy* gave a classic depiction of the Neoplatonic world view, may also have translated Ptolemy but the work is lost.

In his commentary on Cicero's *Dream of Scipio*, Macrobius presented the usual characteristics of the planets and quotes Plotinus as saying that the stars do not cause but only signify events on earth – a view which has reverberated down the ages ever since.

In particular, Macrobius gave two astrological ideas which continued throughout the Middle Ages. The first was that as the soul travels down through the spheres to join the body, it acquires characteristics of the seven planets. From Jupiter's sphere, the soul receives reasoning and intelligence; from Mars, 'the fiery ardour of spirit'; from the sun, 'a nature for feeling and opinion'; from Venus, 'the motion of desire'; from Mercury, 'speaking out and interpreting what it feels'; and from the globe of the moon, 'corporeal begetting and growing'.[2]

The second influential idea was that there is a 'birthchart' of the creation, known as the *thema mundi*. This horoscope of the world was long established and appeared in the Babylonian *Epic of Creation* when it was written down around 2200 BC. The idea is often introduced to explain why Aries should be the considered the 'starting-point' of the circle of the zodiac, a circle which has no beginning. 'They say,' Macrobius wrote, 'that when that day began which was the first of all and is therefore rightly called the world's birthday, Aries was in the Midheaven; and because the Midheaven is as it were the vertex of the world, Aries was therefore held to be the first among them all, the one which appeared like the head of the world at the beginning of light.'[3]

While there may have been some practising astrologers in Spain at the time, Bishop Isidore of Seville treats astrology mainly as if it were past history. In his vast *Etymologiae* he distinguished between *astronomia* and *astrologia*. The former deals with 'the turning of the heavens, and the risings, settings and motions of the stars, and why they are called what they are.' He then makes a distinction between physical astrology which deals with 'the courses of the sun and moon, or the fixed seasons of the stars', and superstitious astrology pursued by the *mathematici* who prophesy by the stars and who 'distribute the twelve heavenly signs among the parts of the soul and body, and attempt to foretell the births and characters of men from the courses of the stars.'[4] Despite the neatness of Isidore's definitions, the Latin words *astrologia* and *astronomia* continued to be used interchangeably for both branches of the subject.

From copies of the works of the Roman historian Pliny, scholars such as the English monk Bede (c.673–735) knew of the notion that the earth is a sphere orbiting the sun, but the weight of the early Church fell in favour of the idea that the earth is a scale model of the Tabernacle of Moses. This idea was first put forward allegorically by Clement of Alexandria in about 200 but it came to be taken literally.

Cosmas, a merchant seaman turned monk, had taken up the idea in the mid sixth century. In his *Topographica Christiana*, he declared that the earth was flat and rectangular, twice as long as wide, and surrounded by ocean. Beyond this ocean, was a second earth, the original home of humanity until Noah crossed the ocean in his Ark after the Flood. Four vertical walls rose from the edges of the outer earth holding up the cylindrical roof of the heavens. The sun disappeared at night behind a high conical mountain in the north and the stars and planets were carried around by angels. This world view, taken from the Bible, had strong echoes of ancient Mesopotamia.

The virtual disappearance of astrology during the Dark Ages was due as much to the disapproval of the early Christian Church as to the destruction of Roman civilization by the German invaders. The monks of the Celtic Church in Ireland, the light of the Western world at the time, were in touch with the Coptic Church in Egypt and would have had some sense of the debates taking place in Alexandria, until it fell to the Arabs in 642.

St Augustine and Free Will

The Algerian Christian Augustine (d.430) remained an unparalleled authority throughout the Middle Ages and his works were among the most widely read. In his *Confessions* (397), he records how he had in his youth 'devoted my time to astrological books' and 'did not cease to consult openly those impostors called astrologers'. Given the close association between astrology and medicine, he had at first studied astrology and intended to make it a career. But his doubts grew and he was finally convinced of his error when he discovered the very different fates of two children born with the precisely the same natal chart: a very wealthy landowner had been born at the same moment as one of his slaves on his estate. He concluded that astrologers were 'right by chance' and not because of their skill in inspecting the stars. And then there was always the thorny question of free will. If the astrologer's art was based on the assumption that human beings were shaped by forces beyond their control, he wondered in one of his letters, why was it that an astrologer could beat his wife? 'I won't say if he catches her being improperly playful, but even if she stares too long through a window? Could she not reply that it was not her fault, but Venus?'[5]

In Book V of *The City of God*, written twenty years after the *Confessions* and after the sack of Rome in 410, Augustine set out his more considered refutation of astrology. He acknowledged that there was a widespread link between 'fate' and the influence of the stars. Aware of Ptolemy's discussion of the relative importance of the moment of conception and the moment of birth, Augustine insisted that neither could be measured accurately enough. Taking up the Biblical story of Jacob and Esau, he focused again on the case of twins. 'Is it not true,' he asks, 'that the will of those who are now living changes the fates decreed at their nativity, when the order in which they are born changes the fates decreed at their conception?' Astrologers would argue that the Ascendants of twins are different because they are born at different times under different constellations. But if their Ascendants are different, 'in which that power is located which causes them to have different fates,' Augustine asks, 'how can this happen, when their conceptions cannot have occurred at different times?'[6]

In a treatise against 'Faustus the Manichee' (c.397–8), Augustine further argues: 'Now we (as opposed to the Manichees) set the birth of no man under the fatal rule of the stars, so that we can loose from any bond of necessity the free choice of his will, by which he lives well or ill, for the sake of the just judgment of God.' Since this is the case, the Star of Bethlehem which the Magi saw when Christ was born was 'not a lord governing his nativity but a servant bearing witness to it.' It follows that 'Christ was not born because it shone forth, but it shone forth because Christ was born; so if we must speak of it, we should say not that the star was fate for Christ, but that Christ was fate for the star.'[7]

Augustine's final position on astrology has echoed down the ages in the Roman Catholic Church: astrology is undeniably false. How else could one explain the different fortune of twins who have the same horoscope? The Stoic conception of fate must also be erroneous since angels and humans have free will. God may know that we are going to sin, but we do not sin because He knows it. We sin from our own free will as wayward and fallen creatures.

The Revival of Astrology

The revival of astrology in Western Europe has been traced back to the English monk Alcuin (735–804), a native of York.[8] His teacher was Bede's pupil Egbert. After a meeting in the 770s with the future Emperor Charlemagne, founder of the Holy Roman Empire, Alcuin agreed to join him in Germany as his private tutor. He then went on to establish the first great medieval school at the Abbey of St Martin near Tours, where among other subjects he taught astrology. He probably based his course on what he could find in the works of Latin authors about eclipses, comets, the planets, lunar phases and other celestial phenomena. Alcuin quoted the great African writer Tertullian on the subject: 'Astrology was allowed only until the time of the Gospel, so that no one from then on, after Christ's appearance, should interpret anyone's nativity from the heavens. For the Magi offered incense and myrrh and gold to the infant Lord as it were to mark the passing of this world's glories and rites, which Christ was to remove.'[9] Charlemagne himself took a great interest in astrology and had a map of the heavens made in the form of a 'celestial table' in silver.

This first 'renaissance' which followed the gradual revival of learning in Europe was wholly Latin. It began in the ninth and tenth centuries with the renewal of the cathedral schools. Astrology became a 'Liberal Art' as part of the *quadrivium*. Despite the ambivalence of the Church to pagan learning, there had been a growing interest in the *quadrivium* in general and *astrologia* in particular in the eleventh and early twelfth centuries. Scholars worked with the old Latin sources and their cosmology came mainly from Macrobius, Boethius and Plato's *Timaeus*. Although never happy with pagan learning, and aware of Augustine's strictures, the Church now accepted astrology as long as it did not threaten God's omnipotence and man's free will.

At the time of the Crusades, Christian scholars were fully aware of their own ignorance and the wealth of learning to be acquired from their Muslim enemies. Writing about the prognostications of the fall of Jerusalem in his history of the First Crusade, Guibert of Nogent observed in the twelfth century: 'The knowledge of the stars is as poor and rare in the West as it is flourishing through constant practice in the East, where indeed it originated.'[10]

In order to redress the balance, encyclopaedic writers like Hugh of St Victor (1097–1141) felt obliged to explain the meaning of astrology to their educated readers.

> The difference between astronomy and astrology is that astronomy is so called from the laws of the stars, astrology is as it were dis-course about the stars: *nomos* means law and *logos* means discourse. So it seems that astronomy deals with the laws of the stars and the turning of the heavens, the positions and the circles, the courses and risings and settings of the constellations, and why each is called what it is. Astrology considers the stars with relation to the observation of birth and death and all sorts of other events, and is partly natural and partly superstitious.[11]

The confusion between *nomos* and *logos*, astronomy and astrology, continued, the term *astrologia* being used to describe the two com-plementary aspects, theoretical and practical, of the same enquiry. Astrology as *horoscopia* was linked by Hugh and others to haruscopy and augury among the magic arts. Medicine, herbalism, geomancy, alchemy and astrology were all intertwined at the time. 'Natural Philosophy' and 'Natural Magic' were both terms for the empirical study of nature. Nature, revealing the hand of God, was a book to be read by all.

The renewed interest in astrology created a demand for astrological texts. It so happens that the awakening of the European mind coincided with the flowering of Moorish civilization in Spain and Sicily. It was there that Arabic and Hebrew translations of Greek classics and original Muslim works on astrology were to be found. The first to translate one of these works into Latin was Lupitus of Barcelona. He was contacted in 984 by Gerbert, a leading scholar of the time and the future Pope Sylvester II (999–1003). Educated in Spain, he was the first to discover the *Mathesis* of Julius Firmicus Maternus. In Rome, Sylvester converted part of the Lateran Palace into an observatory and it was rumoured that he was a magician. The first European book on astrology, *Liber de*

Planetis et Mundi Climatibus, was published early in the eleventh century, possibly written earlier by Gerbert.

By the twelfth century, the trickle of works had become a stream. A growing number of translations from the Arabic were being circulated in Europe. Christian scholars from the North-West travelled to the Muslim centres of learning in Spain and Sicily in search of Greek and Arabic texts. For the development of European astrology the key translations came fast and furious: in 1120–30, Adelard of Bath translated Al-Khwarizmi's *Tables*; in 1136, Hugh of Santalla brought to light the *Centiloquium* (a collection of a hundred astrological aphorisms); and in 1140, Hermann of Corinthia translated Abu Ma'shar's *Introductorium* which became the most widely used Arabic source. Ptolemy was soon rediscovered: Plato of Tivoli translated his *Tetrabiblos* in 1138 and the prolific translator Gerard of Cremona produced a version of his *Almagest* from the Arabic in Toledo in 1175.

Instruments and Tables

By the end of the twelfth century the key astrological texts of antiquity were available in Europe. The theory of astrology was being built on a firm foundation. What was now needed were some reliable instruments and tables.

The art of computing the calendar, and especially the date of Easter, was essential for the agricultural and liturgical year – on the farm and in church. Although he is not known to have written on astrology, Bede was the main authority on what was known as *computus* – that is, the computation or reckoning of the calendar, in particular the date of Easter.

There were no almanacs and no calendars. There were hour-glasses and marked candles and even a few water-clocks (*clepsydrae*), but they could only tell you 'how long' (like an egg timer) and not 'when' (like a modern clock). Without clocks and calendars, people told the time by the positions of the sun and moon. Thus Chaucer in his Prologue to the *Canterbury Tales* could tell that April had arrived with 'his shoures sote' because 'the yonge Sonne/hath in the Ram his halfe cours y-ronne'. And how could he tell that? By looking at a zodiac sundial on a church or town hall, as can still be seen in the Old Court of Queen's College, Cambridge, the Town Hall of Prague or on the wall of the Royal Observatory at Greenwich. The sundial in Queen's College is also a moondial, which was painted in 1733 to replace an earlier dial which had occupied the same position since 1642.[12]

Such sundials date back to at least the second century BC and were widely used by the Greeks and Romans. The principle of the sundial was known to the Chinese as early as 2500 BC. The angle of the arm to the horizontal must be the same as the latitude in which the dial is set up. To tell the time by the moondial it is necessary to know the angular position of the moon relative to the sun. The sign of the zodiac can be read off the dial in Queen's College by observing the position of the shadow in the green curves. An old rhyme was used as an aid to memory:

> The Ram, the Bull, the Heavenly Twins,
> And next the Crab, the Lion shines,
> The Virgin and the Scales,
> The Scorpion, Archer and the Goat,
> The Man that bears the Watering Pot,
> And Fish with glittering scales.

The shadow of the sun at noon would tell you where the sun was in the zodiac. But what about the time? This could be read by the way the shadow fell on the sundial during the day, and by the positions of the stars at night. From the twelfth century onwards, the zodiac appeared in countless 'Books of Hours', which contained a calendar of the dates and times of feasts and prayers as well as psalms and prayers. They were used by clergy and the laity all over Europe.

The most important instrument for the independent development of astronomy and astrology in Europe was the astrolabe which was acquired from the Arabs in the twelfth century. They in turn had obtained it from the Greeks. The astrolabe enabled the projection of the observed sphere of the heavens on to a plane. It was essential for drawing up the tables of the celestial bodies, for observing the heavenly bodies and for finding the time, latitudes, heights and distances. For the horoscope, it provided accurate observations of the heavens at the moment of birth. Combined with the tables, it enabled the astrologer to work out the position of the Ascendant and to divide the chart into the twelve Houses.

Accurate tables were essential. In his kingdom recently reconquered from the Moors in Spain, Alfonso X (1252–1284), King of Castile and Leon, gathered together Muslim, Jewish, and Christian scholars to draw up and codify existing astronomical data. The resulting *Alfonsine Tables* remained the standard work in Europe until revised by Copernicus in the sixteenth century.

Medieval Scholars

Nearly all the medieval scholars who became interested in astrology were churchmen of some sort. They therefore had to come to terms with the Church's attitude to astrology. The early Christian Church had fought what it considered pagan idolatry and superstition. In the twelfth century, Aristotle joined Plato as a revered philosopher and for the next 200 years, the philosophy of the educated in Europe was primarily Aristotelian. *Astrologia* was acceptable as part of *scientia*, knowledge, along with alchemy and medicine. As we have seen, however, the Church had a problem with its implied determinism which seemed to undermine the Christian doctrine of free will and moral responsibility. A person's physical make-up might be determined by celestial influences, but not his conscience and will. In 1277 Bishop Stephen Tempier of Paris issued a list of 219 heretical propositions, six of which clearly concerned astrology:

143 That by different signs in the heavens there are signified different conditions in men both of their spiritual gifts and of their temporal affairs.

161 That the effects of the stars on free will are hidden.

162 That our will is subject to the power of the heavenly bodies.

195 That fate, which is a universal disposition, proceeds from the divine providence not immediately but by the mediation of the movement of the heavenly bodies . . .

206 That anyone attribute health and sickness, life and death, to the position of the stars and the aspect of Fortune, saying that if Fortune is well-aspected to him he will live, and if not, he will die.

207 That in the hour of the begetting of a man in his body and consequently in his soul, which follows the body, by the ordering of the causes superior and inferior there is in a man a disposition including him to such and such actions and

events. This is an error unless it is understood to mean 'natural events' and 'by way of a disposition'.[13]

In a letter in 1272, Berthold of Regensburg summed up the typical attitude of a churchman to astrology: 'As God gave their power to stones and to herbs and to words, so also gave he power to the stars, that they have power over all things, except over one thing . . . It is man's free will: over that no man has any authority except thyself.'[14]

Astrology was accepted, albeit with some reservations, by the greatest medieval minds known as the 'Schoolmen'. Their philosophy predisposed them to accept the influence of celestial bodies, but their Christianity, with its emphasis on the omnipotence of God and free will, checked their enthusiasm.

Robert Grosseteste, Bishop of Lincoln from 1235 to 1253, whose diocese included the University of Oxford, was a great scholar who not only approved of astrometeorology (forecasting the weather by the state of the heavens) but the use of astrology in both alchemy and medicine. In an early work *On the Liberal Arts*, he wrote; 'Natural philosophy needs the assistance of *astronomia* more than that of the rest; for there are no, or few, works of ours or of nature, as for example the propagation of plants, the transmutation of minerals, the curing of sickness, which can be removed from the sway of *astronomia*. For nature below (*natura inferior*) effects nothing unless celestial power moves it and directs it from potency into act.'[15] Grosseteste noted that the terms *astronomia* and *astrologia* were still being used interchangeably. At the same time, he came to reject judicial astrology and insisted that free will is not under the stars but only under God.

Other great medieval thinkers accepted astrology as much as they accepted alchemy. Indeed, they believed the former was necessary in order to calculate the correct time for experiments in the latter. Influenced by the revival of interest in Aristotle, who had stressed the importance of the scientific method in the pursuit of knowledge, the English philosopher Roger Bacon (1214–1294), sometimes called the first European scientist, stressed the importance of experience and observation. He tried to make a clean break with Ptolemy by asserting that the earth is not the centre of the creation but a small planet in a vast universe. Bacon was also a skilled astrologer and fully accepted the horoscope of the religions, reproducing the words of Abu Ma'shar virtually to the letter: 'The philosophers want Jove (Jupiter), in his conjunction with the other planets, to signify religions and faith.' Since there are six planets, there are six principal religions: Jupiter with Saturn gives Judaism; with Mars, the Chaldean 'law'; with the sun, the Egyptian 'law'; with Venus, the 'law' of the Saracens which is 'pleasure-loving and lascivious'; with Mercury, Christianity, 'until, at last, the "law" of the moon will come to disturb it and that is the sect of the Anti-Christ'.[16]

In part IV of his *Opus Maius*, Bacon defined *astronomia* as 'practical *astrologia*' and goes on to explain the ambiguities of the term 'house' and the differences between the 'fixed' zodiac used by astrologers, with its divisions of 30° from the 'first point of Aries', and the moving zodiac caused by the precession of the equinoxes. No doubt recalling his Arabic sources, he defined the lunar mansions as 'the space of the zodiac which the moon crosses in a day' and points to their usefulness in forecasting the weather and for working out critical days in medicine. In *Secretum Secretorum*, his work on alchemy, Bacon further recognized the link between geomancy and astrology. He also admired the mathematician Campanus of Novara (d.1296) to whom a new method of dividing the heavens into twelve Houses was later attributed.

Albertus Magnus (1193–c.1280), a Dominican monk from Cologne, and one of the greatest minds of his age, fully endorsed both astrology and alchemy. He read Firmicus Maternus and Abu Ma'shar and recommended Ptolemy's *Almagest* and *Quadripartitum* (*Tetrabiblos*). He also approved of astrology in medicine, not only for selecting suitable timings but even recommended engraving stones with astrological images to speed up natural processes. He was uncertain about the possibility of predicting the future of individual human lives and believed that Jesus wholly escaped the influence of the stars.

His most outstanding pupil was Thomas Aquinas (1227–1274), who tried to reconcile the new Aristotelianism with the Catholic faith in his celebrated *Summa Theologia*. Aquinas' position was typical of the more thoughtful schoolmen: the body was influenced by the stars but reason and will were not. 'Astrologers, as in many things, can make true predictions, and this especially in general; not however in particular, for nothing stops any man from resisting his passions by his free will. Therefore the astrologers themselves say that "the wise man is master of the stars" (*sapiens homo dominatur astris*), inasmuch he is master of his passions.'[17] The phrase became commonplace in the medieval astrological literature of the time. Aquinas' argument that reason is good as long as it is kept within the confines of faith also became the fundamental dogma of the Church in its attitude to science.

Given the nearly universal acceptance of Aristotle's physics, it is not surprising that he should accept 'general' or 'natural' astrology – that is, the importance of celestial influences in meteorology, medicine and alchemy. Aristotle had made astrology reconcilable with Christianity by denying that the planets were living gods, but stages through which the creative intelligence passed down from beyond the fixed stars to the earth. Aquinas was thus able to claim that, while the stars ruled the body (the property of the sublunary sphere), God ruled the soul (the property of the heavens). From this distinction emerged the view that mundane astrology (which concerns the events of the world) is more determined or 'fated' than natal astrology (which deals with affairs of the soul and free will). Aquinas argued that since groups are more swayed by their passions than individuals, they are more susceptible to the influence of the stars.

The great Spanish physician and alchemist Arnald of Villanova (d.1313) was a fervent believer in the influence of the stars in illness and health. His works were divided into *Medica* and *Exotica*, with the latter subdividing into *Chymica, Astronomica* and *Theologica*. He claimed that Hippocrates emphasized that astrology was an important part of medicine. Indeed, the twin and related sciences of medicine and astrology are both needed by the physician. Astrologers could advise on times to carry out operations and the gathering and uses of herbs. Typical of his interpretation, which no doubt hurried up the patient's outcome, was the judgement: 'If the Ascendant should be in an "obile" sign, and the moon in the same sort of sign – namely Aries, Cancer, Libra or Capricorn – and the Lord of the Ascendant likewise, the sickness will be over quickly, for good or ill.' However, Arnald made it clear that the celestial influences do not necessarily determine but dispose and 'habituate' all things in the sublunary realm. Like Aquinas, he believed that humans, with their reason and free will, could override the influence of the heavens on their passions: 'the wise man will master the stars by his rationality' (*vir sapiens dominabitur astris sua rationabilitate*).[18]

Dante in his *Inferno* (Canto XX.118) mentioned Michael Scot 'who truly knew the game of magic frauds'. Probably born in Scotland towards the end of the twelfth century, he became a Hebrew and Arabic scholar as well as being deeply versed in Latin learning. By the 1220s he was sufficiently well-known to be offered the Archbishopric of Cashel which he declined because of his lack of Irish. Instead, he went down to Sicily, recently recaptured from the Moors, and became the court *astrologus* to Frederick II, a great dabbler in the occult sciences. In 1235, Frederick married Isabella, sister of Henry III of England, but, as Matthew Paris recorded, 'he refused to know her carnally until the fitting hour should be told by the astrologers.'

While in Frederick's employ, Michael Scot wrote several works on astrology, including the widely read *Liber Introductorius*, which was intended 'for student beginners and those not over-burdened with intelligence'. The *horologium* (probably a sundial) and the astrolabe (used at night), he wrote, were essential to establish the hour and the Ascendant and to calculate the Houses. He gave descriptions of constellations and of the planets, as well as an account of the planetary houses and the mundane houses. He included the moon's nodes, *caput draconis* (dragon's head) and *cauda draconis* (dragon's tail), in the lists of planets. The lunar mansions are also mentioned. Well-illustrated and detailed, his work offers a good summary of medieval astrology.

Three lines after the reference to Michael Scot in *Inferno*, Dante mentions the Italian astrologer Guido Bonatti (b.1210). He is among the diviners who are being punished for trying to pry into the future (which belongs to God alone) by having their heads turned on their shoulders to make them face backwards. However, Bonatti confirms the important link between astrology and medicine in the Middle Ages for his name appears on a list of professors at the University of Bologna, one of the oldest medical schools in Europe. The professor of *astrologia* taught a four-year course which medical students were obliged to attend. Bonatti's twelve-book treatise, *De Astronomia* (*astrologia* and *astronomia* were still used interchangeably), summarized the subject at the time, including 'revolutions' (progressions) and elections. It also contained the usual confusion over the House divisions. His *Liber Astronomicus* was considered to be a sufficiently classic work for Henry VII of England to have a deluxe edition in his library 200 years later.

Like many astrologers, Bonatti worked for a patron – in his case, the Italian noble Guido de Montefeltro. The story goes that he would mount the tower above the piazza in Forli with his books and astrolabe and decide the time when his master should march forth with his army against his enemies.

Another thirteenth-century Italian mathematician, Johannes Campanus, is remembered for his method of dividing the Houses in the horoscope. He imagined a great circle passing through the zenith (the point immediately overhead an observer on earth) and at right angles to the meridian. This circle and the meridian cut the sphere used in the horoscope into four quadrants. The quadrants were then each divided into three by circles intersecting at the North and South points of the horizon. As a result, the beginning points (cusps) of the unequal Houses were the degrees of the ecliptic cut by these circles.

The Mastery of the Stars

By the fourteenth century, popes, bishops, kings and princes all had their astrologers. When the Black Death reached Europe in 1347 and raged for three years, it was widely believed to be the result of the configurations of the planets at the time. The Medical Faculty of the University of Paris reported to the king in 1348:

> On 20 March 1345, at 1 p.m., there occurred a conjunction of Saturn, Jupiter and Mars in the house of Aquarius. The conjunction of Saturn and Jupiter notoriously caused death and disaster while the conjunction of Mars and Jupiter spread pestilence in the air (Jupiter, being warm and humid, was calculated to draw up evil vapours from the earth and water, which Mars, hot and dry, then kindled into infective fire). Obviously the conjunction of all three planets could only mean an epidemic of cataclysmic scale.[19]

The growing interest in astrology did not, however, always protect individual astrologers from the wrath of the Church if they stepped out of line. Cecco d'Ascoli, an astrologer and alchemist at the court of Florence who had lectured at Bologna, was burnt at the stake as a heretic on 16 September 1327 for casting the horoscope of Christ and deducing the inevitability of the crucifixion. His heresy was primarily for his work on necromancy, but he also applied his astrology to the coming of Antichrist and to the end of the world, which was all too much for the Vatican. D'Ascoli believed that astrology was the most reliable way of knowing the future – better than magic and divination – and that it made man divine like the angels. It even helped the physician to cure the causes and consequences of an illness without even seeing the patient!

While the Middle Ages had begun with the virtual absence of astro-

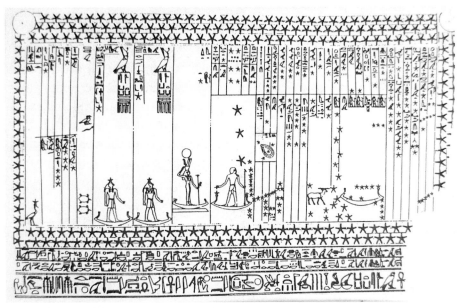

One of the earliest Egyptian star maps (c.1473 BC) on the ceiling of the tomb of Senmut, Dar el-Bahari, Luxor. The bird with a star, on the left, represents Venus, while the figures on the solar boats are Saturn, Mercury, the goddess Isis, with a solar disc, and Orion, with the three stars of his belt above his head. The decans are described on the right.

Circular zodiac from the ceiling of Dendera Temple, Egypt. Dating from the first century BC, it is the first known zodiac in the world. The constellations are arranged around the centre. The original is now in the Louvre, Paris.

A fifteenth-century woodcut showing the dreaded conjunction of Jupiter, grappling with Taurus, and of Saturn: both under the sign of Scorpio. It was thought to forebode disaster.

The astrological hieroglyph of the Great Fire of London in 1666, predicted by William Lilly in 1651. It shows the twins of Gemini, the traditional sign of London, falling headlong into the fire.

Astrological Man, demonstrating the celestial influences on different parts of the body. It reflects the ancient belief in the correspondence between the macrocosm (the universe) and the microcosm (humanity).

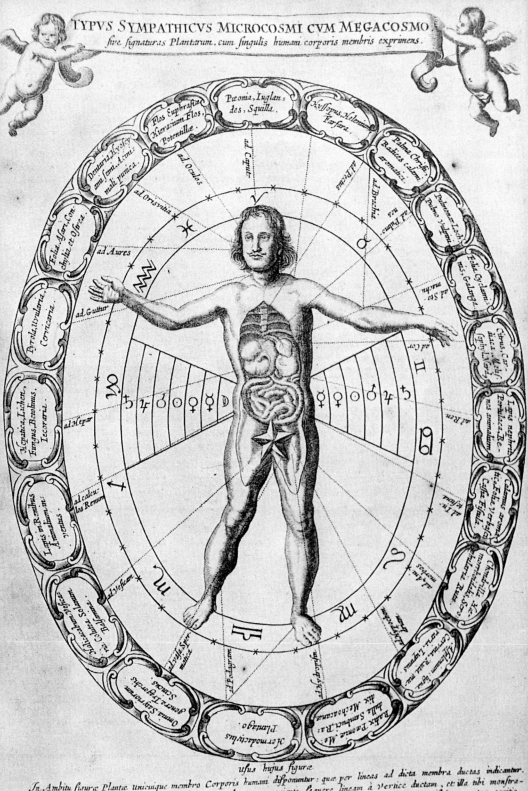

TYPVS SYMPATHICVS MICROCOSMI CVM MEGACOSMO,

sive signaturas Plantarum, cum singulis humani corporis membris exprimens.

usus hujus figuræ

In Ambitu figuræ Plantæ unicuique membro Corporis humani disponuntur: quæ per lineas ad dicta membra ductas indicantur. V.G. si nosse Cupias capitis infirmitatibus quæ plantæ conveniunt, sequere lineam à vertice ductam, et illa tibi monstrabit hic in ambitu, Pæoniam Juglandem, Squillam, quæ uti capitis Signaturam exprimunt: ita quoque potentissima contra capitis morbos à Medicis censentur remedia. Pari pacto in cæteris procede: quæ cum facillima sunt, ea amplius exponenda non duxi.

Author with Choi Park-lai, specialist in feng shui and the Four Pillars of Destiny of Chinese astrology. He also publishes the Chinese Almanac in Hong Kong.

'Yogastrologer' Swami Yogi Prakash lives in Varanasi (Benares), India.

Komilla Sutton, co-founder and chair of the British Association for Vedic Astrology and author of several books on astrology.

David Thomas, astrologer and writer based in North Wales.

logy in the West, they ended with its widespread, if qualified, acceptance. The first half of the fifteenth century was the great age of the illustrated 'Books of Hours'. One of the finest is the Duke of Berry's *Très riches heures* which is often used to illustrate modern books on astrology. Although primarily concerned with the calendar, it contains a beautiful depiction of 'zodiacal man' inspired by medical astrology.

The signs of the zodiac also appeared in the stained glass of churches and cathedrals. They were carved in wood and stone on arches, tympana and misericords. At Vézélay, they surround the figure of Christ on the tympanum above the central doors. Again, their primary intention was to show Christ, like Mithras before him, as the Lord of Time, but the astrological associations would not be lost on those in the know.

In the fifteenth century, Popes Pius II, Sixtus IV and Alexander VI all took a keen interest in astrology. Regiomontanus (Johann Müller, 1436–1476), author of the astrological tables known as *Ephemerides* and connected with the court of the king of Hungary, was asked by Pope Sixtus IV to reform the calendar. He not only anticipated the discoveries of Copernicus but invented a new way of dividing the sky into unequal Houses which is still with us today. His new House system divided the quadrant between the horizon and the meridian. He marked off twelve circles that represented the Houses along the celestrial equator. The cusps were then indicated by the degrees of the ecliptic cut by these circles.

Nevertheless, the Church's acceptance remained qualified. Bishop Nicole Oresme (1320–1382), who had taught theology in Paris, was typically circumspect. He wrote a short work in Latin, *Tractatus Contra Judiciarios Astronomos*, which was expanded into a work in French called *Livre de divinacions* (1361–65). One of his garbled anecdotes mixes up astrology and parricide, but at least it recognizes the importance of Egypt in its origins: 'Nectanebus, King of Egypt, was driven into Macedonia by fourteen nations in rebellion and later he wished to teach astrology to King Alexander who, they say, was his son. Alexander gave him a push and knocked him into a pit where he broke his neck. So it would have served him better to have watched the earth than the heavens.'[20]

While Oresme gave a qualified approval to events flowing from major conjunctions and medical prognostications, he argued that the part belonging to 'Fortune' and more specifically to nativities is unreliable. It is 'not in itself beyond knowledge, so far as the complexion and inclination of a person born at a given time are in question, but cannot be known when it comes to fortune and things which can be hindered by the human will.'[21] It is the old caveat: astrology is fine if it does not interfere with the freedom of the will and the omnipotence of God. It was acceptable if it meant nothing more than that events in heaven signify but do not cause events on earth. It follows that *Sapiens homo dominabitur astris*: the wise man will be master of the stars.

31

Rebirth

Astrology is the most lofty of the branches of knowledge because it deals with celestial things and with the future, knowledge of which is not only divine but very useful.

GIROLAMO CARDANO

IN THE UFFIZI PALACE in Florence hangs the magnificent painting by Botticelli called *Minerva* or *Spring*. In the dark orange grove with its flower-decked floor, Zephyr pursues and holds Flora who has flowers growing out of her mouth. Flora is transformed by Zephyr into the pregnant Hour of Spring, whose diaphanous dress is embroidered with flowers. Thoughtful Venus stands in the middle. To the left the three Graces dance together holding hands.

The whole tableau forms a brilliantly executed allegory, a celebration of the power of nature and of ancient myths. But the most enigmatic and powerful figure stands on the right. With winged sandals, he turns his back to the Graces and points his right hand holding a caduceus wand to the heavens, reminding us of our celestial origins and destination. He is Mercury, the Roman god of travellers; he is Hermes, the Greek messenger of the gods; he is Thoth, the Egyptian god of wisdom. At the heart of the Renaissance, at the heart of Christendom, the ancient father of astrology holds sway.

It is usual to say that the Renaissance began with the discovery of ancient learning after the fall of Constantinople to the Turks in 1453. But, as we have seen, Greek and Roman works of philosophy and science had been filtering into Europe from Arabic translations for centuries. As early as the fourteenth century, a movement was under-way which would eventually lead to the separation of theology from philosophy and metaphysics from science in the so-called Scientific Revolution of the sixteenth and seventeenth centuries. Astrology, bridging both traditions, was inevitably caught up in the intellectual turmoil.

In the fifteenth century in Europe, the horoscopes of children in the wealthier families were drawn up as a matter of course. Astrology also appealed to the newly literate. A fine example of the growth in astrological literature is the *Kalendar and Compost of Shepherds*. Printed in Paris in 1493 and in London in English translation in 1506, only half a century after the art of printing was invented, the work contains marvellous woodcuts. A good summary of medieval astrological lore was put in the mouths of the shepherds, including the lines translated around 1518:

> Saturn is highest, and coldest being full bad,
> And Mars with his bloody sword, ever ready to kill;
> Jupiter very good, and Venus maketh lovers glad,
> Sol and Luna is half good and half ill,
> Mercury is good, and evil verily.[1]

Marsilio Ficino and Stellar Rays

Although not new, there was undoubtedly an upsurge of interest during the Renaissance in ancient Greece and Egypt, especially in Italy. Italian scholars looked back to Stoicism for the notion of cosmic sympathy, Neoplatonism for its belief in the immortality of the soul and to the Pythagoreans for the Harmony of the Spheres and sacred numerology. The remarkable intellectual, Marsilio Ficino (1433–1499), stood in this tradition. Under the patronage of Lorenzo de' Medici in Florence, to whom he gave astrological advice, Ficino set up a school based on the model of Plato's academy which inspired Raphael's painting *The School of Athens* in the Vatican. Like the Platonic philosophers, he believed that 'the world-soul for its own reason has constructed forms beyond the stars in the sky. Parts of these are of such a kind that they themselves are forms too, and the world-soul has impressed its properties on all of them. Every type of lower creation, along with its properties, is contained in the stars, in the forms, in the parts and *in their* properties.'[2]

Ficino was translating a work by Plato, when Medici asked him to look at a recently discovered text in Greek. Entranced by this new document, Ficino dropped his Plato and took up his pen to produce his translation of the *Corpus Hermeticum* which was circulating with the Latin *Asclepius*. The ancient wisdom of Egypt was re-emerging at the centre of Christendom. For Ficino, the Hermetic writings not only appeared in accord with Christianity but confirmed his vision of the dignity of man.

Ficino was keenly interested in astrology, and his reading included Abu Ma'shar, the *Centiloquium*, Bonatti, Campanus, and Ptolemy among others. Manilius had been rediscovered in 1416 and the work of Firmicus Maternus was also available. As a young man Ficino had questioned the claims of divinatory astrology in the unfinished work *Disputatio Contra Iudicum Astrologorum*, but in his later work he expressed few qualms about the influence of the heavens on the physical events on earth. It was, however, *iatromathematica* – astrological medicine – which most appealed to him, for it expressed his Hermetic belief in the correspondence between heaven and earth, and his view of man as a microcosm of the universe. He stated: 'if Galen is the doctor of the body, then Plato is the doctor of the soul.'[3]

'If you value your life you will take medicines approved by the heavens. Confirmed by certain heavenly support,' wrote Ficino in 1489. He believed a particular composition of herbs and vapours made first by the arts of medicine, and then by astrology, produces 'a combination – a harmony, as it were – endowed with the gifts of the stars'.[4]

In his *Theologica Platonica,* written in 1486, Ficino followed his 'divine Plato' and presented the universe as a gigantic, vibrating organism in which the stars were the source of the active forces in matter, plants and animals. Jove, the unique soul of the whole creation, 'placed souls which had a share in intelligence in the purest parts of the spheres, that is the stars and the planets, which he also called gods. In the fiery regions he placed demons and heroes of fire. In those of the clear air, aerial spirits; in those of the dark air, demons and aquatic heroes.' The whole is connected by a Great Chain of Being: 'All the intelligences . . . are so interconnected that, beginning with God who is their head, they proceed in a long and uninterrupted chain, and all the superior ones shed their rays down on the inferior ones.'[5]

Ficino was an accomplished musician and singer, performing on the lyre. Recalling the ancient doctrine of the Harmony of the Spheres, he argued that the stars and planets provide a celestial harmony, the parts of which can be incorporated into music: 'So first from tones chosen in accordance with the standard behaviour of the stars, and then from the tones combined to produce harmony among those same stars, there is made as it were a common pattern and in this patterns emerges a kind of celestial power.' As might be expected, he attributes dreary and plaintive sounds to Saturn, discordant and menacing ones to Mars. The harmonies of Jupiter, by contrast, are melodious and cheerful, and the songs attributed to Venus give sensual pleasure because they are 'wanton and languid'. Mercury, light-hearted and vigorous, lies between the extremes.[6] Such compositions were essential for conducting magical ceremonies. They also later found their supreme expression in Holst's magnificent work *The Planets*.

How did the celestial bodies influence events on earth? Ficino believed that the stars emitted rays which penetrated matter and imprinted characteristics on the things they touched or passed through. In his *Liber de Vita* (1489) he wrote: 'the immense extent of the heavens, their power and their movement mean that every ray of every star penetrates the mass of the earth (which is like a pinpoint in the sky), and in a moment and with the greatest of ease makes its way to the centre.' He based his case for talismanic magic on this: if the stellar rays penetrate the whole earth, they also penetrate metal and precious stones when engraved with images on them which then conserve their power. Celestial power can therefore be harnessed and channelled into talismans, words and songs. For example, 'To fight a fever one sculpts Mercury in marble, in the hour of Mercury, when Mercury is rising, in the form of a man who bears arrows.'[7] And through what vehicle do they affect us? The properties of the heavenly bodies come into our bodies via our spirit.

True to his Neoplatonic and Hermetic sympathies, Ficino felt that the more one transformed the corporal into the spiritual, the more one could escape the physical influences of the celestial bodies: 'The force of fate does not penetrate the mind unless the mind of its own accord has first become submerged in the body, which is subject to Fate . . . Every soul should withdraw from the encumbrance of the body and become centred in the mind, for then Fate will discharge its force upon the body without touching the soul.'[8]

Pico and the Dignity of Man

Another outstanding Italian Renaissance scholar, Count Giovanni Pico della Mirandola (1463–94), took a different path. He died at the age of thirty in 1494, but in his short life he was known for his noble birth, inherited wealth and good looks, as well as for his penetrating intellect. As a very young man, he mastered Arabic and Hebrew and immersed himself in the Cabbala. He appeared in Rome in 1486 and publicly posted up some 900 theses dealing with logic, mathematics, physics and theology which he proposed to defend against all comers. Despite his aristocratic background, he became the friend of Girolamo Savonarola, the scourge of Florentine decadence. Pico is best known for his *Oration on the Dignity of Man* in which he defined man not only as a microcosm of the universe but as the *magnum miraculum* (the great miracle).

After discovering the Cabbala, Pico tried to use the mystical tradition to support Christianity, an attempt condemned by Pope Innocent VIII. Forever seeking controversy, at a time when astrologers were all the fashion in the courts, he launched a twelve-book counterblast, *Disputaciones Adversus Astrologiam Divinatricem*, which he dedicated to the Pope.

However, Pico's celebrated attack was not aimed at all aspects of *astrologia*. Like Aquinas, he made the distinction between natural and judicial astrology and wanted to cleanse true astrology and magic from their superstitious accretions. Although he did not refer to it in his treatise, he would have accepted with reservations 'physical' or 'natural' astrology which foretells natural phenomena such as tides and eclipses. It was 'divinatory astrology' that he attacked, the kind of judicial astrology that seeks to foretell things to come by the stars: natal charts, progressions, elections and interrogations. Apart from stressing the disagreements among astrologers, the main thrust of Pico's attack was that 'the astrologer consults signs that are not signs, and examines causes that are not causes'.[9] He pointed out that astrologers were unable to establish the minute divisions of the zodiac, and that basing a progression on the principle of 'a degree a year' was absurd. He failed to understand why different regions of the sky should produce different effects on earth. As for the 'great conjunctions', stellar rays might affect things below, but how could they possibly affect each other? Since they could not, the aspects between the planets were meaningless. In short, if the astrologers could not get the large things right, how could they be trusted in the small?

Pico further focused on the disagreements between astrologers over House divisions (Campanus versus Regiomontanus), the relative importance of conception and birth (mentioned in Ptolemy), and the different influences of the fixed stars. He raised the question of possible influence from unknown planets. He observed that the precession of the equinoxes meant that the 'first point of Aries' was no longer in Aries at all which made a mockery of the fixed zodiac used by most astrologers. Then there was the problem of inaccurate tables and the difficulty in reliably ascertaining 'the hour of the beginning' and the exact condition of the heavens at the time. Finally, he admitted that sometimes astrologers predicted what actually happened. 'But since a good many predictions do not happen,' he asks, 'why should we not think they came true by chance . . . almost always the lines of the hand, the marks of geomancy and the position of the planets, will not tell him the same thing.'[10]

Pico's principal concern was to restore the liberty of the will and the autonomy of the mind. He sought to separate astrology from medicine and to turn the latter into a science. Above all, he wanted to reform philosophy by eradicating the astrology developed by the Chaldeans and Egyptians as a general conception of reality from the Tree of Knowledge. From his severe pruning, he exempted 'natural magic', not in the sense of necromancy in which one works with daemons, but as 'the practical part of the science of nature, which only teaches us to achieve admirable works by means of natural forces'.[11] Pico's was undoubtedly a devastating attack that exercised the minds of the astrologers who were his contemporaries, and still needs to be considered.

Girolamo Cardano and the Inquisition

For the most part, the Dominicans and Franciscans supported astrology. Even the Jesuits, the most powerful and intellectual order during the Renaissance, were active. Among the Popes, Julius II (1505–1513) used astrology in order to decide the most auspicious time to have a statue of himself erected, while Paul III (1534–1549) regularly consulted astrologers to work out the best time to meet his audiences.

One astrologer who fell foul of the Inquisition was the brilliant Italian physician and mathematician Girolamo Cardano (1501-1576). However, after being released from prison on a charge of heresy,

Cardano lived his final years on a pension from the Pope. He was a prolific writer on astrology. In his view, 'the contemplation of astrology is beautiful in itself, an understanding of how lower things are linked with higher. Its use is to know the future and to be able to take precautions in advance.' He considered astrology to be 'more beneficial and more divine' than any other branch of study because it instructed us about the courses of the stars and the 'gods themselves'.[12] It encompassed all the arts which teach us how to discover the future, namely agriculture, seafaring, medicine, physiognomy, interpretation of dreams and natural magic.

Cardano was clearly going too far when talking about 'the gods' rather than God. The revival of Hermeticism, and an interest in the ancient wisdom of Egypt, once again raised the spectre of paganism. But when in 1586, the former farmworker, Pope Sixtus V, issued a bull prohibiting astrology it was not 'natural astrology' (predictions in relation to agriculture, the art of sailing and medicine) but judicial astrology (natal, horary and electional astrology) which was considered to be a denial of free will and an affront to God. In his bull, *Coeli et Terrae*, Pope Sixtus V railed against the *mathematici* who 'employ an idle, false knowledge of the planets and stars, and with the utmost audacity busy themselves now with anticipating a revelation of God's arrangements of things'. Such divination sprang from the Devil.

Astrologers clearly had to tread carefully. In his reply to the papal bull, the Dominican Tommaso Campanella (1568–1639) observed that it pursued astrologers with more hostility than heretics and schismatics. It even excommunicated them, removed all their property and punished them with a sentence of death. Campanella maintained that astrologers were not offering certain knowledge of the future but were basing their art on physical principles: 'Astrology argues from causes, the reason being that the heavenly bodies work upon the world below like the universal causes of times and temporal things. This is what experience tells us.'[13] Aware of the opposition, he issued his work on astrology in 1629 in Lyons with the title: 'The six books of Astrology of Campanella of the Order of Preachers, in which Astrology, from which all the superstition of the Arabs and Jews has been eliminated, is dealt with on physical principles, according to Holy Scripture and the teachings of Saints Thomas and Albert and the great Theologians, in such a way that it may be read with great profit without coming under suspicion from the Church of God.'

Campanella argued that the physical principles of astrology demonstrate that 'the stars work in lower things by heat, light, motion and aspect'. Bearing in mind Pico's criticism, he insisted that it was absolutely necessary to be sure of the degree and minute of the horoscope. He was equally aware that the precession of the equinoxes meant that the vernal equinox began in Pisces, although astrologers still called it the 'first point of Aries'. Perhaps his most important point was his answer to those who, like Copernicus, thought that the sun and not the earth was the centre of the universe. Far from sounding the death knell for astrology, he argued that what mattered was the relative position of the planets and their angular distances as seen from the earth: 'Whether the sun moves or stands still, it is to be supposed a moving Planet by us, considering the matter from our senses and our description; for the same happens whether it moves or the earth.'[14] As for the planets, he felt that all the planets were propitious in themselves, but some could be favourable and some harmful 'just as a gentle fire is helpful and a big fire a nuisance'. On these grounds, the unlucky planets (Saturn and Mars) were 'helpful to snakes, matters inimical to us, and barbarian peoples who abandon their human status'.[15]

Ironically, Campanella conducted a magical ceremony in the Lateran Palace for the benefit of Pope Urban VIII who felt himself threatened by the approach of a lunar eclipse. In a wonderful summary of the astral magic of the Renaissance, he recommended that for three hours before the eclipse and three hours after one should:

First take every pain to live temperately, according to reason and as closely to God as possible, by dedicating yourself to Him by means of prayer and holy rituals. Secondly, close up your house entirely so that no one else's air may enter therein. Sprinkle the house with rose-flavoured vinegar and waft it with aromatic odours. Make a fire and burn thereon laurel, myrtle, rosemary, cypress and other aromatic woods. There is nothing more powerful than this for dissipating the poisonous operations in the sky, even if they are administered by the Devil. Thirdly, decorate the house with white silk cloths and branches of fern. Fourthly, burn two lights and five torches to represent the planets, so that their places may be filled on earth at the time they are absent from the sky . . . Make representations of the planets from a mixture of aromatic substances, and once you have made copies of the twelve signs of the zodiac (according to the principles of philosophy and not of superstition

as the common people believe) you may proceed . . . Fifthly, have
with you friends and associates whose horoscopes have not been
subject to the evil of an eclipse . . . Sixthly, have people play music
belonging to Jupiter and Venus in the room, so that it can break up
the evil character of the air . . . Seventhly, since the symbols of each
star are found in stones, plants, colours, odours, music and movements . . . provide those which attract the beneficent stars and which
put to flight that of maleficent stars. Liquors distilled under planetary influences should be drunk, as they have a great deal of
power.[16]

Paracelsus and Calvin

Meanwhile, in the North of Europe, the Dutch theologian and humanist
Erasmus (1469–1536) was prepared to countenance astrology as well
as alchemy. The revolutionary Protestant Paracelsus (1493–1541),
remembered as the father of pharmacology, was a physician and
alchemist who used astrology as an essential part of his cures.

Paracelsus named the universal principle which regulated the whole
universe *Magnale-Magnum* and assured the correspondence between the
microcosm and the macrocosm. He believed that man was composed of
three principles – Mercury, Salt and Sulphur – which Hermes called
spirit, soul and body. There were also constellations, stars and planets
(*astra*) in our bodies, as well as in the heavens, and the two needed to
be in harmony in order to enjoy good health. 'For what is more noble
in a doctor,' he asked, 'than a knowledge of the concordance of the
astra? – for there lies the basis of all diseases.'[17]

Like the ancient Greeks, Paracelsus associated the main organs of the
body with the seven planets, and if an organism was out of balance,
the influence of its corresponding planet was to be activated to bring
about a restoration. According to Paracelsus, the sun ruled the heart;
the moon, the brain; Venus, the veins; Saturn, the spleen; Mercury, the
liver; Jupiter, the lungs; and Mars ruled the gall. To bring about a cure,
he insisted that both the right astrological time had to be observed as
well as the correct dosage of the appropriate chemical or herb.

Most of the Protestant reformers were far less enthusiastic about
astrology, partly, no doubt, because of its association with Catholic
decadence. Girolamo Cardano issued Martin Luther's 'true horoscope'
dated 22 October 1483 in which he noted: 'Mars, Venus and Jupiter are

grouped together next to the star Spica, right down by the horizon. From this combination one can discern royal power without the trappings of royalty (because these planets go beneath the earth). This refers to religion.'[18] Although Luther was critical of astrology, his close friend Melanchthon was a staunch supporter, especially of astrological medicine. In his *Initia Doctrinae Physicae* (1549), he argued that 'most of the noteworthy qualities in the temperament are both good and bad and have their origin in the stars.' Turning the tables on Pico, he pointed to the case of two children who inherit the physical characteristics of their parents, yet have very different health and length of life. The cause of this was to be found in the stars. But he would not exclude God from the picture: 'Nature governs a great deal but not everything. One must not remove God from astrological governance, but declare that God moderates many tendencies which originate with the stars, and pray that He help those which are good and suppress those which are bad.'[19]

The French Protestant reformer Jean Calvin (1509–1564) would have none of it. He dismissed judicial astrology as a 'Satanic superstition'. He was ready to acknowledge that 'All earthly bodies and (let me speak in general terms) all inferior bodies have some affinity with the course of the stars and hence derive some kind of distinguishing characteristic.' He accepted 'natural astrology', which shows how inferior bodies like oysters and shellfish grow and shrink with the phases of the moon, and astrological medicine, which tells doctors the opportune moment to draw blood and prescribe medicines. But he would have nothing to do with judicial astrology which investigates what is going to happen to an individual.

Calvin's case was based on two main objections. Firstly, if two women conceived and gave birth at exactly the same moment, the different lives of their offspring would inevitably show that heredity is more important than the influence of the stars. Secondly, if 60,000 men were to die in a single battle, would this mean that all had the same horoscope? That would be patently absurd. Calvin was thus forced to conclude: 'From ancient times, people's minds have been invaded by something like a wasting, contagious disease – the silly eagerness to predict from the position of the sky and the stars what is going to happen to someone and what will be each person's inborn fate.'[20] The same argument reappears in modern attacks on astrology which employ equally vituperative language.

The English Magus

Despite the ambiguous voices coming from the Vatican and the general disapproval of the Protestant reformers, the courts welcomed the astrological insights of the great mathematicians, astronomers and philosophers of the Renaissance. Girolamo Cardano cast the horoscope of Edward VI of England. The remarkable John Dee (1527–1608), brilliant mathematician, navigator, alchemist and secret agent, was court astrologer to Elizabeth I. He predicted a dire fate for Mary, Queen of Scots and chose the date of the coronation of Elizabeth so that it would be 'blessed by the heavens'.

A tall, slender man with a delicate complexion, Dee later grew a long white beard, enhancing his reputation as a magus. He was consulted about the decision of Pope Gregory XIII in 1582 to correct the erring calendar by ten days, but his recommendation to adopt the reform was delayed by 170 years because of the intervention of some Anglican bishops who were suspicious of Rome. Dee was a friend of Gerald Mercator, who invented the map projection which bears his name, and gave the admirals advice on the best time to fight the Spanish Armada.

Dee was a man of enormous erudition who made full use of the new learning of the Renaissance. His library at Mortlake was the best in England at the time and contained at least fifty astrological works, including all the great names. His astrology was based on the influence of stellar rays on earth and the computation of their relative strength emitted at different times and places. Recalling Ptolemy, he argued: 'Every seed (*semen*) has potentially in itself the whole and unchanging order of each act of generation, to be unfolded in the way in which the nature of the place of the conceiver and the power of the surrounding heaven which falls upon it, work and conspire together.'[21] Dee's astrology did not prevent him from being an early advocate of the Copernican theory of a heliocentric universe; indeed, it was in accord with his Hermetic interests.

Dee believed that hidden forces were at work in nature and that the daemons of the spirit world could provide the key to the secrets of the universe. When Edward Kelly, a shady but persuasive would-be alchemist with cropped ears turned up at his home, he began to undertake seances with the help of a scryer or crystal ball which is now lodged in the British Museum. With Kelly as his medium, Dee engaged in 'angelic conversations' with the angels Uriel and Michael. In this way, he claimed to have transcribed the whole lost Book of Enoch. The work exists in a coded language which resembles no known tongue and has yet to be deciphered.

A daemon called Madini told Dee to travel to Poland and then Bohemia in search of the Philosopher's Stone which would transmute base metal into gold and reveal the secrets of nature. At the same time, Dee seems to have been an undercover agent for Elizabeth, for Cabbalistic reasons signing himself 007.

Dee's seances with Kelly became too dangerous and upsetting when they acted on the suggestion that they share their wives. Dee eventually left the court of the Holy Roman Emperor Rudolf II in Prague after being suspected by the papal ambassador of stirring up a Protestant rebellion. He spent the rest of his life in obscurity in Mortlake, rejected by James I as a sorcerer. Although sometimes remembered as a master of darkness, he was in fact a Renaissance magus of the first order. He may well have advised Shakespeare in writing *The Tempest* and inspired the figure of Prospero.

Nostradamus and the End of the World

While John Dee served Elizabeth I, Catherine de Medici, Queen of France, employed Michel de Notre Dame, known as Nostradamus (1503–1566). She first called on him to verify the forecasts of the astrologer Lucus Gauricus, who had predicted the death of her husband Henry II, and then obliged him to draw up horoscopes for all the royal children.

Nostradamus was born in St Rémy in Provence of Jewish parents who had converted to Christianity to avoid persecution. Most of his life he was a physician and alchemist who, like Paracelsus, used astrology as a central part of his healing art. Taught by his learned grandfather, he studied at Avignon and Montpellier, two great centres of medicine. He earned a considerable reputation for his successful treatment of plague victims (although unable to save his own wife and children) and for his eccentric ways, which included maintaining hygiene and not bleeding his patients. He even gave advice on cosmetics and invented fruit preservatives.

His growing reputation as a healer brought him enemies. In 1538, his rivals accused him of heresy and he was summoned before the Inquisition, but he chose to go into hiding and travelled throughout France and Italy. It is said that in Italy he met a group of young monks and knelt down before one of them whom he addressed as 'Your Holiness'. The monk was the former swineherd who later went on to become Pope Sixtus V, the very one who issued the papal bull condemning heresy.

The wandering physician and astrologer eventually settled down with his new wife and after 1550 began issuing his popular annual almanac. Five years later, he finished the first part of his predictions known as the *Centuries*, which were written in a mixture of Latin, French and regional dialects, with astrological and alchemical allusions and symbols. To avoid persecution, he deliberately jumbled the sequence of his quatrains and veiled their meaning and it is these ambiguous and enigmatic 'perpetual prophecies' which continue to excite interest and fear.

He remains the best known prophet of modern times. He appears to have predicted the beheading of Charles I and the death of Marie Antoinette as well as the French and Russian Revolutions. In a remarkable vision, he foretold the Great Fire of London in 1666 – 'Burnt by the fire of three times twenty and six', that is 66! It is said that his prophecy of a coming Antichrist has been fulfilled by Stalin and Hitler. And he even seems to have predicted the ultimate devastation of a nuclear holocaust:

> Leave, leave, go forth out of Geneva all,
> Saturn of gold shall be changed into iron,
> The contrary of the positive rays shall exterminate all,
> Before it happens, the Heavens shall show signs.[22]

As for his apocalyptic vision for the future:

> When a fish pond that was a meadow shall be mowed,
> Sagittarius being in the ascendant,
> Plague, Famine and Death from the military hand,
> The century approaches renewal.[23]

At least, there will be a time for renewal. He predicts a golden age of peace and happiness for mankind following a great war: 'Health, abundance of fruits, joys and mellifluous times.'[24] But it will only last seventy-five years. Nostradamus' final word is that the end of the world will occur in the year 7000 when the sun will destroy the earth:

Twenty years of the reign of the moon have passed.
Seven thousand years another shall hold his monarchy,
When the sun shall resume his days past,
Then is fulfilled and ends my prophecy.[25]

Nostradamus believed that his prophecies were not only revelations
indicated by the 'planetary movements' but also the product of 'divine
inspiration, given that all prophetic inspiration derives from God'.[26]
Most of his visions came through 'scrying'. Whilst sitting on a brass
tripod which had the same angles as the apex of the Great Pyramid, he
contemplated images that appeared in a water-filled flask placed above
a flame. His own horoscope, with the moon in Scorpio, suggested psychic
powers. Reassuringly, Nostradamus did not believe that his prophecies
were inevitable predictions but possible outcomes. Time alone will tell.

Nostradamus has become the world's most famous astrologer
because of his predictions which are still carefully studied. After the
attack on the twin towers in New York on 11 September 2001, his work
hit the bestseller lists. He had, after all, predicted a cataclysmic fire in a
'great new city' on the 45th parallel . . .

32

The New Astronomy

In the midst of all dwells the sun . . . Siting on the royal throne,
he rules the family of planets which turn around him . . . We thus
find in this arrangement an admirable harmony of the world.

COPERNICUS

IN A SMALL MUSEUM near the national library in Florence is the
slightly opaque lens through which Galileo Galilei (1564–1642) first
saw the four moons of Jupiter in 1609. In the following year, he
discovered the rings of Saturn and the phases of Venus, demonstrating
that the latter orbits the sun. The invention of the telescope by the
Dutchman Hans Lippershey in 1608 – or reinvention, for the ancients
may well have already discovered it – revolutionized astronomy in
Europe and had serious consequences for astrology.

With his new telescope which could multiply up to thirty times,
Galileo observed the craters on the moon and the spots on the sun which
undermined the medieval Neoplatonist idea of a perfect universe. His
observations of the planets also confirmed Copernicus' theory that the
sun is at the centre of the universe and the earth travels around it. In a
letter to Monsignor Pietro Dini dated 23 March 1615, he wrote that the
light and the spirit which gives life to matter came together in the 'solar
body, and being placed at the centre of the universe, was thus made more
splendid and vigorous, shining out its light anew'.[1] Although his revolutionary discoveries helped destroy the old cosmology, Galileo was professor of mathematics at Padua and Florence and court astrologer to the
Medicis. When brought before the Inquisition he retracted his views and
publicly rejected heliocentricity in favour of the Ptolemaic system.

In the Middle Ages, the prevailing world view was that of Plato and

Aristotle, which described a 'walled-in' universe with a Chain of Being stretching from God on high to the humblest organism on earth. The motionless earth was at the centre of a perfect universe and Man, created in God's image, was the Lord of the Creation. The observed erratic movement of the planets was explained either by the 'homocentric' spheres of Aristotle or the complex epicycles of Ptolemy. Nicholas of Cusa (1401–64), sometimes called the first modern astronomer, began to undermine the prevailing picture by arguing that the universe is infinite, has no centre and that the earth is a sphere. Nevertheless, George Puerback (1423–61) still wrote a standard work on Ptolemy's epicycles and his pupil Regiomontanus, the founder of a new House system, travelled throughout Europe looking for and translating Greek manuscripts which he believed contained the ultimate truth.

The breakthrough in astronomy occurred due to Nicholas Koppernigk, known to the world as Copernicus (1473–1543). The dour and taciturn Canon of Frauneburg Cathedral in Eermland, North Germany, brought about a revolution – the Copernican Revolution – which had enormous implications for religion and philosophy, as well as for science. Disturbed by the question of the erratic orbits of the planets, he made the Ptolemaic system more complicated by proposing forty-eight circles or wheels within wheels to explain the movement of the seven planets. But the conservative Polish canon had one revolutionary idea: he suggested that the earth did not lie at the centre of the universe. He had the sun, along with the earth and the known planets, orbiting a point close to the sun.

He wrote his theory down in 1510, in a manuscript entitled *Commentariolus* and was only persuaded to publish it after his pupil Rheticus had given the first account of the heliocentric theory in his *Narratio Prima* (1540). Copernicus eventually published his *On the Revolutions of the Heavenly Spheres* in Nuremburg in 1543. He began his treatise boldly by saying that 'in the midst of all dwells the sun . . . Sitting on the royal throne, he rules the family of planets which turn around him.'[2] But he then went on to complicate the picture by placing the sun slightly off-centre. The work had little impact at first, but its implications eventually triggered off one of the greatest paradigm shifts in the history of thought and which finally separated astronomy as a science from astrology as a system of divination.

Tycho Brahe's Uraniborg

The greatest observer of the heavens at the time, Tycho Brahe (1546–1601), remained an astronomer and astrologer. He was at first court astrologer to Frederick II, King of Denmark and Norway, who gave him the island of Uraniborg on which he built an observatory. When the king died in 1588, Brahe was invited to the court of Rudolf II, the Holy Roman Emperor, in Prague, and became his personal astrologer. When I visited his tomb and statue in a church there, I was struck by the depiction of his metal nose that had been made to replace the one he had lost in a duel as a young man.

Brahe equipped his observatory on Uraniborg with massive instruments, many of his own design, including highly accurate sextants and quadrants. He was convinced that the path to true knowledge of the heavens was through observation. He recorded the appearance of a 'new star' in 1572, probably a supernova, which undermined the medieval view that the spheres beyond the moon were perfect and unchanging. He even predicted that it would have its greatest influence in 1592 when a boy would be born in Finland who was destined for great things and would die in 1632 in a religious battle. In 1594 Gustavus Adolphus was born in Sweden and was killed in the battle of Lutzen in 1632. An astrologer's masterstroke or a lucky shot? We shall never know.

Brahe's careful observations and bold reasoning did not lead him to a complete espousal of the Copernican system. Instead, he worked out a half-way house, with echoes of the 'Egyptian system' of the Greek astronomer Herakleides, in which the moon orbits the earth, Mercury and Venus orbit the sun, the sun orbits the earth, and Mars, Jupiter and Saturn orbit both the sun and the earth.

In 1574, Brahe began a series of lectures on astronomy at the University of Copenhagen with an oration arguing the usefulness of astronomy in freeing the mind from earthly preoccupations and directing it towards the heavens: 'To deny the power and influence of the stars,' he declared, 'is to detract from divine wisdom and influence.' He was convinced that ruling planets shaped our character. No doubt with himself in mind, he said that those who have come under 'the fortunate influence of Saturn, the highest star, investigate in solitude matters which are exalted and far beyond the understanding of common people.'

Brahe also offered a persuasive defence of astrology against its detractors. Most people, he argued, are affected by combinations of planets and at different times during their lives are subjected to greater or lesser extent 'to the rays of a planet by means of hidden progressions'. This explains the differences which can be seen in brothers born to the same parents in the same place and brought up in a similar fashion. Brahe did not deny that people can be changed by 'lesser causes such as upbringing, education, conversation, foreign travel and things like that,' but insisted that the reasons for the differences between people can be sought nowhere better than in astrology.

Clearly well-versed in the subject, Brahe addressed the main traditional objections to astrology: that it is difficult to determine the exact moment of birth which leads astrologers to refer back to the moment of conception; that twins born at the same time often have different fortunes; that many die at the same time in war or a natural catastrophe although their horoscopes do not signify identical deaths.

To these objections, Brahe replied that 'astrologers do not claim that the sky acts in precisely the same way upon all those born at one and the same time, but that they are subject to diversity and are altered in different ways by heavenly influences.' In addition, the ability of different individuals to receive the influences or be immune to them varies. Aware of the concerns of theologians and philosophers, Brahe further insisted: 'Nor is man's free will in any way made subordinate to the stars but through it, under the guidance of reason, he can do very many things beyond the influence of the stars, if that is what he wishes.' Indeed, 'if people wish to live as true and supramundane human beings, they can conquer whatever malevolent inclinations they may have from the stars.'[3] In the final analysis, if we develop as rational and spiritual beings we can go beyond the influences of heredity and social and celestial conditioning; we can effectively jump out of our horoscopes. It is a cogent argument which still carries weight today.

Kepler and the Harmony of the World

Brahe's principal collaborator was Johannes Kepler (1571–1630), who followed him as court *mathematicus* (astrologer and astronomer) to Rudolf II in Prague. Born in Württemberg, he studied at Tübingen University. Although he has been called the first of the modern astronomers, he earned his living mainly from his astrological practice.

Steeped in the Hermetic tradition, Kepler's first work, the *Mysterium Cosmographicum* (1596), was largely theoretical. It developed his theory that the nature of the heliocentric planetary system was based on the structure of the five perfect solids of Euclid and the number forms of Pythagoras which all fitted into the harmony of the whole. For instance, the tetrahedron, which is made up of four triangular forms, occupies the space between the spheres of Jupiter and Mars, while the cube separates the spheres of Saturn and Jupiter. In the *Mysterium* he also expressed his conviction that regular simple patterns lie behind the diversity of the world and that number governs every aspect. He noted that God created quantity, and hence the regular solids, the day before he created the heavens.

Kepler believed in the existence of the soul in the sun and that 'the whole world is full of life'.[4] Echoing the Pythagorean doctrine of the Harmony of the Spheres, he believed that as the rays of the stars strike the earth at different angles, they emit different notes, the whole blending into a harmonious chord. Moreover the influences between heaven and earth worked both ways: the only evil to be found in heaven is projected there by the thoughts and actions of humans on earth.

No doubt referring to his own predicament, Kepler lamented the prostitution of astrology in his lifetime: 'Astronomy, the wise mother: astrology, the foolish daughter selling herself to any and every client willing and able to pay so as to maintain her wise mother alive.'[5] The word 'foolish' is somewhat misleading and a more accurate translation from the German would be 'wanton'. Kepler never thought astrology was foolish in the sense of being nonsensical or the pursuit of fools. In *De Stella Nova*, he confessed that against his best reasoning and deepest doubts, 'a most unfailing experience (as far as can be expected in nature) of the excitement of sublunary natures by conjunctions and aspects of the planets instructed and compelled my unwilling belief.'[6]

Rejecting 'superstitious' astrology, he acknowledged that the divisions in the zodiac and the heavens are man-made and not natural. He also stressed that stars are *signs* and not *causes*. But he was keen not to throw the baby out with the bathwater and argued that the influences in the Houses and the different aspects between the planets can be accepted on the basis of experience – that is, if they *work*. Again, the elemental value of the triplicities of the planets might be man-made, but Kepler recognized the significant triplicity of Aries, Leo and Sagittarius in which the 'great conjunctions' of Saturn and Jupiter recur. This led him to consider the 800-year cycles in history; he was not certain that the world would not come to an end in AD 2400. Future generations, be forewarned!

Underlying the adroit mind of this brilliant mathematician was a belief in ancient means of divination – in dreams and celestial omens, all admitted in Scripture – as long as it is understood that they are divine and not natural signs. He not only published astrological calendars, but was actively engaged in mundane astrology, forecasting, among other things, the Austrian retreat from the Turks in 1595. In 1601 he carried out an experiment in mundane astrology by publishing a set of tentative predictions for the following year.

Although welcomed by Platonists, Pythagoreans and astrologers, the *Mysterium Cosmographicum* implied that it was natural forces and not spirits that impelled the planets in their orbits. This was an impressive work for a twenty-four-year-old, and the ageing Brahe invited the author to become his assistant at the court of Rudolf II.

When Brahe died in 1601, Kepler not only took his place as royal astrologer but made great use of his observatory and instruments and his vast array of astronomical data. After eight years of observations of the orbit of Mars, Kepler realized that there was a minor discrepancy between the actual position of Mars and the one calculated according to the Copernican model. From this, he inferred that the orbits of the planets around the sun were not circular, as Copernicus had argued, but elliptical. He went on to demonstrate his hypothesis by comparing his own calculations for planetary positions with Brahe's accurate data. This offered support for the sun-centred model of the solar system. In 1608, Kepler published his aptly named *New Astronomy*. It presented his two famous laws of planetary motion: the first, that planets travel in ellipses with the sun at one focus; the second, that the further a planet is from the sun, the longer it will take to orbit.

A metaphysician and astrologer to the end, Kepler considered his best work to be the *Harmony of the World* (1618) which, as its title implies, sought to interpret and explain the universe in terms of Pythagorean principles of celestial harmony and number. It presented his third law, which described the mathematical relationship between the distances of the planets and the times they took to complete their orbits.

The new astronomy posed a severe dilemma for the Catholic Church which wanted to retain the notion of a perfect creation, with the earth and man at the centre of the universe. Talk of the sun at the centre raised the spectre of pagan religion, especially in its Egyptian form which Ficino and others had helped to revive. The atmosphere was not conducive to free enquiry. Even Kepler's mother had been accused of being a witch and tortured by the Inquisition. Galileo had many patrons in Rome and was well aware of the delicate situation. In a private correspondence with Kepler he agreed that the Copernican system was false, but refused to support the theory in public. In 1613, however, Galileo raised theological arguments which were considered heretical and was obliged to remain silent for fear of his life. When he spoke out again in 1630, it led to his famous trial and subsequent condemnation. He spent the last years of his life, when he was blind, under house arrest and only avoided the fate of a heretic by withdrawing what he knew to be true in 1633. In the same year, the Roman Catholic Church condemned the Copernican heliocentric system.

Isaac Newton's Magic

This did not curb the searching mind of the Protestant Isaac Newton (1643–1727). Ironically, the man who dealt the death blow to medieval cosmology was a great believer in astrology and alchemy – so much so that after reading his voluminous manuscripts, John Maynard Keynes described him as the 'last of the magicians, the last of the Babylonians and the Sumerians . . . the last wonder-child to whom the Magi could do sincere and appropriate homage.'[7]

It was Newton's interest in astrology and astronomy as a student at Cambridge which led him to deepen his mathematical studies. Steeped in the Hermetic tradition, he spent much of his time in alchemical research at Cambridge in pursuit of the Philosopher's Stone. He wrote reams about prophecies based on biblical sources and, in 1728, he published *The Chronology of Ancient Kingdoms Amended*, based on astronomical patterns which he assumed caused historical events.

Newton undoubtedly knew about astrology, especially as many of the alchemists he studied used it in their work. It is known, for instance, that he purchased a book on astrology at Stourbridge Fair in 1663. A famous story, possibly apocryphal, but characteristic of the man, records that when the astronomer Edmund Halley (he who observed the comet) scoffed at Newton's interest in astrology, he replied: 'Sir, I have studied it, you have not.'[8]

In his celebrated *Principia Mathematica* (1687), Newton developed his laws of universal gravitation by bringing together Galileo's mechanics and Kepler's laws. Although profoundly religious, Newton presented a mechanical model of the universe based on natural laws which held sway until Einstein in the twentieth century. His laws of motion gave a simple yet elegant explanation for the movements of the planets without resort to angels, spirits, gods, Ptolemaic epicycles or Pythagorean solids.

Despite the heliocentric revolution, astronomy, astrology and apocalyptic visions continued to go together. The astronomer William Whiston, who succeeded Isaac Newton at Cambridge, gave a public lecture in 1736 in which he predicted that the eclipse of the moon would be accompanied by the appearance of a great comet on the following Thursday at five o'clock in the morning. These portents, he declared, heralded the return of the Messiah and augured the end of the world by fire and earthquake on the following Friday. The lecture was widely publicized and when the comet did appear on time, the city of London was thrown into a panic and thousands fled to the country. The new astronomy may have triumphed, but the old astronomy had its effect.

33

The New Astrology

Trust not to all Astrologers, I saie whie:
for that Art is as secret as Alkimie.

THOMAS NORTON

THE NEW SUN-CENTRED astronomy, developed by astronomers who believed in astrology, did not deter the new astrologers from working according to the geocentric system of Ptolemy. Indeed, in the late sixteenth and early seventeenth century astrology enjoyed a popularity not seen since Roman times. Jean-Baptiste Morin (1583–1656), mathematician, astronomer and physician, practised both astrology and alchemy. He famously suggested – without success – to the 'sun King' Louis XlV that a team of astrologers would give him better advice than his other counsellors. Morin left a vast textbook, *Astrologia Gallica* (1661), in which he simply ignored the new astronomy. It took as fact the old theory of stellar rays which weaken as they become more oblique in relation to the horizon. He celebrated Ptolemy as the *ipse astrologorum princeps* (the prince of astrologers) and declared 'we have demonstrated that the earth does not move in a great orbit, but is fixed in the centre of the World.'[1] Morin not only dismissed the Arabic 'authorities' as false and diabolical but insisted that the divisions of the Houses are natural and determinable points in the heavens. Clearly Kepler passed right over his head.

Culpeper and Medical Astrology

Astrology continued to be used as an integral part of medicine. Acknowledging the correspondence between the planets, the signs of the zodiac and the parts of the human body, treatment was traditionally given by herbal remedies based on their perceived sympathies or antipathies. A Venus herb such as lady's mantle, for instance, could be used by sympathy for gynaecological ailments. On the other hand, a sun herb such as St John's Wort was widely used – and still is – to counteract Saturnine depression.

Nicholas Culpeper (1616–54) was an astrologer and physician whose name still graces countless herb shops. His *Complete Herbal*, which traces the correspondences between plants and planets, has never gone out of print since it was first published in 1653. Reading *The Stars' Own Vegetable Garden*, I found particularly interesting his recommendation that celandine, a herb of the sun and ruled by Leo, is one of the best cures for eye ailments. Lily of the valley is also good for writers and philosophers: 'It is under the dominion of Mercury, and therefore it strengthens the brain, recruiting a weak memory, and makes it strong again.' As for artichokes, well: 'They are under the dominion of Venus, and therefore it is not wonderful that they excite lust.'[2] In his scheme of herbal remedies, Culpeper further suggested that the caraway plant, associated with Virgo, helps digestion, while lavender, a herb of Gemini, is good for headaches. The dock, the bane of farmers, is astrologically connected with Pisces and strengthens the liver, which is governed by Jupiter, the ruler of Pisces.

Culpeper's guidelines are still widely recommended in modern works of astrological medicine: '1 Fortify the body with the herbs of the nature of the Lord of the Ascendant . . . 2 Let your medicine be something antipathetical to the Lord of the Sixth. 3 Let your medicine be something of the nature of the sign ascending. 4 If the Lord of the Tenth be strong make use of his medicines.' He particularly urged a keen regard for the heart: 'keep that upon wheels, because the sun is the foundation of life, and therefore those universal remedies *Aurum Potabile* [liquid gold], and the Philosopher's Stone cure all disease by fortifying the heart.'[3]

Culpeper's *Astrological Decumbiture of Disease* remains a fundamental text in medical astrology. A decumbiture chart is a horoscope cast for the moment of the onset of illness. As such, it represents the patient and her disease, its development, its times of crisis and a possible cure. Culpeper himself chose as the time for the horoscope the moment of receiving a sample of a patient's urine. Even Robert Boyle, one of the founders of the Royal Society and discoverer of the circulation of the blood, accepted the use of astrology in medicine.

Lilly and Christian Astrology

Culpeper lived through the English Civil War and supported the Republican cause with his predictions. Astrologers took sides in the social and political turmoil, although most followed Culpeper in their allegiances. William Lilly (1602–81), the most famous English astrologer of the seventeenth century, became the official astrologer to the Commonwealth Council of State. After receiving a classical education (including Latin, Greek and Hebrew), he was taught the rudiments of astrology by a Welshman called Evans. He married an elderly widow and although she was 'of the nature of Mars', she brought him a handsome fortune and conveniently died five years later. He was now free to turn his hand to both horary and mundane astrology. He first published his predictions based on the motions of the fixed stars under the title of *Merlinus Anglicus Junior* in 1644, followed a few months later by *A Prophecy of the White King and Dreadful Deadman Explained*.

In 1676 Lilly translated from the Italian *The Seven Segments* of 'Jerome Cardan'. This work included the aphorisms which no doubt inspired him to turn a thought to his own Martian wife: 'When the moon is in Scorpio in square of Saturn in Leo, or in his opposition when he is in Taurus partilely, the Native rarely has either Wife or Children, but if Saturn be in Aquarius, he will be a Woman hater . . . When Venus is with Saturn, and beholds the Lord of the Ascendant, the Native is inclinable to Sodomy, or at least shall love old hard-favoured Women, or poor dirty Wenches . . . The Woman that has Mars with the moon is *Right*, I'll warrant her.'[4]

According to Lilly, his *Christian Astrology* (1647) found good acceptance at both universities of Cambridge and Oxford. It proved to be the greatest English work of the seventeenth century and is still regularly consulted. In 'An Epistle to the Student in Astrology', he stressed that the 'heavenly knowledge of the starres' is in keeping with Divine Providence; indeed, 'the more thy knowledge is enlarged, the more doe thou magnify the power and wisdome of Almighty God.' He further sagely advised, 'afflict not the miserable with terrour of a harsh judgment; direct such to call on God to divert his judgments impending over them: be civil, sober, covet not an estate; give freely to the poor, both money and judgment: let no worldly wealth procure an erroneous judgment from thee, or such as may dishonour the art.'[5]

The work itself is a straightforward textbook describing the characteristics of the planets (including the moon's nodes), the signs of the
zodiac and the nature of the twelve Houses. It is particularly good on
horary astrology. The breadth of Lilly's reading is indicated by the
explanation of 'horary questions' in the appendix: 'So named from
the Latin word *hora*, an hour, because the time of their being asked is
noted, and the figure of the heavens for that time is taken to judge the
result. The word *hora* appears to be derived from the Egyptian name for
the sun, which Herodotus informs us was *Horus* or *Orus*; the Hebrew
or, lux, light, or day, the *oriens*, eastern, all appear to have had the same
origin. The Buddhists call the sun *Hiru*, which, with its Braminical name
also, appears equally to have derived from Egypt, the first cradle of
astrology.'[6]

In 1648, Lilly was sent, as the official astrologer to the Commonwealth Council of State, to rally the Republican troops at the siege of
Colchester with his predictions based on the motions of the stars. The
value of astrological propaganda was not lost on the Republicans.
Lilly's newspaper column, begun in March 1649 and the first of its
kind, was penned to the same end.

But Lilly was playing a dangerous game. In 1651, the new Parliament
locked him up against the wishes of Cromwell for thirteen days on
political charges and, after the Restoration of the monarchy, King
Charles II had him imprisoned on charges of high treason. Again in
1655, he was indicted for 'sorceries' for giving judgement to a 'half-
witted young woman' on stolen goods.[7] His most celebrated indictment,
however, was for his unwelcome prediction of the Plague and the Great
Fire of London of 1666 in a pamphlet issued in 1648. The star known
as the Bull's North Horn, similar to Mars, was in the exact Ascendant
of London, which was based on the moment of driving in the first pile
of the new London Bridge:

> In the year 1665 the Aphelium of Mars, who is the general
> significator of England, will be in Virgo, which is assuredly the
> ascendant of the English Monarchy, but Aries of the Kingdom . . .
> There will then . . . appear in this kingdom so strange a revolution
> of fate, so grand a catastrophe and great mutation unto this
> monarchy and government as never yet appeared of which as the
> times now stand, I have no liberty or encouragement to deliver my
> opinion – only it will it be ominous to London, unto her merchants
> at sea, to her traffique on land, to her poor, to all sorts of people

inhabiting in her, or to her liberties, by reason of sundry fires and
a consuming plague.[8]

In his own copy of the pamphlet 'Monarchy or No Monarchy', written
in 1651, Lilly wrote 1665, 1666 and 1667 as the possible dates for the
plague and fire. He illustrated the catastrophe in crude woodcut prints,
with people digging graves and the dead in their winding sheets.
Although he was summoned before a parliamentary committee of
inquiry investigating the predictions, including those of Nostradamus,
he was acquitted, after arguing that he had expressed his predictions in
'hieroglyphicks' to conceal them from the vulgar.

Elias Ashmole (1617–92), one of the leading intellectuals of the day,
and founder of the Ashmolean Museum in Oxford, was a Freemason,
alchemist and astrologer. As astrologer to Charles II, he intervened on
behalf of William Lilly who later wrote his autobiography for him. He
continued to believe in the possibility of true predictions of horary and
judicial astrology. In his *Theatrum Chemicum Britannicum* (1652),
Ashmole included the lines from Thomas Norton's *Ordinall of Alchimy*:

> Trust not to all Astrologers, I saie whie:
> for that Art is as secret as Alkimie.

In a commentary, Ashmole agreed that 'Iudiall Astrologie is the Key to
Natural Magick, and Natural Magick the Doore that leads to this
Blessed Stone.' 'Natural Magick' was of course another name for science
and the 'Blessed Stone' was the Philosopher's Stone, the Holy Grail of
alchemy. 'Astrologie is a profound Science,' Ashmole continued: 'The
depth of this Art lyes obscure'd in, and is not reach't by every vulgar
Plumet that attempts to sound it. Never was any Age so pester'd with a
multitude of Pretenders . . . not worthy to weare the Badge of illustrious
Urania.' Yet for all his faith in the true science, Ashmole lamented 'ere
long Astrologie shall be cried down as an Impostor, because it is made
use of as a Stale to all bad Practises, and a laudable Faculty to bolster
up the legerdimane of a Cheate.'[9]

The Age of Enlightenment

Astrology undoubtedly went into decline in the following centuries. But
Jim Tester is quite wrong in *A History of Western Astrology* to say that
in the seventeenth century 'astrology died, like an animal or plant left

stranded by evolution'.[10] Despite the triumph of the mechanical universe of Newton and the rationalism of the French philosopher René Descartes, astrology survived in educated circles as a strand in the Hermetic tradition and among the masses as part of the folklore of seamen, farmers and healers. The sales of almanacs, first printed in 1469 and today kept alive by Old Moore, continued.

The fact that in the seventeenth century, the philosopher Pierre Bayle and Jonathan Swift both felt compelled to attack astrologers attests to the continuing popularity of astrology. Swift had in his sights one John Partridge who made a comfortable living from publishing astrological almanacs entitled *Merlinus Liberatus*. The great Irish satirist made his own deadpan *Predictions for the Year 1708*, allegedly written by Isaac Bickerstaff, in which he forecast the death of Partridge. When the day had come and gone, Swift returned with another pamphlet describing the poor man's death, following up his intention 'to show how ignorant these sottish pretenders to astrology are in their own concerns'.[11] In a similar satirical vein, Voltaire also later published a pamphlet when he was sixty-six apologising for drawing breath after two astrologers had predicted that he would die at thirty-two.

In the so-called 'Age of Reason' in the eighteenth century, the era of Enlightenment based on analytical reason and humanist fervour, there was a 'Zodiac Club' at Cambridge University, while the University of Salamanca in Spain continued to teach astrology until 1776. Astrology was an element of Freemasonry which was in fashion with the leaders of the American Revolution, notably Jefferson, Adams and Franklin, and at the court of Louis XV. The poets Thomas Chatterton and William Blake were both interested in the subject. Blake was a friend of the physician Ebenezer Sibly, author of *The Celestial Art of Astrology* (1784) and the *New and Complete Illustration of the Occult Sciences* (1790). Blake possibly drew his picture of the 'Human Flea' for him as an example of the Gemini type.[12]

The first Astronomer Royal John Flamstead (1649–1719) chose the date and time for the founding of the Royal Observatory at Greenwich according to electional astrology. Sir Hans Sloane, President of the Royal Society, held astrology in high esteem, although he was not himself a practitioner. These were thoughtful, practical men, some of the best minds of their age, and yet they did not dismiss the subject out of hand like many modern scientists. But just as an earlier age had distinguished between 'natural' and 'judicial' astrology, so it was not long before the distinction was firmly established between 'scientific' astronomy, which restricted itself to describing the movement of the planets, and astrology, which attempted to interpret their influence on human affairs. The astrologers themselves were undismayed. They fell back on the old argument that astrology is a conjectural art like medicine. The heliocentric and geocentric views of the universe were nothing more than frames of reference for different purposes. The crucial point was whether astrology works or not. And if the planets were not *causes* of human affairs in the real world, at least they could be read as *signs* in a symbolic universe.

34

The Psychology of Antiquity

Astrology represents the summation of all the psychological knowledge of antiquity.

CARL JUNG

WHILE ASTROLOGY LANGUISHED in the shade during the bright light of the false Enlightenment of the eighteenth century, nineteenth-century Romanticism, with its love of the magical and the marvellous, predisposed the public to astrology. It was no accident that the astrologer Ebenezer Sibly should have been a friend to the greatest Romantic poet of the starry universe, William Blake. One of Blake's most exquisite engravings, *I Want a Star*, shows a man climbing a ladder to the heavens, beautifully illustrating the yearning for union with the cosmos.

In Britain, the astrological almanacs, often recycling old predictions, continued to be published: the *Vox Stellarum* sold 560,000 copies in 1839. The first man to offer mass-produced astrology in Britain was one Raphael, whose real name was Robert Cross Smith (1795–1832) from Bristol. Arriving in London in 1820, he soon launched *The Straggling Astrologer of the Nineteenth Century* and managed to persuade Princess Olive of Cumberland to be a contributor. When it failed, Raphael edited *The Prophetic Messenger* with a series of predictions. It took off but its creator died soon afterwards.

Richard Morrison (1795–1874), the other celebrated astrologer of the century, was an educated former lieutenant in the Royal Navy. He adopted the Hebrew name of Zadkiel. Morrison saw astrology as an integral part of the 'occult sciences' and claimed that his own crystal ball which he used for 'scrying' was controlled by Michael, Archangel of the sun. He had a flourishing practice and in 1849 launched *Zadkiel's Magazine*, subtitled *Record and Review of Astrology, Phrenology, Mesmerism and Other Sciences*. Raphael and Zadkiel, hiding under their pseudonyms, founded the first British astrological organization, aptly called the Society of the Mercurii.

Zadkiel also edited and introduced William Lilly's *Christian Astrology* (1647) under the title *Introduction to Astrology* and published it in 1853 with his own *Grammar of Astrology* and Tables for calculating nativities. He considered that it could be 'speedily learned by any person of even moderate abilities'. He dedicated his work 'To the University of Cambridge, the seat of Mathematical and Philosophical Learning . . . this little effort at opening a road for the mathematical investigation of the elementary Philosophy of Plato and Aristotle, as taught by the "divine" Claudius Ptolemy.'[1]

Undeterred by the previous 200 years of astronomy and the discovery of the planets Uranus by William Herschel in 1781, and of Neptune in 1846, Zadkiel still took the earth to be the centre of the universe in his calculations. He won some notoriety and the opprobrium of the *Daily Telegraph* in 1861 for predicting ill-health for Prince Albert who died soon after.

That astrology was once more considered worthy of study, albeit on the intellectual fringe, is shown by the open interest at the end of the nineteenth century by the scholar Richard Garnett (1835–1906), Keeper of Printed Books in the British Museum. Rejecting the mystical view of astrology, he saw it as an exact science based on mathematical calculations. At the same time, he valued it not so much as a means of predicting the future, but rather as an attempt to classify the diverse elements of human character in one all-embracing system. Once the mother of astronomy and sister of mathematics, astrology was now finding a new home in the family of psychology.

Blavatsky and the Theosophists

In the USA the first American astrological literature appeared around 1840. Luke Broughton (1828–99), an emigrant from Leeds in England, was the first major American astrologer. His pupils included W.H. Chaney, the father of the novelist Jack London. Madame Blavatsky (1831–91), young widow of a septuagenarian Russian and founder of the Theosophical Society in 1875, ensured that astrology became an integral part of the occult sciences and essential hand luggage on the path to spiritual enlightenment.

It was a time when Spiritualism was spreading throughout America and Madame Blavatsky rode the wave. A long-standing medium, she claimed to be guided by the masters Koot Hoomi and Morya of Tibet, who conversed with her by means of their astral bodies. Tibet, India and Egypt were her chief inspiration. Her *Isis Unveiled* (1886) was followed up two years later by her magnum opus *The Secret Doctrine*, which sought to crystallize the hidden essence of spiritual experience from the great religious traditions. Her wedding of Eastern and Western astrology made the subject acceptable among her well-heeled and educated followers.

Astrology is an underlying refrain of *The Secret Doctrine*. Blavatsky makes clear that she is referring to 'esoteric' astrology as opposed to the 'exoteric astrology' practised in the West. While the former is a divine science for the initiate, the latter is a 'superstitious astrolatory for the profane'.[2] Following her exploration of occult and ancient mysteries, she concluded that the zodiac was of very great antiquity. The twelve constellations of the zodiac have a powerful energy and the seven chief planets are the spheres of spirits. They affect us through their rays, emanations and vibrations. The seven spirits (also called angels and logoi) who preside over the seven planets are the 'Builders of the Universe'. Apart from the four exoteric planets (Saturn, Jupiter, Mercury and Venus), there are three others that remain nameless which have direct astral and psychic communication with the Guides and Watchers on Earth. Vulcan is a sensed planet hidden behind Mercury. In addition, there are seventy other unnamed planets that preside over the destiny of nations. While the sun is positive and alive, the moon is a cold residual quantity, symbol of evil: 'she is *dead*, yet a *living body*,' her decaying, soulless corpse full of destructive life.[3]

According to Blavatsky, it is not only the planets that influence us. The seven stars of the Great Bear have planetary spirits, known as the Rishis, who mark the passage of time and the duration of events. Moreover, the seven sisters of the Pleiades (the supposed wives of the Rishis) at one time dwelt in Atlantis and are the source of energy. And as far as Dog Star Sirius is concerned, it is the origin of the 'Logoic mind' and the great instructor of mankind. Together, the asterisms form a cosmic triangle in the heavens with a powerful force which reaches us on earth via the 'cosmic mental plane'.

Blavatsky wrote in no uncertain terms: 'Yes, our destiny is written in the stars! . . . This is not superstition, least of all is it fatalism . . . It is now amply proved that even horoscopes and judiciary astrology are not quite based on fiction, and that stars and constellations consequently have an occult and mysterious influence on, and connection with, individuals. And if with the latter, why not with nations, races and mankind as a whole?'[4] But however powerful the occult influences of the heavenly bodies, Blavatsky is no determinist. She insists that 'All the great astrologers have admitted that man could react against the stars.'[5]

Following in Blavatsky's tradition, in 1922 the Presbyterian minister Marc Edmund Jones founded the 'Sabian Society' in the USA, borrowing the name from a mystical brotherhood which flourished in the city of Harran in North-West Mesopotamia until the tenth century. In his *Key Truth of Occult Philosophy*, published in Los Angeles in 1925, Jones declared that the key truth is that 'Time is Illusion' and the second is that 'Space is Relationship'. His astrological Sabian Symbols offer a separate symbolic image for each of the 360° of the zodiac. He further halved each sign to make 24 'spans' of 15° with different characteristics or qualities attributed to them. For instance, in Aries (the 'Span of Realization') the symbol of the eighth degree is a woman's hat 'with streamers blown by the East wind'. Reverend Jones interpreted this as 'the first real attempt at self-exteriorization and embodiment in consciousness. Individualizing Eastern forces are suggested.'[6]

Just before Madame Blavatsky died in 1891, a young Englishman was introduced to her Inner Group who was to transform Theosophical astrology into a practical, popular pursuit for the masses in the twentieth century. His name was William Allen (1860–1917), a travelling sweet salesman with ambition. Transforming himself into the more suggestive Alan Leo, he launched the magazine *Modern Astrology* with his ardent Theosophical wife (who insisted on a Platonic relationship). This helped to reintroduce to astrology the spiritual dimension which is widespread today. Leo clearly fulfilled a popular need for his magazine flourished and his team of astrologers sent out by post thousands of horoscopes at a shilling a go (Zadkiel had charged his own clients in guineas). But Leo fell foul of the law and was twice charged with fortune-telling. On the second occasion, he was fined £5 with £25 costs.

Leo was undeterred. As an indefatigable organizer and publicist, he not only founded three astrological societies but his Astrological Lodge of the Theosophical Society, founded in 1917, became the parent of all subsequent British organisations. He was the first to produce a series of DIY books intended for the mass audience which enabled readers to understand the rudiments of astrology. The titles *Astrology for All*, *The Key to Your Own Nativity* and *Practical Astrology* are typical. In the first work, Leo outlined an 'Astrology without Calculations' in which individual and personal characteristics were represented by the sun and moon. Tracing the origins of astrology to the Chaldeans (who, he claimed, taught the Egyptians), he argued that astrology was 'the beginning of nearly all that we hold valuable in art, literature, religion and science'.[7] He was undoubtedly responsible for the new emphasis on personality in the horoscope and on astrology as a spiritual practice.

Rejecting the notion that astrology is merely the decadent revival of an ancient superstition, Leo attempted to give a rational basis to the subject. He argued that it was based on two principles. The first was that the whole universe, as the term implies, is a unity, and a law which operates in one part of the universe must be operative throughout the whole. The second principle was that by 'a study of the motions and relative positions of the planets the operations of these laws may be observed, measured and determined'.[8] While the first is readily admitted by most scientists, the latter claim is the stumbling block. We may be able to observe and measure the laws of the celestial bodies – the subject of astronomy – but to interpret them is the aim of astrology.

Leo presented practical astrology as a science which demanded 'a highly organized brain and a metaphysical trend of thought' to grasp its meaning. But more than that, he called it the 'soul of astronomy' and the 'most practical and scientific exposition of Fate and Destiny the world has ever known'. It was none other than 'The Law which Governs our Solar System'. Indeed, just as Judaism had been the religion of the Age of Virgo and Christianity that of the Age of Pisces, astrology was destined to become 'the religion of the race' in the coming Age of Aquarius, 'the sign of the MAN, who will soon arise, his mission being to prepare the way for the age of perfected manhood in whom God may dwell.'[9] Heady stuff indeed!

Yet with his Theosophical background and esoteric interests, Leo's astrology was far from being deterministic. 'Character,' he liked to say, 'character alone, determines destiny.' The real ego, he insisted, was beyond the horoscope. It was possible to improve character by the growth of the soul whose magic power is the will: 'its password, I will be what I WILL to be; and, when it *wills* to pass the limitations of the stars, then it is freed from the wheel of re-birth.' Astrology contains the secret: 'He who loses his life shall find it.'[10] He ended the work with the medieval adage: 'Wise Man Who Rules His Stars.'

Leo's profitable activity proved truly alchemical when his writings reached the high-minded composer Gustav Holst. In the process, they were transmuted by his celestial imagination into one of the most sublime expressions of astrology ever: *The Planets*. Each of the musical pieces reflect the astrological character of the planets. Holst was undoubtedly inspired by astrology, although he liked to keep quiet about his source in the work of the salesman-cum-fortune-teller-cum-felon.

Alice Bailey and Esoteric Astrology

The American Theosophist Alice A. Bailey was another writer strongly influenced by Madame Blavatsky's *Secret Doctrine* and proposed a 'New Group of World Servers'. She developed her own version of *Esoteric Astrology* (1934) which she considered to be a form of 'intuitional astrology' based on 'ancient science'. Like her great mentor, she claimed to be in touch with the Tibetan masters Morya and Koot Hoomi and considered herself as a member of the 'creative aristocracy' of seekers scattered throughout the world. In her view, the universe was under the control of certain 'Lives' whose purpose was outside the comprehension of the most illumined minds of this planet. Aware that astrology was based on illusion (the zodiac, for instance, is the imaginary path of the sun through the heavens), she nevertheless argued that it was 'the purest presentation of occult truth in the world' because it dealt with the energies and forces which play through the whole field of space.[11]

Bailey espoused the ancient view that the heavenly bodies influence us through 'stellar rays'. But she maintained that esoterically there are not only five non-sacred planets but seven sacred planets (of which ours is not one) which correspond to the seven energy centres in man. There are also seventy 'hidden planets' in our solar system, which is just one of the seven solar systems that form seven energy centres of the 'One About Whom Naught Can Be Said'.[12]

In a note to a chart of the 'Seven Creative Hierarchies in Active Planetary Expression', Bailey rightly acknowledged that much in it may seem obscure and erroneous. She made it even more complicated by adding that the placing of Sagittarius between Capricorn and Aquarius is 'a temporary emphasis and will change in another world cycle'.[13] But only the initiated would be fully able to grasp the meaning. Indeed, Bailey offered new rulers of the planets and constellations for those who are on 'the Path'.

According to Bailey, humans are not influenced by the planets but by the constellation of the Great Bear, the seven sisters of the Pleiades and the Dog Star Sirius. Together, they form a Sacred Triangle in the heavens, that is 'an aggregation of centres in the body of the One about Whom Naught may be Said'.[14] Again, the seven stars of the Great Bear (known as the seven Rishis) are the sources of the seven rays of our solar system. But the moon has lost its power. In the days of Lemuria (a legendary civilization like Atlantis), the moon was a vital entity but now it is a dead form, the source of decay and destruction. All this has strong echoes of Madame Blavatsky.

When it comes to interpreting the birthchart in Bailey's esoteric astrology, the sun sign indicates the present problem of the individual and is related to his or her life tendencies; the Ascendant indicates the intended life and holds the secret of the future; the moon indicates the past and summarizes limitations and handicaps. Yet, like Blavatsky, she also recognizes that we can go beyond the influences of the stars by the force of our will – the distinctive feature of the 'Shamballa force'. It is part of the divine nature of man which knows that good will inevitably triumph over evil.[15]

According to Bailey, in their many incarnations a person passes through the zodiacal circle backwards from Pisces to Aries. But this is not the end of the matter. If the individual emerges out of the 'Great Illusion' then the great 'Wheel of Life' is reversed and she will be able to work in the opposite direction and eventually emerge as an enlightened person and world Saviour.[16] Clearly Bailey's work went against the grain of contemporary 'exoteric' astrology, but it did attempt to restore the beauty and wisdom of ancient astrology which depicted the universe as a living organism with a world soul. It also recovered the ancient belief that astrology is the most important means to enlightenment.

Jung and Psychological Astrology

Despite the interest of writers like Goethe, astrology as a practice took longer to catch on in Germany. Aquilin Backmund (1876–1938), known as Alexander Bethor, founded the first German astrological magazine

Zodiakus in 1909. Alfred Witte (1878–1941) gave it a degree of intellectual respectability and founded the 'Hamburg School', which uses eight hypothetical trans-Neptunian planets and has even produced ephemerides for them. Dr Reinhold Ebertin (b.1880) became the doyen of scientific astrologers and founded the Cosmobiological Institute. The German tradition has developed the radical technique of 'mid-points', which sees the middle point of the zodiac between two planets as expressing their energies. The method usually dismisses the intermediate houses and the zodiac signs.

Although a number of leading Nazis, notably Rudolf Hess, Heinrich Himmler and Joseph Goebbels consulted astrologers, Hitler himself seems to have expressed little interest. Fearful of inauspicious forecasts, he had the Swiss astrologer Karl Ernest Krafft (who had interpreted Nostradamus for Goebbels) held in police custody from 1941. Only when Germany was facing defeat in May 1945 was Goebbels able to persuade Hitler to have a look at his horoscope and that of the Republic drawn up in 1933.[17] During the Second World War, the German astrologer Louis de Wohl, who had came to Britain in 1935, was employed by the British government to counteract any possible negative influences.

A number of German-speaking psychologists were attracted to astrology both as a means of understanding the self and as a method of self-transformation. It was this aspect which attracted one of Sigmund Freud's friends, the physician Wilhelm Fleiss. Believing in the Hermetic doctrine of correspondences and Pythagorean numerology, Fleiss tried to establish a causal relationship between the rhythms of human metabolism and movements of the planets. He was unable to convince Freud, but Freud's own pupil Carl Jung (1875–1961) took up astrology with the zeal of a convert. In a letter to Freud written in June 1911, he described his evenings as 'taken up largely with astrology. I make horoscope calculations in order to find a clue to the core of psychological truth.' Jung remained enthralled by astrology for the rest of his life.

Where Freud emphasized the importance of early sexual dynamics in determining adult personality, Jung felt that the process of becoming truly individual involved developing a meaningful relationship with the cosmos. This inevitably led him to a sympathetic study of both alchemy and astrology: 'If some authors of mediocre education have believed until now that they could [dismiss] astrology as having vanished long ago, this same astrology, rising in the soul of the people, presents itself once again today at the gates of the university that it left three hundred years ago.'[18]

He was deeply impressed by the psychological insights of the ancients and concluded that astrology was assured of being recognized without reservations because 'astrology represents the summation of all the psychological knowledge of antiquity'.[19] Jung's interest was not merely theoretical for he sometimes used the horoscopes of his patients to help in his analyses.

Jung's own world view was echoed by that of traditional astrology. His notion of 'archetypes' embedded in the collective unconscious is similar to Plato's universal 'ideas' or 'forms', which provide the template for all existing objects. From this perspective, Jung saw the signs of the zodiac as twelve 'archetypal images' or manifestations of the collective unconscious, such as the Old Man Saturn and the Young Maiden Venus. This no doubt explains the power of astrological symbolism to inspire the imagination.

Given the precession of the equinoxes, Jung recognized that the birth data in a horoscope never depends on the actual astronomical constellations, but upon 'an arbitrary, purely conceptual time-system'. Yet it does not follow that the horoscope is meaningless for 'whatever is born or done this moment of time, has the qualities of this moment of time.'[20] In a foreword to the *I Ching* in 1949, he added that just as there are antiquarians who can name the time and place of origin and maker of an *objet d'art*, so there are astrologers 'who can tell you, without any previous knowledge of your nativity, what the position of the sun and the moon was and what zodiacal sign rose above the horizon at the moment of your birth. In the face of such facts, it must be admitted that moments can leave long-lasting traces.'[21] On the face of it, the concept recalls Ptolemy's view of the moment of birth as a seed of the future personality. Although Jung later modified the formulation, it has been taken up by countless astrologers as an explanation for the significance of the horoscope.

This complex idea has to be understood in the context of Jung's celebrated notion of 'synchronicity' which he later developed in *Synchronicity: An Acausal Connecting Principle* (1950). He recognized that the connections between events in certain situations may not be causal – that is, they may not be like one ball mechanically hitting another and sending it into the pocket of a pool table. Instead, there may be truly non-causal combinations of events, events which have 'a kind of meaningful cross-connection' which is recognized by the mind perceiving them. He thus defined synchronicity to be 'a psychically conditioned relativity of space and time' in which outer and inner events (physical and psychical events) are not causally connected.[22]

This 'acausal connecting principle' explains the common experience of meaningful coincidences. A classic example is when a clock stops – never to start again – on the death of its owner. Another example is when Lord Caernarvon, the desecrator of Tutankhamon's tomb, died in a Cairo hotel, his dog in North Wales howled and dropped dead. Yet another example given by Jung is that of a golden beetle making a noise at the window at the precise moment that one of his patients mentioned that she had dreamed about a beetle the night before.

The principle of synchronicity would also explain the relationship between events in heaven and events on earth; one does not necessarily cause the other, but they do have a meaningful connection. The idea also echoes the Stoic idea of universal sympathy. Certainly Jung himself did not see it in terms of 'magical causality' (a view held by earlier astrologers) but preferred the hypothesis of natural philosophy which assumes 'a secret correspondence or meaningful connection between natural events'.[23] Synchronicities occur when archetypal contents in the collective unconscious erupt into consciousness, that is to say, when they are 'constellated'. The Great Years, defined in relation to constellations in the heavens, exemplify the process on a huge collective scale.

Jung claimed to take a scientific interest in astrology and supported statistical research into the subject. In the early 1950s he even tried to demonstrate synchronicity at work by investigating the synastry of couples – that is, their compatibility as revealed by comparing their birthcharts. He made a statistical study of 483 marriages, drawing up 966 horoscopes. The object was to establish differences between married and non-married couples. In their horoscopes, he looked for three traditionally compatible contacts: moon-sun (the ideal 'cosmic marriage' of Sol and Luna), moon-horizon and moon-moon. In the first batch of 180 married pairs, he found the most common aspect showed moon conjunct sun (10 per cent) and in the second batch of 220 pairs moon conjunct moon (10.9 per cent). Taking both batches together, of 400 married pairs moon conjunct moon came out at 9.2 per cent while moon conjunct sun and moon opposition sun both at 7 per cent.

Jung saw that, although taken separately, the results reflected the combinations he was looking for, when taken together they cancelled each other out. He declared the experiment to be inconclusive and pronounced: 'If astrologers had concentrated more on statistics to justify scientifically the accuracy of their forecasts, they would have found out long ago that their pronouncements rest on unstable foundations.'[24] At the same time, he was struck by the observation that the predictions of a few astrologers were so accurate they were statistically disturbing. Drawing on the research of Dr Rhinem, of Duke University in the USA, on telepathy and clairvoyance, he suggested that the astrologer was like a seer who could occasionally have a glimpse of the future.

Jung recognized in his own experiments that the researcher tended to find what he was seeking. In the case of astrology, it suggested 'a secret mutual connivance exists between the material and the psychic state of the astrologer.'[25] Despite his desire to appear scientific, by placing astrology in a psycho-physical world of human meaning, Jung demonstrated that the methods of the purely physical sciences are not appropriate in understanding the subject. The relationship between the events in heaven and those on earth is not causal; they coincide and correspond.

Jung was instrumental in creating the widespread contemporary view of the natal horoscope as a 'map of the psyche' in which celestial bodies are correlated to aspects of the mind. In *Jung and Astrology* (1992), the astrologer Maggie Hyde pointed out that the psychology of the unconscious applies to the astrologer as well as the client in their relationship.[26] As with any therapist or counsellor, the astrologer cannot hide behind a cloak of objectivity.

Despite his interest in the unconscious forces of the psyche and their spiritual dimension, Jung liked to think that his approach to psychoanalysis was scientific. In fact, there have been two main trends in modern astrology. One is the attempt to demonstrate that astrology is an objective science, and the other is to see it as a valuable tool in psychological growth. This psychological approach rejects the determinism of the scientific school of astrology, which traces causes to the celestial bodies rather than seeing them as signs and symbols. Psychologically-inclined astrologers focus almost entirely on the birthchart and see the horoscope as a seed bank of possibilities waiting to be realized.

Dane Rudhyar and Humanistic Astrology

In France the revival of astrology began with Dr Gerard Encausse (1865–1916) who wrote under the name of Papus. Professor Paul

Choisnard (1867–1920), known as Paul Flambert, was the first to place astrology on a statistical basis and spent his lifetime trying to get astrology accepted by the scientific world. His work was taken up and developed later by the psychologist Michel Gauquelin who has contributed more than any other to a statistical justification for astrological claims of extra-terrestrial influence.

Apart from Gauquelin, whose work will be considered in the following chapter, the most influential French astrologer of the twentieth century was Daniel Chennevière who went to the US at the age of twenty-one and adopted the pseudonym of Dane Rudhyar (1895–1985). He combined an interest in Theosophy and psychology with a humanistic concern for the individual. Rejecting the 'scientific method' of astrology, which uses 'rays' or 'waves' to explain the influence of the celestial bodies, he saw astrology as first and foremost a symbolic system, a kind of 'algebra of life'. His first influential book *The Astrology of Personality* (1936) mentioned Jones' 'Sabian Symbols' and was published at the request of Alice Bailey. It laid down the foundations for his new approach. 'The revolutions of celestial bodies,' he insisted, 'constitute in their totality a vast and complex symbol, which, of itself, is made up solely of cyclically changing patterns of relationships.'[27] The planets and stars used in astrology are therefore merely symbols and not causes. Indeed, Rudhyar argued that it makes sense for the individual to allow the symbols to organize themselves into significance.

While setting up the International Committee for Humanistic Astrology, Rudhyar developed his views in *The Practice of Astrology: As a Technique in Human Understanding* (1968). He presented the subject in terms of thirteen steps, emphasizing the need 'to assume personal responsibility for the use of one's knowledge'. The knowledge which could be acquired included self-understanding and the wisdom of attaining a harmonious relationship with the universe. What the sky reveals, he reiterated, is 'nothing but *raw materials for human understanding*'.[28] Far from causing events to happen on earth, a conjunction of planets only *indicates* the possibility of a certain type of event occurring in a certain place at a certain time. It does not predict 'events' but only outlines phases in a person's development. Astrology is therefore a technique of understanding, a method of interpreting the relationship between causally unrelated sets of phenomena. It is a process as symbolic as making a painting, writing a musical score or calculating complex mathematical formulae.

More than any other astrologer, Rudhyar was responsible for the shift of the astrological attitude towards psychology in the twentieth century.[29] He also stressed its spiritual dimension. In his *The Astrology of Transformation* (1980), he suggested that the 'individual-in-the-making' should see the birthchart as a mandala, a means of meditation on the self, as well as a symbol of individual karma. But while Rudhyar's transpersonal astrology is aimed at creating a fully autonomous individual, its ultimate goal is to transcend the individual consciousness, leaving biology and culture behind. This involves the marriage of mind and soul, the 'descent' of spirit and the 'ascent' of matter.[30] The fulfilment of individual selfhood is understood as an illusionary goal before the final transformation into a fully realized person who unites with universal consciousness where the centre and circumference are one. Indeed, from this perspective the birthchart is the first stage in the Great Work of spiritual alchemy: 'an altar on which the fire of constant overcoming must burn.' Rudhyar finally ends in pure mysticism: the alchemical fire is 'the Whole singing Itself "I" in a myriad of silences.'[31]

Alan Oken and Astrological Awareness

Another influential American astrologer who has taken the psychological and spiritual road is Alan Oken. As the title of his book *As Above, So Below: A Primary Guide to Astrological Awareness* (1973) shows, he was well aware of the law of correspondences at the heart of the Hermetic Tradition. The opening epigram is by the Stoic Marcus Aurelius: 'Ever consider the Universe as One Living Being, with material substances and one Spirit.' He stressed that the individual is a microcosm of the universe: in all creation there is a repetition of the same pattern in all structures, from the tiniest atom to the greatest unit of the universe. One of the main reasons 'Man' is on earth is to become increasingly self-realized. Astrology is a method of such progressive awareness, a means to expand consciousness and to help one on the 'Path of Enlightenment'.[32]

Writing in the 1970s, Oken was convinced that a merger was taking place between the esoteric and exoteric communities, between the occultist and the natural scientist, and that astrology, which links the intuitive and rational minds, was leading the way. In *The Horoscope, the Road and its Travelers* (1974), he stressed again that astrology is a practical tool to understand oneself and help others as well as a spiritual path toward greater understanding of universal law. Viewing astrology as a vehicle for ancient wisdom, Oken now thought it was time in the coming Age of Aquarius for astrology's 'inner temple' of esoteric teaching, hitherto reserved for the initiated, to be presented to the 'masses'.[33]

Seeds Packet and the Fallen Stick

The modern psychological approach to astrology sees the correlations in a birthchart between the planets and personality traits as being mainly symbolic. A symbol reaches beyond the objective and empirical realm to the realm of the unconscious and of the imagination. At the same time, a symbol can organize and illuminate any experience to which it refers.

From this perspective, astrology offers a rich symbolic language which can be used to interpret human experience and to order and understand our feelings. Astrology can provide a vehicle for interpreting the complexity of human experience and the deeper rhythms of the human condition. It can increase self-knowledge. By helping us to become more aware of our limits and possibilities, it can help us to act more decisively and purposefully. The horoscope at its best is a chart of our potentiality. Just as the ancients saw stars as 'windows' or 'doors' to another world, so it can give us a glimpse of possible futures.

Having our strengths and weaknesses delineated by the stars can be liberating. What we do with the knowledge is up to us. It can help in the process of the awakening and transformation of the self. We may be born with certain characteristics, but we do not have to be their slaves. We can channel our negative energies into a positive direction, transforming our difficulties and problems into opportunities for growth and fulfilment.

Modern 'person-centred' astrology focuses on interpreting the subjective experience of the individual rather than predicting external events. It therefore transcends the old debate about fate and free will by presenting the horoscope as a blue-print of possibilities without predicting that any one possibility will be realized. From this perspective, the horoscope is like a seed packet which we are given at birth. Whether the seeds land on stony or fertile ground, whether they wither or flourish, whether they develop into flowers or weeds is largely up to us. We can cultivate or neglect the garden of our self.

There is, of course, a danger that by such a loose psychological definition of astrology, it can became all things for all beings. Ouspensky gives an interesting anecdote about his spiritual teacher, the Armenian G.I. Gurdjieff. A pupil once asked him about astrology, but the master continued the walk with a group of other students through a wood. Suddenly he dropped his walking stick. Each pupil reacted in a different way. One did not notice it, one jumped for it, one jumped too late, and another saw that he had dropped it intentionally and observed everyone's reaction. When they discussed their instinctive reactions, Gurdjieff observed: 'That is astrology.'[34]

35

Science or Superstition?

*The most persistent hallucination that ever
haunted the human brain.*

Franz Cumont

IN AN UNPRECEDENTED ATTACK, nineteen Nobel Prize-winners
included their names with '186 leading scientists' at the end of an article
titled 'Objections to Astrology', which was printed in the American
magazine *The Humanist* in 1975. Happily treading on ground outside
their fields, they declared the subject to be a gross superstition with no
scientific basis and that astrologers were mere charlatans for pretending
anything else:

> Scientists in a variety of fields have become concerned about the
> increased acceptance of astrology in many parts of the world. We,
> the undersigned – astronomers, astrophysicists, and scientists in
> other fields – wish to caution the public against the unquestioning
> acceptance of the predictions and advice given privately and
> publicly by astrologers. Those who wish to believe in astrology
> should realise there is no scientific foundation for its tenets . . . Why
> do people believe in astrology? In these uncertain times many
> people long for the comfort of having guidance in making decisions.
> They would like to believe in a destiny predetermined by astral
> forces beyond their control. However, we must face the world, and
> we must realise that our futures lie in ourselves and not in the stars.
>
> One would imagine in this day of widespread enlightenment
> and education, that it would be unnecessary to debunk beliefs based
> on magic and superstition. Yet, acceptance of astrology pervades
> modern society.[1]

The manifesto not only showed the humanist arrogance that 'our futures lie in ourselves' but implied that modern science is the only means of discovering the truth about the nature of the mind and the universe. More disturbing was their attack on book publishers and the media for disseminating the findings of astrology which can only contribute to 'the growth of irrationalism and obscurantism'. This new Inquisition came not from religious fanatics but from the supposedly cool and rational community of scientists who get decidedly hot under the collar when faced with a subject which does not fit into their preconceived understanding of the world. As the American philosopher of science Paul Feyerabend observed, the virulent manifesto against astrology 'shows the extent to which scientists are prepared to assert their authority even in areas in which they have no knowledge whatsoever.'[2]

The most extraordinary aspect of this manifesto is that it should have ever been written in the first place. A hundred years earlier it would have been unthinkable, for astrology was considered to be dead and buried, crushed for ever by the twin pillars of Reason and Science. Before the Second World War, Harold Spencer Jones, the Astronomer Royal of the Observatory at Greenwich in Britain declared: 'Astrology is rubbish, a mere collection of empirical rules that have come down through the dim mists of the past . . . whereas astronomy is the Queen of the Sciences, astrology is the Queen of Humbug.'[3] Similar sentiments were expressed in the entry on astrology in the 1957 edition of the *Encyclopaedia Britannica*: 'A pseudoscience which . . . still flourishes, however, in Asia and Africa and is a means of livelihood to many charlatans who prey upon the ignorant classes in all countries.' Following in the same footsteps, the British TV astronomer Patrick Moore declared that astrology is 'medieval hocus-pocus' which is 'without scientific foundation and may be aptly summed up by the word, "rubbish".'[4] Indeed, astrology has been called 'the most persistent hallucination that ever haunted the human brain'.[5]

It is easy for the rational and scientific mind (including mine at one stage in my life) to dismiss the whole subject as mumbo-jumbo, as a form of rampant superstition dangerously persisting in an age of reason and enlightenment. After all, how can the position of the planets at birth possibly influence our character and life? Clearly astrology must be unscientific, irrational nonsense.

But is it? Is the scientific evidence as clear-cut as its detractors claim? Not all scientists are prepared to close their mind to the possibility of extraterrestrial forces affecting living organisms on earth. Celestial bombardment and influences are inevitably part of our larger environment. Modern science is catching up with ancient lore in recognizing that the cosmos influences the weather, vegetation, and the quality of the air we breathe. It might even influence our moods and personality.

Solar Influence

Without the sun, there would of course be no life on earth. Its daily rising and setting provides the basic rhythm of our lives, shaping our periods of sleeping and wakefulness. We are entirely programmed to follow the cycle of night and day, sleep and work. The sun not only has a physical effect on our well-being (as a source of vitamins), but also a psychological one. It is the movement of the sun travelling between the Tropic of Cancer and the Tropic of Capricorn which brings about the seasons. And the seasons in which we are born and grow up will affect our personality. After studying cycles at work throughout nature, Harvard Professor Ellsworth Huntington acknowledged: 'All this may suggest astrology . . . Nevertheless, the cold fact as to millions of births leaves no doubt that on the average people born in February or March differ decidedly from those born in June and July.'[6] Death rates in London go up 30 per cent in winter. Some people in Northern climes find they become depressed by the lack of sun in the winter, so much so that the condition known as S.A.D. (Seasonal Affective Disorder) has recently been diagnosed. It is not only daisies and celandines that open up to the sun.

There is a growing body of evidence to suggest that the cyclical activity of the sun has a widespread effect on earth. It has been argued that solar flares have a definite relationship with Jupiter-Saturn alignments, which might cause a maximum tide on the sun, thereby provoking an abundance of sunspots which in turn could trigger off earthquakes through a massive injection of particles in the upper atmosphere.[7]

There has also been some interesting work done on the influence of sunspot activity. Sunspots are intense magnetic storms which appear as dark areas on the sun's surface and which emit huge amounts of radiation. They come and go in an irregular way within a regular 11.6 year cycle. The Japanese haematologist Dr Maki Takata developed an index to measure the level of albumen in the blood, an organic colloid that encourages clotting. He found that that there was a definite link

between worldwide variation in albumen level and sunspot activity –
now known as the Takata effect. He concluded that fluctuations in solar
radiation profoundly affect the level of albumen: the index increased
during periods of heightened sunspot activity and just before sunrise,
while it decreased during solar eclipses. After seventeen years of work,
Maki Takata concluded: 'Man is a kind of living sundial.'[8]

Lunar Influence

The moon also has considerable influence on life on earth. Galileo
declared that the theory that the tides are caused by the moon was
'astrological nonsense'.[9] Shakespeare knew better when he wrote in
Hamlet: 'The moist star/Upon whose influence Neptune's empire
stands/Was sick almost to doomsday with eclipse.' Every sailor and
scientist now knows that the spring tides occur twice a month two days
after the new and full moons. Neap tides occur two weeks later. The tide
will be at its maximum (which occurs about twice a year) when a spring
tide coincides with the moon's closest proximity.

Newton's law of universal gravitation explains the phenomenon of
tides. Spring tides occur when the sun, moon and earth line up to create
the maximum degree of gravity at the new and full moons. The part of
the earth's surface closest to the moon is subject to the strongest upward
pull, so that the sea there bulges up, leaving it flatter in those areas
where the gravitational attraction is the least. The delay of two days is
created by the resistance of the water. The size of the tide depends on
two things: the moon's distance from the earth and its position relative
to the sun. When the moon is closest to the earth its tidal force is 30 per
cent higher than when it is furthest away. The tidal force of the sun is
only half that of the moon.

There are of course two major lunar cycles. The progression from
new moon (when the moon is between the earth and the sun and reflects
little sunlight) to full moon and back is known as the *synodic* lunar cycle
and takes about twenty-nine and a half days. The other cycle is the time
taken for the moon to make one complete revolution around the earth
relative to the 'fixed' stars. Because the earth is moving on its own orbit
around the sun, this *sidereal* cycle takes a little less time, approximately
27.3 days.

According to the ancient writer Lucilius, 'The moon feeds oysters,
fills sea urchins, puts flesh on shellfish and on beasts.' What has been

found to be true is that the sea urchin in the Red Sea and the palolo sea worm in the Pacific have a sexual cycle linked to the lunar month. Even the activity of a rat in a dark room varies according to the position of the moon.[10]

Experiments undertaken by Frank A. Brown, Professor of Biology at Northwestern University, led him to conclude that organisms may be exquisitely sensitive receivers of even the weakest impulses from the moon. He took oysters in light-proof containers from New Haven, Connecticut, to Evanston, Illinois, and found that within two weeks the oysters adjusted their opening and closing rhythms to the lunar phases of Evanston. Organisms as different as the potato and fiddler crab show yearly (solar) and monthly (lunar) periodicities. Studies of living organisms, from algae to plants, from invertebrate to vertebrate animals, show that metabolic rates are quite independent of immediate external conditions. Brown concluded: 'It has now become quite clear that under such constant conditions all living things have continuously imposed upon them from the environment metabolic rhythms of exactly the nature of geophysical frequencies.'[11]

After a long series of experiments under controlled conditions, the Theosophist Lily Kolisko, a follower of Rudolf Steiner's system of Bio-Dynamics, concluded that there is a relationship between the rate of growth in plants and the phases of the moon under which they were planted.[12] As a rule of thumb, vegetables grow faster when planted shortly before the full moon and slower when planted under the waning moon. According to trials by other advocates of Bio-Dynamics, it has been found that leafy vegetables grow best when planted under the full moon and root vegetables under the waning or new moon.

Humans, it would seem, are not exempt from the influence of the moon. Countless women find their menstrual cycle coinciding with the phases of the moon; it is not arbitrary that the word *menses* means moon. Darwin observed: 'Man is descended from fish . . .why should not the twenty-eight day feminine cycle be a vestige of a past when life depended on the tides, and therefore the moon?'[13] It has long been observed that some mentally disturbed individuals are often more agitated during the period of the full moon; indeed, the word 'lunatic' comes from *luna*, the Latin word for moon. Again, the word epilepsy comes from the Greek for 'to seize upon from the moon'. The legend of the werewolf, of the man being turned into a wolf, was believed to be a form of madness (known as lycanthropy) which was caused by the moon.

Recent studies in the USA would seem to support the ancient practice of Ayurvedic surgeons in India who delay operating until the moon begins to wane in order to get less scarring. The Florida surgeon Edson Andrews found that excessive bleeding from operations for tonsils and peptic ulcers often coincided with the full moon. 'These data have been so conclusive and convincing to me,' he wrote, 'I threaten to become a witch doctor and operate on dark nights only, saving the moonlit night for romance'.[14]

Planetary Influences

It is not too difficult to accept that the sun and the moon influence life on earth but what about the further planets and the cosmos as a whole? Again, some scientists have come up with some intriguing results and theories. The experiments of Professor Giorgio Piccardi at the University of Florence with 'activated water' (used to scour boilers) have shown that extraterrestrial forces change the properties of water. In particular, Piccardi found that the reaction speed of oxychoral bismuth varies at the time of solar eruptions, powerful magnetic disturbances or large collections of cosmic rays. On an annual basis, it varies as the earth spirals on a corkscrew trajectory through different fields of force on its journey across the galaxy. It is also affected by the activity of sunspots over the eleven-year cycle.[15]

If such chemical reactions are influenced by extraterrestrial forces, why should not organic life, including we humans, be similarly touched? Transmissions of electromagnetic waves have been detected from the moon, Venus, Mars, Jupiter and Saturn. Could the planets themselves be responsible for the vagaries of the sun which affect us? As Piccardi has observed: 'It is not necessary for us to project a man into inter-planetary space, or even for him to leave his country or his house, in order to subject him to the effects of the cosmos. Man is always in the middle of the universe, for the universe is everywhere.'[16]

From a different perspective, the controversial British astronomer Percy Seymour has argued that organic life responds through its nervous system to the magnetic properties of the earth, moon and planets: 'The magnetic field of the earth vibrates with a wide range of natural frequencies' and the 'tidal forces' of the planets are able to make the natural frequencies 'keep in step' with them. He likens the solar system to a huge transmitter of cosmic music: the planets, sun and moon are its broadcasting 'stations', each sending out signals of a specific frequency. All the elements of the cosmos interact together through a kind of 'resonance'. The earth's magnetosphere receives and amplifies the music. Human beings respond to certain 'stations' rather than others according to their birth and genetics. This would seem to be a modern version of the ancient theory of the Harmony of the Spheres.

But how does it affect an individual at birth? Seymour's hypothesis is that the orbits of the planets cause changes in the earth's magnetic field. The resulting electrical activity will affect the evolving human foetus through 'resonance' (the cornerstone of his theory), thereby shaping its personality. 'I am suggesting,' he wrote, 'that a foetus with a given set of inherited characteristics has a nervous system genetically tuned to receiving specific fluctuations of the geomagnetic field, and that it will not respond to others of greater strength to which it is not tuned.'[17] Whatever the nature of the individual personality, it will automatically be tuned to those fluctuations for the rest of its life.

Michel Gauquelin and the 'Mars Effect'

Seymour's work is largely theoretical, but that cannot be said of the researches of the French psychologist and statistician Michel Gauquelin (1928–1991) who spent three decades investigating whether the planets have an effect on human personality. He set out to be rigorously scientific in his method: 'Let us first of all throw out all occult explanations whereby the rising planets would "cast a spell" of an invisible or symbolic kind on the new-born child, a spell that which would be connected to his whole life and decide his fate. This kind of pronouncement is not pertinent, for scientifically, only concrete, limited and precise hypotheses can be formulated.'[18]

His first discovery was that in a group of 508 eminent doctors there was an odd preference for them to be born at a moment when Mars or Saturn had just risen or was at its highest point (zenith or culmination). But his most celebrated finding was the so-called 'Mars effect' on sportsmen. If Mars were to give no indication of a baby becoming a sports champion, then one would expect thirty-two champions for each of the eighteen sectors into which he divided their birthcharts. Analysing the position of Mars at the birth of 570 French champions, Gauquelin found 355 had the planet in a 'hot zone' – that is, in the sectors of the heavens just after rising (above the Ascendant), culminating (the MC) and, to a lesser extent, at the opposite points (near the Descendant and the IC). The probability of deviations like this coming up by accident is more than 1,000-1 against. He found no correlation for drug-induced births.

The Belgian Committee for the Investigation of Reputedly Paranormal Phenomena (Le Comité Belge pour l'Investigation Scientifique des Phénomènes Réputés Paranormaux), founded in 1949, repeated the experiment in 1965 with a sample of 535 athletes and confirmed the 'Mars effect'. They chose not to publish the results, despite the resignation of one of its professors. A similar body in the USA, the Committee for the Scientific Investigation of Claims of the Paranormal (SCICOP) – founded in 1976 by *The Humanist* magazine which had printed the 'Objections to Astrology' – replicated the 'Mars effect' in athletes, but again the findings were not published, which led to more resignations and recriminations.[19]

Collecting data for 25,000 prominent Europeans, Gauquelin further discovered a connection between the moon and writers and politicians, Venus and writers, Mars and athletes and soldiers, Jupiter and actors, soldiers and writers, and Saturn and doctors and scientists. There was a clear distinction between the traditionally 'tough' planets, Mars and Saturn, with the 'tough' professions of sports, armed services and science, and the 'soft' planets, the moon, Venus and Jupiter, with the 'soft' professions of the arts.

Is it more than a coincidence that the traditional astrological interpretation of the planets should fit the professions? Mars traditionally goes with soldiers; Jupiter is associated with 'top brass' as well as actors; Saturn is appropriate for the cautious and rational scientist. On the face of it, Gauquelin's research would seem to suggest that individuals tend to choose professions which fit their temperamental type as indicated by the planets at the time of birth.

In addition to his study of 25,000 prominent Europeans, Gauquelin also found that in 15,000 matchings of parents with their children, the data indicated a correlation between the 'birth sky' of parents and that of their children.

Although Gauquelin's work has been broadly welcomed by astrologers, he overlooked some of the most important aspects of traditional astrology. For example, he divided horoscopes into eighteen sectors as opposed to the conventional twelve. His 'hot' zones fall into the cadent houses (twelfth, ninth, sixth and third) and not the angular houses as might be expected by astrologers. He found no evidence for the traditional claims about sun signs, nor did he find that the position of the planets made a difference to people's personalities. He maintained that half of the planets – Mercury, Uranus, Neptune and Pluto – play no role at all.

Whilst working in the Psychophysiological Laboratory at Strasbourg University, Gauquelin wrote *L'astrologie devant la science* (1966) which denounced popular astrology. In his view it had become 'an arid doctrine of prices and rates ordered according to arbitrary rules'.[20] Fearful of losing his academic respectability, he distanced himself from astrology. Indeed, after a lifetime of statistical research into the subject, he declared that since 'the most painstaking studies have shown the inanity of horoscopes, there should be a strong backlash against this exploitation of public credulity.'[21] He concluded that commercial astrology should be combated as a psychological and social danger.

Yet for all his scepticism, he insisted that the ancient astrologers deserved our respect and that there is a place for a new and different 'cosmobiology'. Animal life on earth, after all, is only a fragment of the total life of the universe.

In general, astrologers have been keen to promote Gauquelin's research to give scientific weight to their subject. John Addey asserted that what Gauquelin's work had done for astrology was comparable to what Darwin's had done for biology.[22] In his spirited defence of astrology, John Anthony West has further argued that the 'Mars effect' proves astrology's fundamental premiss. He even goes so far as to declare: 'Gauquelin's work amounts to the *scientific* vindication of the ancient metaphysical doctrine of the Harmony of the Spheres; that doctrine that recognizes the planets and stars as both embodiments and transmitters of Divine and Cosmic Principles.'[23]

Astrology and Psychology

Other experiments in the USA were less conclusive than Gauquelin's. The US psychologist Vernon Clark tested the ability of astrologers to determine biographical details of individuals from their natal charts. They managed to show a significant ability to match biographical sketches to the right horoscopes and to discern high IQ and cerebral palsy, but this could have been due to their intuition rather than astrological skills. Attempts to repeat the experiments failed. Following up Vernon Clark's work, Shaun Carlson at Berkeley, California, tested astrologers' judgements against Personality Inventories derived from questionnaires. The astrologers showed an ability to detect fake inventory descriptions from the horoscope evidence, but according to the level of statistical significance of the experiments, they failed. The findings were published in the journal *Nature* in December 1985 with the questionable inference that the experiment 'clearly refutes the astrological hypothesis'.

John Addey applied statistical research to traditional astrology and applied his 'theory of harmonics' to reinterpret Gauquelin's findings. A modern version of the ancient doctrine of the Harmony of the Spheres, his mathematically-based theory attempted to address the harmonious correspondences of the cosmos. The principal elements of the birthchart were interpreted as 'wave forms' in the periodic cycles of the heavens – signs (the ecliptic), houses (the daily rotation of the earth) and aspects (the orbits of the planets). The wave forms themselves are expressed in numbers. For example, the trine aspect (the division of the 360° circle into segments of 120°) gives the number three, the four angles express the number four, and so on. In addition, Addey was particularly interested in how astrology might work. Despite his Pythagorean inspiration, he used the mechanical analogy of a lock to explain the imprint of the astrological signature at birth.

The work of Gauquelin, Vernon Clark and others was carefully analysed by the British psychologists H.J. Eysenck and D.K.B. Nias at the British Institute of Psychiatry at London University in the 1970s. Although sceptical from the beginning, they were unable to find anything seriously wrong with Gauquelin's methods, statistics or conclusions linking certain planets with professions, especially as his work could be replicated. Indeed, they concluded that he had made 'a very convincing case' for the basic astrological premiss that there is a connection between the affairs of humanity and the position of the planets at the time of birth: 'The findings are inexplicable but they are also factual, and as such can no longer be ignored.'[24]

Using Jung's concepts of introversion and extroversion, Eysenck and the astrologer Jeff Mayo tested the hypothesis that outward-going people tend to be born under the odd-numbered signs of the zodiac (Aries, Gemini, Leo, Libra, Sagittarius, Aquarius) and inward-looking people under the even-numbered signs (Taurus, Cancer, Virgo, Scorpio, Capricorn, Pisces). That is to say, people born with the sun in Leo should be far more likely to develop an extroverted type of personality than those born with the sun in Cancer. The results were striking and exactly in accord with astrological prediction, although Eysenck cautioned that they could be a result of self-fulfilling prophecies since the subjects knew they were participating in an astrological experiment.[25]

Eysenck and Mayo also tested whether individuals born under the three water signs (Cancer, Scorpio and Pisces) tended to be more emotional and neurotic than those born under the signs representing the other elements. Again, when the results were passed through a computer the predicted relationship between personality and date of birth came out 'very clearly'. Confessing his 'instinctive scepticism and dislike of anything mystical', Eysenck wrote: 'To find some solid fact in the astrological field was surprising and not entirely welcome . . . Perhaps our arrogance has been misplaced: there may indeed be more things in heaven and earth that we have dreamt of!'[26]

While dismissing the wilder claims of popular astrology, Eysenck and Nias acknowledged that extraterrestrial forces influence life on earth and called for more research in the field of cosmobiology. 'Perhaps the time has come,' the hard-nosed scientists concluded, 'to state quite unequivocally that a new science is in the process of being born. Amid all the dross, there does seem to have been a nugget of gold.'[27]

Astrology and Science

By disposition and training, conventional scientists tend to be hostile to astrology. To acknowledge such mysterious and invisible forces at work in the cosmos undermines their predominantly mechanical and materialist world view. If their findings suggest there may be something in astrology, they tend to be either ignored or not published. If they are inconclusive, they draw conclusions condemning astrology outright which are not backed up by their fragmentary evidence. Some astrologers believe that there has been a concerted effort in the scientific community to suppress any evidence supporting the claims of astrology.

The scientists and Nobel prize winners who objected to astrology were clearly venturing outside of their own fields of competence in a way which would have caused outrage if they had done the same for the work of their fellow scientists. Moreover, even in astronomy and medicine, modern scientists clearly have little knowledge of the history of their subjects, and even less of the enormous contribution astrology has made to their development. They overlook the fact that some of the greatest astronomers in the past, such as Ptolemy, Tycho Brahe and Kepler, were practising astrologers. They have forgotten that astrology was the mother of science and the psychology of the ancient world.

Science itself is not the ultimate authority and the only means to knowledge. As every philosopher and historian of science knows, science develops by disproving earlier theories. This often results in a sudden paradigm shift, when an existing theory can no longer take into account a growing number of anomalies thrown up by empirical evidence and logical inconsistencies, as occurred in the so-called Copernican and the Darwinian Revolutions. Moreover, the laws of nature are not iron-clad rules, but simply observed regular patterns in nature. Its theories are based on statistical probabilities, not certainties. As the mathematician and philosopher A.N. Whitehead wrote: 'The Certainties of Science are a delusion. They are hedged around with unexplored limitations. Our handling of scientific doctrines is controlled by the diffused metaphysical concepts of our epoch.'[28]

Ironically, the cutting edge of much of the new science confirms the ancient world view of the astrologers. Relativity theory describes a much more fluid and indeterminate universe than Newton's mechanical model which was governed by eternal laws. Quantum physics shows that systems can suddenly change in an unpredictable manner – make quantum leaps – from one state to another. Heisenberg's 'Uncertainty Principle' further suggests that the observer inevitably affects what is being observed.

More recently, chaos theory has shown how complex the clusters of causes and effects can be. An insignificant event in one part of our planet earth can easily influence another part in a major way: a butterfly flapping its wings in Tokyo may affect the weather in New York. Chaos theory has stressed the apparently random behaviour of regular systems at certain levels, such as the ticking of a clock or the dripping of a tap. The form of every snowflake is unique. It is possible to predict the orbit of Jupiter but not the movement of rain down a window. The same might be said of humans: we know that we are born to die but the details of our life appear open-ended.

Nevertheless, while there might appear to be a great deal of chaos and infinite unpredictability in nature, there is an underlying order. Patterns eventually emerge in chaotic and complex systems in computers. Certain shapes, known as fractals, can be discerned in nature, as in a jagged coastline. In a new version of the Hermetic doctrine of 'as above, so below', the British physicist David Bohm has argued that there is an 'implicate order' in the universe in which every part of what exists is enfolded within every other part. It is not to be understood in terms of a regular arrangement of objects or of events; rather 'a total order is contained, in some implicit sense, in each region of space and time'.[29] Indeed, as with yin and yang and the Tao, while nature flows between the opposite poles of order and chaos, there is an overall harmony. As Einstein observed, God does not play dice with the universe. If he did, it would be with loaded dice.

Where astrology is concerned, it is as difficult to predict exactly the future character and life of a person as it is to predict the movement of a river, a stock market or a horse race because so many variables are involved. At the same time, certain tendencies can be deduced from the blueprint of the horoscope. It offers a platform for the journey of life, a seed packet of possibilities.

At the very least, the moment of a person's conception and birth must remain an important part of his or her make-up. If we were conceived in love, I believe we will carry that security and warmth with us for ever. If our birth experience was happy, it will tell in adult life. Indeed, what goes before affects what comes after: we inevitably interpret our later encounters in terms of our earlier experiences. In a sense, it might be said that character is fate as much as fate is character.

Ultimately, however, what we make of the seeds we are given at birth is up to us. As with chess, there are certain rules and parameters in the game of life, but the outcome depends on our rational and intuitive choices. We are products of our celestial environment as well as our natural, social and cultural environments. Our genetic make-up, our upbringing and education will all affect us. But while we adapt to our environment, we can also change it. Our early experience will affect us, but we can say 'no' to our conditioning. In our consciousness lies our freedom. We are not just passive objects manipulated by external forces but active subjects with consciousness, will and foresight who are capable of shaping our own destiny. The more we develop as conscious and spiritual beings, the more we free ourselves from the physical influences of heaven and earth. We can take up our past and launch ourselves into the future through our present conscious choices and actions. Ultimately, we can jump out of our horoscope and create a work of art of our self.

The Mystery of Heaven and Earth

Astrology offers, like religion and philosophy, an interpretation rather than a description of reality. It is an interpretation which is fundamentally symbolic and imaginative, rather than rational and descriptive. As a system of belief, it is not based in the objective physical world but in a psycho-physical realm of human meaning. Having first developed as part of a system of initiation, it embodies cosmic principles. As such it is closer to the 'mythopeic' way of thinking – that is, the myth-making mentality of early and pre-industrial societies. Myths can contain not only disguised elements of historical fact but also psychological and metaphorical truths. They reveal deep patterns of meaning from the collective unconscious.

Symbols have the quality of embodying the thinking of ages, the experience of generations and the reveries of the human species. They fire the imagination and evoke visions of the beyond. They speak a wordless language which all can understand. The sun sign symbols, for instance, act for us like the totems of North American Indians. My sign Leo refers to a natural object – a group of stars which looks like a lion in the night sky – but it is also my 'spirit-animal' to which I bear a resemblance. By saying 'I am Leo,' I am saying that not only was I born in a certain month but also that I have the characteristics of the lion which symbolizes my personality. By saying that 'I am a Dog' in the Chinese astrological scheme, I am saying that I was born in a certain year and have certain dog-like characteristics.

Clearly, the most popular form of astrology – the sun signs – are the most superficial. It is hardly rational or scientific to say that at any one time a twelfth of the population will share the same fate in love, work and play. Yet if these symbols and totems are meaningful to those who read their 'stars' in the newspapers, I cannot see why they should not be acceptable as useful myths in helping people understand themselves and to work out their priorities.

In the final analysis, astrology is closer to divination than science, to poetry than physics. It appeals more to the imagination than to reason. Because it escapes neat definition, it is supremely frustrating to the orderly and rational mind, but highly attractive to the creative and intuitive person. But its unique quality is that it encompasses all of these things; hence its appeal to the numerically and artistically inclined, to the observer of the night sky as well as the explorer of the psyche, to the mathematician and the artist.

At the centre of astrology lies the unfathomable mystery of the correspondence between heaven and earth, of the relationship between ourselves, time, and the cosmos. With the collapse of the old scientific and religious certainties and the growing troubles of the soul, it will no doubt respond to the profound psychological and spiritual needs of humanity for a long time to come.

36

Unresolved Issues

Chaos gives birth to a dancing star.

NIETZSCHE

THERE ARE MANY unresolved issues concerning astrology, many of which are openly admitted by the more thoughtful astrologers. Even John Addey, former President of the Astrological Association of Great Britain, has recognized the difficulties:

> So far as the practical rules of horoscopy are concerned, they're a host of uncertainties – the zodiac, the houses, aspects – all present intractable problems which can only be solved by careful, persistent work; the philosophical basis has yet to be adequately re-expressed in modern times; the metaphysical laws and principles of our subject are uncoordinated; our records are scattered and contain many errors.[1]

As widely practised today, astrology is based on an astronomically false view of the universe and follows arbitrary rules established 2,000 years ago. It still operates within the Ptolemaic world view which places the sun at the centre of the universe. This, of course, only affects the practice of astrology that is based on the assumption that the influences of the planets are relative only to the earth.

Again, it does not consider the inclination of the ecliptic on the celestial equator above the polar circle where the ecliptic coincides with the horizon and therefore crosses no Houses. This means that children born in Siberia, Lapland, Alaska and Finland cannot have a normal horoscope. In these regions, the midnight sun, which neither rises nor sets, graphically illustrates the problem. Because of the tilt of the Earth's axis, the length of time spent under each constellation or sign of the zodiac for a given place on Earth varies according to its latitude and longitude. As a result, the Houses vary and some are entirely absent.

Houses are one of the most difficult areas in astrology. House divisions vary according to different traditions and schools: some divide the birthchart up into eight houses, most into twelve. In ancient Egypt, the astrologers worked with 10° sectors – the decans – on the ecliptic; in India, they operate with fields of 3°; and in the West, with 30°, although this too can vary. Some use the methods of Campanus or Regiomontanus while most follow the seventeenth-century semi-arc system of the Italian monk Placidus de Titis. A semi-arc is defined as half the time (converted into degrees and minutes of space) that a planet remains above or below the horizon. One-third of the semi-arc is the extent of each House for that planet. The competing House systems produce different zodiac positions for the intermediate House cusps, which is clearly awkward.

This leads to the question of aspects, the arc in degrees between any two planets or points in the zodiac. The 'orb', the number of degrees on either side of an exact aspect, varies according to different astrologers; more traditional astrologies vary the orbs depending on the planet involved. In horary astrology, the period to reach exactitude for an 'applying aspect' (used to show future events) can be hours or days after the time of the horoscope. A 'separating aspect' (used to show the past) comes before the time of the horoscope.

The timing of directions and progressions also seems somewhat arbitrary. Directions are methods of moving planets and other factors forward into new positions and aspects in the birthchart. 'Primary directions' result from the diurnal rotation of the earth in the hours after birth. 'Secondary directions' or 'progressions' are derived from the planetary motions along the ecliptic in the days after birth. The position of the planets one *day* after birth are said to signify life conditions one *year* after birth. Why should this be the case apart from convention?

There are other astrological directions that are even more question-able: 'solar arc directions' which add the arc of the sun's secondary progression for a particular date to all factors in the horoscope; 'tertiary directions' which equate lunar months after birth with years of life; and 'symbolic directions' (so called because the increment is not linked to any astronomical motions), which add fixed increments to horoscope factors for each year. In horary astrology, one degree is usually equivalent to a day, month, or year according to the context.

Perhaps the most telling criticism of Western astrology is that it does not take into account the precession of the equinoxes. Most Western astrologers use the 'tropical' zodiac which is fixed. Each astrological year begins with 0° Aries, known as the first point of Aries. But because of the precession of the earth's axis, the sun on the vernal equinox actually now rises in 7° Pisces. For most Western astrologers a child born on 24 March is Arian, but the sun is actually rising far into Pisces at the moment of her birth. An ancient Egyptian 'Arian' born in the Age of Taurus would presumably be even more different from one born today.

Indian astrologers use the 'sidereal' zodiac, which aligns the starting point of the twelve signs with the beginning of the fixed star constellation of Aries. The sidereal zodiac is not entirely absent in Western astrology for the precession of the equinoxes brings about the Great Years. We are now in the Age of Pisces, but about to enter the Age of Aquarius.

Where does this leave sun-sign astrology? Which is the best zodiac to use, the tropical or the sidereal? Personally, I think the sidereal is preferable since it corresponds more closely to the actual situation in the heavens at the moment of birth. But what about the Chinese Circle of Animals which is entirely imaginary?

Does this mean that one tradition is right and the other wrong? One way out of the dilemma is to recognize that the zodiac itself is a creation of the human imagination, a projection of unconscious archetypes into shapes which resemble certain human figures and creatures in the heavens. Astrology offers a celestial language with which to express feelings, thoughts and images about ourselves. The zodiac might vary according to cultural traditions – as we are, so we see – but it does not mean that one is best.

Although most dictionaries say the word 'zodiac' comes from the Greek for 'Circle of Animals', it can also be translated as 'Wheel of Life'. As such, the zodiac may be seen as a symbolic representation of seasonal transformation and of endless cycles of creation.[2] Indeed, it offers a symbol of the Many in the One.

While astrology is no longer an integral part of astronomy, astrologers have taken into account some of the findings of astronomers. They have embraced three new planets, Uranus (discovered in 1781), Neptune (1846) and Pluto (1930), and given them characteristics which reflect the spirit of the times when they were discovered. Uranus, the sky god, is associated with revolution, disruption and intuition; Neptune, the god of the sea, with idealism, confusion and refinement; Pluto, lord of the underworld, with destruction, transformation and transcendence. Following in the footsteps of Alice Bailey, a few astrologers continue to work with hidden planets still waiting to be discovered. Indian astrologers often work with twelve planets with increasing spiritual roles corresponding to the twelve signs of the zodiac.

Some astrologers have also embraced Chiron, the planetoid – possibly a trapped comet – which lies between the orbits of Saturn and Uranus and was discovered in 1977. Ephemerides which track its movements have been printed. The son of Saturn, Chiron is seen as an exemplar of the wounded healer who teaches the art of survival in a hostile world.[3] More controversial is the use of asteroids in horoscopes. They form a belt of vast numbers of fragments thought to be a disintegrated planet between the orbits of Mars and Jupiter. Ephemerides of some of the better-known asteroids, such as Ceres, Pallas, Juno and Vesta, have been published. Where will the list of celestial bodies end?

Virtually all astrologers drew a line at the attempt of astronomers in 1995 to throw out the time-honoured division of the zodiac into twelve signs by introducing a thirteenth called Ophichus (associated with the Greek healer Asclepius). The feet of Ophichus reach down on to the ecliptic between the constellations of Scorpio and Sagittarius with a span of 18.5°. The sun travels through the constellation between 30 November and 18 December each year. But while it makes a thirteenth constellation on the ecliptic, it does not follow that there should be a thirteenth sign. The signs of the zodiac, although ancient, have always been a pattern projected into the heavens; as such they are a convention, not a reality. While the addition of the three new planets Uranus, Neptune and Pluto makes an interpretation of a birthchart more subtle and richer, to accept a thirteenth sign would throw the whole symbolism of the zodiac into confusion.

There remain three other principal concerns. The first is the question raised by St Augustine of why the personalities of twins are different. This is also true of 'time twins' – that is, babies who are born at the same place and time with different fathers and mothers. According to traditional astrology, the horoscopes of the twins should be identical and yet experience shows that twins tend to differ as much as any other siblings. On the other hand, twins born of the same parents are not born exactly at the same time, and this could have an effect on their horoscopes. Most contemporary astrologers would say that the birthchart is not a strict catalogue of predetermined characteristics but rather a map of tendencies. Time twins will share the same tendencies, but they will also be influenced by biology and culture, by their genetic inheritance and upbringing.

A related issue is that of the most appropriate moment in time to use in casting a horoscope. Should it be the moment of conception or the moment of birth? Ptolemy was well aware of the dilemma but opted for the latter. On the face of it, the moment of conception would seem to be more appropriate, the time when the ovum and sperm unite and the genetic code is laid down. According to some spiritual traditions, that is the time when the soul enters the body. Esoteric astrologers sometimes work with the moment of conception, but the vast majority of modern astrologers follow Ptolemy and take the moment of birth as most significant. The exact time is usually considered to be the moment of the baby's first breath. If this is the case, artificially induced births can alter the future personality of a child.

An associated problem is knowing one's exact time of birth. Where it is not known within half an hour or not known at all (often the case in places like India and Africa where births are not always registered), an astrologer can draw up a chart of the approximate time and look for pointers to the actual time. The horoscope can be tested with certain timing measures to indicate major past events to complete the process of rectification. A traditional method for finding out the moment of conception is called the 'Pre-Natal Epoch' or, more grandly, the 'Trutine of Hermes'. This involves interchanging the degree of the Ascendant or Descendant at birth with the position of the moon ten lunar months before birth.

Next there is the question of mass tragedies. Did all the Jews gassed by the Nazis or the citizens of Hiroshima bombed by the Allies have their fates written in the stars? Did the sole survivor of the volcanic eruption in St Pierre in Martinique have a different birthchart from those of his fellow citizens? Clearly the victims of natural catastrophes such as floods and earthquakes cannot all share the same horoscopes. Other factors are at play.

This raises the issue of mundane astrology. Mundane astrologers continue to cast horoscopes for important events, such as coronations, the signing of treaties or the starting up of businesses. They draw up horoscopes for organizations and nations usually on the basis of founding documents or treaties which represent their 'birth'.

William Lilly accurately predicted both the Plague and the Great Fire of London in the seventeenth century and was even brought before the House of Commons for having provoked the catastrophes. The enigmatic prophecies of Nostradamus are regularly interpreted to fit recent events. Yet the most famous of astrological prophecies – the prediction of a deluge following the grand conjunction of all the planets in Pisces in 1524 – did not occur. Similarly, the financial crash on the stock market expected on 3 May 2000, when the heavy planets of Uranus and Neptune lined up, conspicuously failed to materialise.

Determinism and Free Will

The most vexed issue in astrology is that of determinism and free will. This question has exercised the best philosophers and theologians and has been the stuff of tragedy. 'It is the stars/The stars above us, govern our conditions,' we are told in Shakespeare's *King Lear*. But then in *Julius Caesar*, Cassius declares:

> Men at some time are master of their fates.
> The fault, dear Brutus, is not in our stars,
> But in ourselves, that we are underlings.

Fate means 'It has been written.' It assumes an orderly, interconnected, determined universe. For Hindus, it appears in the form of karma; for Muslims, the will of Allah. The Greeks called the troubling face of fate *Moira*, represented by the three goddesses who turn the Spindle of Necessity, while the Christians called its bright face Providence.

Certainly when I first began to study astrology, the chief stumbling block for me was its apparent denial of personal freedom. If the chief traits of our personality are decided at birth, then surely that denies personal responsibility for our actions? The kind of hard determinism which says that our fates are entirely 'written' in the skies completely undermines the role of personal choice in individual lives and in history.

The most extreme version of this was put forward by the French astrologer Morin de Villefranche in the seventeenth century: 'the birth dates and the events in the lives of men are enchained by Providence in view of a necessary concourse of the communal realization of destiny, in such a way that he who is by birth destined, for example, to die by assassination does not fail to encounter his assassin, and that he who must be unhappily married will invariably seek out the woman who shall see to it that it is so.'[4] If this is the case, the assassin can be held no more responsible for the act than his dagger; both are in the grip of superior forces, mere links in the chain of necessity.

A few modern astrologers like Liz Greene still find room for fate, or *Moira*. For her, there is 'something' that retaliates when its boundaries are transgressed and which seems to possess 'a kind of "absolute knowledge" not only of what the individual needs, but of what he is *going* to need for his unfolding in life.'[5]

Some modern astrologers take up the old Neoplatonic and Hermetic argument that while fate may be represented by the influence of the stars above, it does not follow that humans are not free. The more people identify with their physical selves, the more they will be subject to the influences of the planets. Conversely, the more people develop their state of consciousness, the more they will be able to develop their free will and thus shape their lives.

In this tradition, Margaret Hone writes:

> Inasmuch as a man identifies with his physical self and the physical world around about him, so he is indissolubly part of it and subject to its changing pattern as formed by the planets in their orbits. Only by the recognition of that which he senses as greater than himself can he attune himself to what is beyond the terrestrial pattern. In this way, though he may not escape terrestrial happenings, by the doctrine of free will and willing 'acceptance' he can 'will' that his real self is free in its reaction to them.[6]

Most contemporary astrologers adopt a more psychological approach and see the horoscope as a blueprint of future possibilities. As Jeff Mayo and Christine Ramsdale have written: 'You may think that if the future can be foretold we have no free will, being enmeshed in an inescapable fate. The birth-chart shows our *potentially* strongest features and drives and our most likely limitations. Within the overall pattern of the chart (of our psychological make-up) we have complete freedom of choice.'[7]

In my view, a belief in the correspondence between heaven and earth does not deny the possibility of self-transformation. The development of our state of consciousness is undoubtedly the path to liberation: the more conscious we become, the more our lives become creative and purposeful. As Hermes tells Tat in the *Hermetica*, those who follow the principle 'Mind is Guide' do not suffer the evils of fate. The medieval scholars sympathetic to astrology concluded that 'the stars incline but do not compel'. The wise person is not the slave but the master of the stars.

A question that is often asked is whether astrology can really predict the future. For me, the heavenly bodies are not *causes* of events on earth nor even *signs* conveying specific information, but rather they are *symbols* which only evoke the possibility of a certain type of event occurring in space and time. Astrology can give an idea of the broad picture but each individual fills in the details of his or her life. Again, the stars incline but do not compel.

Some astrologers have been able to predict both social and individual events with uncanny accuracy. But the ability to predict the future might be based more on an insightful reading of history and personality – on informed guesses – rather than an accurate reading of the future. In my view, the future is not sufficiently predestined and there are too many unknown variables at work to be able to predict exactly what will happen. And the shaping power of the human mind and imagination ensures that, to a degree, we create our own lives. Free will is an integral part of our personalities, however established they may be at birth.

The birthchart is like a warning: it points out what could happen in our lives if we follow a particular path. It tells us about the passage of time and the opportunities that might open up to us at different stages in our lives. It shows the cards that fate may have dealt us, but we can still influence the outcome of the game. The more skilful we are, the more successful we will be. At the same time, there is no such thing as a bad chart: hardships can inspire positive attitudes and actions and obstacles can be seen as challenges to overcome. Both are means of self-transformation. We forge our selves in the fire of suffering on earth and reveal our true selves when things go badly. Even the acceptance of certain limitations – we are born, grow old and die – can lead to wisdom and peace of mind.

Although we are born into a certain situation – social, historical, environmental, terrestrial and celestial – it does not mean that we are merely a product of our circumstances and that our lives are predestined to follow a particular direction. Indeed, by a supreme act of will, I believe we can jump out of our astrological charts and reject the indications of our horoscopes. Our passionate nature may 'incline' us to become excited, but we can train ourselves to remain calm. Because of their exceptional natures, Socrates and Christ chose voluntary deaths; they were not predestined to be killed by the ruling powers at a certain time. As the example of Zen masters and Hindu mystics show, we can go beyond our karma and become self-revolving wheels.

37

Bringing it All Together

WHILE STUDYING THE history and philosophy of Western astrology and working out its complex principles, I was fortunate enough to have as my neighbour a man who had been practising astrology for twenty-five years. David Thomas was a quietly spoken, warm-hearted man who enjoyed sailing. We had been discussing Ibn Arabi, the Sufi philosopher and poet, when he first mentioned his interest in astrology. He was even finishing a book on the subject.

For David, astrology was neither an esoteric discipline nor a science, but a very matter-of-fact and down-to-earth subject. He was the first person I met who made me feel that there was 'something' in astrology.

I asked him one day how he had become an astrologer.

'When I started reading astrology text books at the beginning, it was as though I was not learning something new, but was remembering something I had forgotten. Astrology just took over my life – it pushed everything else out of the way.'

'And its value?'

'The value of having a chart done is that it helps people, if they will, to understand themselves better.'

I expressed my concern about the implications of astrology for free will. He had considered the subject carefully: 'It's a very old-fashioned idea to say that we are influenced by the planets. I'm sure that is not how it works. I think Jung's idea of synchronicity best explains it. Jung said that at any given moment of time a co-relationship exists between everything in existence at that moment of time. Applying this to astrology, the position of the planets at the time of a person's birth may be said to form a co-relationship with the birth.'

'So it's not a case of cause and effect?'

'No. Planets do not cause things to happen to people; they only indicate what is happening.'

I could hear the echoes of the medieval schoolmen who said that the stars incline but do not compel: *astra inclinant non determinant.*

He went on, 'Astrologers stand on firm ground. Planets always, always manifest according to their principles – always. During twenty-five years of practice – on a busy day-to-day basis – I have never found this not to be so.'

David used the equal House system, that is marking out twelve Houses of 30° each from the Ascendant on the birthchart. He had honed down their meaning to: first, self-expression; second, possessions and feelings; third, communication (mental and physical); fourth, home (caring for, looking after, protecting); fifth, creativity, leadership, love, love affairs, children, sports, games, taking risks; sixth, work and service for others, duty, responsibility; seventh, relationship; eighth, intensity, depth of feeling; ninth, wide-rangingness; tenth, outside world and standing therein; eleventh, unorthodoxy; twelfth, the unconscious, the values, the arts. He found the best way to express the two ideas of 'feelings and possessions' in the second House as 'emotional security'.

While recognizing the importance of the interaction of the planets with one another, he did not use all the aspects between them. He looked for trines and sextiles (helpful), oppositions, squares, semi-squares and quincunxs (unhelpful) and considered conjunctions to be either helpful or unhelpful depending on the situation. He had found from long experience that the quincunx aspect in a chart is particularly significant.

He made use of the Part of Fortune inherited from the Muslims but had dispensed with the moon's nodes, which had been developed by the Greeks and had come back into fashion.

'I once caused a scandal at an astrological summer school at a Cambridge college,' he told me with a sparkle in his eye. 'I was sitting at table when I said I had done away with the nodes. You could hear the cutlery fall in the shocked silence!'

In his view astrology is not a science but an art based on interpretation.

'It involves a cat's cradle of factors and the various strands have to be teased out and taken into consideration. As I get older, I use my intuition more and more. The thrust of a chart is quickly discernible, although it takes longer to get a subtle chart right. When considering a chart, it's a mistake to be dogmatic. A particular activity could result in a number of different interpretations, depending on the circumstances of the person involved.'

Peter Marshall's Horoscope

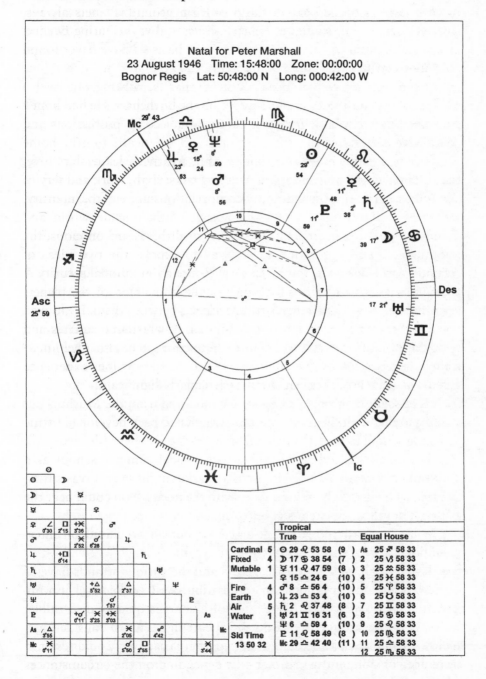

Natal for Peter Marshall
23 August 1946   Time: 15:48:00   Zone: 00:00:00
Bognor Regis   Lat: 50:48:00 N   Long: 000:42:00 W

	Tropical	
	True	Equal House
Cardinal 5	☉ 29 ♌ 53 58 (9)	As 25 ♐ 58 33
Fixed 4	☽ 17 ♋ 38 54 (7)	2 25 ♑ 58 33
Mutable 1	☿ 11 ♌ 47 59 (8)	3 25 ♒ 58 33
	♀ 15 ♎ 24 6 (10)	4 25 ♓ 58 33
Fire 4	♂ 8 ♍ 56 4 (10)	5 25 ♈ 58 33
Earth 0	♃ 23 ♎ 53 4 (10)	6 25 ♉ 58 33
Water 1	♄ 2 ♌ 37 48 (8)	7 25 ♊ 58 33
	♅ 21 ♊ 16 31 (6)	8 25 ♋ 58 33
Air 5	♆ 6 ♎ 59 4 (10)	9 25 ♌ 58 33
	♇ 11 ♌ 58 49 (8)	10 25 ♍ 58 33
Sid Time	Mc 29 ♎ 42 40 (11)	11 25 ♎ 58 33
13 50 32		12 25 ♏ 58 33

When I met David to have my horoscope drawn up, I asked him if he could clarify two questions about my birthday. Being born on the 23 August 1946, I found that in the popular newspapers I was usually defined as a Leo but sometimes placed in Virgo. On the 'cusp' was the usual interpretation.

David clarified the issue: 'You are either a Leo or a Virgo, depending on the time of your birth. You can't be one and the other.'

He looked up the day and year of my birth in his Ephemeris and confirmed that I was definitely a Leo – by hours. In another year, it could have been different.

The other problem was my time of birth. My mother thought it was four o'clock in the afternoon but at eighty-six could not be absolutely certain. David's response was that the birthchart would tend to confirm the time.

Before drawing it up, he asked me what I considered important in my childhood and upbringing. I told him how I had been born after the Second World War in Bognor Regis on the South coast of England and grew up with my older brother and mother in the large house of my grandparents who had retired from running hotels. My parents had divorced before my second birthday. My father, who had been a fighter pilot during the war and went on to become a successful race-horse trainer, never contacted me afterwards. It did not worry me at the time, and I felt somehow 'special' for not having a dad like all my other friends at school.

My idyllic childhood by the sea was shattered when I went to a boarding school in a small village nestling in the Downs and discovered how cruel people could be.

While talking to David, I found that I focused on a key event in my late teens. One winter's evening, I was lying in front of a coal fire reading a French novel, when my uncle burst in and put on the bright light.

'What do you think, you're doing!' he barked. 'You should be doing your homework. You'll never come to anything in your life. You're hopeless!'

He wanted me to become an accountant like himself, but I decided instead to go to sea.

After sailing around the world and spending a year teaching in West Africa, I came back to Britain and spent ten years at university doing three degrees, and, I now realize, partly trying to prove my uncle wrong. Rejecting the authoritarian figures of my uncle, teachers and officers, I became a libertarian. Rejecting the narrow and hypocritical Christianity of my school, I became a humanist. Rejecting my family's obsession with property, I became a free-wheeling writer. Now in my fifties, having brought up two children, divorced, and begun a new relationship, I was on a more spiritual path, seeking harmony with the cosmos while not forgetting the well-being of the planet. No doubt conscious of my father's own neglect, I had tried to be a good father to my own children.

That was enough for the first session. When I next saw David, he gave me a copy of my chart.

'Well, Peter,' he said, smiling warmly. 'I was going to mark this chart "Speculative" but such a clear picture of you emerges from it that I am very confident that we have arrived at a birth time that is fairly close to the proper one.'

That was reassuring at least.

'To begin with,' he went on, 'there are two heavily populated areas in the chart. You have four planets in Libra in the Tenth House and three in Leo in the Eighth House with the sun next door in the Ninth. There are only ten planets altogether so you can see how emphasized these two areas are.'

'What does it all mean?'

'The Tenth House represents your activities in the outside world. The Tenth House is Libra which indicates that these activities involve contact with other people – very many, in your case. Venus rules Libra so this is much strengthened. Jupiter, which is well aspected, shows much opportunity and success. Mars provides energy, initiative and enterprise and Neptune is not only the sea but gives great sensitivity and awareness of the "Values".'

'And the other cluster of planets in the Eighth House?'

'The other collection represents inwardness. The Eighth House is in Leo which is leadership, creativity, love, love affairs, children, sports, games and pastimes that are slightly risky, such as battling through the Irish Sea in a gale! The Eighth House is associated with Scorpio – the deepest, most intense sign of the zodiac. Pluto rules Scorpio, so again there is an emphasis of this factor, and Mercury represents your mental processes. So we have Scorpio twice, once by ruler and once by House. Scorpio appears again this time as itself containing the Part of Fortune. The intensity of Scorpio is being combined with the originality and unorthodoxy of Uranus as represented by the Eleventh House.'

'What about Saturn in the Eighth House?'

'The only spectre at the feast is grumpy old Saturn, who is not aspected to any other planet, which paradoxically makes it all the more powerful. The negative effect of Saturn is to be inhibiting and limiting. Saturn also represents the father and, as the aspect to the Midheaven is a square, what is indicated is either a non-existent relationship with the father, as is your case, or a bad one.'

'And the other aspects?'

'I was coming to that. There is a small triangle of helpful aspects joining with your sun, Jupiter and Midheaven and your Ascendant, Sagittarius. You will not be surprised to hear that Sagittarius is all about wide-rangingess of all sorts – physical, mental and spiritual – and that Jupiter rules both Sagittarius and the Ninth House. Your sun, which represents creativity and purpose, is in the Ninth House. Uranus joins in the valediction from Gemini in the Sixth House. It is connected to all the outgoing elements. Uranus is the innovative, original and unorthodox element: Gemini is communication and the Sixth House is work.'

'I notice that my moon is alone in Cancer in the Seventh House.'

'Your moon – your emotions, your mother and women in general – is not well-aspected. It make squares to Venus (relationship) and Jupiter (opportunity). However, the squares are really helpful aspects in disguise. They draw attention to an area that needs to be worked on. The moon rules Cancer and it is in the Seventh which is relationship. Cancer is about the home, but it's also about caring for, looking after, nurturing, feeding, protecting, etc. My feeling about this is that it is pointing to difficulties you had in your relationships in your original home and that the suggestion is that these will continue to afflict you until you resolve them.'

David was clearly of the school which believes that no chart is bad. Any negative elements can be transformed into positive outcomes, and difficulties can be seen as opportunities for growth. What he said about the need to come to terms with early home difficulties struck a deep chord.

'So how would you sum things up?'

'The chart indicates opportunity and ease and is a very helpful chart in that sense and there is only one really difficult aspect. That is the opposition, which means what is says, between Uranus in Gemini in the Sixth House and your Sagittarius Ascendant. Uranus in difficult aspect means very marked disruption and upheaval. The Sixth House is work – also health – and is directly opposed to all this outgoingness. I don't know what it means. What does it suggest to you?'

I liked the way David was reluctant to offer advice or a definitive interpretation. He encourages people to discover things for themselves. But he is happy to discuss the sometimes elusive meaning of the chart and its implications for present trends. He encourages his clients to keep in touch and come back to consider future trends through progressions and transits of the chart. Many of his clients consult him when they have difficult choices to make in their lives, whether about their relationships or their work. He also works with the *I Ching*, the ancient Chinese method of divination.

When working on progressions and transits, David is keen to stress that nothing is fixed and encourages his clients to accent the positive and eliminate the negative.

David wrote down for me his interpretation of my horoscope and gave me the notes he had made during the process. They seemed surprisingly accurate and apt:

> Uneasy expression of affections and lack of harmony in the home (your original home, presumably). Optimism, extremely helpful situations; perhaps tendency to trust to luck. Cheerful, happy disposition. Male and female sides combine very well. Originality in the Arts. Frequent good opportunities. In connection with Uranus opposition Ascendant aspect, there is a suggestion that self-discipline and restraint are called for.

David also added some notes taken from his textbooks on some of the aspects he found in my chart:

> Mercury sextile Venus. The mind and mental outlook are improved by this contact. . . A writer or speaker benefits in this way.

> Mercury sextile Mars. Mercury receives the strength of Mars, hence the mind is forceful, incisive, forthright and good at debate.

> Mars conjunct Neptune. Interest in the sea, in mysticism, in hidden things pursued with energy and with desire to experiment in new ways. Psychic sensitivity or any form of idealism.

> Mercury conjunct Pluto. A desire to study those things which lie beneath the surface.

> Sun trine Ascendant. Creative ability, will to achieve, power of leadership, sense of independence and enterprise.

Again, I was deeply impressed by the astrological confirmation of these known attributes of my character and interests.

Elizabeth Ashton Hill's Horoscope

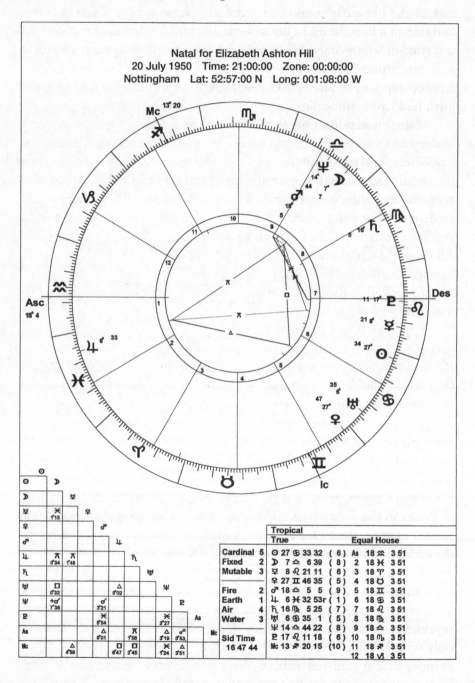

Natal for Elizabeth Ashton Hill
20 July 1950   Time: 21:00:00   Zone: 00:00:00
Nottingham   Lat: 52:57:00 N   Long: 001:08:00 W

Tropical		
True		**Equal House**
Cardinal 5	☉ 27 ♋ 33 32 (6)	As 18 ♒ 3 51
Fixed 2	☽ 7 ♎ 6 39 (8)	2 18 ♓ 3 51
Mutable 3	☿ 8 ♌ 21 11 (6)	3 18 ♈ 3 51
	♀ 27 ♊ 46 35 (5)	4 18 ♉ 3 51
Fire 2	♂ 18 ♎ 5 5 (9)	5 18 ♊ 3 51
Earth 1	♃ 6 ♓ 32 53r (1)	6 18 ♋ 3 51
Air 4	♄ 16 ♏ 5 25 (7)	7 18 ♌ 3 51
Water 3	♅ 6 ♋ 35 1 (5)	8 18 ♍ 3 51
	♆ 14 ♎ 44 22 (8)	9 18 ♎ 3 51
Sid Time	♇ 17 ♌ 11 18 (6)	10 18 ♏ 3 51
16 47 44	Mc 13 ♐ 20 15 (10)	11 18 ♐ 3 51
		12 18 ♑ 3 51

When Elizabeth met David I was not present, so I do not know exactly what they discussed. Nevertheless, I learned later that she had told him about her early work as a teacher in further education, how she had rebuilt a Porsche and a house with previous boyfriends, how she had travelled in South America and Japan, how she had worked in television and taught photography and film at degree level, and how she was now a practising photographer. She had held down a number of responsible jobs, had five major relationships and had no children.

At their initial meeting, David felt there was something he could not understand, but having drawn up her chart, he realized what it was.

'There are powerful forces at work here and the trouble with powerful forces is that they need to be controlled and channelled. There is much outwardness and inwardness. Yang and Yin. The former is very evident in what you told me about yourself and I wonder to what extent you are conscious of the latter and how much it plays a part in your life. All over the chart there are contradictions which could either work harmoniously together or be in conflict.'

He looked at the outwardness first, running through the things she had done in her life.

'This is all pretty up-front stuff,' he commented. 'It is not surprising that your Part of Fortune is in Aries in the Third House, indicating that the area in which you would find true fulfilment and satisfaction is in a very strong desire to communicate.'

Next he examined the area of inwardness as revealed by the chart.

'There is a considerable amount of "caringness" present. You have three planets – a Stellium – in the Sixth House which is concerned with work and services for others; and two in Cancer which involves looking after, caring for, feeding, nurturing and protecting. Uranus, one of the planets in Cancer, makes a trine aspect – the best you can get – to Jupiter in Pisces in the First House. Uranus is unorthodoxy and individuality. Jupiter is opportunity for expansion and development and Pisces has to do with all hidden things, including the unconscious.

'The contradiction here is that Aquarius, your Ascendant and a very important factor in the chart, is quincunx Saturn in Virgo in the Seventh House and opposition Pluto in Leo in the Sixth. The quincunx represents something that absolutely has to be dealt with, but can be so only with considerable difficulty. Aquarius in difficult aspect, as this is, is independent and self-willed: but it is ruled by Uranus which is an important part of the caring syndrome. Also, Virgo is work and service for others and Saturn is limitation. So there is limitation in the Sixth House concerned with work and service for others due to the negative characteristics of Aquarius. Pluto on the other hand supplies a thera-peutic element: it removes obstacles and leads to rebirth.'

There were more helpful aspects, David pointed out, between Pluto and Mercury in Leo and the moon, Mars and Neptune in Libra in the Eighth House, which indicated a harmonious coming together in relation-ships involving intense feelings.

Her Midheaven, the area concerned with outward activity, in Sagittarius, also concerned with wide-ranginess, made excellent aspects with Mercury, Neptune and Pluto, which emphasized communication and sensitivity. Together they suggested inner wide-ranginess.

'Putting it all together,' he concluded, 'I wonder if a single-minded pursuit of this up-front activity is masking the caring, sensitive, creative side of your nature which is, perhaps, not getting much of a look-in. I think the caring element must be given more emphasis.'

He also gave her the notes he made while interpreting her chart. On the difficult side was a tendency to be all caution and control or none at all, and a question mark over her judgement. On the helpful side, she was of great sensitivity as well as being intuitive and emotional. She had energy, drive and a desire for independence. With a visionary nature, she would always be conscious of some great ideal.

His last words to her were: 'My general impression is that you are about to experience a new beginning and the best thing you can do is to be very, very aware of impressions and intuitions and be awake to guidance.'

Synastry for Peter Marshall and Elizabeth Ashton Hill

Elizabeth and I had our charts done with David before I began this book and before we finally decided to live together. We therefore asked him to do a synastry for us – that is, a comparison of our charts with a view to their compatibility. A symbolic composite chart can be derived from the midpoints from the common factors between two horoscopes but he mainly compared our two charts side by side and looked at the aspects between our planets.

The situation appeared clear-cut if not entirely welcome: 'This is a relationship that will need to be worked on in order to keep balanced. To start with, you both have a lot of Libra in your natal charts:

Elizabeth has three planets in Libra and one in the Seventh (Libra's) House; Peter has four in Libra and one in the Seventh – a very heavy loading for each of you. People necessarily bring their own baggage to a relationship and it is important to see that it is used constructively, or at least not allowed to cause trouble.

'As we know, Libra does not impart balance, as many think. On the contrary it indicates imbalance and the consequent need to achieve balance.

'This balance is indicated perfectly in the comparison of your natal charts. There are six helpful aspects and six unhelpful; and in the area in which one looks for the possibility of a long-lasting happy relationship, there is the best aspect you can get – a trine – and the worst you can get – an opposition. In addition to that, there are four conjunctions, each of which is in Libra. So you see what I mean. I can only show you what is indicated. You will know how this manifests in your life together.

'Taking the six helpful aspects, Libra appears in all of them and this indicates the sharing you have in outwardness. As counterpoint to all this go-go activity is a gentle, caring, loving aspect indicating on your side, Elizabeth, steadiness and caring; and on Peter's side, emotional response to this end and also the element of caring, looking after, feeding, nurturing and protecting. So, here we have a harmonious and loving relationship, which is what Libra is all about.

'Now, on the unhelpful side we have the same elements working together but in disharmony. The aspects show desire for domesticity and to perform caring work for others on one side, and a desire for independence and work in the outside world on the other. The last aspect more or less combines the caring, sensitive sides of both your natures but still causes trouble for some reason. The four conjunctions follow exactly the same pattern.

'What is interesting is that these elements swop over from one of you to the other, so it isn't one-sided. I have never seen in twenty-five years such a clear example of Libra at work!'

So that was the basic situation. It was the 'baggage' we brought with us which caused it to be so. David recommended that we looked at our natal charts to see if we could see the answers.

We're working on it. So far so good! Things are getting more balanced every day. We suspect that the trine is even growing stronger than the opposition . . .

38

The Age of Aquarius

All of us are in the gutter, but some are looking at the stars.

OSCAR WILDE

AT THE END OF the nineteenth century, the French historian Bouché-Leclerq declared that astrology had permanently disappeared; he was writing the history of a dead superstition.[1] The revival of astrology started in England at the beginning of the twentieth century, with Alan Leo's books on practical astrology, but has since spread throughout the Western world. Its popularity in the mass media can be dated to August 1930 when R.H. Naylor wrote an astrological profile of Princess Margaret, daughter of the future George VI, for the *Daily Express*. The enthusiastic response which helped sell copies led other dailies to follow suit.

The most popular form of astrology based on the sun signs fills the columns of newspapers and magazines throughout the world. Since they predict the love life, financial affairs and happiness of millions who share one of the twelve sun signs, few, including the readers, take it seriously. Then there are astrologers who offer their services through the post without even meeting their clients. Their work has been greatly helped by computer software which not only cuts out the time-consuming calculations but provides print-outs of the interpretation of a chart at the press of a button.

Astrology in the West has been taken up not only by millions of readers but by influential movers in society. During the Second World War, De Gaulle regularly consulted a fellow general in the Free French Army who was an astrologer. Thanks to his wife Nancy, President Ronald Reagan took astrological advice before making key decisions, especially in relation to the Soviet Union. The *New York Post* ran a headline on 9 May 1987 declaring, 'Astrologer Ran the White House'. Stock-market analysts and horse-racing punters consult astrologers. Police departments in the US use astrologers to help track down criminals. Even hostile critics recognize 'the astrological phoenix' has created 'the greatest resurgence astrology has ever known since the scientific revolution' of the seventeenth century.[2]

In India, every wealthy family has its own astrologer and horoscopes are a key element in deciding on arranged marriages. There are even calls to restore astrology to the university curriculum. In Egypt, politicians and diplomats do not make a move before consulting their astrologers. In rural China, young computer scientists will consult their local astrologer and 'fortune-teller' for advice about their love life and career prospects.

Despite the vociferous attacks of scientists and religious leaders in the twentieth century, astrology has hardly ever been in better health. It is a valuable technique of understanding human character and experience. It provides us with a language to understand who we are and how we might develop and a body of concepts to discuss and appreciate our feelings and relationships. Perhaps the reason why women are more sympathetic to astrology than men is because they are more in touch with their emotions and intuition. Yet an increasing number of men from Mars are beginning to appreciate the insights of Venus.

Above all, astrology offers a path of transformation since it can lead us from the confusion of everyday life to a deeper understanding of ourselves and of our place within the universe. It is transpersonal because it sees the fully individualized person as part of the cosmic whole. At this level, the 'I' of individual consciousness is transformed into the 'We' of universal consciousness. From this perspective, the birthchart is the *prima materia* in the Great Work of spiritual alchemy. Descended from the stars, we can return to the stars. We can pass again through the gates of heaven.

At the dawn of the new millennium, on the threshold of the Age of Aquarius, we are undoubtedly entering a period of transformation and uncertainty. Millions of people are looking afresh at astrology as a possible guide to understanding themselves and to planning the future.

There are good reasons why this should be so. Astrology not only stretches back beyond the Stone Age but its fundamental beliefs are the same throughout the world. My world-wide study of astrology has confirmed my hunch that the astral knowledge of China, India,

Mesopotamia and Egypt has common roots, possibly as a legacy from an earlier lost civilization. The core of astrology, the language of the stars, is a *lingua franca,* expressed in geometrical shapes and numbers and embodied in myths and symbols, which covers the whole world and transcends local cults and beliefs.[3] It not only conveys the psychological understanding of antiquity but carries in a disguised form much of the lost sacred science of the ancient world, which is highly relevant to our times.

Above all, astrology embodies two key truths common to all philosophical and religious traditions. The first is that there is an inextricable correspondence between heaven and earth. As the greatest document to come out the Hermetic Tradition, the anonymous *Emerald Tablet,* puts its: 'True it is, without falsehood, certain and most true. That which is above is like to that which is below, and that which is below is like that which is above, to accomplish the miracle of the one thing.'[4] The second truth is that the human microcosm not only mirrors the macrocosm of the universe, but they are ultimately one. By understanding ourselves we can understand the universe. As the Oracle at Delphi declares: 'Man, know thyself and thou wilt know the Universe and the Gods.'

As expressed in myths and temples, signs and symbols, astrology further teaches us that life is a preparation for what is to come and death is but a change in our continuous journeying. It reminds us that life is sacred and that all beings deserve our compassion. It tells us that matter can be transformed into spirit and that the ultimate purpose of life is to develop our consciousness and realize ourselves as spiritual beings. It assumes that there is order, meaning and consciousness in the universe. It asserts that not only is Gaia alive but there is a World Soul. It shows us that everything is independent and interconnected in the world: All is One and One is All.

My long study of astrology has undermined for ever my youthful belief in inevitable progress. It has shown me that as a species we have in many ways regressed rather than evolved. By becoming slaves of instrumental reason, we have lost the intelligence of the heart. By becoming wedded to materialism and relentlessly pursuing pleasure, we have lost our spiritual bearings. By being earth-bound, we have lost our archaic link with the heavens. By becoming fragmented, we no longer see ourselves as part of the whole.

There can be no doubt that our present world is increasingly devoid of mysteries. Ours is an age of information rather than knowledge, let alone wisdom. Reason and science claim to be able to understand and explain everything. There is little room left for the magical, the miraculous, the marvellous and the supernatural.

Astrology, like alchemy and magic, belongs to an older – and a newer – way of perceiving the world. It is an offshoot of the primordial world view which still exists among some remote peoples and which is beginning to re-emerge among the most thoughtful and sensitive in urban societies. It does not distinguish between the inner and the outer, the subject and object. It experiences the human soul as participating in the *anima mundi*, the World Soul. It believes the secret of Being is hidden in the skies. It sees spirits playing in the woods and angels flying in the clouds. It finds meaning in the flight of birds across the setting sun and the conjunction of planets.

Astrology accepts that there is a Harmony of the Spheres and that the stars are gateways to another world. Rather than a Black Hole of ignorance and superstition, it holds out a Milky Way of visionary thinking. It is undoubtedly part of the archaic way of thinking which recognizes that beauty, enchantment and mystery are essentials elements of the universe.

Astrology began when humans first looked up at the vast star-studded canopy of the night sky and wondered what it all meant. It was born out of puzzlement and curiosity. It was the first attempt of our ancestors to understand the mystery of the universe and to discover the purpose of life. This universal and primordial experience helped form – and still does – the central questions of philosophy and religion: Who are we? Where do we come from? Why are we here? Where are we going? By attempting to understand the relationship between heaven and earth and our place within the cosmos, astrology has tried to interpret the meaning of human destiny and the riddle of existence.

While not a religion, astrology suggests that there is a spiritual and magical dimension to life. Like the *anima mundi* of the ancient alchemists, the world of the astrologers is charged with symbolic meaning. It sees a place for soul in the universe. Astrology stands out in our cold and mechanical culture like a brilliant star on a frosty night. Inspired by a yearning for harmony amongst the chaos of everyday life and for permanence in a changing world, it has tried to understand the human condition by correlating the main experiences of life on earth to the great and permanent cycles of the heavens. By reconnecting us with the cosmos, it holds forth the possibility of becoming fully realized human beings. By aligning us once again with the deep rhythms of nature, it shows us how we can attain wholeness, wisdom and peace.

Notes

Introduction

1 In John Anthony West, *The Case for Astrology* (London: Arkana, 1992), pp. 142–3.
2 Franz Cumont, *Astrology and Religion Among the Greeks and Romans* (New York: Dover, 1912), p. 30.
3 Bart J. Bok and Lawrence E. Jerome, *Objections to Astrology* (Buffalo, N.Y.: Prometheus Books, 1976), pp. 9–10.
4 Richard Dawkins, *Independent on Sunday* (31 December 1995), article reworked in *Unweaving the Rainbow* (London: Allen Lane, 1998).
5 Johannes Kepler, *De Stella Nova* (1606), ch. 28; also in John Anthony West, *The Case for Astrology* (New York: Viking Arkana, 1991), p. 106.
6 In David Brewster, *Memoirs of the Life, Writings and Discoveries of Sir Isaac Newton* (Edinburgh, 1855), vol. 2, p. 408.
7 See Jane Ridder-Patrick, *A Handbook of Medical Astrology* (London: Arkana, 1990), p. 10.
8 See Maggie Hyde, *Jung and Astrology* (Wellingborough: Aquarian Press, 1992).

1 Into the Dragon's Mouth

1 See Roderick Whitefield, Susan Whitefield and Neville Agnew, *Cave Temples of Dunhuang* (London: British Library, 2000).
2 Cf. Joseph Needham, *Science and Civilisation in China* (Cambridge: Cambridge University Press, 1959), vol. 3, p. 276. The Dunhuang star map is in the Stein Collection, no. 3726, British Library, S612/1 (vol. 14 of catalogue, P 6/2).
3 *Sik Sik Yuen Guide* (Hong Kong: Sik Sik Yuen, 1996).

2 The Dog and the Tiger

1 See Bridget Giles and the Diagram Group, *Chinese Astrology* (London: HarperCollins, 1996), p. 104.
2 See Man-Ho Kwok, *Chinese Astrology: Forecast Your Future from Your Chinese Horoscope* (London: Blandford, 1997), p. 46; Giles, *Chinese Astrology*, p. 76.
3 Giles, *Chinese Astrology*, p. 226.
4 See Man-Ho Kwok, *Chinese Astrology*, p. 72.
5 Ibid., pp. 64–5, 60–61.
6 See Anistatia R. Miller and Jared M. Brown, *The Complete Astrological Handbook for the Twenty-first Century* (New York: Schocken Books, 1999), pp. 93–5.
7 Giles, *Chinese Astrology*, pp. 8–9.
8 Jean-Michel Huon de Kermadec, *The Way to Chinese Astrology: The Four Pillars of Destiny*, trans. N. Derek Poulsen (London: Unwin, 1983), p. 138, n. 24; Joseph Needham, *Science and Civilisation in China* (Cambridge: Cambridge University Press, 1959), vol. 3, p. 405. For Tibetan astrology, see Miller and Brown, *The Complete Astrological Handbook*, pp. 119–139.

3 The Way and its Virtue

1 Lao tsu (Lao Tzu), *Tao Te Ching*, trans. Gia-fu Feng and Jane English (New York: Vintage, 1972), ch. 1.
2 *Huai Nan Tzu* (c.120 BC) in *Sources of the Chinese Tradition*, ed. Theodore de Bary (New York: Columbia University Press, 1960), vol. I, pp. 192–3.
3 Lao tsu, *Tao Te Ching*, ch. 4.
4 See Huon de Kermadec, *The Way to Chinese Astrology: The Four Pillars of Destiny*, trans. N. Derek Poulson (London: Unwin, 1983), p. 33 and n. 25.
5 See Joseph Needham, *Science and Civilisation in China* (Cambridge: Cambridge University Press, 1954), vol. 2, pp. 216ff.
6 Anistatia R. Miller and Jared M. Brown, *The Complete Astrological Handbook for the Twenty-First Century* (New York: Schocken Books, 1999), p. 49.
7 Chu Hsi in Needham, *Science and Civilisation in China*, vol. 2, pp. 479–10.
8 *I Ching or Book of Changes*, trans. Richard Wilhelm into German and rendered into English by Cary F. Baynes, 3rd edition (London: Arkana, 1989), pp. 318–19.
9 Ibid., Hellmut Wilhelm, Preface, p. xiv.
10 Ibid., pp. 328–9.
11 Ibid., Carl Jung, Foreword, p. xxi.

4 Surveying the Infinite

1 Matthew Ricci, *China in the Sixteenth Century: The Journals of Matthew Ricci: 1583–1610*, trans. Louis J. Gallagher (New York: Random House, 1953); Joseph Needham, *Science and Civilisation in China* (Cambridge: Cambridge University Press, 1959), vol. 3, p. 367.

2 Robert Temple, *The Genius of China: 3,000 Years of Science, Discovery and Invention* (London: Prion, 1991), p. 38.

3 *T'ai shang chiu yao hsin yin miai ching*, 4a; in Edward H. Schafer, *Pacing the Void: T'ang Approaches to the Stars* (Berkeley, Calif.: University of California, 1977), p. 179. For the works of Chang Kuo, see also Needham, *Science and Civilisation in China* (1954), vol. 2, p. 356.

4 See Temple, *The Genius of China*, p. 36.

5 Needham, *Science and Civilisation in China* (1959), vol. 3, p. 444.

6 Robert Temple, *The Crystal Sun: Rediscovering the Lost Technology of the Ancient World* (London: Century, 2000), pp. 59, 116.

7 In Fung Yu-Luan, *A History of Chinese Philosophy: The Period of the Philosophers*, trans. Derk Bodde (Peiping: Henri Vetch, 1937), p. 397.

8 Needham, *Science and Civilisation in China* (1959), vol. 3, p. 213.

9 Ibid. (1962), vol. 4, part 1, pp. 320–1.

10 Ibid. (1959), vol. 3, pp. 219–24.

11 Ibid., p. 427.

12 See Temple, *The Genius of China*, pp. 33–4.

13 Needham, *Science and Civilisation in China* (1959), vol. 3, p. 433.

14 Ibid. (1957), vol. 2, p. 264.

15 Ibid. (1959), vol. 3, p. 278.

5 As Above, So Below

1 See Joseph Needham, *Science and Civilisation in China* (Cambridge: Cambridge University Press, 1974), vol. 5, part 3, pp. 21–2.

2 See Edward H. Schafer, *Pacing the Void: T'ang Approaches to the Stars* (Berkley, Calif.: Unversity of California, 1977), pp. 35–6.

3 Needham, *Science and Civilisation in China* (1959), vol. 3, pp. 361–2.

4 Ibid. (1962), vol. 4, part 2, p. 479.

5 Schafer, *Pacing the Void*, p. 68.

6 Ibid., p. 124.

7 Li Po, 'Teng T'ai po feng', *Chiu T'ang shu*, in ibid., p. 129.

8 See Schafer, *Pacing the Void*, p. 100.

9 Ibid., pp. 135–6.

10 Ibid., p. 230.

11 Ibid., p. 39.

12 Ibid., p. 71.

6 The Temple of Heaven

1 Joseph Needham, *Science and Civilisation in China* (Cambridge: Cambridge University Press, 1954), vol. 2, p. 353.
2 Ibid., pp. 378–9.
3 Ibid. (1962), vol. 4, part 2, p. 478.
4 Edward H. Schafer, *Pacing the Void: T'ang Approaches to the Stars* (Berkeley, Calif.: University of California, 1977), pp. 13,75.
5 Nicholas Trigault, *De Christiana Expeditione apud Sinas* (Vienna, 1615), trans. in *Purchases his Pilgrimes* (London, 1625), vol. 3, p. 384.
6 Needham, *Science and Civilisation in China* (1954), vol. 2, p. 384. See also A. Forke, 'Lun Hêng', *Philosophical Essays of Wang Chhung*, part 1, (Shanghai, London, Leipzig, 1907); Part 2 (Berlin,1911).

7 The Four Pillars of Destiny

1 See Raymond Lo, *Feng Shui and Destiny for Managers* (Singapore: Times Books International, 1997), p. 14.
2 See Anistatia R. Miller and Jared M. Brown, *The Complete Astrological Handbook* for the Twenty-first Century (New York: Schocken Books, 1999), pp. 54, 64.
3 Ibid., p. 78.
4 Ibid., p. 81.
5 Raymond Lo, *Feng Shui and Destiny for Managers* (Singapore: Times Books International, 1997), p. 18.
6 See Jean-Michel Huon de Kermadec, *The Way to Chinese Astrology: The Four Pillars of Destiny*, trans. N. Derek Poulson (London: Unwin, 1983), p. 39. See also Miller and Brown, *The Complete Astrological Handbook*, p. 107.
7 See Joseph Needham, *Science and Civilisation in China* (Cambridge: Cambridge University Press, 1959), vol. 3, p. 246.
8 Miller and Brown, *The Complete Astrological Handbook*, p. 90.
9 Ibid., p. 98.

8 Know All Things

1 See Charles Windridge, ed., *Tong Sing: The Chinese Book of Wisdom* (London: Kyle Cathie, 1999), p. 7.
2 Matthew Ricci, *China in the Sixteenth Century: The Journals of Matthew Ricci: 1583–1610,* trans. from the Latin by Louis J. Gallagher (New York: Random House, 1953), pp. 82–3.

9 Wind and Water

1 Stephan D. R. Feuchtwang, *An Anthropological Analysis of Chinese Geomancy* (Taipei: Southern Material Center, 1974), p. 15. See also Raymond Lo, *Feng Shui and Destiny for Families* (Singapore: Times Books International, 1999), p. 126.

2 See Man-Ho Kwok with Joanne O'Brien, *The Elements of Feng Shui* (Shaftesbury: Element Books, 1991), p. 3.

3 Ricci, *China in the Sixteenth Century: The Journals of Matthew Ricci: 1583–1610*, trans. from the Latin by Louis J. Gallagher (New York: Random House. 1953), pp. 82 ff.; Ernest Eitel, *Feng-shui or The Rudiments of Natural Science in China* (Hong Kong: Lane, Crawford, 1873), pp. 1, 4ff; Joseph Needham, *Science and Civilisation in China* (Cambridge: Cambridge University Press 1954), vol. 2, pp. 359–61.

4 Paul Wheatley, *The Pivot of the Four Quarters* (Chicago: Aldine, 1971), p. 450; Steven Bennett, 'Patterns of the Sky and Earth: The Chinese Science of Applied Cosmos', *Chinese Science*, vol. 3 (March 1978), p. 2.

5 See Eugene Anderson and Marja Anderson, 'Changing Patterns of Land Use in Rural Hong Kong', *Mountains and Water: Essays on the Cultural Ecology of South Coastal China* (Taipei: Orient Cultural Service, 1973), pp. 34, 50.

6 Kwang-chih Chang, *Shang Civilization* (New Haven: Yale University Press, 1980), p. 159.

7 See Sang Hae Lee, *Feng Shui: Its Context and Meaning*, Cornell University Ph.D. thesis, 1986 (Ann Arbor, Michigan: UMI, 1999), p. 10.

8 Lo, *Feng Shui and Destiny for Families*, p. 129.

9 In Lee, *Feng Shui*, p. 341.

10 See Needham, *Science and Civilisation in China* (1954), vol. 2, p. 361.

11 Man-Ho Kwok, *The Elements of Feng Shui* , pp. 41–2.

12 See Feuchtwang, *Chinese Geomancy*, pp. 18 ff.

13 See Man-Ho Kwok, *The Elements of Feng Shui*, pp. 61–7.

14 Ibid., p. 57.

15 See Peter Marshall, *The Philosopher's Stone: A Quest for the Secrets of Alchemy* (London: Macmillan, 2001), pp. 223–4.

10 Star House

1 Raymond Lo, *Feng Shui and Destiny for Families* (Singapore: Times Books International, 1999), p. 10.

2 Ibid., p. 57.

3 *I Ching or Book of Changes*, trans. Richard Wilhelm into German and rendered into English by Cary F. Baynes, 3rd edition (London: Arkana, 1989), Carl Jung, Foreword, p. xxiv. See also Carl Jung's 'Synchronicity: An Acausal

Principle', *The Structure and Dynamics of the Psyche, Collected Works* (Princeton, N.J.: Princeton University Press, 1960), vol. 8.

4 Raymond Lo, *Feng Shui and Destiny for Managers*, (Singapore: Times Books International, 1997), p. 148.

5 Jean-Michel Houn de Kermadec, *The Way to Chinese Astrology: The Four Pillars of Destiny*, trans. N. Derek Poulsen (London: Unwin, 1983), p. 2.

6 Man-Ho Kwok, *Chinese Astrology: Forecast Your Future from Your Chinese Horoscope* (London: Blandford, 1997), p. 9.

7 See Peter Marshall, *The Philosopher's Stone: A Quest for the Secrets of Alchemy* (London: Macmillan, 2001), p. 46.

11 Wisdom of the Heavens

1 Nehru, *Letters to his Sister* (1963), in Louis MacNeice, *Astrology* (London: Aldus, 1964), p. 287.

2 *Independent* (London: 31 March 2001).

3 See www.vedicfuture.com.

4 B. V. Raman, *Astrology for Beginners* (1940) (New Delhi: UBS, 1998), p. xiii.

5 Hart Defouw and Robert Svoboda, *Light on Life: An Introduction to the Astrology of India* (London: Arkana, 1996), p. xxiv.

6 See ibid., p. ix; Komilla Sutton, *The Essentials of Vedic Astrology* (Bournemouth: The Wessex Astrologer, 1999), p. 1.

7 In Defouw and Svoboda, *Light on Life,* p. 20.

8 *Bhagavad Gita,* trans. Juan Mascaró (Harmondsworth: Penguin, 1975), 2:22, p. 50.

9 Raman, *Astrology for Beginners,* p. xxvii; Sutton, *The Essentials of Vedic Astrology,* p. 4.

10 Raman, *Astrology for Beginners,* p. 2.

11 See ibid., p. 5.

12 Sutton, *The Essentials of Vedic Astrology,* p. 16.

13 Defouw and Svoboda, *Light on Life,* Vasant Lad, Foreword, p. xx.

14 Defouw and Svoboda, ibid., p. 13.

15 Valerie J. Roebuck, *The Circle of Stars: An Introduction to Indian Astrology* (Shaftesbury: Element Books, 1992), p. 12.

16 Ibid., p. 16.

12 Far-seeing Eyes

1 B. L. Dhama, *A Guide to the Jaipur Astronomical Observatory*, Preface, (Jaipur, n.d).

2 Ibid., p. 3.

3 P. C. Sengupta, *Surya Siddhanta*, trans. Ebenezer Burgess, (Calcutta, 1935), p. viii; Rupert Gleadow, *The Origin of the Zodiac* (London: Jonathan Cape, 1968), pp. 137, 139.

4 See Shil-Ponde, *Hindu Astrology: Jyotisha-Shastra* (New Delhi: Sagar, 1968); Valerie J Roebuck, *The Circle of Stars: An Introduction to Indian Astrology* (Shaftesbury: Element, 1992), p. 152, n.7.

5 Gleadow, *The Origin of the Zodiac*, pp. 138.

6 See B. V. Raman, *Astrology for Beginners* (New Delhi: UBS, 1998), pp. xiii–xiv.

7 Giorgio de Santanilla and Hertha von Dechend, *Hamlet's Mill: An Essay on Myth and the Frame of Time* (1967), (Boston: David R. Godine, 1977), pp. 3, 301, 346. See also John E. Mitchener, *Traditions of the Seven Risis* (New Delhi: Motilal Banarsidass, 1982).

8 *Brihat Parashara Hora*, 97:1–2a, in Hart Defouw and Robert Svoboda, *Light on Life: An Introduction to the Astrology of India* (London: Arkana, 1996), p. 14.

9 *Vrddhayavanajataka of Minaraja*, ed. David Pingree, 2 vols., (Baroda: Oriental Institute, 1976), vol. I, pp. 1–4; Roebuck, *The Circle of Stars*, p. 21.

10 de Santanilla and von Dechend, *Hamlet's Mill*, p. 138.

11 *Rig Veda*, trans. W. D. O'Flaherty (Harmondsworth: Penguin, 1981), 5.13.6.

12 *A Sourcebook in Indian Philosophy*, ed. S. Radhakrishnan and C. A. Moore (Princeton, NJ: Princeton University Press, 1971), p. 7.

13 Ibid. p. 13.

14 *Rig Veda*, 10.127; Roebuck, *Circle of Stars*, p. 3.

15 *Hymns of the Atharva Veda*, trans. M. Bloomfield (New Delhi: Motilal Banarsidass,1992) 10.7.12. See de Santanilla and von Dechend, *Hamlet's Mill*, pp. 140, 233.

16 Roebuck, *Circle of Stars*, p. 5.

17 See Gleadow, *The Origin of the Zodiac*, p. 143.

18 *A Sourcebook in Indian Philosophy*, ed. S. Rodhakrishnan and C. A. Moore (Princeton, NJ: Princeton University Press, 1971), p. 77.

19 Svetasvatara Upanishad, Vl, 11–12.

20 *The Upanishads*, trans. Eknath Easwaran (London: Arkana, 1988); Prashna, Vl, 3–4, p. 280.

21 See Komilla Sutton, *The Essentials of Vedic Astrology* (Bournemouth: The Wessex Astrologer, 1999) pp. 256–7.

22 Ibid., p. 6.

23 Dhama, *A Guide to the Jaipur Astronomical Observatory*, preface.

24 See David Pingree, *Jyotishsastra: Astral and Mathematical Literature* (Wiesbaden: Otto Harrassowitz, 1981); and Roebuck, *The Circle of Stars*, pp. 5–6.

25 Roebuck, *The Circle of Stars*, p. 7.

26 Gleadow, *The Origin of the Zodiac*, p. 140.

27 See ibid., p. 141.

28 O. Neugebauer, 'Tamil Astronomy', *Osiris*, X (1952), pp. 252–76.

29 See www.loudoun-net.com/kamesh/NadiAstrology.

13 The Wheel of Life

1 Raman, *Astrology for Beginners* (New Delhi: UBS, 1998) p. 5.

2 See ibid., pp. 18–23.

3 See Sutton, *The Essentials of Vedic Astrology* (Bournemouth: The Wessex Astrologer, 1999), pp. 74–92.

4 Ibid., p. 238.

5 Varahamihira, *Brhajjataka*, ed. Sastri (1981), 27:1–3, pp. 518–19, in Roebuck, *The Circle of Stars: An Introduction to Indian Astrology* (Shaftesbury: Element, 1992), p. 124.

6 See ibid., pp. 124–7.

7 Hart Defouw and Robert Svoboda, *Light on Life: An Introduction to the Astrology of India* (London: Arkana, 1996), p. 115.

8 See Raman, *Astrology for Beginners*, p. 16. For a more detailed account, see Defouw and Svoboda, *Light on Life*, pp. 129–149.

9 Ibid., p. 116.

10 See Sutton, *The Essentials of Vedic Astrology*, p. 25.

14 The Family of Planets

1 Hart Defouw and Robert Svoboda, *Light on Life: An Introduction to the Astrology of India* (London: Arkana, 1996), p. 33.

2 Ibid., pp. 8–9.

3 Sutton, *The Essentials of Vedic Astrology* (Bournemouth: The Wessex Astrologer, 1999), p. 53. See also her *The Lunar Nodes: Crisis and Redemption* (Bournemouth: The Wessex Astrologer, 2001).

4 *Vrddhayavanajataka of Minaraja*, ed. David Pingree (Baroda: Oriental Institute, 1976), vol. 2, p. 16.

5 See Sutton, *The Essentials of Vedic Astrology*, p. 22.

6 See Raman, *Astrology for Beginners* (New Delhi: UBS, 1998), pp. 11, 12.

7 See Sutton, *The Essentials of Vedic Astrology*, p. 21.

8 See ibid., p. 27; Raman, *Astrology for Beginners*, p. 13.

9 Defouw and Svoboda, *Light on Life*, pp. 278–306; Sutton, *Essentials of Vedic Astrology*, pp. 265–76.

10 See ibid., pp. 212–16.

15 Lunar Mansions

1 *Hymns of the Atharda Veda*, trans. M. Bloomfield (New Delhi: Molital Banarsiduss, 1997), 19:7 and 8.
2 See Rupert Gleadow, *The Origin of the Zodiac* (London: Jonathan Cape, 1968), p. 144.
3 See Komilla Sutton, *The Essentials of Vedic Astrology* (Bournemouth: The Wessex Astrologer, 1999), pp. 228–9.
4 See Valerie J. Roebuck, *The Circle of the Stars: An Introduction to Indian Astrology* (Shaftesbury: Element, 1992), p. 94.
5 See Hart Defouw and Robert Svoboda, *Light on Life: An Introduction to the Astrology of India* (London: Arkana, 1996), pp. 204–246; Sutton, *The Essentials of Vedic Astrology*, pp. 168–209; Roebuck, *The Circle of the Stars*, pp. 90–121.

16 Yogastrology

1 Varahamihira, *Brihat Samhita*, trans. H. Kern (1913), ch. 2:3.

18 By the Waters of Babylon

1 See W. B. Emery, *Archaic Egypt* (Harmondsworth: Penguin, 1987), p. 192; E. A. Wallis Budge, *From Fetish to God in Ancient Egypt* (Oxford: Oxford University Press, 1934), p. 155.
2 Michael Baigent, *From the Omens of Babylon: Astrology and Ancient Mesopotamia* (London: Arkana, 1994), p. 27.
3 *The Epic of Gilgamesh*, trans. N. K. Sanders (Harmondsworth: Penguin, 1972), p. 111.
4 See Baigent, *From the Omens of Babylon*, p. 29.
5 E. Reiner, *The Venus Tablet of Ammisaduqa* (Malibu, 1975), p. 29.
6 Baigent, *From the Omens of Babylon*, p. 62.
7 *The Epic of Gilgamesh*, p. 80.
8 Ibid., p. 25.
9 Ibid., p. 26.
10 See Baigent, *From the Omens of Babylon*, pp. 160–1.
11 Austen Henry Layard, *Discoveries in the Ruins of Nineveh and Babylon* (London: John Murray, 1853), pp. 196–8.
12 Robert Temple, *The Crystal Sun: Rediscovering a Lost Technology of the Ancient World* (London: Century, 2000), p. 31, see also pp. 7–24.
13 See ibid., pp. 17–18.
14 See Nicholas Campion, *An Introduction to the History of Astrology* (London: Faculty of Astrological Studies, 1989), p. 11.

15 See Tamsyn Barton, *Ancient Astrology* (London: Routledge, 1994), p. 14; Gleadow, *The Origin of the Zodiac* (London: Jonathan Cape, 1968), pp. 163–74.

16 See B. L. Van der Waerden, 'History of the Zodiac', *Archiv für Orientforschung*, vol. 16, p. 219.

17 In Baigent, *From the Omens of Babylon*, pp. 51, 52.

18 See B. L. Van der Waerden, *Science Awakening II: The Birth of Astronomy* (Leiden, 1974), pp. 103–8.

19 Ibid., p. 126. Gleadow gives a date of 419 BC, *Origin of the Zodiac*, p. 163.

20 Campion, *Introduction to the History of Astrology*, p. 12.

21 A. Sachs, 'Babylonian Horoscopes', *Journal of Cuneiform Studies*, vol. 6 (1952), pp. 54–7.

22 Ibid.

23 See A. Sachs and H. Hunger, *Astronomical Diaries and Related Texts from Babylonia*, 2 vols. (Vienna,1988–9).

24 Sachs, 'Babylonian Horoscopes', p. 69.

25 See O. Neugebauer and H. B. Van Hoeson, *Greek Horoscopes* (Philadelphia, 1959), p. 17.

19 Let There Be Light

1 See J. C. Cooper, *An Illustrated Encyclopaedia of Traditional Symbols* (London: Thames & Hudson, 1999), p. 198.

2 Michael Baigent, *From the Omens of Babylon: Astrology and Ancient Mesopotamia* (London: Arkana, 1994), p. 99.

3 R. Thompson, *The Reports of the Magicians and Astrologers of Nineveh and Babylon in the British Museum*, 2 vols. (London: Luzac, 1900), vol. 2, 119, p. lvi.

4 Baigent, *From the Omens of Babylon*, p. 108.

5 Diodorus Sicilus, *Diodorus of Sicily*, trans. C. H. Oldfather *et al.*, 9 vols. (London, 1933), vol. 2, p. 30.

6 Baigent, *From the Omens of Babylon*, p. 114.

7 Ibid., p. 117.

8 Ibid., p. 119.

9 Herodotus, *The Histories*, trans. Robin Waterfield (Oxford: Oxford University Press, 1998), pp. 87–8.

10 S. Parpola, *Letters from Assyrian Scholars to the Kings Esarhaddon and Assurbanipal*, 2 parts, (Neukirchen-Vluyn, 1983) part 2, p. 11.

11 Thompson, *Reports of the Magicians*, vol. 2, 243B, p. lxxvi.

12 Sicilas, *Diodorus of Sicily*, vol. 2, p. 30.

13 See Baigent, *From the Omens of Babylon*, pp. 129–30.

14 Thompson, *The Reports of the Magicians and Astrologers*, vol. 2, 100, p. Ixiii.
15 Ibid., vol. 2, 103, p. liv; 272, p. Ixxxviii.
16 A. Livingstone, *Mystical and Mythological Explanatory Works of Assyrian and Babylonian Scholars* (Oxford: Oxford University Press, 1986) p. 123, line 8.
17 Thompson, *The Reports of the Magicians*, vol. 2, 186, p. Ixvi.
18 Ibid., vol. 2, 218, p. Ixxi; 221, p. Ixxii.
19 H. C. Rawlinson, 'On the Birs Nimrud, or the Great Temple of Borsippa', *Journal of the Royal Asiatic Society* (1861), vol. 18, p. 17.

20 The Image of Heaven

1 E. A. Wallis Budge, *The Book of the Dead* (1899) (London: Arkana, 1986), p. xxi.
2 See Plato, *Timaeus*, trans. H. D. P. Lee (Harmondsworth: Penguin, 1965), p. 37.
3 See John Anthony West, *Serpent in the Sky: The High Wisdom of Ancient Egypt* (Wheaton, Ill.: Quest Books, 1993), p. 104.
4 In John Anthony West, *The Traveller's Key to Ancient Egypt: A Guide to the Sacred Places of Ancient Egypt* (London: Harrap Columbus, 1987), p. 157.
5 Alexandre Piankoff, *The Pyramid of Unas,* in vol. 5 of *Egyptian Religious Texts and Representations* (New York: Bollingen Foundation, 1964), Utterance 219, Spells 192–3, p. 68.
6 R. O. Faulkener, 'The King and the Star Religion in the Pyramid Texts', *Journal of Near Eastern Studies*, vol. 25, No. 3 (July 1966), p. 154.
7 Alexandre Piankoff, *Pyramid of Unas,* Utterance 214, Spell 138, p. 60.
8 Alexandre Moret, *Mystères Égyptiens* in Wm. R. Fix, *Star Maps* (London: Octopus, 1979), p. 98.
9 Herodotus, *The Histories*, trans. Robin Waterfield (Oxford: Oxford University Press, 1998), p. 109.
10 *The Ancient Egyptian Pyramid Texts*, trans. R. O. Faulkener (Warminster: Aris & Phillips, 1969), Utterance 467, p. 156.
11 Ibid., Utterance 419, p. 138.
12 See Robert Bauval and Adrian Gilbert, *The Orion Mystery* (London: Heinemann, 1994).
13 See Graham Hancock and Santha Faiia, *Heaven's Mirror: Quest for the Lost Civilization* (London: Michael Joseph, 1998), p. 94.
14 See Richard A. Proctor, *The Great Pyramid: Observatory, Tomb and Temple* (London, 1883) and West, *The Traveller's Key to Ancient Egypt*, pp. 91–2.
15 In Rupert Gleadow, *The Origin of the Zodiac* (London: Jonathan Cape, 1968), p. 204.

16 See West, *The Traveller's Key to Ancient Egypt*, pp. 95–7.

17 See Fix, *Star Maps*, p. 32.

18 Giorgio de Santillana and Hartha von Dechend, *Hamlet's Mill: an Essay on Myth and the Frame of Time* (Boston: David R. Godine, 1977), pp. 245–6.

19 Sir Norman Lockyer, *The Dawn of Astronomy* (London: Macmillan, 1894), p. 100.

20 Ibid. (Boston, Mass.: MIT Press, 1973), p. 119.

21 See Robert Temple, *The Crystal Sun: Rediscovering the Lost Technology of the Ancient World* (London: Century, 2000), pp. 213, 443.

22 See Ibid., pp. 348, 364, 440–2.

23 See Alan W. Shorter, *The Egyptian Gods* (London: Kegan Paul, Trench, Trubner & Co., 1937), pp. 9–10.

21 The Return of the Phoenix

1 Robert A. Armour, *Gods and Myths of Ancient Egypt*, (Cairo: The American University in Cairo Press, 1986), pp. 154–5.

2 *The Book of the Dead*, trans. E. A. Wallis Budge, (London: Arkana, 1986), p. 622.

3 R. O. Faulkner, ed.,*The Ancient Egyptian Coffin Texts*, (Warminster: Aris & Phillips, 1994), vol. I, pp. 179–80.

4 *Pyramid Texts* in R. T. Rundle, *Myth and Symbol in Ancient Egypt* (London: Thames & Hudson, 1993), p. 58.

5 See S. R. K. Glanville, *The Legacy of Egypt* (Oxford: Clarendon Press, 1942), pp. 161–2.

6 Diodorus of Sicily, in Christian Jacq, *Egyptian Magic,* trans. Janet M. Davis (Warminster: Aris & Phillips, 1985), p. 34.

7 Rupert Gleadow, *The Origin of the Zodiac* (London: Jonathan Cape, 1968) p. 171.

8 I. E. S. Edwards, *The Pyramids of Egypt* (London: Penguin, 1993), p. 286.

9 See John Anthony West, *Serpent in the Sky: The High Wisdom of Ancient Egypt* (Wheaton, Il.: Quest, 1993), p. 95. Gleadow, *The Origin of the Zodiac*, pp. 177–78, opts for the date 2780 BC.

10 In Gleadow, *The Origin of the Zodiac*, p. 179.

11 Robert Eisler, *The Royal Art of Astrology* (London: Herbert Joseph, 1946), p. 80.

12 Gleadow, *The Origin of the Zodiac*, p. 185.

13 Tamsyn Barton, *Ancient Astrology* (London: Routledge, 1974), p. 28.

14 See Athanasius Kircher, *Oedipus Aegyptiacus* (Rome, 1653), vol. 2, part 2, pp. 182–6.

15 Jacq, *Egyptian Magic*, p. 34.

22 The Horoscope of Eternity

1 See Rupert Gleadow *The Origin of the Zodiac* (London: Jonathan Cape, 1968), pp. 188–9. For the map, see opp. p. 192.

2 Ibid., p. 188.

3 In West, *The Traveller's Key to Ancient Egypt*, p. 393.

4 J. Norman Lockyer, *The Dawn of Astronomy* (1894) (Boston, Mass.: MIT Press, 1973), p. 176.

5 See John Anthony West, *Serpent in the Sky: The High Wisdom of Ancient Egypt* (Wheaton Il.: Quest, 1993), pp. 101–2.

6 See Alexander Gurshtein writing in *Scientific American* (May 1997), reported in the *Sunday Telegraph* (London, 25 May 1997). See also Graham Hancock and Santha Faiia, *Heaven's Mirror: Quest for the Lost Civilization* (London: Michael Joseph, 1998), pp. 29–30.

7 See Gleadow, *The Origin of the Zodiac*, p. 209.

8 See S. R. K. Glanville, ed., *The Legacy of Egypt* (Oxford: Clarendon, 1942), p. 162; Geraldine Pinch, *Magic in Ancient Egypt* (London: British Museum Press, 1994), p. 167.

9 See West, *Serpent in the Sky*, pp. 99–100.

10 See Gleadow, *The Origin of the Zodiac*, pp. 192, 197, 204.

11 See R. A. Schwaller de Lubicz, *The Temple in Man: Ancient Egypt in Architecture and the Perfect Man* (1949), trans. Deborah and Robert Lawlaw (Rochester, Vt.: Inner Traditions International, 1988) p. 110.

12 E. A. E. Reymond, *The Mythical Origin of the Egyptian Temple* (Manchester: Manchester University Press, 1969), p. 110.

13 In R. A. Schwaller de Lubicz, *Sacred Science: The King of Pharaonic Theocracy*, trans. A. and G. VandenBroeck (Rochester, Vt.: Inner Traditions International, 1988), Appendix V, pp. 277–8.

14 Ibid., p. 159.

15 See Hancock and Faiia, *Heaven's Mirror*, p. 67.

16 E. A. E. Reymond, *The Mythical Origin of the Egyptian Temple* (Manchester: Manchester University Press, 1969), p. 77.

17 In Robert Bauval and Graham Hancock, *Keeper of Genesis: A Quest for the Hidden Legacy of Mankind* (London: Heinemann, 1996), p. 197.

18 See ibid., p. 201.

19 See Nicholas Campion, *An Introduction to the History of Astrology* (London: n.d.), p. 26.

20 Gleadow, *The Origin of the Zodiac*, p. 209.

21 See Geraldine Pinch, *Magic in Ancient Egypt* (London: British Museum Press, 1994), p. 167.

22 Campion, *Introduction to the History of Astrology*, p. 26.

23 Herodotus, *The Histories*, trans. Robin Waterfield (Oxford: Oxford University Press, 1998), p. 126.

23 The Harmony of the Spheres

1 Franz Cumont, *Astrology and Religion among the Greeks and Romans* (New York: Dover, 1912), p. 53.

2 See Jack Lindsay, *The Origins of Astrology* (London: Muller, 1971), p. 91.

3 Rupert Gleadow, *The Origin of the Zodiac* (London: Jonathan Cape, 1968), p. 209. See also Robin Waterfield, 'The Evidence for Astrology in Classical Greece', *Culture and Cosmos*, vol. 3, no. 2 (1999), pp. 3–15.

4 See M. R. Wright, *Cosmology in Antiquity* (London and New York: Routledge, 1995), p. 122.

5 See Waterfield, 'The Evidence for Astrology in Classical Greece', p. 3.

6 Hesiod, *Works and Days*, in J. B. Pritchard, ed., *Ancient Near Eastern Texts* (Princeton, NJ.: Princeton University Press, 1955), pp. 564–7.

7 Hesiod, *Works and Days*, trans. Samuel Butler (London, 1923), p. 20.

8 O. Neugebauer, *The Exact Sciences in Antiquity* (New York: Dover, 1957), p. 170; S. J. Tester, *A History of Western Astrology* (London: Boydell Press, 1987), p. 12.

9 Pritchard, ed., *Ancient Near Eastern Texts,* p. 23–6.

10 Nicholas Campion, *An Introduction to the History of Astrology* (London: n.d.), p. 17.

11 See Waterfield, 'The Evidence for Astrology in Classical Greece', pp. 5, 9.

12 Plutarch, *Alcibiades*, in ibid., p. 10.

13 In Wright, *Cosmology in Antiquity,* p. 53.

24 The Moving Image of Eternity

1 Diogenes Laertius, *Lives of Eminent Philosophers* , trans. R. D. Hicks, 2 vols. (London, 1925), vol. 1, p. 175.

2 In Michael Baigent, *From the Omens of Babylon: Astrology and Ancient Mesopotamia* (London: Arkana, 1994), p. 177.

3 Plato, *Timaeus*, trans. H. D. P. Lee (Harmondsworth: Penguin, 1965), p. 34.

4 Nicholas Campion, *An Introduction to the History of Astrology* (London: n.d.), p. 20.

5 Plato, *Timaeus*, pp. 44, 45.

6 Ibid., p. 53.

7 Ibid., p. 50.

8 Ibid., p. 54.

9 Plato, *The Statesman* 269c4–d2, in M. R. Wright, *Cosmology in Antiquity* (London and New York: Routledge, 1995), pp. 140–1.

10 Plato, *Timaeus*, pp. 57–8.

11 Plato, *Timaeus*, (40c–d), trans. Robin Waterfield. Waterfield makes a strong case for the mistaken addition of a 'not' in 'those who are *not* capable of

calculation' in the translation of Lee (used elsewhere) and others, which completely changes the meaning. See Robin Waterfield, 'The Evidence of Astrology in Classical Greece', *Culture and Cosmos*, vol. 3, no. 2 (1999), pp. 7–8.

12 Plato, *The Republic*, trans. Desmond Lee, 2nd edn. (Harmondsworth: Penguin, 1981), p. 450.
13 Ibid., p. 451.
14 Ibid., pp. 451–2.
15 Ibid., p. 452.
16 See ibid., pp. 360–1. See also Waterfield, 'The Evidence for Astrology in Classical Greece', p. 9; James Adams, *The Nuptial Number of Plato* (1891) (Wellingborough: Thorsons, 1985).
17 Plato, *Phaedrus*, trans. Walter Hamilton (London: Penguin, 1973), p. 31.
18 Ibid, p. 33.
19 Plato, *The Republic*, p. 453.
20 In Wright, *Cosmology in Antiquity*, p. 129.
21 Aristotle, *De Caelo*, trans. Guthrie, Loeb edition, vol. 2, p. 9.

25 The Hellenistic World

1 Nicholas Campion, *An Introduction to the History of Astrology* (London: n.d.), p. 23.
2 Cicero, *De Divinatione* in Michael Baigent, *From the Omens of Babylon: Astrology and Ancient Mesopotamia* (London: Arkana, 1994), p. 178.
3 See B. L. Van der Waerden, *Science Awakening II: The Birth of Astronomy* (Leyden: Brill, 1974), vol. 2, p. 81.
4 See Tamsyn Barton, *Ancient Astrology* (London: Routledge, 1994). p. 9.
5 Jim Tester, *A History of Western Astrology* (London: Boydell, 1987), pp. 15–16.
6 See Barton, *Ancient Astrology*, p. 25.
7 See ibid., p. 27.
8 *Stobaei Hermetica*, in Garth Fowden, *The Egyptian Hermes: A Historical Approach to the Late Pagan Mind* (Princeton, NJ.: Princeton University Press, 1993), p. 92.
9 Clement, *Stomata*, Book V, Ch. 4, in R. A. Schwaller de Lubicz, *Sacred Science: The King of Pharonic Theoracy*, trans. André and Goldian VandenBroech (Rochester: Inner Traditions International, 1985), p. 274.
10 Firmicus Maternus in ibid., pp. 158–9.
11 In *Hermetica*, trans. Brian P. Copenhaver (Cambridge: Cambridge University Press, 1995), p. xxxvii.
12 *Corpus Hermiticum*, ibid., pp. 14, 2.

13 Ibid., p. 52.
14 Ibid., p. 35.
15 Ibid., pp. 60–1.
16 *Asclepius*, ibid., p. 89.

26 The Poetry of the Stars

1 Pliny, *Natural History*, 35.199, in Tamsyn Barton, *Ancient Astrology* (London: Routledge, 1994), p. 34.
2 Cicero, *On Divination*, 1.130, in ibid., p. 36.
3 In M. R. Wright, *Cosmology in Antiquity* (London and New York: Routledge, 1995), p. 125.
4 Pliny, *Natural History*, 30.1.1–2
5 Suetonius, *Augustus*, 94.5, in Barton, *Ancient Astrology*, p. 40.
6 Juvenal, *The Sixth Satire,* in ibid., p. 173.
7 Manilius, *Astronomica*, trans. G.P. Goold (Cambridge, Mass.: Harvard University Press, 1997), p. 7.
8 Ibid., pp. 25–6.
9 Ibid. p. 223.
10 Ibid., pp. 26–7.
11 *Dorethei Sidonii Carmen Astrologicum*, ed. David Pingree (Leipzig, 1976), in Jim Tester, *A History of Western Astrology* (London: Boydell, 1987), p. 89.
12 Otto Neugebauer and H. B. Van Hoesen, *Greek Horoscopes* (Philadelphia, 1959), p. 80.
13 *Vettii Valentis Anthologiarum Libri,* ed. W. Kroll (Berlin, 1908), in Tester, *A History of Western Astrology*, p. 48.
14 In Eric Russell, *History of Astrology and Prediction* (London: New English Library, 1974), pp. 28–9.

27 The Ambient

1 Geoffrey Cornelius, *The Moment of Astrology* (London: Arkana, 1994), pp. 97–8.
2 Ptolemy, *Tetrabiblos*, trans. F. E. Robbins (Cambridge, Mass:. Harvard University Press, 1998), p. 3.
3 Ibid., pp. 3–4.
4 Ibid., p. 13.
5 Ibid., pp. 21, 23.
6 Ibid., pp. 135, 156–7.
7 Ibid., p. 221.
8 Ibid., p. 439.

 9 Ibid., p. 225.
10 Ibid., p. 345.
11 Ibid., p. 369.
12 Ibid., pp. 395, 397.
13 Ibid., pp. 426–7.
14 Ibid., p. 447.
15 Ibid., p. 449.
16 Paul Henry, 'The Place of Plotinus in the History of Thought', in Plotinus, *The Enneads*, trans. Stephen MacKenna, 3rd ed. (London: Faber & Faber, 1962), p. xxxv.
17 Porphyry in Plotinus, *The Enneads*, ibid., p. 2.
18 Plotinus, *The Enneads*, IV.8, p. 357.
19 Ibid., II.3.11, p. 99.
20 Ibid., I.6.9, pp. 63–4.
21 Ibid., II.3.5, p. 95.
22 Ibid., II.3.7, p. 96; IV.4.33, p. 316; II.3.95, p. 95.
23 Ibid., IV.4.33, p. 317.
24 Ibid., II.3.3, p. 93; II.3.7, p. 96.
25 Ibid., II,3.9, p. 97.

28 Myriogenesis

 1 Galen, *Prognostics from the [Time of the Patient's] taking to Bed*, in Tamsyn Barton, *Ancient Astrology* (London: Routledge, 1994), p. 185.
 2 *Papyri Graecae Magicae. Die griechischen Zauberpapyri*, ed. and trans. K. Preisendanz, 2 vols. (Leipzig,1928–31), 36.320–32.
 3 See ibid., 7.795–845.
 4 Ibid., 7.284–99.
 5 Ibid., 13.705–15.
 6 Porphyry, *The Cave of the Nymphs*, in Barton, *Ancient Astrology*, p. 198.
 7 In Garth Fowden, *The Egyptian Hermes: A Historical Approach to the Late Pagan Mind* (Princeton, N.J.: Princeton University Press, 1993), p. 92.
 8 In Barton, *Ancient Astrology*, p. 65.
 9 Julius Firmicus Maternus, *Mathesis: Ancient Astrology – Theory and Practice*, trans. Rhys Bram (New Jersey: Noyes, 1975), 2.30.
10 Ibid., 1.6.1–2.
11 Ibid., 4.22.2.
12 In Jim Tester, *A History of Western Astrology* (London: Boydell, 1987), p. 139.
13 Iamblichos, *Theurgia or The Egyptian Mysteries,* trans. Alexander Wilder (London: William Rider & Son, 1911), p. 269.
14 Ibid., pp. 266, 268.

15 In G. R. S. Mead, *Thrice Greatest Hermes*, 3 vols. (London: John M. Watkins, 1949), vol. 3, p. 298.

16 E. M. Forster, *Alexandria: A History and a Guide* (London: Michael Hagg, 1982), p. 56.

17 In Barton, *Ancient Astrology*, p. 72.

18 Ibid., p. 74.

19 Ibid., p. 77.

29 The Stargazers of the Middle East

1 In Peter Marshall, *The Philosopher's Stone: A Quest for the Secrets of Alchemy* (London: Macmillan, 2001), p. 216.

2 In Seyyed Hossein Nasr, *Science and Civilization in Islam*, 2nd ed. (Cambridge: Islamic Texts Society, 1987), p. 61.

3 See ibid., pp. 147–8.

4 In Jim Tester, *A History of Western Astrology* (London: Boydell, 1957), p. 159.

5 In Michel Gauquelin, *Dreams and Illusions of Astrology* (London: Glover & Blair, 1980), p. 43.

6 See Tester, *A History of Western Astrology*, p. 163.

7 See Frances Yates, *Giordano Bruno and the Hermetic Tradition* (London: Routledge, 2002). See also Vivian E. Robson, *The Fixed Stars and Constellations in Astrology* (1923) (Wellingborough: Aquarian, 1979), pp. 236–9.

8 Abu Ma'shar, *De Revolutionibus Nativitatum*, Bk. 5, in Tester, *A History of Western Astrology*, p. 171.

9 See Anistatia R. Miller and Jared M. Brown, *The Complete Astrological Handbook for the Twenty-first Century* (New York: Schocken, 1999), pp. 263–332.

10 Al-Biruni, *Elements of Astrology*, trans. by R. Ramsay (London: Wright, 1934) in Tester, *A History of Western Astrology*, pp. 157–8n.

11 In Marshall, *The Philosopher's Stone*, pp. 250–1.

12 In Eugenio Garin, *Astrology in the Renaissance: The Zodiac of Life* (London: Arkana, 1983), p. 49.

13 In Tamsyn Barton, *Ancient Astrology* (London: Routledge, 1994), p. 69.

14 See Rabbi Joel C. Dobin, *The Astrological Secrets of the Hebrew Sages: To Rule Both Day and Night* (Rochester, Vt.: Inner Traditions International, 1977).

15 Miller and Brown, *The Complete Astrological Handbook*, p. 334.

16 See Rabbi Joel C. Dobin, *The Astrological Secrets of the Hebrew Sages: To Rule Both Day and Night* (Rochester Vt.: Inner Traditions International, 1977), Ch .20.

17 Shabbath,153a, in Miller and Brown, *The Complete Astrological Handbook*, pp. 335–6.
18 Ibid., pp. 336–345.
19 Dobin, *The Astrological Secrets of the Hebrew Sages* in ibid., pp. 344–5.
20 See Warren Kenton (Zev ben Shimon Halevi), *The Anatomy of Fate: Kabbalistic Astrology* (London: Rider, 1978), pp. 31–33.
21 Ibid., p. 93.
22 Ibid., p. 192.

30 At the Beginning of Light

1 Jim Tester, *A History of Western Astrology* (London: Boydell, 1987), pp. 200, 129. See also T. O. Wedel, *The Medieval Attitude toward Astrology* (New Haven: Norwood,1920)
2 Macrobius, *Ambrosii Theodisi Macrobii Commentarii in Somnium Scipionis*, ed. James Willis (Leipzig, 1963).
3 Ibid., I.21, 23 ff.
4 Isodore, *Etymologiae*, III, 27. In Tester, *A History of Western Astrology* (London: Boydell, 1987), p. 125.
5 In Eric Russell, *The History of Astrology and Prediction* (London: New English Library, 1972), p. 43.
6 Augustine, *The City of God*, V. In Tester, *A History of Western Astrology* (London: Boydell, 1987), pp. 108–9.
7 Augustine, *Contra Faustum Manichaeum*, II, 5. In Tester, *A History of Western Astrology* (London: Boydell, 1987), p. 111.
8 Nicholas Campion, *An Introduction to the History of Astrology* (London, n.d.), p. 43.
9 Tertullian, *De Idolatria*, c.9. In Tester, *A History of Western Astrology* (London: Boydell, 1987), p. 112.
10 Guibert of Nogent, *Gesta Dei per Francos*, VIII.8. In Tester, *A History of Western Astrology* (London: Boydell, 1987), p. 143.
11 Hugh of St Victor, *De Eruditione Docta*, bk. II, ch.11. In Tester, *A History of Western Astrology* (London: Boydell, 1987), p. 143.
12 See M. M. Scarr, *The Dial: Its Background, History and Use* (Cambridge: Queen's College, n.d.).
13 In Tester, *A History of Western Astrology*, p. 177.
14 Ibid, p. 178.
15 Robert Grosseteste, *De Artibus Liberalibus*, ibid., p. 179.
16 *The 'Opus Maius' of Roger Bacon*, ed. J. H. Bridges (London, 1900), Part IV.
17 Thomas Aquinas, *Summa Theologia*, Ia.q.115, a.4. In Tester, *A History of Western Astrology* (London: Boydell, 1987), p. 181.

18 In Tester, *A History of Western Astrology*, p. 186.

19 In Philip Ziegler, *The Black Death* (London: Pelican, 1970), p. 38.

20 In Louis MacNeice, *Astrology* (London: Aldus, 1964), p. 278. See also G. W. Coopland, *Nicole Oresme and the Astrologers* (Liverpool: Liverpool University Press, 1952).

21 In Tester, *A History of Western Astrology*, p. 198.

31 Rebirth

1 In Louis MacNeice, *Astrology* (London: Aldus, 1964), p. 272.

2 Marsilio Ficino, *Liber de Vita* (1489), Bk. III, Ch. 1. See also Thomas More, *The Planets Within: The Astrological Psychology of Marsilio Ficino* (New York: Lindisfarne, 1990).

3 Ficino, *Liber de Vita*, dedication to Lorenzo de' Medici.

4 In Eugenio Garin, *Astrology in the Renaissance: The Zodiac of Life,* trans. Carolyn Jackson and June Allen (London: Arkana, 1990), p. 63.

5 Ficino, *Theologica Platonica,* X 2, ed. R. Marcel (Paris: Les Belles Lettres, 1964), vol. 2, pp. 208–9.

6 Ficino, *De Vita Coelitus Comparanda* (1489).

7 Ficino, *Liber de Vita,* III, 19.

8 *The Letters of Marsilio Ficino,* trans. London Language Department of the School of Economic Science (London: Shepheard-Walwyn, 1978).

9 Giovanni Pico della Mirandola, *Disputationes Adversus Astrologiam Divinatricem,* ed. E. Garin (Florence: Vallecchi, 1946), p. 19.

10 Ibid., vol. p. 10.

11 *Apologia,* in Garin, *Astrology in the Renaissance*, p. 91.

12 Girolamo Cardano, *De Libris Propriis* (1562); *Encomium Astrologiae* in *The Occult in Early Modern Europe: A Documentary History*, ed. and trans. P. G. Maxwell-Stuart (London: Macmillan, 1999), pp. 68, 83.

13 Tommaso Campanella in ibid., p. 113.

14 Campanella, *The Six Books of Astrology of Campanella* (Lyons, 1629) bk. 1, ch. 2, art. 1, 3; Jim Tester, *A History of Western Astrology* (London: Boydell, 1987), p. 214.

15 Campanella, *Astrologicorum Libri VII* (1630), bk.1, ch. 2, art. 3, in *The Occult in Early Modern Europe*, p. 92.

16 Ibid., p. 106.

17 Paracelsus, *Paragranum* (c.1530–4) in Peter Marshall, *The Philosopher's Stone: A Quest for the Secrets of Alchemy* (London; Macmillan, 2001), p. 352.

18 Cardano, *De Exemplis Centum Geniturarum Liber* (1547) in *The Occult in Early Modern Europe*, p. 87.

19 Melanchthon, *Initia Doctrinae Physicae* (1549), ibid., p. 94.

20 Jean Calvin, *Avertissement contre l'astrologie judiciaire* (1549), in ibid., p. 74.
21 *John Dee on Astronomy: Propaedeumata aphoristica* (1558–1568), in Latin and English, ed. and trans. Wayne Shumaker (Los Angeles, 1978), Aphorism XXI.
22 Nostradamus in Bill Anderton, *Prophecies for the Millennium* (London: Parragon, 1999), Century I, verse 44.
23 Ibid., verse 16.
24 Ibid., verse 89.
25 Ibid., verse 48.
26 Ibid., p. 30.

32 The New Astronomy

1 Galileo Galilei to Monsignor Pietro Dini (23 March 1615), in Eugenio Garin, *Astrology in the Renaissance: The Zodiac of Life,* trans. Carolyn Jackson and June Allen (London: Arkana, 1990), p. 10.
2 Copernicus, *On the Revolutions of the Heavenly Spheres* (Nuremberg, 1543), Bk. I, Ch. 1.
3 Tycho Brahe, *De Disciplinis Mathematicis Oratio* (1574) in *The Occult in Modern Europe: A Documentary History,* ed. and trans. P. G. Maxwell-Stuart (London: Macmillan, 1999), pp. 84–5.
4 Johannes Kepler, *De stella Nova in Pede Serpentarii* (1606), in Garin, *Astrology in the Renaissance,* p. 9.
5 In Eric Russell, *The History of Astrology and Prediction* (London; New English Library, 1972), p. 60. See also John Anthony West, *The Case for Astrology* (New York: Viking Arkana, 1991), p. 105.
6 Kepler, *De Stella Nova,* cap. 28; ibid., pp. 105–6.
7 John Maynard Keynes, 'Newton the Man', *Royal Society: Newton Tercentenary Celebrations* (Cambridge: Cambridge University Press, 1947), 27–34. See also Peter Marshall, 'The Ultimate Magus' in *The Philosopher's Stone: A Quest for the Secrets of Alchemy* (London: Macmillan, 2001), pp. 398–409.
8 In Brewster, *Memoirs of the life . . . of Isaac Newton,* vol. 2, p. 408.

33 The New Astrology

1 Jean-Baptiste Morin, *Astrologia Gallica* (Hagae-Comitis, 1661), p. 161, in Jim Tester, *A History of Western Astrology* (London: Boydell, 1987), p. 235.
2 Nicholas Culpeper, *The English Physician Enlarged* (1653) in Louis MacNeice, *Astrology,* (London: Aldus, 1964), p. 282.
3 In Jane Ridder-Patrick, *A Handbook of Medical Astrology* (London: Arkana, 1989), p. 139–140. See also Graeme Tobyn, *Culpeper's Medicine* (London: Element Books, 1996).

4 Jerome Cardan, *The Seven Segments* (London, 1676), trans. William Lilly, in MacNeice, *Astrology*, p. 274.

5 William Lilly, *Introduction to Astrology* (1647) ed. Zadkiel (with his own *Grammar of Astrology*) (London: G. Bell & Sons, 1939), p. 11.

6 Ibid., p. 342.

7 Zadkiel, 'Life of William Lilly', ibid., p. 7.

8 In Derek Parker, *Familiar to All: William Lilly and Seventeenth-Century Astrology* (London: Jonathan Cape, 1975), p. 227.

9 Elias Ashmole, *Theatrum Chemicum Britannicum* (London, 1652).

10 Jim Tester, *A History of Western Astrology* (London: Boydell, 1987), p. 240.

11 Isaac Bickerstaff (i.e. Jonathan Swift), *Predictions for the Year 1708* (London, 1708).

12 See Nicholas Campion, *An Introduction to the History of Astrology* (London: n.d.), p. 60.

34 The Psychology of Antiquity

1 Zadkiel, *Grammar of Astrology* (1853), published with William Lilly's *Introduction to Astrology* (1647) (London: G. Bell & Sons, 1939), pp. v, 351.

2 Madame Blavatsky, *The Secret Doctrine* (New York, 1888) 3rd edition, vol. 3, p. 337.

3 Ibid., vol. 3, p. 115, vol. 1, p. 180.

4 Ibid., in John Anthony West, *The Case for Astrology* (New York: Viking Arcana, 1991), p. 125.

5 Blavatsky, *The Secret Doctrine*, vol. 3, p. 339.

6 In Louis MacNeice, *Astrology*, (London: Aldus, 1964), p. 21.

7 Alan Leo, *Astrology for All*, 9th edition (Edinburgh: International Publishing, n.d.), pp. vii–ix.

8 Ibid., prelims.

9 Leo, *Practical Astrology*, 2nd edition (London: William Reeves, 1910), pp. ix–xi.

10 Ibid., p. 220.

11 Alice A. Bailey, *Esoteric Astrology* (London: Lucis Press, 1951), p. 5.

12 Ibid., p. 12.

13 Ibid., p. 35.

14 Bailey, *A Treatise on Cosmic Fire*, given in an appendix to her *Esoteric Astrology*, p. 658.

15 Ibid., p. 581.

16 Ibid., pp. 20–1.

17 See Howe, Ellic, *Urania's Children* (London: William Kimber, 1967) and Neil Spencer, *True as the Stars Above: Adventures in Modern Astrology* (London: Victor Gollancz, 2000), ch.13.

18 Carl Jung, *Collected Works of C. G. Jung* (Princeton, N.J.: Princeton University Press, 1964), vol. 10.

19 Carl Jung, 'In Memory of Richard Wilhelm', *The Secret of the Golden Flower*, trans. into German, Richard Wilhelm, into English, C. F. Baynes (London: Kegan Paul, Trench, Trubner, 1947), p. 143.

20 Ibid.

21 Jung, Foreword (1949), *I Ching,* trans. Cary F. Baynes (London: Arkana,1989), pp. xxiii–xiv.

22 Carl Jung, 'Synchronicity: An Acausal Connecting Principle' (1950) in *The Structure and Dynamics of the Psyche, Collected Works,* trans. R. F. C. Hull (Princeton, NJ.: Princeton University Press, 1960), vol. 8. See also M. L. von Franz, 'The Process of Individuation', *Man and his Symbols*, ed. Carl Jung (1964) (London: Picador, 1978), pp. 226–7.

23 In MacNeice, *Astrology*, pp. 222–3.

24 Carl Jung, *Interpretation of Nature and the Psyche,* written with W. Pauli (Princeton N.J.: Princeton University Press, 1955).

25 See Geoffrey Cornelius, Maggie Hyde and Chris Webster, *Astrology for Beginners* (London: Icon Books, 1995), pp. 158–9.

26 See Maggie Hyde, *Jung and Astrology* (Wellingborough: Aquarian, 1992), p. 193.

27 Dane Rhudyar, *The Astrology of Personality* (New York: Lucis Press, 1936).

28 Dane Rhudyar, *The Practice of Astrology: As a Technique in Human Understanding* (1968) (Baltimore, Maryland: Penguin, 1970), p. 9.

29 See Geoffrey Cornelius, *The Moment of Astrology: Origins in Divination* (London: Arkana, 1994), p. 103.

30 Dane Rhudyar, *The Astrology of Transformation: A Multilevel Approach* (Wheaton, IL: Quest, 1980), p. 99.

31 Ibid., pp. 198, 199. See also Rhudyar, *Beyond Individualism: The Psychology of Transformation* (Wheaton, IL: Quest Books, 1979).

32 Alan Oken, *As Above, So Below: A Primary Guide to Astrological Awareness* (New York: Bantam, 1973), p. 11.

33 Alan Oken, *The Horoscope, the Road and its Travelers* (New York: Bantam, 1974), p. 7.

34 P. D. Ouspensky, *In Search of the Miraculous* (London, 1950), pp. 366–7.

35 Science or Superstition?

1 Bart J. Bok and Lawrence C. Jerome, *Objections to Astrology* (London: n.d.), pp. 9–10. See also John Anthony West, *The Case for Astrology* (New York: Viking Arkana, 1991), pp. 177–8.

2 Paul Feyeraband, *Science in a Free Society* (New York: Schocken, 1978).

3 In West, *The Case for Astrology*, pp. 142–3.

4 Patrick Moore, *Naked Eye Astronomy* (London: Lutterworth, 1966), p. 2.

5 Franz Cumont, *Astrology and Religion among the Greeks and Romans*, (New York: Dover, 1912), p. 30.

6 Ellsworth Huntington, *Mainsprings of Civilization* (London: J. Wiley,1945).

7 See John Gribbin and Steven H. Plagemann, *The Jupiter Effect* (London: Macmillan, 1974).

8 In Michel Gauquelin, *Astrology and Science* (1966), trans. James Hughes (London: Peter Davies, 1970), p. 224.

9 In H. J. Eysenck and D. K. B. Nias, *Astrology: Science or Superstition?* (Harmondsworth: Penguin, 1982), p. 163.

10 See Gauquelin, *Astrology and Science*, pp. 192–3.

11 *Science* (4 December 1959); see also West, *The Case for Astrology*, pp. 329–30.

12 See Lily Kolisko, *The Moon and Plant Growth* (London: Anthroposophical Foundation, 1936)

13 In Eysenck and Nias, *Astrology*, p. 176.

14 Ibid., p. 180.

15 See Gauquelin, *Astrology and Science*, pp. 216–8, 238–40.

16 In Gauquelin, *Dreams and Illusions of Astrology* (1969) (London: Glover & Blair, 1980), p. 172.

17 Reply of Percy Seymour to Nigel Henbest's review of his work in the *New Scientist* (12 May 1988) in West, *The Case for Astrology*, pp. 383–4. See also Percey Seymour, *Astrology: The Evidence of Science* (London: Lennard, 1988), pp. 116–18.

18 Gauquelin, *Astrology and Science*, p. 165.

19 See Geoffrey Cornelius, Maggie Hyde and Chris Webster, *Astrology for Beginners*, (Cambridge: Icon,1995), p. 153.

20 Gauquelin, *Astrology and Science*, p. 208.

21 Gauquelin, *Dreams and Illusions*, p180.

22 See Eysenck and Nias, *Astrology*, p. 208.

23 West, *The Case for Astrology*, p. 312.

24 Eysenck and Nias, *Astrology*, p. 208.

25 See ibid., p. 166.

26 *Evening Standard* (London, 2 March 1977).

27 Eysenck and Nias, *Astrology*, p. 209.

28 A. N. Whitehead, *Adventure of Ideas* (Cambridge: Cambridge University Press, 1933), p. 198.

29 David Bohm, *Wholeness and Implicit Order* (London: Routledge & Kegan Paul, 1980).

36 Unresolved Issues

1 John M. Addey, *Address to the Astrological Association of Great Britain* (1959), in John Anthony West, *The Case for Astrology* (New York: Viking Arkana, 1991), p. 227.

2 See J. C. Cooper, *An Illustrated Encyclopaedia of Traditional Symbols* (London: Thames & Hudson, 1999), p. 198.

3 See Eve Jackson, *Astrology: A Psychological Approach* (London: Dryad Press, 1987), pp. 120–22; Melanie Rheinhart, *Chiron and the Healing Journey* (London: Arkana, 1989).

4 In West, *The Case for Astrology*, p. 474.

5 Liz Greene, *The Astrology of Fate* (London: Unwin, 1986), p. 8.

6 Margaret Hone, *The Modern Textbook of Astrology* (London: Fowler, 1951), p. 7.

7 Jeff Mayo and Christine Ramsdale, *Astrology* (London: Teach Yourself Books, 1996) p. 4.

38 The Age of Aquarius

1 See A. Bouché-Leclerq, *L'astrologie grecque* (Paris: Le Roux, 1899), vol. 2.

2 R. B. Culver and P. A. Ianna, *The Gemini Syndrome: A Scientific Evaluation of Astrology* (Buffalo, N.Y.: Prometheus, 1984), p. v.

3 See Georgio de Santillana and Hertha von Dechend, *Hamlet's Mill: An Essay on Myth and the Frame of Time* (1969) (Boston: Nopareil, 1998), p. 74.

4 *Emerald Tablet* in Peter Marshall, *The Philosopher's Stone: A Quest for the Secrets of Alchemy* (London: Macmillan, 2001). p. 250.

Select Bibliography

Astronomy

Dunlop, Storm, *Night Sky* (London: HarperCollins, 1999)

Hodson, F. R., ed., *The Place of Astronomy in the Ancient World* (Oxford: Oxford University Press, 1974)

Koestler, Arthur, *The Sleepwalkers: A History of Man's Changing Vision of the Universe* (1959) (Harmondsworth: Pelican, 1982)

Krupp, E. C., ed., *In Search of Ancient Astronomie* (London: Chatto & Windus, 1980)

Lockyer, J. Norman, *The Dawn of Astronomy* (1894) (Boston, Mass.: MIT Press, 1973)

Moore, Patrick, *Naked Eye Astronomy* (London: Lutterworth, 1966)

Staal, Julius, *Patterns in the Sky* (London: Hodder & Stoughton, 1961)

Temple, Robert, *The Crystal Sun: Rediscovering a Lost Technology of the Ancient World* (London: Century, 2000)

Toulmin, S., and Goodfield, J., *The Fabric of Heavens: The Development of Astronomy and Dynamics* (New York: Harper Row, 1965)

Van der Waerden, B. L., *Science Awakening II: The Birth of Astronomy* (Leiden: Brill, 1974)

Whipple, Fred. L., *Earth, Moon and Planets*, 3rd edn (Harmondsworth: Pelican, 1971)

Astrology: history and general

Allen, Richard Hinckley, *Star Names: Their Lore and Meaning* (New York: Dover, 1963)

Anderton, Bill, *Prophecies for the Millennium* (London: Parragon, 1999)

Baigent, Michael, Campion, Nicholas and Harvey, Charles, *Mundane Astrology* (London: Thorsons, 1995)

Barbault, Arnauld, *Défense et illustration d'astrologie* (Paris, 1955)

Bok, Bart. J. and Jerome, Lawrence E., *Objections to Astrology* (New York: Prometheus, 1976)

Campion, Nicholas, *An Introduction to the History of Astrology* (London: n.d)
   *The Great Year: Astrology, Millenarianism and History in the Western
   Tradition* (London: Arkana, 1994)
   and Eddy, Steve, *The New Astrology: The Art and Science of the Stars*
   (London: Bloomsbury, 1999)
Cooper, J. C., *An Illustrated Encyclopaedia of Traditional Symbols* (London:
   Thames & Hudson, 1999)
Coopland, G.W., *Nicole Oresme and the Astrologers* (Liverpool: Liverpool
   University Press, 1952)
Cornelius, Geoffrey, *The Moment of Astrology: Origins in Divination* (London:
   Arkana,1994)
   and Devereux, Paul, *The Secret Language of the Stars and Planets: A Visual
   Key to Celestial Mysteries* (London: Pavilion, 1996)
Crow, W. B., *A History of Magic, Witchcraft and Occultism* (London: Abacus,
   1972)
Culpeper, Nicholas, *The English Physician Enlarged* (London, 1653)
Culver, R. B. and Ianna, P. A., *The Gemini Syndrome: A Scientific Evaluation of
   Astrology* (Buffalo, N.Y.: Prometheus, 1984)
Curry, Patrick, *Prophecy and Power: Astrology in Early Modern England*
   (London: Polity, 1989)
Davidson, Ronald C., *Astrology* (London: Mayflower, 1963)
de Santillana, Giorgio and von Dechend, Hertha, *Hamlet's Mill: An Essay on
   Myth and the Frame of Time* (1969) (Boston: Nonpareil, 1998)
Eisler, Robert, *The Royal Art of Astrology* (London: Herbert Joseph, 1946)
Eysenck, H. J., and Nias, D. K. B., *Astrology: Science or Superstition?*
   (Harmondsworth: Pelican, 1984)
Feyerabend, P., *Science in a Free Society* (New York: Schocken, 1978)
Fix, Wm R., *Star Maps* (London: Octopus, 1979)
Garin, Eugenio, *Astrology in the Renaissance: The Zodiac of Life,* trans. Carolyn
   Jackson and June Allen (London: Arkana, 1990)
Gauquelin, Michel, *Astrology and Science* (1966), trans. James Hughes (London:
   Peter Davies, 1970)
   Cosmic Influences upon Human Behaviour (London: Garnstone, 1974)
   Dreams and Illusions of Astrology (1969) (London: Glover & Blair, 1980)
   Written in the Stars: The Best of Michel Gauquelin (Wellingborough:
   Aquarian, 1988)
   Neo-Astronomy: A Copernican Revolution (London: Arkana, 1991)
Gettings, Fred, *The Arkana Dictionary of Astrology* (London: Arkana, 1990)
Greene, Liz, *The Astrology of Fate* (London: Unwin, 1985)
Gribbin, John, and Plagemann, Steven H., *The Jupiter Effect* (London:
   Macmillan, 1974)
Harpur, Patrick, *The Philosophers' Secret Fire: A History of the Imagination*
   (London: Penguin, 2002)

Howe, Ellic, *Urania's Children* (London: William Kimber, 1967)

Hyde, Maggie, *Jung and Astrology* (Wellingborough: Aquarian, 1992)

Jackson, Eve, *Astrology: A Psychological Approach* (London: Dryad Press,1987)

Jung, C. G., Introduction and Appendix 'In Memory of Richard Wilhelm', *The Secret of the Golden Flower*, trans. into German, Richard Wilhelm; into English, C. F. Baynes (London: Kegan Paul, Trench, Trubner, 1947)

Foreword (1949), *I Ching*, trans. Cary F. Baynes (London: Arkana, 1989)

'Synchronicity: An Acausal Connecting Principle' (1950) in *The Structure and Dynamics of the Psyche, Collected Works*, trans. Hull, R. F. C., vol. 8 (Princeton, N.J.: Princeton University Press, 1960)

Collected Works, vol. 10 (Princeton, N.J.: Princeton University Press, 1964)

Memories, Dreams, Reflections, ed. Aniela Jaffé, trans. R. and C. Winston (London: Fountain, 1977)

ed., *Man and his Symbols* (1964) (London: Picador, 1978)

with Pauli, W., *Interpretation of Nature and the Psyche* (Princeton, N. J.: Princeton University Press, 1955)

Kenton, Warren, *The Anatomy of Fate: Kabbalastic Astrology* (London: Rider, 1978)

Astrology: Celestial Mirror (London: Thames & Hudson, 1989)

Kolisko, Lily, *The Moon and Plant Growth* (London: Anthroposophical Foundation, 1936)

MacNeice, Louis, *Astrology* (London: Aldus, 1964)

Mann, A. T., ed. *The Future of Astrology* (London: Unwin Hyman, 1987)

Marshall, Peter, *The Philosopher's Stone: A Quest for the Secrets of Alchemy* (London: Macmillan, 2001)

Maxwell-Stuart, P. G., ed., *The Occult in Early Modern Europe: A Documentary History* (London: Macmillan, 1999)

Mayo, J., White, O. and Eysenck, H. J., 'An Empirical Study of the Relation between Astrological Factors and Personality', *Journal of Social Psychology* (1978), vol. 105, pp. 229–36.

More, Thomas, *The Planets Within: The Astrological Psychology of Marsilio Ficino* (Hudson, N. Y.: Lindisfarne, 1989)

Naylor, Phylis, *Astrology: An Historical Examination* (London: Maxwell, 1967)

Parker, Derek, *Familiar to All: William Lilly and Seventeenth-Century Astrology* (London: Jonathan Cape, 1975)

Pico della Mirandola, Giovanni, *Disputationes Adversus Astrologiam Divinatricem*, ed. E. Garin (Florence: Vallecchi, 1946)

Ramesey, William, *Astrology Restored* (London, 1653–5)

Russell, Eric, *The History of Astrology and Prediction* (London: New English Library, 1972)

Robson, Vivian E., *The Fixed Stars and Constellations in Astrology* (1923) (Wellingborough: Aquarian, 1979)

Ross, J. C. and McLauglin, M. M., eds, *The Portable Renaissance Reader* (Harmondsworth: Penguin, 1985)

Roob, Alexander, *The Hermetic Museum: Alchemy and Mysticism* (Köln: Taschen, 1997)

Rudhyar, Dane, *The Practice of Astrology: As a Technique in Human Understanding* (1968) (Baltimore, Maryland: Penguin, 1970)
Psychology of Transformation (Wheaton, IL: Quest, 1979)
The Astrology of Transformation: A Multilevel Approach (Wheaton, IL: Quest, 1980)

Seymour, Percy, *Astrology: The Evidence of Science* (London: Lennard, 1988)

Spencer, Neil, *True as the Stars Above: Adventures in Modern Astrology* (London: Victor Gollancz, 2000)

Tester, Jim, *A History of Western Astrology* (London: Boydell, 1987)

Thomas, Keith, *Religion and the Decline of Magic* (Harmondsworth: Penguin, 1991)

Thorndike, Lynn, *A History of Magic and Experimental Science*, 6 vols (New York: Columbia University Press), vols 1 and 2 (1923); 3 and 4 (1934); 5 and 6 (1941))

Tillyard, E. M. W., *The Elizabethan World Picture* (1943) (Harmondsworth: Penguin, 1966)

Tobyn, Graeme, *Culpeper's Medicine* (London: Element, 1996)

Wedel, T. O., *The Medieval Attitude toward Astrology* (New Haven: Norwood, 1920)

West, John Anthony, *The Case for Astrology* (New York: Viking Arkana, 1991)

Yates, Francis, *Occult Philosophy in the Elizabethan Age* (London: Routledge, 2001)
Giordano Bruno and the Hermetic Tradition (London: Routledge, 2002)

Guides and handbooks

Addey, John, *Harmonics in Astrology* (London: Fowler, 1976)
A New Study of Astrology (London: Urania Trust, 1996)

Bennett, Judith, *Sex Signs* (London: Pan, 1981)

Blavatsky, Madame, *The Secret Doctrine*, 3 vols (New York, 1888)

Campion, Nicholas, *The Ultimate Astrologer* (London: Rider, 2002)

Cardan, Jeremy, *The Seven Segments*, trans. William Lilly (London, 1676)

Carter, Charles E. O., *Astrological Aspects* (London: C. W. Daniel, 1960)
The Principles of Astrology (Wheaton, IL: Quest, 1985)

Cornelius, Geoffrey, Hyde, Maggie and Webster, Chris, *Astrology for Beginners* (Cambridge: Icon, 1995)

Freeman, Martin, *Forecasting by Astrology* (Wellingborough: Aquarian, 1983)

Gilchrist, Cherry, *Astrology* (London: Batsford,1982)
  Planetary Symbolism in Astrology (London: Saros Foundation, Astrological Association of Great Britain, n.d.)

Goodman, Linda, *Linda Goodman's Love Signs* (London: Macmillan, 1979)
  Linda Goodman's Sun Signs (London: Pan, 1988)
  Linda Goodman's Relationship Signs (London: Pan, 1999)

Greene, Liz, *Saturn: A New Look at an Old Devil* (Wellingborough: Aquarian, 1976)
  Star Signs for Lovers (London: Arrow, 1980)

Hand, Robert, *Planets in Transit: Life Cycles for Living* (Rockport, Mass.: Para Research, 1976)
  Horoscope Symbols (London: Whitford, 1987)

Harvey, Charles and Suzi, *Astrology* (London: Thorsons, 1999)

Hone, Margaret, *The Modern Textbook of Astrology* (London: Fowler, 1951)

Kempton-Smith, Debbi, *Secrets from a Stargazer's Notebook: Making Astrology Work for You* (New York: Bantam, 1984)

Jones, Marc Edmund, *How to Learn Astrology* (New York: Doubleday, 1971)

Leo, Alan, *Astrology for All*, 9th edn. (Edinburgh: International Publishing, n.d.)
  The Art of Synthesis (London: Fowler, 1968)
  Practical Astrology, 2nd edn. (London: William Reeves, 1910)

Lilly, William, *Christian Astrology* (1647), reprinted by Zadkiel (i.e. Richard Morrison) as *Introduction to Astrology* with his own *Grammar of Astrology* and Tables for calculating nativities (1853) (London: G. Bell & Sons, 1939)

Lyle, Jane, *The Complete Handbook of Astrology* (London: W. H. Smith, Marshall Cavendish, 1992)

MacNaughton, Robin, *How to Transform your Life through Astrology* (New York: Bantam, 1983)

Marks, Tracy, *The Art of Chart Interpretation* (London: CRCS, 1986)

Martens, Ronny and Trachet, Tim, *Making Sense of Astrology* (New York: Prometheus, 1998)

Mayo, Jeff, *Astrology: A Key to Personality* (Saffron Walden: C. W. Daniel, 2000)
  and Ramsdale, Christine, *Astrology* (London: Teach Yourself Books, 1996)

Miller, Anistatia R. and Brown, Jared M., *The Complete Astrological Handbook for the Twenty-first Century* (New York: Schocken, 1999)

Musaios (Charles Muses), *The Lion Path: You Can Take it With You* (Berkeley, CA.: Golden Scepter Press, 1987)

Nostradamus, *The Complete Prophecies of Nostradamus*, ed. Ned Halley (London: Wordsworth, 1999)

Oken, Alan, *As Above, So Below: A Primary Guide to Astrological Awareness* (New York: Bantam, 1973)

The Horoscope, the Road and its Travelers (New York: Bantam, 1974)

Alan Oken's Complete Astrology (New York: Bantam, 1980)

Parker, Julia and Derek, *Kiss Guide to Astrology* (London: Dorling Kindersley, 2000)

Parkers' Astrology (London: Dorling Kindersley, 2001)

Rheinhart, Melanie, *Chiron and the Healing Journey* (London: Arkana, 1989)

Ridder-Patrick, Jane, *A Handbook of Medical Astrology* (London: Arkana, 1990)

Sakoian, Francis and Acker, Louis S., *The Astrologer's Handbook* (Harmondsworth: Penguin, 1981)

Thornton, Penny, *Synastry* (Wellingborough: Aquarian, 1982)

Weingarten, Henry, *Investing by the Stars* (New York: MacGraw-Hill, 1996)

White, Suzanne, *The New Astrology* (London: Macmillan, 1986)

Zadkiel, (i.e. Richard Morrison) *Grammar of Astrology*, with William Lilly's *Introduction to Astrology* (London: G. Bell & Sons, 1939)

China

Chen Zungui, *History of Astronomy of China*, 4 vols (Shanghai, n.d.)

Craze, Richard, with Billy Lee, *Chinese Astrology* (London: Teach Yourself Books, 1998)

Eitel, Ernest, *Feng-shui or The Rudiments of Natural Science in China* (Hong Kong: Lane, Crawford, 1873)

Elliot, Roger, *Peking Lunch. Your Guide to Chinese Astrology* (London: Coronet, 1973)

Feuchtwang, Stephan D. R., *An Anthropological Analysis of Chinese Geomancy* (Taipei: Southern Material Center, 1974)

Fung Yu-lan, *A Short History of Chinese Philosophy*, trans. Derk Bodde (Princeton, N.J.: Princeton University Press, 1938)

Giles Bridget and the Diagram Group, *Chinese Astrology* (London: HarperCollins, 1996)

Gleadow, Rupert, *The Origin of the Zodiac* (London: Jonathan Cape, 1968)

Huon de Kermadec, Jean-Michel, *The Way to Chinese Astrology: The Four Pillars of Destiny*, trans. N. Derek Poulsen (London: Unwin, 1983)

Heavenly Pennies, trans. N. Derek Poulsen (London: Unwin, 1985)

I Ching or Book of Changes, trans. Cary F. Baynes from the German translation of Richard Wilhelm (London: Arkana, 1989)

Kwang-chih Chang, *Shang Civilization* (New Haven: Yale University Press, 1980)

Lau, Theodora, *The Handbook of Chinese Horoscopes* (London: Souvenir Press, 1980)

Lee, Sang Hae, *Feng Shui: Its Context and Meaning*, Cornell University Ph.D. thesis, 1986 (Ann Arbor, Michigan: UMI, 1999)

Lo, Raymond, *Feng Shui and Destiny for Managers* (Singapore: Times Books International, 1997)
  Feng Shui and Destiny for Families (Singapore: Times Books International, 1999)
Man-Ho Kwok, *Chinese Astrology: Forecast Your Future from Your Chinese Horoscope* (London: Blandford, 1997)
  Chinese Face and Hand Reading (London: Piatkus, 1995)
  with O'Brien, Joanne, *The Elements of Feng Shui* (Shaftesbury: Element, 1991)
Michio, Kushi, with Esko, Edward, *Nine Star Ki* (Becket, Mass.: One Peaceful World Press, 1991)
Needham, Joseph, *Science and Civilisation in China* (Cambridge: Cambridge University Press), vol. 2 (1954); vol. 3 (1959); vol. 4 (1962); vol. 5 (1974).
Palmer, Martin, *Yin and Yang* (London: Piatkus, 1997)
Pan Nai, *History of Observation of Stars in China* (Shanghai: Scholar Press, 1989)
Ricci, Matthew, *China in the Sixteenth Century: The Journals of Matthew Ricci: 1583–1610*, trans. from the Latin by Louis J. Gallagher (New York: Random House, 1953)
Rigby, Paul and Bean, Harvey, *Getting it Together with Chinese Astrology* (Hong Kong: South China Morning Post, c.1981)
Schafer, Edward H., *Pacing the Void: T'ang Approaches to the Stars* (Berkeley, Calif.: University of California, 1977)
A Source Book in Chinese Philosophy, trans. Wing-Tsit Chan (Princeton, N.J.: Princeton University Press, 1963)
Sun Xiaochun and Kistemaker, Jacob, *The Chinese Sky during the Han* (Leiden: Brill, 1997)
Temple, Robert, *The Genius of China: 3,000 Years of Science, Discovery and Invention* (London: Prion, 1991)
Tung Jen, *Chinese Astrology* (London: Foulston, 1998)
Walters, Derek, *Chinese Astrology: Interpreting the Revelations of the Celestial Messengers* (Wellingborough: Aquarian, 1987)
Wheatley, Paul, *The Pivot of the Four Quarters* (Chicago: Aldine, 1971)
White, Suzanne, *The New Chinese Astrology* (London: Pan, 1994)
Windridge, Charles, ed., *Tong Sing: The Chinese Book of Wisdom* (London: Kyle Cathie, 1999)

India

The Bhagavad Gita, trans. Juan Mascaró (Harmondsworth: Penguin, 1975)
Bhat, M. Ramakrishna, *Fundamentals of Astrology* (Delhi: Motilal Banarsidass, 1967)

Bihari, Bepin, *Myths and Symbols of Vedic Astrology* (Salt Lake City: Passage Press, 1990)
    Fundamentals of Vedic Astrology (Salt Lake City: Passage Press, 1992)
Defouw, Hart, and Svoboda, Robert, *Light on Life: An Introduction to the Astrology of India* (London: Arkana, 1996)
Dhama, B. L., *A Guide to the Jaipur Astronomical Observatory* (Jaipur, n.d)
Dreyer, Ronnie Gale, *Vedic Astrology: A Guide to the Fundamentals of Jyotish* (York Beach, Maine: Samuel Weiser, 1997)
Harnass, Dennis, *Nakshatras: The Lunar Mansions of Vedic Astrology* (Twin Lakes, WI.: Lotus Light, 1999)
Hymns of the Atharva Veda, trans. M. Bloomfield (New Delhi: Motilal Banarsidass, 1997)
Minaraja, *Vrddhayavanajataka of Minaraja*, ed. David Pingree, 2 vols, (Baroda: Oriental Institute, 1976)
Mitchiner, John E., *Traditions of the Seven Risis* (New Delhi: Motilal Banarsidass, 1982)
Narasimha, *Kalaprakashika*, trans. N. P. Subramania Iyer (New Delhi: Asian Educational Services, 1982)
Parasara, Maharashi, *Brihat Parasara Hora Sastra*, 2 vols, trans. G.C. Sharma (New Delhi: Sagar, 1991)
Pingree, David, *Jyotishsastra: Astral and Mathematical Literature* (Wiesbaden: Otto Harrassowitz, 1981)
Raman, B.V., *Astrology for Beginners* (1940) (New Delhi: UBS, 1998)
    How to Judge a Horoscope (Bangalore: IBH Prakashana, 1981)
    Muhartha: Electional Astrology (New Delhi: UBS,1993)
Rawson, P., *Tantra* (London: Arts Council of Great Britain, 1971)
Rig Veda, trans. W. D. O'Flaherty (Harmondsworth: Penguin, 1981)
Roebuck, Valerie J., *The Circle of Stars: An Introduction to Indian Astrology* (Shaftesbury: Element, 1992)
Sharma, Vishwanath Deva, *Astrology and Jyotir Vidya* (Calcutta: Vishwa Jyotirvid Samgha, 1973)
A Sourcebook in Indian Philosophy, ed. S. Radhakrishnan and C. A. Moore (Princeton, NJ: Princeton University Press, 1971)
Surya Siddhanta, trans. Ebenezer Burgess, intro. P.C. Sengupta (Calcutta, 1935)
Shil-Ponde, *Hindu Astrology: Jyotisha-Shastra* (New Delhi: Sagar, 1968)
Sutton, Komilla, *The Essentials of Vedic Astrology* (Bournemouth: The Wessex Astrologer, 1999)
    Vedic Astrology (London: Collins & Brown, 2000)
    The Lunar Modes: Crisis and Redemption (Bournemouth: The Wessex Astrologer, 2001)
    Vedic Love Signs (London: Pan, 2003)
The Upanishads, trans. Eknath Easwaran (London: Arkana, 1988)

Varahamihira, *Brihat Samhita*, trans. H. Kern (1913); trans. M. Ramakrishna
 Bhat (Delhi: Motilal Banarsidass, 1981)

Mesopotamia

Baigent, Michael, *From the Omens of Babylon: Astrology and Ancient
 Mesopotamia* (London: Arkana, 1994)
Black. J., and Green, A., *Gods, Demons and Symbols of Ancient Mesopotamia*
 (London: British Museum, 1992)
The Epic of Gilgamesh, trans. N. K. Sanders (Harmondsworth: Penguin, 1972)
Hooke, S. H., *Babylonian and Assyrian Religion* (London: Blackwell, 1962)
Kramer, S. N., *The Sumerians: Their History, Culture and Character* (Chicago:
 University of Chicago Press, 1963)
Layard, Austen Henry, *Discoveries in the Ruins of Nineveh and Babylon*
 (London: John Murray, 1853)
Livingstone, A., *Mystical and Mythological Explanatory Works of Assyrian and
 Babylonian Scholars* (Oxford: Oxford University Press, 1986)
Neugebauer, Otto, ed., *Astronomical Cuneiform Texts*, 3 vols (London: Lund
 Humphries, 1955)
Oates, J., *Babylon* (London: Thames & Hudson, 1986)
Oppenheimer, A. L., *Ancient Mesopotamia*, rev. edn. (Chicago: University of
 Chicago Press, 1977)
Parpola, S., *Letters from Assyrians Scholars to the Kings Esarhaddomn and
 Assurbanipal*, part I, texts (Neukirchen-Vluyn, 1970); part II, commentary
 (Neukirchen-Vluyn,1983)
Reiner, E., *The Venus Tablet of Ammisaduqa* (Malibu, 1975)
 Enuma Anu Enlil, Tablets 50–51 (Malibu, 1981)
Sachs, A., 'Babylonian Horoscopes', *Journal of Cuneiform Studies*, (1952),
 vol. 6, pp. 54–7
 and Hunger, H., *Astronomical Diaries and Related Texts from Babylonia*,
 2 vols. (Vienna,1988–9)
Thierens, A. E., *Astrology in Mesopotamian Culture* (Leiden: Brill, 1935)
Thompson, R. C., ed.,*The Reports of the Magicians and Astrologers of Nineveh
 and Babylon in the British Museum*, 2 vols. (London: Luzac, 1900)
Van der Waerden, B. L., 'History of the Zodiac', *Archiv für Orientforschung*,
 vol. 16

Egypt

Antoniadi, E. M., *L'astronomie égyptienne depuis les temps les plus reculés*
 (Paris: Gauthiers-Villars, 1934)

The Ancient Egyptian Pyramid Texts, trans. R. O. Faulkener (Warminster: Aris & Phillips, 1969)

Armour, Robert A., *Gods and Myths of Ancient Egypt* (Cairo: The American University in Cairo Press, 1986)

Bauval, Robert, and Gilbert, Adrian, *The Orion Mystery* (London: Heinemann, 1994)

    and Hancock, Graham, *Keeper of Genesis: A Quest for the Hidden Legacy of Mankind* (London: Heinemann, 1996)

The Book of the Dead, trans. E. A. Wallis Budge (London: Arkana, 1986)

Cumont, F., *L'Égypte des astrologues* (Paris, 1937)

Edwards, I. E. S., *The Pyramids of Egypt* (London: Penguin, 1993)

Fowden, Garth, *The Egyptian Hermes: A Historical Approach to the Late Pagan Mind* (Princeton, N.J.: Princeton University Press, 1993)

Faulkener, R. O., 'The King and the Star Religion in the Pyramid Texts', *Journal of Near Eastern Studies*, vol. 25, no. 3 (July 1966)

Fix, Wm. R., *Star Maps,* (London: Octopus, 1979)

Ghalioungui, P., *Magic and Medical Science in Ancient Egypt* (London: Hodder & Stoughton, 1963)

Glanville, S. R. K., ed., *The Legacy of Egypt* (Oxford: Clarendon, 1942)

Hancock, Graham and Faiia, Santha, *Heaven's Mirror: Quest for the Lost Civilization* (London: Michael Joseph, 1998)

Jacq, Christian, *Egyptian Magic,* trans. Janet M. Davis (Warminster: Aris & Phillips, 1985)

Kircher, Athanasius, *Oedipus Aegyptiacus* (Rome, 1653)

Neugebauer, O., and Parker, Richard A., *Egyptian Astronomical Texts,* 2 vols. (London: Lund Humphries, 1960)

Piankoff, Alexandre, *The Pyramid of Unas,* vol. 5 of *Egyptian Religious Texts and Representations* (New York: Bollingen Foundation, 1964)

Pinch, Geraldine, *Magic in Ancient Egypt* (London: British Museum Press, 1994)

Proctor, Richard A., *The Great Pyramid: Observatory, Tomb and Temple* (London, 1883)

Reymond, E. A. E., *The Mythical Origin of the Egyptian Temple* (Manchester: Manchester University Press, 1969)

Rundle Clark, R. T., *Myth and Symbol in Ancient Egypt* (London: Thames & Hudson, 1959)

Schwaller de Lubicz, R.A., *The Egyptian Miracle: An Introduction to the Wisdom of the Temple*, trans. André and Goldian VandenBroeck (Rochester, VT.: Inner Traditions International, 1985)

    Sacred Science: The King of Pharaonic Theocracy, trans. André and Goldian VandenBroeck (Rochester, VT.: Inner Traditions International, 1988)

    The Temple of Man: Ancient Egyptian Architecture and the Perfect Man, trans. Deborah and Robert Lawlow (Rochester, VT.: Inner Traditions International, 1988)

Shorter, Alan W., *The Egyptian Gods* (London: Kegan Paul, Trench, Trubner & Co., 1937)

Wallis Budge, E. A., *From Fetish to God in Ancient Egypt* (Oxford: Oxford University Press, 1934)

  Egyptian Religion: Egyptian Ideas of the Future Life (London: Arkana, 1991)

West, John Anthony, *The Traveller's Key to Ancient Egypt: A Guide to the Sacred Places of Ancient Egypt* (London: Harrap Columbus, 1987)

  Serpent in the Sky: The High Wisdom of Ancient Egypt (Wheaton, IL.: Quest, 1993)

Greece and Rome

Adams, James, *The Nuptial Number of Plato* (1891) (Wellingborough: Thorsons, 1985).

Aristotle, *De Caelo*, trans. W. K. C. Guthrie, Loeb edn (London: Heinemann, 1939)

Barton, Tamsyn, *Ancient Astrology* (London: Routledge, 1994)

Bouché-Leclerq, A., *L'astrologie grecque* (Paris: Le Roux, 1899)

Diodorus Sicilus, trans. C. H. Oldfather et al., Loeb edn. (Cambridge, Mass.: Harvard University Press, 1989)

Cumont, Franz, *Astrology and Religion among the Greeks and Romans* (New York: Dover, 1912)

  Les religions orientales dans le paganisme romain (Paris, 1937)

Fagan, Cyril, *Astrological Origins* (Llewellyn, 1971)

Hermetica, trans. Brian P. Copenhaver (Cambridge: Cambridge University Press, 1995)

Firmicus Maternus, Julius, *Mathesis: Ancient Astrology – Theory and Practice,* trans. Rhys Bram (New Jersey: Noyes, 1975)

Herodotus, *The Histories*, trans. Robin Waterfield (Oxford: Oxford University Press, 1998)

Hesiod, *Works and Days*, in J. B. Pritchard, ed., *Ancient Near Eastern Texts* (Princeton, NJ.: Princeton University Press, 1955)

Iamblichos, *Theurgia or The Egyptian Mysteries,* trans. Alexander Wilder (London: William Rider & Son, 1911)

Lindsay, Jack, *The Origins of Astrology* (London: Muller, 1971)

Manilius, *Astronomica*, trans. G. P. Goold (Cambridge, Mass.: Harvard University Press, 1997)

Mead, G. R. S., *Thrice Greatest Hermes*, 3 vols (London: John M. Watkins, 1949)

Papyri Graecae Magicae. Die griechischen Zauberpapyri, ed. and trans. K.
    Preisendanz, 2 vols (Leipzig, 1928–31)
Neugebauer, Otto, *The Exact Sciences in Antiquity* (New York: Dover, 1969)
    and van Hoesen, H. B., *Greek Horoscopes* (Philadelphia, 1959)
Plato, *Timaeus,* trans. H. D. P. Lee (Harmondsworth: Penguin, 1965)
    Phaedrus, trans. Walter Hamilton (London: Penguin, 1973)
    The Republic, trans. Desmond Lee (Harmondsworth: Penguin, 1981)
Plotinus, *The Enneads,* trans. Stephen MacKenna, 3rd edn (London: Faber &
    Faber, 1962)
Ptolemy, Claudius, *Tetrabiblos,* trans. F. E. Robbins (Cambridge, Mass.: Harvard
    University Press, 1998)
Waterfield, Robin, 'The Evidence for Astrology in Classical Greece', *Culture and
    Cosmos,* vol. 3, no. 2 (1999), pp. 3–15
Wright, M. R., *Cosmology in Antiquity* (London and New York: Routledge,
    1995)

Middle East

Abu Ma'sar, *The Abbreviation of the Introduction to Astrology* (Leiden: Brill,
    1994)
Abu Ma'sar on Political Astrology, ed. Keiji Yamamoto et al, 2 vols. (Leiden:
    Brill, 1995)
Al-Biruni, *Elements of Astrology,* trans. R. Ramsay (London: Wright, 1934)
Burckhardt, Titus, *The Mystical Astrology according to Ibn Arabi* (London: Fons
    Vitae, 2001)
Dobin, Rabbi Joel C., *The Astrological Secrets of the Hebrew Sages: To Rule
    Both Day and Night* (Rochester, VT.: Inner Traditions International, 1977)
Forster, E. M., *Alexandria: A History and a Guide* (London: Michael Hagg,
    1982)
Kennedy, S. Edward, ed., *Astronomy and Astrology in the Medieval Islamic
    World* (London: Varorium, 1998)
Kenton, Warren (Zev ben Shimon Halevi), *The Anatomy of Fate: Kabbalistic
    Astrology* (London: Rider, 1978)
Nasr, Seyyed Hossein, *Islamic Science: An Illustrated History* (Kazi, 1995)
    An Introduction to Islamic Cosmological Doctrines (London: Thames &
    Hudson, 1978)
    Science and Civilization in Islam, 2nd edn. (Cambridge: Islamic Texts
    Society, 1987)

Index

Ba. = Babylonian; Ch. = Chinese; Eg. = Egyptian; In. = Indian; Is. = Islamic; Ro. = Roman. Main sections are in **bold**. Diagrams are indicated by *italics + d*. Tables are indicated by *italics + t*.